Praise for *Gorbachev's Gamb*

T0087435

'The ultimate, definitive and conclusive account ~ ~
most transformative periods in modern history. As we continue to be shaped by the consequences of the critical years
examined by Grachev, we shall continue to learn from this
masterful book.'
Amitai Etzioni, George Washington University

'Andrei Grachev, an important member of Gorbachev's foreign
policy team, writes as a participant-observer. His penetrating
and well-informed account of the end of the Cold War, as seen
from the Soviet side, offers a subtle and persuasive interpretation which will be a valuable corrective to much Western conventional wisdom.'
Archie Brown, University of Oxford

'A major contribution to our understanding of the last years of
the Soviet Union and to the end of the Cold War.'
Australian Journal of Political Science

'This gripping book is one that deserves the attention of students of politics, international relations and history.'
Slavonic and Eastern European Review

'A sympathetic and detailed analysis of how the last Soviet
leader's "new political thinking" brought about the break-up
of the Warsaw Pact and of the Soviet Union itself in 1991.'
Europe-Asia Studies

'A highly readable and very convincing account of the evolution of a new political thinking ... [and a] well-informed and
moving account of Gorbachev's perestroika.'
International Affairs

'Andrei Grachev is uniquely qualified to recount the end of the
Cold War from the Soviet side with lessons for all. This important book provides fresh analysis... and shatters myths about
how and why the Cold War ended as and when it did.'
The Russian Review

THE CHINESE ECONOMIC REFORMS

Edited by
STEPHAN FEUCHTWANG AND
ATHAR HUSSAIN

Routledge
Taylor & Francis Group

LONDON AND NEW YORK

First published in 1983 by Croom Helm Ltd

This edition first published in 2019
by Routledge
2 Park Square, Milton Park, Abingdon, Oxon OX14 4RN

and by Routledge
711 Third Avenue, New York, NY 10017

Routledge is an imprint of the Taylor & Francis Group, an informa business

British Library Cataloguing in Publication Data
A catalogue record for this book is available from the British Library

ISBN: 978-1-138-32344-5 (Set)
ISBN: 978-0-429-43659-8 (Set) (ebk)
ISBN: 978-1-138-34391-7 (Volume 5) (hbk)
ISBN: 978-1-138-34392-4 (Volume 5) (pbk)
ISBN: 978-0-429-43882-0 (Volume 5) (ebk)

Publisher's Note
The publisher has gone to great lengths to ensure the quality of this reprint but points out that some imperfections in the original copies may be apparent.

Disclaimer
The publisher has made every effort to trace copyright holders and would welcome correspondence from those they have been unable to trace.

The Chinese Economic Reforms

Edited by
STEPHAN FEUCHTWANG AND ATHAR HUSSAIN

CROOM HELM London & Canberra
ST. MARTIN'S PRESS New York

© 1983 S. Feuchtwang and A. Hussain
Croom Helm Ltd, Provident House, Burrell Row,
Beckenham, Kent BR3 1AT

British Library Cataloguing in Publication Data

The Chinese economic reforms.
   1. China — Economic policy — 1949-
   I. Feuchtwang, S.   II. Hussain, A.
   330.951'05   HC427.9
   ISBN 0-7099-1022-3

First published in the United States of America in 1983

Library of Congress Cataloging in Publication Data
Main entry under title:

The Chinese economic reforms.

   Bibliography: p.
   Includes index.
   1. China — Economic policy — 1976-   — Addresses,
essays, lectures. I. Feuchtwang, Stephan. II. Hussain,
Athar.
HC427.92.C4665   1982   338.951   82-10703
ISBN 0-312-13385-5

Printed and bound in Great Britain by
Biddles Ltd, Guildford and King's Lynn

CONTENTS

LIST OF TABLES AND LIST OF FIGURES

Tables

ADDITIONAL INFORMATION

Abbreviations

ACFTU   All China Federation of Trade Unions
BMA   Bureau for Materials Allocation
BPM   Bureau of Price Management
CCC   Capital Construction Commission
CCP   Chinese Communist Party
CITIC   China International Trust and Investment
        Corporation
CPPPC   Chinese People's Political Consultative
        Committee
FYP   Five Year Plan
GUTIC   Guangdong Trust and Investment Corporation
GVIO   Gross Value of Industrial Output
MNC   Multinational Corporations
PB   People's Bank
PLA   People's Liberation Army
PRC   People's Republic of China
SEC   State Economic Commission
SEZ   Special Economic Zone
SPC   State Planning Commission
SSB   State Statistical Bureau

Bibliographic abbreviations are listed with the
  list of References

Pronunciation

Chinese names and words in this book are trans-
literated by the system which is in widest use.
That is pinyin, or the Chinese Phonetic Alphabet.
Some of the initial letters used in pinyin may at
first present difficulties of pronunciation. For
these the following guide should help.
q   is pronounced as in cheer but at the front of the
    palate.
x   is pronounced as in ship but at the front of the
    palate
zh is pronounced as in judge but with the tip of the
    tongue curled back
z   is pronounced as in reads and without being
    voiced
c   is pronounced as in hats
The currency of the PRC (renminbi) is given in den-
ominations of the Yuan (¥). In December 1980
£ = 3.6¥, US$ = 1.5¥.

MAP OF CHINA

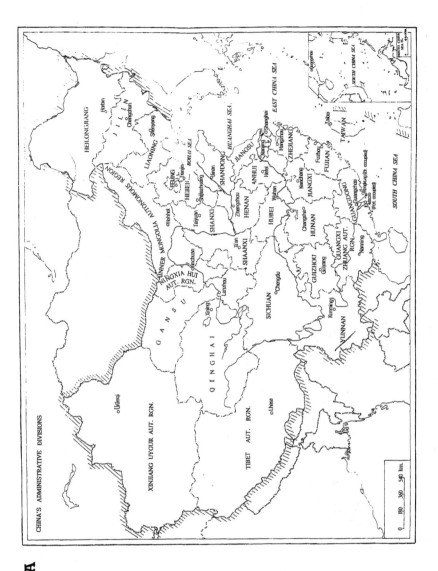

CHINA'S ADMINISTRATIVE DIVISIONS

INTRODUCTION

Stephan Feuchtwang
Athar Hussain

What was once denounced as the 'capitalist road' is now the line in China. Commencing in 1978, the 'readjustments' to the longer-standing aims of modernisation have wrought extensive changes in economic organisation and management. The Chinese have set out to learn from foreign economies, especially those in Eastern Europe, and elicit the help of Japanese companies and overseas Chinese to modernise the economy. How profound are these departures from the traditional stance towards the economy? How do the Chinese economic reforms compare with those that have taken place in the Soviet Union and Eastern Europe and which were once denounced by the Chinese Communist Party? What are the Chinese economists' own conceptions of the necessity for the changes which are occurring?

These are the questions addressed by this book. Chapters on the Chinese debates and differences in conceptions of economic policy are followed by extensive accounts of East European and Japanese economies in order to furnish the background against which the recent developments in China, described in Part 2, are to be evaluated. To introduce them, we will provide an overview of and then assess the nature and the extent of changes which have taken place in China since the downfall of the Gang of Four.

The Chinese divide their political history into periods of switches in policy and their

* We are grateful to Terry Cannon, Maisie Gray, Paul Hare, Martin Lockett and Vella Pillay for comments.

Introduction

complementary campaigns - a process of the start
and re-start of divergent lines of political
development. Changes in the direction of
development are announced by a shift in slogans, by
the launching of new campaigns and the enforced
obsolescence of old campaigns. The new (after the
change) and the old (before it) are stated
dramatically. This is no less true of the present
leadership than it was of the leadership it
replaced. With each change in direction, history
is re-assessed and re-divided into periods of
healthy and morbid development. Following the
accession of the present leadership, Chinese
political history has gone through yet another
periodisation. The ten years of the Cultural
Revolution and its aftermath (1966-1976) and the
years of the High Tide of Socialism and Great Leap
Forward (1957-59) have been condemned as wasted
years. And the rest, in particular the years
1961-64, have been re-evaluated as the years of
development along the right lines.

In assessing whether the recent changes in the
leadership, in political direction and in targets
of denunciation constitute strategic changes in
policy, one should not let the slogans currently
in circulation in China dictate terms. There has
indeed been an overhaul of the leadership, but
what changes in policy does that imply? A shift
in the direction of economic policy indeed there is,
but what institutional transformation does that
entail? Perhaps they point to the beginnings of a
permanent and far reaching economic and political
reform, but what is the range and the objective of
that reform? Are the recent changes any more than
a phase of the familiar pattern of profound
changes which are introduced but later reversed?
These are the questions which the reader needs to
address to the essays collected here. As yet, no
full and coherent assessment is possible. But
these essays provide a basis for identifying the
direction of the economic reforms. They
concentrate not so much on the politics of policy
making as on the changes in policy - of economic
policy, in particular - and their effects. Moreover, they provide detailed coverage of the main
areas of economic reform while at the same time
they are written from different perspectives. So
they each raise anew the questions of assessment
we have put.

Introduction

A Genealogy of Current Policies

The policies which have been introduced in China
since 1976 - in particular since 1978 - are not all
new. Most have either been tried - albeit for a
short period of time - or proposed before - albeit
rejected and denounced. Though the present
policies are seen by the present Chinese leadership
as a clean break from the regime of the decade
1966-76, a significant proportion of them were in
fact promulgated during the years of retrenchment
after the excesses of the first phase of the
Cultural Revolution in 1971-72. These policies
include a shift of emphasis away from capital
works towards production for immediate use in rural
areas, payment according to work rather than
according to needs and the accent on economic
rationality rather than on ideological rectitude in
industrial enterprises. However, by 1973 the
tide once again turned away from economic
stabilisation towards political struggle and the
transformation of the social relations of
production (M.Bastid and J.Domenach, 1976).
   In policy debates in China, and indeed in
socialist economies of Eastern Europe, a number of
themes and alternatives constantly recur. Broadly
speaking they are: the division of economic
administration and decision-making between central
and sub-central authorities, the division of
responsibility between the Party cadres and the
administrative personnel, the extent of autonomy
to be granted to enterprises, the nature of
instruments to be used to secure the implementation
of plans (directive vs. economic instruments), the
disposition towards the non-state sector of the
economy, the form of incentives (material vs. moral
incentives) and the importance to be accorded to
international trade, in particular with capitalist
economies. This recurrence arises because the
possibilities of changes within the parameters of
central planning, social ownership of means of
production and the one-party state are limited.
Policy debates tend to reiterate the possible
alternatives. Moreover, because policies have often
been cyclical rather than cumulative, the same
debates have periodically recurred. In China, for
instance, after the delegation of some economic
decisions to the provinces, following the First Five
Year Plan (1953-57), a large number of changes were
introduced only to be reversed later. And the
reversals of policies have been coupled with changes

3

in the political leadership and the balance of
power between different factions of the Party.
Today's helmsmen in China are the condemned men of
previous years. As we point out later, many of the
policies which have been implemented since 1978
were proposed by them during earlier periods.

There are a number of different strands to the
genealogy of present policies. The shifting course
of policies announced by successive leaderships is
one. A second is the actual effect of announced
policy changes and the stances towards economic
institutions and economic management. And the
third is the course of debates about policies and
the direction of economic reforms. The first two
need distinguishing because there always has been a
gap between the policy dispositions of the
leadership and the actual changes in the economy.
For instance, despite all the emphasis on moral
incentives during the Cultural Revolution, economic
incentives remained important - in the form of
differentiation of salaries and wages and
particularly the use of prices to stimulate
agricultural production. Similarly, despite all
the polemics against the Soviet Union, the method
of management of industrial enterprises and
techniques of central planning remained similar to
those in the Soviet Union. Moreover, Chinese
economics still leans heavily on Soviet economics.
An adequate analysis of these three strands would
be no less than a comprehensive history of the
People's Republic of China (PRC), a task which is
beyond the scope of an editorial introduction. We
have decided to be selective and concentrate on the
third strand. For that we rely on an outstanding
article by Cyril Lin[1], which is an extensive survey
of policy debates in China since the mid 50s and
of the views of today's leading economic policy
makers.

Debates about economic policy have not been
debates among professional economists alone. From
time to time party leaders, in particular Mao,
Liu Shaoqi, Zhou Enlai and Deng Xiaoping have
pronounced on economic issues, and have laid down
criteria for the assessment and validation of
economic analyses. This indeed has not been
peculiar to China. Stalin in his Economic Problems
of Socialism in the USSR adjudicated among rival
views on whether the Law of Value holds under
socialism, and assayed the official text book on
political economy. Politicians in capitalist
countries also pronounce on economic issues;

economic policy everywhere is too important
politically to be left to professional economists.
Yet there is an important difference: politicians
of capitalist countries do not perform the role of
adjudicator among rival economic analyses. Nor do
they perform the epistemological function of
differentiating the scientific from the non-
scientific. Rather they appeal to the authority of
a particular school of economics. Professional
economists have an autonomy in capitalist economies
which they have not had in socialist economies.
From this, writers on socialist economies have
drawn the conclusion that from time to time
professional economists in their analyses have been
constrained and deflected by political interventions.
This indeed has been the case.

The important question, however, is not whether
non-professional adjudications have helped or
hindered economic analyses; rather it is to ask,
why have they taken place? To answer this question
one has to start by specifying the contexts in
which economic arguments are deployed. Here, it is
worth repeating the truism that socialist economies
were founded by a break away from capitalism, and
they are meant to follow a path of development
different from that of capitalist economies. This
in itself opens up two areas of dispute and
argumentation. First, what are the characteristics
which identify an economy as socialist and not as
capitalist? Second, do the changes and
developments in the economy resuscitate what is
meant to have been superseded, that is do they
recreate a capitalist economy in a different guise?
The specification of what is socialist and the
delineation of socialist from capitalist is built
into the very structure of socialist economies.
These, one may note, are also the prime concerns of
the Marxist commentators on socialist economies.
These two concerns delineate one of the two areas
in which economic arguments are deployed.
Following Cyril Lin one may describe this as
diagnostic.

For obvious reasons professional economists do
not have a monopoly of diagnostic arguments. This
traditionally is the area in which politicians have
intervened. Stalin's Economic Problems and Mao's
economic writings were in effect a delineation of
what is specific to socialism and what is specific
to capitalism, and of differences between stages of
socialism. Not only do economists not have a
monopoly in this field but also the position they

occupy in it is governed by politics and not economics. This still remains the case when they are accorded primacy, as has been the case in China since 1978.

The second area of deployment of economic argument is in the management of planned economy, and problems encountered during the course of formulation and implementation of plans. One may term such arguments functional. The two areas are obviously interconnected, and the relationship between them has been historically variable. One effect of diagnostic arguments is to set limits to economic problems. However, since diagnostic arguments themselves are contentious such limits are variable. Moreover, the causation does not always run from the diagnostic to the functional; in specific cases diagnostic arguments themselves have been adapted to validate certain types of functional arguments. An example of that is Mao's criticism of Stalin's hostility towards the peasantry and his re-classification of the peasantry - at least certain sections of it - as a force for socialism.

In China economic arguments have for a long period been characterised by an orthodoxy which emphasises state and collectivist forms of ownership, stresses moral incentives and distrusts market relationships, profit and material incentives. As a result it has been identified with administrative planning by directives rather than planning with the help of prices and profit. However, in contrast to orthodoxy in Eastern Europe, mass mobilisation and the delegation of some initiative to enterprises and to provincial and local authorities have been central components of the Chinese orthodoxy. Historically, as we point out later, challenges to orthodoxy have originated directly in the guise of projects for reforms of the planning mechanism; and they, in turn, have been assessed and denounced on the basis of general diagnostic arguments. Malfunctions of planning have, therefore, furnished the ground for the emergence of heterodox notions of reform.

Schematically, the central objective of traditional planning has been to maximise gross output without much regard for efficiency, and it set out to do so by a massive rate of investment buoyed up with state ownership and the restriction of personal consumption either by coercion - that is by the non-availability of commodities and by rationing - or by ideological persuasion. In view

of the historical record of such planning in
socialist economies one can argue that certain
types of economic problems ,such as imbalances
between the sectors of production, the neglect of
qualitative aspects of products and inefficiency
in the use of resources have been endemic to it.
It is precisely these problems which have been the
targets of the heterodoxy. One could then argue
that challenges to the orthodoxy are potentially
built into the traditional planning system.

The traditional type of planning, which was
practised in the Soviet Union till the end of the
fifties and then continued with some alterations,
was emulated in all socialist economies. It did
not leave much room for an economic analysis of
problems of planning. For it rendered the
formulation and the implementation of plans mainly
an administrative problem. Orthodox stances in
diagnostic arguments and the traditional style of
planning together squeezed out economic analysis.
This is what happened in the Soviet Union. In the
1920s when the foundations of a planned economy
were being laid in the Soviet Union there was a
profusion of economic discussion on the
formulation and the methods of implementation of
the plan. But all that was then set aside. For
almost thirty years economists did no more than to
interpret the texts of the founding fathers. It
was only in the sixties that Soviet economics
started to move again towards problems of planning.

The Chinese did not copy the Soviet model
completely, and during the periods of the Great
Leap Forward and the Cultural Revolution they set
out to depart from it. In the process the
planning system was paralysed and all economic
problems were turned into political problems to be
solved by mass mobilisation and the emulation of
exemplary models. Economics was of no great help
in proposing solutions to economic problems. The
Chinese distanced themselves from the Soviet Union
and Eastern Europe precisely at the time of the
renaissance of economics in those countries; as a
result, they missed out on it.

One is tempted to treat the diagnostic
arguments as ideological and the functional
arguments as objective. But ideological (or
doctrinal) problems are usually regarded as
illusory: problems which do not exist and which
objective economics would do well to neglect.
The qualification 'objective' is taken to valorise
the problem as real. In fact doctrinal problems

are no less real than functional problems. For, as we have pointed out, doctrinal disputes are built into the very foundation of socialist economies. Moreover, functional problems do not exist independently of doctrinal disputes; frequently the latter suggest the former. Here, one may point to the profusion of the economic analyses of the problems of planning in the Soviet Union of the 20s, some of which were highly original. They could not have happened but for the doctrinal disposition to cast an economy radically different from capitalism.

Doctrinal verdicts have indeed set the limits of economic analysis in China. But it would be wrong to regard them as anti-scientific. For they have been inspired by the confidence that Marxism furnishes the science of society and a general methodology for all sciences. It is this assumption which has prompted political adjudications in professional arguments. Thus the argument that what Chinese economics needs is a shift away from ideology and doctrine towards scientific economics begs the question of the direction of that shift.

The scope for economic debates and experiments in organisation and policy is now much wider than at any time since 1949. Professional economic analysis, and indeed a professional analysis of other issues, is revalued. Listening to professional arguments and empirical analysis rather than learning from the masses is now the watchword. The current flowering of economic journals and the ability of economists, including those who are not members of the Party, to broach the issues which were previously taboo is, nevertheless, politically determined. Politics still remains firmly in command after the death of Mao and the downfall of the Gang of Four, though in the form of the elevation of economics. The changes in economic policy which have ocurred in China have been accompanied by a re-structuring of the Party and a strengthening of the chains of government command, a preliminary codification of criminal, civil and public law, and an emphasis on professionalism in all domains.

Far from being purely economic, this indicates a far reaching change of 'line'. Moreover, the style of arguments has undergone a marked transformation: changes in policy are evaluated less in class than in functional terms. From the perspective of the analytical framework which was

8

in currency during the decade of the Cultural
Revolution (1966-76) these changes amount to 'taking
the capitalist road'. But this judgement begs the
question of the validity of that analytical framework. The changes which have been introduced seem
to command a wide support, and the top leadership
of the Party is more united in its policy stance
than it has been for a long time. But it would be
premature to take these as the end of political
struggles over economic policy. Not only are there
differences in emphases in the arguments of
supporters of the change, but also the attitudes
towards economic change and the denigration of
ideological struggle have become noticeably more
cautious during the last two years.

Lin divides the ebb and flow of debates on
general economic issues and economic policy into
periods, the last of which started in 1978. In the
earlier periods the economists and thus professional
economics were officially relegated to specific
tasks of planning. On wider issues of the
organisation of the economy their professional
expertise was not solicited. There is now a reversal
in their ranking: in the past it was the pronounce-
ments of the political leadership which laid down the
guidelines for professional economic analyses. But
now it is economists' proposals for economic
solutions to the problems of planning which inform
the dispositions of the political leadership. The
political leadership now is impatient for economic
reforms but it lacks the wherewithal of the requisite
theory and blueprints. But it still needs to be
emphasised that economists do not have an unlimited
tether; there are clear limits to the type of
economic solutions which the political leadership
would accept.

Following the reconstruction after 1949
(Liberation) the years up to 1956 constituted the
first period of economics. This period witnessed
the formulation of the First Five Year Plan, the
first census of population and the nationalisation
of major industrial, commercial and financial
companies. The range of the industrial sector under
state ownership was extended further by importing
large numbers of complete plants from the Soviet
Union. The transformation in agriculture during this
period took the form of first the land reform which
eliminated the landlords, and then of the establishment of 'mutual-aid teams' followed by the 'lower-
stage' and the 'higher-stage' cooperatives (similar
to the Soviet Kolkhoz). The latter was the first

step towards a collectivist agriculture. That, in all, was the period when the foundations of a planned economy were laid and transition from capitalism to socialism was completed. The economic tasks during that period were clearly laid out, and economic analysis contributed little to the accomplishment of those tasks beyond the statistical work of planning. The Soviet Union furnished the model of the socialist economy which was to be followed in its essentials. The Chinese Communists did indeed adapt the Soviet model to their conditions, but that adaptation was carried out by political leaders rather than by economists. Departures from the Soviet model during this period were, however, discreet and limited.

That was also the period of the re-education of economists in socialist economics. Chinese were sent for training to the Soviet Union to add to the stock of economists trained in Europe, the United States and Japan who were themselves to some extent being retrained. The pilgrimage of Chinese economists towards the Soviet Union was supplemented by a large scale translation of Soviet texts on political economy and treatises on planning and management. Even today these form the backbone of Chinese economics. Prominent among translated texts was Stalin's Economic Problems of Socialism in the USSR, whose reverberations on Chinese economic analyses is analysed by Clausen in Chapter 1. Austere in tone and sparse in economic analysis, Stalin's text is structured around the two laws which have been the staple diet of traditional economic analysis in socialist economies: the Law of Value and the Law of Balanced and Proportional Development. Neither of them have a precise content. The former is a general rubric for the discussion of prices and markets and their role in the determination of production and the distribution of labour. The latter simply refers to the balanced development of sectors of production in a planned economy. The essential feature of Stalin's text is that planning is not regarded as a problem, but rather as an activity which requires little more than common sense and elementary bookkeeping. This feature is not peculiar to Stalin but is characteristic of traditional Marxism.

There is a paradox here. Despite the emphasis which Marxism has placed on the superiority of a planned over a non-planned economy, for a long time socialist economies put the formulation and

applied to socialism as well as
took the law to be a law of effi
resources (in particular labour)
mutandis was valid for all modes
then went on to use his interpre
Value to make a case for market
schema of market socialism,enter
full financial autonomy and thei
be assessed by the profit each
planning bureau was to set the p
to equate their supply and deman
make use not of directives but of
like taxes, interest rate and th
credit to control the activities
The choice of inputs and outputs
enterprises.

In fact Sun's schema is ide
suggested by the famous Polish e
in the late '30s in response to
and von Mises that the planning
be made impossible by the Promet
ting and processing information
and implement the plan. What La
it is possible for a socialist e
perfect market system, and there
same efficiency in the allocatio
the same economy in the requirem
as that claimed for the perfect
critics of socialism. Moreover,
socialist economy would be bette
perfect market system than a cap
cause the former, unlike the lat
the distorting influences of mon

Lange's solution did no mor
objections of the critics of soc
His schema of market socialism i
it raises more problems than it
assumes rather than demonstrates
planning bureau would in fact ge
prices through a process of grop
ond, he neglects what is likely
economy during the time when the
groping for the equilibrium pric
assumes that enterprises will bel
rules and regulations of the perf
an assumption which arguably is
socialist economy as it is for a
In general it needs to be said tl
al economy which has been claime
ism is not as valid as it might
turns out that the determination

implementation of plans outside the purview of a
systematic economic analysis. It is no exaggeration
to say that for a long time there was an assumption
that the socialisation of means of production in
itself furnished the conditions for the planning
of the economy, and the problems encountered during
the course of planning did not call for their
economic analysis since they were administrative
and political problems. After the economic
discussion of the 1920s in the Soviet Union, it was
left to the critics of Marxism and socialism (Hayek
and von Mises) to raise problems about the
possibilities of formulating and implementing plans.

The Eighth Congress of the Chinese Communist
Party (CCP) in September 1959 (first since 1956)
heard criticisms of bottlenecks in the supply of
means of production, shortages of means of consumption , imbalances in the output of different sectors
of production and the lack of coordination in the
execution of the First Five Year Plan (FYP). Such
complaints have been a commonplace in all socialist
economies. Among the prominent critics of the
First FYP was Chen Yun, then Minister of Commerce
and a Vice-Premier of the State Council - the
highest organ of government in China. To avoid
the recurrence of such problems he suggested
radical measures like the granting of financial
autonomy (known as khozraschet in Eastern Europe)
to state-owned enterprises, and reliance on economic
rather than administrative instruments to secure
the implementation of plans. These indeed are the
principal features of economic reforms which have
been introduced in Eastern Europe. Chen Yun's
proposals were not accepted in 1956. Instead the
reform took the form of not a transformation of
the planning mechanism but of a territorial
decentralisation of economic administration. Such
a redistribution of economic administration has
been common in all socialist economies. In fact a
similar decentralisation of economic administration
took place in the Soviet Union and in some other
East European countries around the same time.
However, the views put forward by Chen Yun then are
of some interest, because he is now a Vice-Chairman
of the CCP. What he proposed in 1956 has now been
finally put into practice.

The main importance of the Eighth Congress
lies in the fact that it marked the beginning of a
period of widespread debate on economic as well as
a large number of other issues. It was a period -
termed the second period by Lin- when a hundred

prices have no place in socialism. Rather he linked
their existence and necessity under socialism to the
co-existence of different forms of property: those
of the state and of collectives. That co-existence
was for him a transitory phenomenon; socialism, he
thought, would eventually grow out of different
forms of property. This indeed has been the position of Mao. The position of market socialists like
Sun Yefang and Oskar Lange was fundamentally different from this. For them prices and markets are not
transitory phenomena but a permanent feature of a
fully developed socialist economy. In fact, the
model of market socialism is based on the assumption
that there is but one form of property.

Prices and markets were only one aspect of the
debates which flourished when a hundred flowers
blossomed. The debate was launched under the general heading of 'Problems Concerning Basic Economic
Laws During the Transition Period'. A large number
of distinct issues were discussed under this general
rubric; of them the trajectory of development of
socialist economy in China was one of the most important. Luo Gengmo traced the path of socialist
development from centrally planned production
(either by state-owned or collective enterprises) to
a decentralised socialist economy with decision-
making power vested in financially autonomous enterprises managed by workers. He characterised the
former as the phase of 'great ownership' and the
latter as that of 'small ownership'. One may note
that this scheme of development of a socialist economy is the exact reverse of the usual Marxist sketch
of the path of development of capitalism: competitive capitalism which is characterised by the lack
of any centralised direction eventually gives way to
monopoly capitalism which, in turn, is characterised
by the dominance of a few large firms and centralised direction of the major sectors of the economy
by the state.

However, it is not this contrast which is of
interest but the implication that a decentralised
socialist economy cannot be introduced ab initio
but only after a period of centralised direction of
the economy. In our view there is something of importance in this implication. It is all too commonly
assumed that centralised planning through administrative directives was simply a creation of Stalin;
it is spoken of as Stalinist planning. This over-
looks the fact that the assumption of political
power involves bringing economic activity under political control, and that control by administrative

15

edicts, though crude, is a quick way of ensuring
that. A decentralised socialist economy with a monopoly of political representation by the communist
party does presuppose that enterprises in whom the
power of economic decision-making is vested are politically trustworthy - a condition which has not
existed at the outset of the assumption of power by
Communists. Therefore, it can be argued that, at
least initially, socialist planning under a one-
party state cannot but be what is called 'Stalinist
planning'.

The economic discussion during the period of a
hundred flowers was generally within the parameters
of Marxist economics and centralised planning.
However, there were a few economists who questioned
the pertinence of Marxist economics. Among them was
Chen Chenhan who cast doubt on the ability of
Marxist economics to supply answers to economic problems of planning; he advocated the teaching of
bourgeois economics in Chinese universities. All
these different views and critiques of them were
aired within the pages of Economic Research
(Jingji Yanjiu), New Construction (Xin Jianshe) and
Economics of Planning (Jihua Jinji) and other established journals. The criticism of heterodox views
was more political than economic: it took the familiar form of their condemnation as rightist.
Battle lines were drawn between advocates of the
Law of Balanced and Proportional Development and
those of the Law of Value under socialism. But
there was another division, between those who gave
priority to the transformation of relations of production: the recasting of forms of ownership and an
overhaul of incentive structure and wage and salary
scales. The two divisions ran parallel. Those who
advocated reliance on the Law of Value, on prices
and profit, as the instruments of planning, were
also the ones who put the accent on the development
of productive forces. The battle was finally won by
the side fighting under the joint banner of the Law
of Balanced and Proportional Development, or directive planning, and the transformation of the relations of production. With this the period of a
hundred flowers (the second period of economic discussions) ended.

As for economic policy, that became distinctly
radical in 1955. The room for manoeuvre left to
private capitalists was severly curtailed. And by
1956, well ahead of the official time-table, nearly
all of peasant households (83%) had been incorporated into the 'higher stage cooperatives'; the rest

followed suit soon after that. Thus, on the economic policy front the Eighth Congress marked the
beginning of a series of events which revolutionised
the Chinese countryside. These events culminated
in the Great Leap Forward of 1958-59, which witnessed the merger of the newly established cooperatives into communes, and a vast mobilisation of rural
labour for infrastructural projects and for the
establishment of a wide variety of rural industries.
In the early 1950s it was envisaged that the cooper-
ativisation of agriculture alone would take 15 to 20
years. In industry, the Eighth Congress marked a
break from the one-man management imported from the
Soviet Union; Workers' Congresses, which were to
participate in the management of enterprises, were
set up in 1957.

After a successful start because of the good
crop in 1958, the Great Leap Forward turned out to
be too ambitious. Hasty as their formation was,the
communes lacked the appropriate organisational
structure. The emphasis that was put on the spontaneous mobilisation of mass effort cut the ground
from underneath the planning of the economy. In
fact, the Second FYP was set aside almost as soon as
it was formulated. The problems created by the
Great Leap were further compounded by natural disasters. Grain production declined steeply in 1959,
and then again in 1960. As Rosenberg and Young
(1982:282) point out, such a series of setbacks only
fifteen years earlier would have resulted in widespread famine, epidemics and death. But now, though
people were hungry and there were some deaths from
malnutrition, there was no massive famine. The
collectivisation of agriculture had made it
possible to spread the shortage of food thinly.

An attempt to move mountains though it was,
the Great Leap was not devoid of economic logic.
As Eckstein (1977:56-57) has pointed out the
Great Leap resembled what many economists have
prescribed for less developed countries with surplus
labour: the employment of surplus labour for capital
projects, and the utilisation of primitive and
advanced technologies in tandem. In addition, the
Great Leap was an attempt to reduce the dependence
of rural on urban areas for the supply of
industrial goods.

The chaos caused by the Great Leap furnished
the ground for yet another re-evaluation of
economic policy and planning. In response to the
unregulated mass mobilisation of the Great Leap,
the pendulum swung towards centralised planning and

a tight control of economic activities from the
centre. This is what happened during the emergency
years of 1959-61. With the stablisation of the
economic situation in 1961, there were once more
demands for the decentralisation of planning and
economic decisions. These proposals trod the same
ground covered during the hundred flowers period in
1956-57, and they were aired in the same journals.
This time, however, the policy implications of
reliance on prices and profit were considered in
greater detail than before. Moreover, a detailed
proposal for the reform of the organs of economic
management was put forward. It suggested the
replacement of branch ministries by industrial
trusts with their own budget - holding companies, in
fact. The other suggestions of the proposed reform
were : the institution of a clearly defined structure of responsibility and authority of organs of
economic management, an increase of enterprise
autonomy in drawing up production programmes, the
granting to enterprises of the right to retain their
depreciation funds and a part of their profits, the
encouragement of lateral contacts between enterprises, the separation of the Party from the
management of the enterprises and a greater reliance
on material incentives. This proposal of reforms
was indeed very similar to the ones being aired in
Eastern Europe around the same time. And, generally
speaking, this is the model of economic reform
which has been implemented in Eastern Europe since
the mid 1960s (discussed by Hussain in Chapter 3),
and of the economic reforms in China since 1978.
Aside from this, there were proposals for rolling
back the frontiers of rural collectivisation.

In fact, none of the proposals for a radical
transformation of industrial management were
implemented in China then. In industry there was
merely a shift in emphasis towards economic
efficiency and adherence to plans. The main
changes were in agriculture. The size of rural
communes was reduced, and, therefore, there was an
increase in their number. In addition, the commune
was formally turned into a federal organisation
consisting of the now familiar three tiers: the
commune, the production brigades and the production
teams. Except for the execution of huge capital
projects and the management of large scale rural
industry, most economic activities (in particular
cultivation) were devolved to teams. During the
emergency years of 1959-61 the devolution of
cultivation went down even further to groups of

households smaller than teams. From 1959 onwards, the accent was on increasing agricultural production for immediate sustenance. To that end private plots, that were in places on the verge of obsolescence during the Great Leap, were restored and expanded. The enthusiasm of rural Party cadres for mobilising peasants for capital works was reined back, and private side-line production was encouraged. However, the notable feature of retrenchment policies in agriculture during the period 1959-64 is that they did not reverse but simply consolidated rural communes. Thus, the departure from the Soviet model in agriculture which had started with the Great Leap became irrevocable. None the less, aside from workers' participation, industrial management remained similar to that in the Soviet Union.

The major theoretical product of the third (1959-61) and the fourth period (1961-64) of economic discussions was Mao's notes on Stalin's Economic Problems and the Soviet text book on political economy, then in currency in China in its 1959 edition (Mao, 1977). Clausen discusses Mao's critique in Chapter 1. Like his earlier Ten Great Relationships, the critique sanctioned and indeed encouraged departures from the established orthodoxy. But now Mao took the orthodoxy head-on rather than undermining it by allusion.

Although during the period 1959-64, which straddles the three phases of economic discussions in China, Mao pronounced on a great many topical issues, he laid down general guidelines for economic policy rather than specific programmes of action. A set of distinct themes runs through those guidelines. Among them four stand out. First, the peasantry should not be regarded as an alien force, and treated as a milch cow in the service of socialist industrialisation. Second, he rejected the strategy of the 'modernisation' of China's huge countryside through pre-programmed step-by-step institutional transformations and the application of modern inputs produced by urban industry in favour of a strategy of letting the movement in the countryside itself set the targets and dictate the pace of institutional transformations, and of producing within the countryside at least some of the technical means needed for its development. Third, drawing on the experience of East European economies he cautioned against neglecting the development of light industry and agriculture in favour of, he thought, only a short-term acceleration of heavy industry . Finally,

Introduction

the faith that he put in the creative potential of
the mass movement made him suspicious of detailed
planning from the centre. In fact, there is in Mao
an uneasy relationship between the necessity of
planning, which he always accepted, and letting the
mass movement set the pace of change.

Although he towered over other leaders of the
Party, the official policy of the Party was far from
decided by Mao alone. Instead it was frequently an
outcome of the factional struggle in the Party. At
times he managed to outflank his opponents and
forced them to toe his 'line' - as indeed he did
when he forced the Party leadership to go along with
the tide of collectivisation in agriculture - while
at others he, like a shrewd general, retreated when
the balance of forces was against him - as he did
after the debacle of the Great Leap.

Widely divergent though the strategies of
development of the Chinese economy of different
factions were, all of them were against overemphasis on heavy industry and the neglect of
agriculture. The policy towards agriculture started
to change in 1955, when compulsory grain quotas for
delivery to the state were sharply reduced. There
was yet another reduction in them, and an improvement in the terms of trade in favour of agriculture,
in 1957. In 1962 Zhou Enlai launched the slogan
'taking agriculture as the foundation and industry
as the leading factor' as the Party policy. Between
1960-65 investments in agriculture and in industries
supplying inputs to agriculture were sharply
increased. However, there remained wide differences
over policies to develop agriculture and to
ameliorate the low living standards of rural
inhabitants, some suffering famine.

In the debates and arguments over economic
issues between 1956-64, one can, following Cyril Lin,
discern three strands. One was devoted to the
economic development of China through the continual
transformations of relationships of production. It
favoured sustaining the momentum of collectivisation
gained during the Great Leap; and it saw in the
restoration of capitalism the dragon threatening
socialist China. This was the position of what may
be termed the Shanghai school, discussed at length
in Chapter 2 by Christensen, and it was associated
with Chen Boda, Zhang Chunqiao and Kang Sheng
the big names of the Cultural Revolution. The ideas
of this school were nearest to those of Mao. In the
disputes over policy, however, they did not always
have his support.

20

Introduction

The second school advocated balanced development through reliance on markets, and a shift of emphasis of planning towards agriculture and consumer goods. Foremost, this school saw the periodic mass movements to transform social relations of productions as disruptions rather than as means for an accelerated development of the Chinese economy. This school dismissed the dangers of the restoration of capitalism in China as illusory, and, therefore, it favoured the granting of economic initiative to individual or small groups of peasant households. It stressed planning and the control of activities by the government over local movements for the democratisation of industry and collectivist experiments. This school was not against transformations of social relations, and nor was it for the restoration of capitalism. Rather it envisaged the development of the economy in stages: first the development of forces of production by a tight governmental planning and by granting entrepreneurial freedom to petty commodity producers in rural and urban areas, and then measured step-by-step social transformation. Chen Yun and Bo Yibo were linked with this school; and among political leaders they had the support of Liu Shaoqi and Deng Xiaoping. This school exercised a decisive influence over economic policy during the years of economic stabilisation in 1961-63. They are now once again prominent in the management of the Chinese economy.

The third school included Sun Yefang and Gu Zhun. On policy issues they supported the second school. What distinguished them was their concern with theoretical research on problems of planning, and the use of mathematical techniques. They elaborated Marx's schema of extended re-production in order to sketch the growth path of a socialist economy. The other main areas of their interest were targets and instruments of planning, criteria for the allocation of investment and the computation of prices.

During the period 1956-64 neither the first nor the second school had complete sway over economic policy, which alternated between building on the experience of the Great Leap, and retrenchment and stabilisation. After a temporary retreat, Mao returned in 1962 to what he called the 'front line', and made the continuation of the class struggle and combating 'revisionism' the immediate aims of the Party policy. In order to clean up corruption in the countryside and to combat renascent capitalism the 'Socialist Education Movement' was launched

in 1963. This movement, in fact, had a greater rep-
ercussion in the countryside than the Cultural Revolution. And it brought the Shanghai school into prominence. The alternating 'lines' of economic and
social policies of the Party sharpened the differences between the two schools. And, from 1964 onwards, it came to be labelled 'the two line'
struggle by the Shanghai school. Aside from the
mobilisation of masses for more production, the
Shanghai school put a special stress on the disper-
sal of industry in the interior of China, and a de-
professionalisation of technical expertise through
the popularisation of technical education. Their
general aim was to at least attenuate the three
divisions, which, among others, Mao had singled out
for eventual abolition in his Ten Great Relationships. They were, the divisions between mental and
manual labour, between the countryside and the city
and between agriculture and industry.

What for the Shanghai school was the 'two line
struggle' is for the present leadership 'the two
line trauma'. Not only does 'trauma' refer to the
divergences in economic policy between the period
1960-76, but also to the whimsical justice meted out
to Party stalwarts, during the high tide of the
Cultural Revolution in 1966-69, and then later during various campaigns in 1972-76. On the economic
front it alludes to what the present leadership
regards as the dismal economic record of the decade
1966-76: the paralysis of planning, capricious
economic policies, chaos in industry and a near
stagnation and even periodic declines in agricultural production. The main charge against the decade is that there was no perceptible amelioration in
the precarious living standards of a large section
of the rural population. In fact, it is claimed now
that there was no increase in living standards of
the population in the twenty years between the on-
set of the Great Leap (1958) and the increase in
wages and agricultural prices in 1978.

The last may well be true. But in assessing
the significance of this claim one may keep in view
the two facts: first, the crop in 1958 was exceptionally good; and, second, the professed policy
during the decade of the Cultural Revolution was to
keep constant or even to decrease the higher wages
and to increase the lower wages. Moreover, there is
an additional problem: what is now claimed about
the decade of the Cultural Revolution is in contradiction with the claims of the Chinese authorities
after 1969. That is, production did not suffer

during the upheavals of 1966-69, and that both industrial and agricultural production was increasing.
Although it is portrayed as such now, the decade
1966-76 was far from uniform. In 1969 there was a
concerted attempt to reverse the excesses of the
Cultural Revolution, and to increase production. As
pointed out earlier, a number of measures introduced
since 1978 were affirmed as the Party policy in
1972-73. In view of what was said and stressed
then, it is difficult to accept that production and
the amelioration of living standards (especially in
rural areas) was completely neglected in favour of
quixotic struggles during 1966-76. The difference
between the period after 1978, and the period 1966-
76, in our view, does not consist in the development
of forces of production versus the transformation of
social relations of production. Rather, it is more
fruitful to look at it in terms of two distinct
strategies of economic development and the amelioration of living standards.

A key component of the strategy, which could be
said to be ascendant during 1966-76 was the slogan
'self-reliance', which was taken in a variety of
senses. So far as internal economic organisation
was concerned, the slogan was taken to mean that
provinces and even lower units, with some exceptions, would strive towards self-sufficiency in the
basic items of sustenance, in particular grain. It
was in fact a strategy for a geographical decentralisation and dispersion of economic activities. The
essential idea behind it was the development of activities using local inputs and producing for local
use, and that provinces and lower units would ask
higher authorities for only those resources which
could not be supplied locally. The implication was
that provinces and local units could independently
draw up their own targets so long as they could meet
them by mobilising local resources. Moreover,
'self-reliance' was also applied to the national
economy. It was used by some as a caution against
dependence on foreign trade and foreign investment,
and by others to mean almost total opposition to
foreign trade and any involvement in the international financial network.

The other dimension of the strategy was to develop a more integrated local economy by furthering
lateral contacts between enterprises, units of distribution and consumers within the locality. These
lateral contacts in the early 1970s took the form of
mutual visits and inspections to tailor local production to local demand. As a consequence of these,

enterprises used their resources, surplus to those
needed for meeting planned targets, to branch out
into activities to meet local demand. At times
these activities were far removed from the area of
their specialisation. Apart from this, there was a
proliferation of collective enterprises (mostly
small units), geared to producing for the local market.

Aside from an economic, there was an obvious
military rationale to the strategy. During the decade 1966-76 the Chinese leadership did regard a war
involving China as a serious possibility.It is, however, a separate question, how well did the strategy
in fact work? Leaving aside its actual implementation, when assessing the strategy one needs to keep
in view its following general implications. To the
extent that the strategy mobilised the resources which
would have been left unutilised,it obviously furth-
ered economic.development. But such a strategy always involves some element of diverting resources
to less efficient uses. This is corroborated by the
waste engendered by the attempts to manufacture
steel in rural areas during the Great Leap. In addition to that,the present Chinese authorities point
out,that the preoccupation with local self-sufficiency in grain led to a neglect of cash crops, and
diverted to grain production land not suited for
the purpose.

The strategy of 'self-reliance' was not simply
a production strategy, but also a strategy of consumption, of the distribution of income and transformations of social relations of production. For,
given the technical backwardness of China and the
concentration of its large scale industry in a few
coastal centres, geographical self-reliance could
only work provided consumption was restricted to a
few basic commodities. Therefore, it could be argued that 'self-reliance' meant not only tailoring
local production to local use but also consumption
to local production. Austerity in consumption was
an essential component of the strategy; and it was
achieved by ideological exhortation and by restricting high incomes. The strategy went hand in hand
with an egalitarian distribution policy, and stress
on putting collective above individual interests.

The strategy in operation now is in certain
essential respects very different, though not a
clean break, from the self-reliance strategy. In
agriculture local self-sufficiency in grain is no
longer the aim. There is some re-diversion of land
from grain to other uses. The bias now is in favour

24

of specialisation according to comparative advantage
at the national level. In the state-owned industry
the emphasis is on rationalisation and specialisation and against the proliferation of products to
meet local needs. 'Payment according to work'
rather than 'according to needs' has always been
professed, if not uniformly applied, in China.
Therefore, the main change which has taken place in
China is not in the general principle of payment.
It consists in a noticeable increase in the thresh-
hold of tolerance of economic inequality. This is
manifested in the 'responsibility system' being
introduced in rural communes, in the positive encouragement now given to the private side-line production by rural households, and to collective enterprises geared to 'making money' in urban areas, and
in the wage policy. The emergence of inequality is
justified on the grounds that it is paid for by an
increase in production, and that it is associated
with an increase in the income of poor households.
The accent of the distributional strategy now is not
so much on containing inequality within certain
bounds as on ensuring that poor households do not
fall below a minimal standard of living.

There is decentralisation, but now it takes the
form of granting autonomy to enterprises. Lateral
contacts are encouraged, but as part of the extension of market relationships. There is a shift away
from the ideology of 'serving the people' towards
economic rationality, which is seen as the quickest
way of raising the low standards of living of the
masses. Arguably, the Chinese economy of 1966-76
was only partially planned: key sectors and activities were planned by the government but the rest
was left to local initiative. Since 1978, the network of planning has become more taut as well as
more extensive. Local initiative is far from out of
fashion; its direction, however, has shifted. During the cultural revolutionary years it was directed
towards collectivist experiments and capital projects, but now it is more oriented towards attempts
by households to increase their incomes. The most
striking change is perhaps in education and the
attitude towards intellectuals: the stress now is
on academic standards and not on the popularisation
of technical education.

In all there are significant departures from
some of the cardinal principles of the decade 1966-
76; but it would be wrong to look at the changes
which have taken place in China as a complete shift
from one strategy to another. Economic policy

during 1966-76 was far from consistent, and it did contain within it some elements which have become prominent since 1976. Moreover, when registering the changes one should not overlook what has remained of the past attitudes towards the building of socialism and the development of the economy. An important component of the changes which have taken place since 1976 is the end of political uncertainty and sudden shifts in 'line'. This in itself may partially account for the improvement in the performance of the Chinese economy during the period 1978-80. It is also important from the point of view of the future evolution of the economy: the changes which have taken place are likely to be cumulative rather than reversible.

The changes in policy after 1976 have not been sudden. During the first two years after the downfall of the Gang of Four there was little change in the professed principles of economic policy; it was mainly a period of rehabilitation of those accused during the Cultural Revolution of taking 'the capitalist road'. Initially the main feature of the 'new economic policy' was the ambitious 'Four Modernisations' plan announced by Hua Guofeng (then the new, and since demoted Party Chairman) in 1977. It was a plan of the modernisation of agriculture, industry, defence and scientific research and education; it was no more than a massive programme of investment in the four sectors. Apart from its scale, it was identical to the one suggested by Zhou Enlai as far back as 1964. During the course of debates after 1978 it was criticised as too ambitious. The emphasis now is no longer on a massive investment within a short period of time. Lately, capital investment in industry has been curtailed. In fact the modernisation plan is no longer mentioned; the present economic policies are described as modest-sounding 'Re-adjustments'.

There has been some improvement in economic performance since 1976. 'How much of that is due to changes in economic policy and organisation?' is an open question. The rates of growth of industrial output have been as follows:[2]

1974-76	5.5%	(average yearly rate)
1977	14.3%	
1978	13.5%	
1979	8.5%	
1980	8.7%	
1981	4.0%	

Introduction

As one can see there has been a deceleration in industrial growth; and the high rates of growth in the
two years to 1978 could be attributed to the political stabilisation alone. So far as agriculture is
concerned, grain output in 1981 was 15% up on 1978,
despite a reduction of 6 million acres in grain crop
area (Beijing Review 3, 18th Jan. 1982:8). This
compares favourably with a 7.4% increase in grain
production during the cultural revolutionary years
of 1970-73, or even the increase of 10% between
1973-75.3 To this must be added the far greater
improvement in production since 1978 of non-grain
staples and agricultural side-line products.
    Moreover, there has been a pronounced shift in
the composition of industrial production from heavy
to light industry, as shown by the following table
of rates of growth.

Year	Light	Heavy
1979	9.6%	7.7%
1980	18.4%	1.4%
1981	13.6%	-4.5%

As a result, the share of light industry in industrial output has increased from 43.1% in 1978 to
51.3% in 1981 (Xinhua, 11th Jan. 1982). This shift
is associated with a large increase in household income on the one hand, and the curtailing of investment, on the other. The proportion of national income going to consumption went up from 63.5% in 1978
to 70% in 1981. In the three years to 1981, real
wages rose by 30.8%, and rural incomes by 60%. It
is, however, interesting to note that during the
same period rural and urban savings grew even faster
than incomes (Beijing Review 17, 26th April 1982:15-
16). Although the increase in savings is regarded
by the Chinese authorities as a sign of material
well-being (op.cit), it is not necessarily salutary.
For it may be an index of unsatisfied demand for
consumer goods (especially of some newly introduced
articles) and, therefore, of repressed inflation.
Here one may point out that high household savings
are commonplace in socialist economies of Eastern
Europe and that they are a monetary counterpart of
the shortage of consumer goods.
    The share of investment in national incomes is
shown by the following table:

Introduction

1976	31.1%
1977	32.3%
1978	36.5%
1979	33.6%
1980	Not available
1981	30.0% (approximate)

(Compiled from Beijing Reviews 12, 23rd March 1981:
25, and 17, 26th April 1982:15).

One may note that the share went up initially, as a
result of the ambitious investment policy. And it
only started to decrease in 1979. The aim is to
decrease the share further to 25% (Beijing Review 14
6th April 1981:3). Beside these changes, the composition of investment has also undergone a change.
The share of, what is termed, investment in production in total investment declined from 82.6% in 1978
to 58.9% in 1981; while that of investment in housing, health, education and research and culture
(non-productive investment) went up from 17.4% in
1978 to 41.1% in 1981. (Beijing Review 17, 26th
April 1982:15). The new bias towards 'non-productive' investment is in fact a belated attempt to redress the previous neglect of housing and the economic and social infrastructure.
     It is clear that there is a marked shift away
from the previous policy of austerity in consumption
and the glorification of investment in the name of
the collective interest towards an increase in
household incomes. But as we have just seen,an increase in money income may give rise to inflationary
pressures in the economy as well as increase consumption. Moreover, the increase in household incomes which has taken place in China has been coupled with an increase in income inequality. It still
remains to be seen whether present economic policies
are able to improve the standard of living of a significant proportion of poor households.

Recent Developments

It is time now to consider the extent of changes in
economic policy and organisation since 1976. How
far has enterprise autonomy and the loosening of
directed planning gone?
     Markets have existed at all times in China
since 1949. With an overwhelming proportion of its
population (between 75 and 80%) employed in communes
under collective rather than state ownership,the domain of operation of market relationships in China

has always been wide. The reform introduced since 1978 is amongst other things a cautious attempt to extend market relationships to carefully selected enterprises in the industrial sector.

However, it needs emphasising that nothing specific can be deduced from the simple fact of the extension of the domain of market relationships. For 'market' is an ambiguous term; it encompasses a wide variety of commercial relationships between economic agents of different status. Moreover, it can be associated with a disparate set of effects. Therefore, rather than just registering the fact of the scale and purchase of commodities, one needs to go further and look at the following:

1) the formal status of economic agents participating in market transactions,
2) the effect of market transactions on the behaviour of economic agents,
3) the non-market constraints to which economic agents are subject and
4) the general macroeconomic environment in which market transactions take place.

Following the usual practice we take market transactions to mean the transactions which take place among financially autonomous units. Thus the granting of financial autonomy is a pre-condition for the extension of market relationships. This is what has happened in China. Reform has taken the form of granting financial autonomy to an increasing number of industrial enterprises which simply means that they have a budget of their own.

This formal change has been coupled with a change in the indices used to control the activities of enterprises and an enlargement of the room for manoeuvre open to enterprises. Following the reform, profit has become the main index of the performance of enterprises, and there is a greater stress on technical efficiency. In addition, the financially autonomous enterprises have been given the right of disposal over their depreciation funds as well as a part of their profits. A large part of the profit of enterprises is still clawed back by the government, and on average they are left with 20% of their profit which can be used for bonuses and premia to employees, for the provision of social services to employees, and for investment. The variation around 20% is great , ranging between 2% and 100%, but it is still worth noting that on average the proportion of profit left in the hands of enterprises is smaller than in East European economies.

Introduction

Apart from these, enterprises have acquired
some power of choice - more nominal than real -
over their inputs and outputs. As Hare's chapter
makes clear this choice is constrained by the output quotas which organs of economic management set
to enterprises and by the administrative allocation
of scarce means of production. Generally speaking,
the scarcity of commodities, which is a characteristic of China as well as of other planned economies, sets a limit to the range of exercise of
market relationships. For it necessitates the
rationing of commodities through administrative
means, and therefore implies that it is not only
money but also the relevant document which is
needed for the acquisition of means of production.
Despite all the extension of market relationships
which has taken place in China during the last four
years it still remains in part a 'documentary'
economy. On the basis of the experience of
East European economies one can predict that it is
likely to remain so in future. Therefore, one can
argue that, given the scarcity of commodities which
historically has been a problem in centrally
planned economies, the effective scope for the
exercise of market relationships will remain
limited.

As for the effects of market transactions on
the activities of enterprises, they depend crucially
on the configuration of prices and the method by
which they are determined, and on the extent to
which financial constraints restrict the activities
of enterprises.

There is now widespread acceptance in China
that prices - at least those of the means of
production - should be equal to the cost of
production plus a profit margin,namely what Marx
termed prices of production. But the issue of how
prices should be calculated is still debated among
reformers. Prices in China are determined in some
cases by the government and in others by enterprises or by both of them. The latter set 'free
prices', while the former sets the 'fixed' and the
band of variation of 'controlled' prices. One may
note that this division of labour in the determination of prices is unlikely to result in prices of
production. As we see it, the main importance of
the acceptance of the prices of production consists
in the recognition of the need to charge for fixed
capital. That recognition has paved the way for the
charging of interest on investment funds supplied
to enterprises. This in turn has opened the way

for banks to play an active role in the allocation
of investment funds rather just being a 'cloakroom'
for funds.

It is important to emphasise that under conditions of scarcity, prices of production do not
perform the function of equating the supply and
demand for commodities. They do no more than to
restrict the variation in the rate of profit earned
by enterprises, and they necessitate some non-market
mechanism for the rationing of commodities. If
prices are to perform the function of equating the
supply and demand for commodities in China, inflation is inevitable. The Chinese economy went
through the rare experience of a 6% inflation in
1980, and a 2% inflation in 1981 (Beijing Review
23 Nov 1981:3). That inflation was no more than
a partial manifestation of the gap between the
demand and supply of commodities, which arguably
has always existed in China. But it has become
wider since 1978 because of the sharp increases
in household incomes. In the past the authorities
attempted to neutralise the gap by encouraging
austerity and the rationing of commodities - both
consumer and production goods. This then points to
the dilemma of the Chinese authorities. If they
wish to give a free rein to market relationships
then they have to accept inflation, which may well
be much higher than that in 1981. On the other hand
if they want to restrain inflation then they have
to resort to ideological exhortation and rationing
to bridge the gap between the demand and supply.
But rationing can lead to disguised inflation in
black marketing. The implication is, then, that
authorities cannot extend the scope of the market
by a simple judicial fiat; they are constrained by
macroeconomic conditions. In our view it is
highly unlikely that the Chinese authorities will
opt for an uncontrolled inflation, and therefore
they will have to settle for a limited play of
market forces.

The system of directive planning is still very
much intact in China. It owes its survival to two
factors. First, as a paper on the relationship
between planning and market in China by three
Chinese economists at an International Atlantic
Economic Conference in May 1979 points out, directive planning is needed to accomplish the large
scale structural transformation of the Chinese
economy and to secure socio-economic objectives
(Liu Guogang et al, 1980). The long term plan for
the Chinese economy announced by the leadership is

31

in fact the agenda for centralised directive
planning. The latter is not being disputed in
China. Secondly, directive planning is needed
because, as we have just argued, the leadership is
not willing to accept the full consequences of
giving the market a free rein. Therefore, as we
see it, planning through the market is less a
substitute for directive planning than a supplementary instrument of directive planning.

Until September 1980 only 16% of industrial
enterprises were elevated to financial autonomy.
But these enterprises accounted for about 60% of
the industrial output of the state sector. In that
month the State Council accepted the principle of
the extension of autonomy to all industrial enterprises in the state sector. Since then some form
of financial responsibility and profit retention
has been extended to all state enterprises in
Sichuan province and to a lesser extent in other
provinces. However, as the chapters by Lockett and
Hare point out, the 16% of enterprises selected to
pioneer the reform were the best equipped for
autonomy. Therefore their experience is not an
accurate index of the success of future reforms.
The enterprises left out during the first stage
include those which for various 'objective'
reasons cannot make profit and are thus dependent
on government subsidies, as well as those which do
not have the managerial expertise to make use of
autonomy.

This brings us to the limits of operation of
enterprise autonomy in China. In principle the
grant of financial autonomy to enterprises is a
method of imposing discipline on them by rewarding
the profit-makers and penalising the loss-makers.
However, since for socio-economic reasons it is
often impossible for Chinese authorities to let
persistent loss-makers go bankrupt, the financial
penalities which can be imposed on loss-makers are
necessarily limited. There has been some closure
of enterprises, but that has been a result of
mergers engineered by the authorities. Moreover,
the authorities use differential rates of taxation
or profit retention in order to equalise the
'objective' advantage. One may note that government subsidies to loss-making enterprises are in
effect a suspension of the principle of financial
autonomy. Therefore it can be argued that the
proportion of potentially profitable enterprises
sets limits to the range of extension of financial
autonomy for enterprises and the concomitant use of

profit as an instrument of control. This is not
peculiar to China; as Hussain points out in his
chapter, it is borne out by the experience of
financial autonomy in East European economies.
There have been recent signs of concern over
technical efficiency itself, where the discipline
of financial autonomy was supposed to be particularly effective. Industrial output may have
increased but so has the cost of production;
stockpiling and the poor quality of products are
still problems (Renmin Ribao editorial 27 Feb. 82,
tr. in SWB, 6970, BFI:10).
     Chinese writers talk of enterprises as a
'community of immediate producers' - a team of
managers and workers in the parlance of American
behavioural theorists. And they rationalise the
initial phase of the reform in terms of the pursuit
of material benefit by that community and the
concomitant gain to the economy in general in the
form of higher efficiency (Lin Zili, 1980: 173 &
175). In its general outline this rationlisation
is, one may note, a variant of the Adam Smith
argument that through the market economic agents,
each pursuing its own narrow material interest,
end up maximising social welfare. This is to be
expected since any rationalisation of the extension
of market relationships cannot but be a variant of
Adam Smith's classic argument.
     Since the industrial enterprise is at the centre
of urban economic reform it is worth looking closely
at what this 'community of immediate producers' is.
The enterprise is not a 'spontaneous' organisation
but is brought into existence by an administrative
decision or permission. Further, since there is
no financial market in ownership and the activities of enterprises are at least broadly regulated
by plan directives, the contours of the enterprise
are administratively determined. Mergers and
administrative reorganisation are decided by organs
of economic management rather than by enterprises
themselves. This has a crucial bearing on the
relationship between organs of economic management
and enterprises and on the 'objective' environment of
the enterprise, and therefore its profit potential
is determined by administrative decisions. The
implication is that the enterprise cannot be made
solely responsible for its financial performance.
     The economic unit in China - as indeed in other
socialist economies - is not just an economic unit
but also a political unit. The grassroot Party
organisation is anchored in the workplace. Most

managers are Party members; qualifications include
political reliability as well as economic competence.
That the enterprise is a crucial node in the
political network means that government policy towards enterprises cannot be based solely on economic
criteria. Besides, the enterprise is the locus of
provision of a wide variety of social services,
including housing, medical care and child care, the
significance of which we discuss later. The community of direct producers within the enterprise is
hierachical rather than egalitarian, and it cannot
be said to have a unified material interest. The
interests of workers are not necessarily the same
as those of managers. Some managers - but not all -
are in favour of increased autonomy for the enterprise, but it is not clear that workers will go
along with all the consequences of financial autonomy. Strictly speaking it entails the earnings of
employees varying with the financial performance of
the enterprise. However, there is a limit to the
range of variation - in particular that of decrease
- in earnings which workers would accept. As
elsewhere, workers in China like higher but also
stable earnings. This puts a brake on the principle
of financial autonomy in two ways. First, basic
wages have to be guaranteed independently of the
financial performance of the enterprise. Second,
the principle of 'each according to his work',
which has traditionally meant similar wages for
similar work regardless of the locus of employment,
indirectly restricts the variation in earnings
between workers in successful and less successful
enterprises. As far as wages are concerned the
reform has implied an increase in the earnings of
workers employed in profitable enterprises selected
to pioneer the reform. However, when the reform is
extended to unprofitable enterprises ,it is not
likely to lead to an equivalent decrease in
earnings of workers in those enterprises. Since
the downfall of the Gang of Four there has been a
general increase in the earnings of labourers; it
is that, rather than the link between earnings and
profit, which accounts for the popularity which the
economic reform has enjoyed in China.

In China the notion of the enterprise as the
community of immediate producers entails the
election of leading enterprise personnel by the
workforce. As pointed out earlier, the participation of workers in the operation of the enterprise was first introduced in 1957. During the
Cultural Revolution workers' participation was

extended to the highest enterprise level, and came
to be embodied in Revolutionary Committees. They
were abolished after the downfall of the Gang of
Four, and for a time the responsibility for the
running of the enterprise was placed solely with
the manager. This reversion back to 'one-man
management' (rejected in 1957 as a discreditable
Soviet practice) was a part of the restoration of
the chains of economic command which, according to
the present leadership, had broken down during the
cultural revolutionary years. More recently, however, the leadership has started to re-introduce
workers' participation, albeit in the form of a
resuscitation not of Revolutionary Committees but
of Workers' Congresses prior to the Cultural
Revolution. Not only are they different in name
but also the range of intervention of new Workers'
Congresses is more circumscribed than that of the
defunct Revolutionary Committees.

Since the re-introduction of workers' participation, as Lockett points out in his chapter, some
40% of enterprises in the state sector have
operated procedures for the election of officials
at one or more tiers of the enterprise. The scope
for the election of officials is, however, limited
by the appointment of officials by the government
in order to maintain the chains of economic command.
As yet, in only 44 cases is the ultimate authority
for electing the factory director formally given
to the Workers' Congresses, and even then the
election requires higher approval. There is
evidence that middle managers resent the whole idea
of workers' participation. The function assigned
to workers' management now is different from that
during the period of the Cultural Revolution. Then,
workers' participation - which was less formal than
it is now - was seen as a mechanism for putting
politics in command. But now workers' participation
is seen more as an instrument for improving
technical efficiency - a device for putting economics in command. Workers' Congresses as they exist
now are, generally speaking, more consultative than
'legislative' bodies: most regulations within which
enterprises work are decided by higher organs of
management rather than by Workers' Congresses.

State enterprises account for a small proportion of economic units, and employ an even smaller
proportion of the labour force. Therefore, reforms
directed towards them can only have a limited
effect. In contrast to the state sector the collective sector is very varied in size of units,

earnings of labourers and conditions of work. Apart
from rural communes, there are a large number of
collective enterprises in urban areas: factories,
workshops, repair shops, retail and catering outlets. They come under the aegis of municipalities
and neighbourhood organisations. The largest are
included in a plan. The rest, the majority, are
'guided' rather than directed by authorities. In
addition to collective enterprises, there are private establishments in urban areas. Though urban
collective and private enterprises are financially
autonomous, municipal authorities exercise a strong
indirect influence on their revenue through price
control, taxes and by restricting them to certain
branches of activity.

Though such enterprises have always existed in
China, the present leadership has encouraged their
further proliferation. Moreover, the stance towards them has undergone a radical change. During
the period of the Cultural Revolution they were expected to 'serve the people', and the emphasis was
on the rapid transformation of private into collective enterprises. But now they are licenced to conduct themselves as commercial organisations, and the
pressure on private enterprises to collectivise has
been removed. On the ideological plane collective
enterprises have been elevated in rank, and are considered by some to be almost as socialist as the
state enterprises (Jiang Yiwei 1980:66; Xue Muqiao,
December 1981).

As White points out in his chapter the strategy
behind the encouragement of collective and private
enterprises is that their proliferation will help
mop up urban labour exceeding the requirements of
the state sector. Chinese authorities have always
recognised that for a long time to come the state
sector will remain incapable of absorbing all the
urban labour force. In the past, especially during
the period of the Cultural Revolution, the export
of urban youth to the countryside, work-sharing
through overmanning in state enterprises and the
encouragement of collective enterprises were the instruments for tackling the massive problem of unemployment. The first is now regarded as undesirable and socially infeasible, and the second a
recipe for inefficiency and inculcating the mental-
ity of 'eating from the same iron bowl'. The result
is that the proliferation of collective and private
enterprises is the sole solution for what is in fact
a massive problem of unemployment.

Since 1976 employment in the urban collective

sector has grown faster than in the state sector. This development extends the dualism which has always been the central feature of the Chinese economy. That dualism is, of course, the co-existence of a state sector - with relatively high earnings, and relatively secure and stable conditions of employment - with a collective sector characterised by relatively low average earnings. As Lockett points out (Table 7:1) the average earnings in the urban collective sector is 77% of that in the state sector. The difference is not large, but the range of variation of earnings is wider in the urban collective than in the state sector. Many neighbourhood and young people's collectives pay wages to their workers lower than the lowest state enterprise wage.

China Daily (14 Feb. 1982) reports an increase in Shanghai City's collective sector workforce of 5.5% in 1981, making it a fifth of the total five million. This may not include a number of 'temporary residents', estimated as 200,000,who are probably contract workers.4 These are workers contracted to industrial collective or state enterprises, but without security of employment. As yet the urban collective sector accounts for only 23% of urban employment (Table 7:1); but the recent development implies a continued growth in this percentage. Zhejiang province is taken as a model, with its growth of urban collectives, by 17.6% in 1979 & 34.5% in 1980 (Jingji Guanli, 11, 1981:3-6).

One effect of this would be to increase the inequality of incomes in urban areas. Economic dualism is a commonplace and elsewhere is far more pronounced than in China. It remains to be seen whether China can encourage the rapid growth of the urban collective sector without incurring the problems usually associated with urban dualism, and whether the urban collective sector will grow fast enough to absorb the labour force in excess to the state sector. In his chapter White discusses the labour and employment policies in detail.

Since the provision of welfare services is intertwined with enterprises, any reform of enterprises raises the general problem of social welfare. Social services are distributed through two distinct channels: through the work-place and through the municipal organisations. For example, ration cards are issued either by the local police station or by the trade union organisation of the place of work. Apart from that, large enterprises have their own clinics (some even hospitals), educational and recreational facilities, housing and holiday

resorts. There are no uniform rules for access to
enterprise social services. In some cases they are
available to all inhabitants of the locality. In
addition, pensions are paid out of the social fund
of the enterprise and administered by the trades
union organisation. A large enterprise often resem-
bles a rural commune in that it is a unit of habit-
ation, a locus for provision of social services as
well as a production unit.

Since resources at the disposal of enterprises
vary, the provision of social services through work
places implies a variation in the standards of provision. With a shift in the direction of financial
autonomy this variation is bound to increase. More
profitable enterprises will have more to spend on
social services than the less profitable. In addition, the growth of the collective sector, composed
as it is of small establishments with few or no resources for providing social services, necessitates
the extension of social services provided by municipal authorities or by state insurance corporations, being introduced on a trial basis in Shanghai.
Otherwise, the gap between the standards of provision in the state sector and the collective and private sector is bound to grow. At a general level
one may note that because of the importance of social services and wide variations in the standards of
their provision, standards of living vary much more
than indicated by differences in money incomes.
Means to prevent the growth of social service inequalities do exist. One is to transfer the welfare
and insurance schemes of state enterprises to municipal authorities, as suggested by Jiang Yiwei
(1980). Less drastic would be a regulation limiting
the extent to which bonuses and welfare funds can be
increased. But it is not possible to say whether
either have been put into effect.

Self-reliance is the watchword of Chinese economic policy now, as it was of the policies prior to,
during and after the Cultural Revolution. However,
the interpretation put on 'self-reliance' has
changed. During the period of the Gang of Four, it
was taken to mean minimal participation in international trade, prohibition of foreign investment in
China and no foreign borrowing. But now 'self-
reliance' is to be achieved, in Premier Zhao Ziyang's
words, 'through equal and mutually beneficial exchange with other countries', and more importantly,
'through a bold advance into the world markets'
(quoted in China Trade and Economic Newsletter, Dec.
1981). The 'bold advance' has spurred export-

oriented agriculture, mineral extraction and industry. Cannon points out that much of the recent private investment in China has flowed into this sector. Besides household saving, Hong Kong and overseas Chinese are the biggest source of private investment in China. Though private investment contributes to the development of the Chinese economy, it raises the problem of the emergence of a sector which is outside the ambit of the plan. Foreign private investment raises the additional problem of the emergence of enterprises not under the control of the citizens of the PRC. Much private foreign investment is flowing into the hinterlands of Guangzhou and Hong Kong in the Pearl River delta. That region of China is likely to become an economic satellite of Hong Kong. Private foreign investment is not confined to Southern China; a part of it has gone to Shanghai and Tianjin. The inflow of private foreign investment has also influenced consumption patterns in China.

An interesting recent development in China is the emergence of various kinds of joint venture, in particular of joint Chinese and Japanese ventures. Littler in his chapter mentions several Japanese corporations which have established production facilities in China. The emergence of such ventures opens up the possibility of the importation of the two tier production system which is common in Japan. It is a system whereby large corporations contract out a part of their production to small establishments which pay out low wages and are completely dependent on their large customers. There is the possibility that a similar relationship might develop between joint ventures and urban and rural collective and private enterprises in China. Littler goes on to consider the far reaching implications of that development. In all, foreign investment in China is likely to give rise to economic differences and economic relationships which have not existed in China since Liberation. Cannon analyses some of their implications.

However, one needs to keep in view the scale of these developments. Private enterprises and export-oriented economic activities are still very small in relation to the whole of the Chinese economy. New imported consumer goods still have not penetrated deep into the Chinese economy, and their spread owes as much to the easing of restrictions on the visits of overseas Chinese as it does to importation or production of those goods in China. The penetration of new consumer goods implies an increase in differences in consumption patterns as well as an increase in the general consumption level. The former is of some significance because until recently consumption patterns, especially in urban areas, have by international standards been highly uniform.

With this in mind, what will be the effects of the spur to collective and private enterprise and the welcome given to foreign investment? First, there will be an increase in economic and productive activity at the margin of the planned economy. Second, there is likely to be an increase in differences in earnings and conditions of work in enterprises. As to the benefits, they do add to the development of the Chinese economy and permit a more flexible and a wider market in consumer goods. It is easy to condemn them as blemishes on China's socialist record, but the question which has to be answered then is whether the state sector by itself is capable of meeting the socialist aims of providing employment to all and satisfying consumer needs. As we see it, during the period of the Cultural Revolution these problems were not solved but were obscured by political slogans. The ease with which the present leadership first devalued the Cultural Revolution and then condemned it altogether is something which has to be taken seriously. That cannot be simply attributed to the political astuteness of the present leadership; it is, as we see it, an index of general dissatisfaction with the way in which economic problems were conjured away by 'putting politics in command'.

Recent developments in China have indeed extended the role of the market, and that extension owes as much to the developments in the collective and the private sector as to the grant of financial autonomy to state enterprises. The growth of the collective and the private sectors is of special importance because, by and large, they are not covered by the state resource allocation system. Their growth and the increased financial autonomy of state-owned enterprises point to a wide extension of markets in means of production, which until recently have been very rudimentary. Where they existed in the past, they were part of a black economy or of informal arrangements among enterprises. The encouragement now given to market transactions has led to a formal recognition of such transactions. Nevertheless, the state resource allocation system is, and is likely to remain, important. What this implies is that collective enterprises outside the range the system are

limited in the range and scale of their activities.
And as they grow and diversify they may, as they do
now, seek incorporation as state enterprises to secure resources.

None of the developments which have taken place
in China imply a dismantling of the planning system.
The growth of the market by itself does not imply an
end of planning. There is no incompatibility between planning and the market, unless, of course, one
identifies planning with quantitative planning. The
collective and the private sector which has grown
has not so much displaced the planned sector as
taken on what the planned sector cannot do. Further
there is no likelihood of the collective and the
private sector dwarfing the state sector. Foreign
investment in China is likely to be very limited,
and that is not because of the attitude of the
Chinese government but because of the attitude and
the caution of foreign investors.

To start with the main focus of the reform was
on the industrial-urban sector,but in time it shifted to agriculture. The changes which have taken
place in agriculture could be divided into four categories: experiments with alternative structures of
the commune, stress on diversifying agriculture, a
devaluation of collective capital projects and the
creation of a climate favourable to private side-
line production.

Since shortly after their foundation communes
have been a three-tier structure. The hierarchy of
importance attached to each tier has varied historically. Generally speaking, the 'left' has placed
emphasis on the higher tiers of the commune and
brigade, and the right on the lowest tier, the
team. The assumption has been that the team and
then the brigade would eventually disappear leaving
the commune to be both the administrative and the
sole productive organisation. Since the formalisation of the commune structure in the early 60s, the
team has been the accounting unit as well as the
principal unit of agricultural production in most
cases, while the higher tiers of the commune have
been more concerned with administration, and with
managing commune industry and carrying out large
scale capital projects. As the Grays point out in
their chapter the combination of production and
administration in the commune is being reconsidered.

However, the commune will not, even so, die
a sudden death. As Jack and Maisie Gray point out,
during the last two years there have been widespread
transformations in the internal economic relation-

ships of the communes. This has involved the introduction of various systems of so called production
responsibility - in effect a varied range of economic contracts. As a unified unit of cultivation,
the team has been replaced by a looser unit built
around contracts.

In some communes all the land and some capital
of the team have been divided up among constituent
households, who are then responsible for all the
tasks and the costs involved in the cultivation of
the land assigned to them. This amounts to a transfer of effective ownership to households, but only
an incomplete transfer. For households are not allowed to sell or lease the land assigned to them; and
existing agricultural machinery and production support facilities have remained collective. The distribution system associated with this particular
form of production responsibility varies. In some,
each household hands over a pre-assigned quota to
the team which after the deduction of the state
quota is distributed centrally to all constituent
households, working as well as non-working households. This implies a reduction in income inequality among working households, and ensures succour to
households not able to support themselves. In
others, there is no centralised distribution to ·
working households, and each household pays only its
share of the state-quota, and of the accumulation
and public welfare fund. The assignment of collective land to individual households is the extreme
form of the production responsibility system, and
has happened only in those communes where the collective organisation had not struck deep roots
(Beijing Review 48, 30th Nov. 1981:15-20).

In those communes where collective organisation
was already well developed, there has been no par-
celling out of land to households. There the cultivation of land is, as before, organised by the team.
And it is only tasks which are divided among households, who may now specialise in particular work.
As before, the team distributes the income and the
produce, but remuneration to working households is
now strictly according to work. Egalitarian distribution policies, symbolised by the once highly
praised and now discredited Dazhai production brigade, have gone out of fashion. The changes which
have taken place are still regarded as experimental,
though not transitory. Provincial governments have
selected a few communes to try out new institutions
outside the framework of the commune. For example,
in Sichuan, the province which has taken a lead in

granting autonomy to industrial enterprises, agro-
industrial cum commercial complexes and agriculture-
animal husbandry cooperatives have grown up side by
side with the selected communes (Beijing Review 13,
29th March 1982:3-4).

As the Grays point out the commune was meant to
be a collective organisation, but in actual practice
it functioned more like state organisations, though
without their characteristically greater security
and standardisation of personal incomes. The commune has been successful in mobilising the peasantry and bringing peasant agriculture within the ambit of the planned economy without forced collectivisation. Combining production and administration
in one unit was meant to provide a framework for
undertaking large capital projects and the diversification of economic activities, which would, it was
thought, help develop the countryside as well as
absorb surplus rural labour. In that too, the communes succeeded. But the combination of production
and administration has also been a source of problems.

For it resulted in the appointment of commune
officials by the provincial and county authorities,
which cut the ground from underneath the ideal of
the commune as a self-governing and democratic community of producers. Not only are officials and
Party cadres appointed from above but also the commune is at least partially responsible for paying
them. Moreover, the commune is also responsible for
paying teachers in village schools and 'barefoot
doctors'. The burden of paying these personnel ultimately falls on production teams. Lately, the
number of officials and full-time Party cadres in
communes has been sharply reduced, and the policy is
that they should be elected rather than appointed
(Beijing Review 12, 24th March 1980:14-20). There
are proposals to disengage government administration
from the organisation of production and marketing,
turning the commune into a marketing-cum-production
cooperative. The administrative functions of the
communes are to be taken over by the re-created
xiang (district) authorities. With these changes
the key characteristics of the present day communes
would disappear. That, however, would not mean an
end to collective agriculture, which has existed in
China since 1955. The intention, rather, is to
create a realistic and a democratic basis for varied
forms of cooperation among households.

There always have been wide differences between
communes, though the differences within the commune

have been much less. Therefore, the communes did succeed in greatly reducing the economic differences internal to them by redistributing from rich to poor households, or from the rich to the poor teams depending on the level at which redistribution took place. To the extent that redistribution drives a wedge between work performed and remuneration received, it has dampened work-incentives. Hence an oft-repeated remark in communes, 'you get the same regardless the amount of work you do'. Generally speaking, two types of changes in the method of payment have taken place in communes. First, wherever an egalitarian distribution policy has been in force that is set aside in favour of payment according to work. Redistribution is allowed but that is to be restricted to non-self sustaining or poor households. The second change which has taken place is in the way in which work points are calculated. Earlier work was taken in a broad sense: everybody doing similar work got the same work-points. But now there is a greater differentiation among the types of work, and work-points are graded according to the efficiency of work (Beijing Review 3, 19th January 1981:23-29, and 15, 12th April 1982:18-28).

During the decade 1966-76 the accent was on grain production for the justifiable reason that the provision of staple food was - and indeed is - a pressing problem. In that China has been a singular success among Third World countries, and in the main it has succeeded in feeding its rapidly growing population. But now in China it is argued that this near self-sufficiency in grain was achieved at the cost of neglecting non-staple crops, and of inefficient use of land. Since 1978 the official policy is not to 'prescribe' but merely to 'recommend' cropping patterns to teams (Beijing Review 35, 31st August 1981:15-18). The production of non-staples by collective organisations and households is encouraged, and households can get loans for side-line production. So far the policy has succeeded: the production of non-staples as well as grain has increased. Given the bias of the new policy, the production of the former has grown faster than the former. In appraising the shift in cropping patterns one has to keep in view the fact pointed out by a Chinese agronomist who questions the logic of the current enthusiasm of his peers for animal husbandry: annual per capita grain consumption has been around 300 kilogrammes (below the world average of 350) for some time (Beijing Review 7, 15th February

1982:26-28). The official target is to increase per
capita consumption to 400 kilogrammes per year
(Beijing Review 2, 11th January 1982:24). What this
points to is that the shift in cropping patterns
away from grain may pose a food problem in future.
The attainment of the official target for grain consumption in the foreseeable future cannot be taken
for granted, especially since the present pricing
policy of the government makes the production of
non-food crops more lucrative than growing grain.
This also was the case during the cultural revolutionary decade, but then 'putting the collective
interest first' and 'taking grain as the key link'
inhibited peasants from responding to price signals.
    What, in all, are likely effects of new trends
in rural communes? Chinese authorities repeatedly
emphasise that the production responsibility system
has not undermined the foundations of collective
agriculture, and that in some ways it has strengthened the rural collective economy. Collective agriculture in China does not refer to one but to a wide
variety of socio-economic relationships. Therefore
the question 'whether the production responsibility
system has undermined collective agriculture?' is
not illuminating. Rather the important issue is one
of specific changes in the multiple relationships
which together have constituted the rural collective
economy.
    So far as the cultivation of land is concerned
it is clear that the introduction of production
responsibility has led to a decrease in the scale of
cooperation from a team (consisting of around 20
households) to smaller 'integrated units' (consisting of 3 to 5 households). The team, however, still
remains the unit of account, distribution and taxation. Although the Chinese authorities stress that
land and means of production remain collective (team
or brigade or commune) property, it is worth point-
ing out that the newly emergent 'integrated units'
can purchase agricultural machinery out of their
savings. Therefore, agricultural implements owned
by groups of households and not the team have increased and will continue to increase. Previously,
accumulation meant accumulation by one of the three
tiers of the commune, but now in addition to that
there is accumulation by individual households or
'integrated units'. Prior to the current changes
when the land and means of production were collectively owned, the economic differences among households eventually consisted in the number of able-
bodied persons they each had. But because of the

45

Introduction

present changes households will differ not only with
respect to the amount of labour but also with respect to ownership of agricultural implements and
other forms of capital. One likely effect of this
will be that the households well-endowed in labour
and poor capital will hire labour to the households
well-endowed with capital. The hiring of labour is
allowed, but its scale is limited.

That China is sparse in cultivable land and
abundant in labour is central to any assessment of
the commune and the current changes. The total
farmland is 100 million hectares, and the rural
workforce is around 300 million and rural population
around 800 million. The implication is that with
land per worker equal to a third of a hectare, there
is just not enough land to employ all rural labourers. It is estimated that with the present technology only 50% of the available workforce is actually
needed for agriculture, and that mechanisation would
decrease the percentage even further to 20 and 30%
(Beijing Review 41, 12th October 1981:3). One may
therefore identify two distinct problems which China
faces: feeding its population and producing non-
food crops for internal consumption and exports, and
second, the diversification of economic activities
in order to absorb surplus labour. Since the Great
Leap Forward capital projects like schemes to con-
serve and distribute water and terracing of hills,
and the establishment of industries at brigade
and at commune level,have helped to absorb surplus
rural labour - but only to a degree. Collective
capital projects still remain on the agenda, but
now, according to the official guidelines on agriculture, the participation in them is to be voluntary and remunerated (Beijing Review 12, 24th March
1980:14-20). During the cultural revolutionary
years, private side-line production was frowned upon
because it distracted from collective capital projects. Now the former has a priority over the latter; and side-line production outside the aegis of
the commune is seen as one of the two principal
mechanisms for diversifying and absorbing surplus
rural labour. The other, as before, is the establishment of more rural industries. The state has
taken over a greater responsibility for financing
large-scale capital projects. Non-communal side-
line production has increased the income of at least
a proportion of households, but it still remains to
be seen whether its growth will make a significant
contribution to the absorption of surplus labour.
Collective accumulation funds still remain - even in

those communes where the team land has been parcell-
ed out;furthermore, they have, as Chinese writers
point out, increased because of the increase in
household incomes. But one also has to take into
account the fact of increase in the cost of capital
projects because of the shift from voluntary to
remunerated work on such projects. The effect of
the changes on capital projects is of special importance because they not only put surplus labour to
work but also they indirectly raise the productivity of agriculture.

The changes in organisation of work and the
method of distribution in communes open up the problems of an increase in economic differences among
rural households which have not been great until
now (Nolan and White, 1981), and of provision for
poor households. There is no doubt that the recent
changes have increased the differences as well as
the level of rural incomes. The main reason for the
former is that households are not equally well-endowed with labour and savings. Historically, China
has guaranteed its population food, clothing,
housing, medical care and burial expenses - the so
called 'five guarantees'. It is estimated that now
10% of rural households are not able to provide
these out of their own income (Beijing Review 52,
28th December 1981:17-18). When a commune or a
lower tier distributes 'to each according to needs',
provision for such households poses no special problem. But when payment is according to work, provision for the poor households does emerge as a separate problem. This is exactly what has happened in
China during the last two years. The problem has
come in for a widespread discussion. At present, as
one can gather from reports in Beijing Review, the
methods of provision to poor households vary from
commune to commune. With the dissolution of the
commune and the separation of diverse activities
which are at present carried out by communes, it is
doubtful that the present informal arrangements will
be able to carry out the five guarantees. In rural
as well as in urban areas municipal authorities will
have to assume a much greater responsibility for
social welfare. The Chinese authorities recognise
this, but as yet there are no definite plans.

Conclusion

An assessment of the reforms is now possible, without aspiring to firm conclusions.
1. There has been a noticeable improvement in the

performance of agriculture and industry after the
downfall of the Gang of Four, but,as we see it,in
industry that is more due to political stability, an
end to conflicting policies and the restoration of
chains of economic command, than due to the economic
reforms which have been introduced in China since
then.

2.   The economic reforms introduced after the downfall of the Gang of Four seem to be popular. But,as
we see it,that popularity is perhaps less a result
of specific changes brought about by the reform and
more due to the general increase in wages in the
state sector,increases in prices which the government pays for agricultural produce and the increase
in the availability of consumer goods.

3.   Economic reforms will undoubtedly increase economic differences: in earnings among state enterprises, between enterprises in the collective sector
and between households in rural areas. The response
to this increase in differentiation has yet to be
seen.

4.   Economic reforms will bring to the surface certain problems which have always existed in China,
and will make certain problems emerge which have
been unknown in China. Among the former, unemployment is the major problem. Leaving aside rural
unemployment, the problem of urban unemployment is
massive in China. It is an open question whether
the collective sector can and will grow fast enough
to absorb surplus urban labour.

5.   The leadership cannot introduce market reforms
by fiat; the extension of market relationships is
constrained by general macroeconomic conditions. In
particular shortages of means of production makes
their administrative rationing, and therefore the
control of enterprises by administrative directives,
inevitable.

6.   The success of market oriented reforms depends
crucially on the managers and the functionaries in
the organs of management. The leadership may be
impatient for market oriented reforms, but it is not
at all clear that all managers and functionaries
are.

7.   One has to be careful not to gauge the future
course of economic reforms by the experience of
pilot schemes. Pilot schemes are always too successful because those selected to pioneer the reform
tend to be the best suited for it. East European
economies are littered with highly successful pioneer experiments. Financial and economic autonomy
works well and may even yield spectacular results

when it comes to profitable enterprises, but it does not with respect to less successful enterprises. On the basis of experience of East European economies which have introduced reforms very similar to those being introduced in China, the most likely outcome is that financial and economic autonomy will be restricted in its effects: it will apply to successful enterprises but not to less successful enterprises, who will have to be subsidised by the government. Subsidies to loss-making enterprises are common even in Hungary, the most market-oriented of East European economies.

8. With increasing differences and economic autonomy,social welfare and the provision of social services is likely to emerge as one of the major problems in China. The point is that politics in command of economics resolved income maintenance and the provision of social services as general problems, and turned them into local problems for enterprises, municipalities and communes. With the increasing emphasis on self-interest, the provision of sustenance and social services to marginal groups will start to emerge as a separate and distinct problem.

9. Since the downfall of the Gang of Four there has been an increase in household incomes, and that increase comes on top of large household savings. This with the introduction of new consumer goods and a shift away from the previous emphasis on austerity raises the problems associated with large unsatisfied consumer demand. In varying degrees this problem is a commonplace in all East European economies, and it is a major cause of dissatisfaction. The emphasis on material incentives accentuates the problem because material incentives take the asymmetric form of an increase in the earnings of more successful rather than a decrease in the earnings of the less successful. Further, as Deng Xiaoping has himself pointed out, bonuses and premia are often not based on higher productivity but simply used as a device for increasing earnings. Therefore, there is no reason to assume that all bonuses and premia are backed by higher productivity. Thus, as we see it, material incentives are a two-edged weapon. The 6% inflation which China experienced in 1980 was not an isolated problem but a manifestation of excess consumer demand in the economy.

10. 'Politics in command' stressed democracy everywhere, but electoral and democratic procedures were rarely formalised. 'Following the mass line' is no longer currency, but electoral and democratic procedures have started to be formalised, and there is

increasing codification of the civil and public law.
11. Wide economic differences have always existed
in the countryside. The emergence of contractual
obligations in place of collective work would accen-
tuate those differences further. The basic problem
is one of provision for those households which are
not able to sustain themselves. The second problem
is one of the execution of capital works and the
provision of agricultural support services which are
beyond the capacity of households and teams.
12. Chinese population is still far from being
well-fed. Ensuring an adequate food supply still
remains a problem in China. The grant of autonomy
to rural households in the choice of cropping
patterns and in pursuing side-line occupations may
create a food problem in future.
13. Foreign investment and deeper involvement in
international trade have attracted much attention
for the good reason that they imply a fundamental
departure from previous policies. But it is unlikely that either of them would assume major proportions in China. That is not simply because of the
attitude which the government might take but also
because of the limited possibilities which exist for
the extension of international trade and attracting
foreign investment. None the less, foreign investment is likely to have important regional effects in
China: the hinterland of Guangzhou is rapidly becoming an economic satellite of Hong Kong. Moreover
investment by the overseas Chinese may well assume a
special economic and social significance.

PART 1

DEBATES AND COMPARISONS

CHINESE ECONOMIC DEBATES AFTER MAO AND THE CRISIS OF OFFICIAL MARXISM

Søren Clausen

Looking back at the debates that have been taking place among Chinese economists since 1978, one is tempted to conclude that Chinese economic thinking is a not altogether alien world. In the various scholarly debates, as they are expressed in the economic journals and at big conferences, one finds protagonists of a 'tight money' policy and cuts in public spending, others arguing in favour of a thorough price reform, general concern about inflationary wage pressures, etc. The acute economic problems of China anno 1981 - unemployment plus inflation - are sadly universal, and China's economic strategists are dealing with those universal problems. No wonder that the economic discourse of China, after the dust clouds of Maoism have by and large settled, gradually takes on a more familiar hue.

This non-uniqueness of Chinese economic thinking is even more striking when one looks at economic developments in the Soviet Union and Eastern Europe in the 1950's and 1960's. It can be argued that the development of China closely follows the precedent of these countries, only with a time lag of some 15 to 20 years; likewise, the post-Mao economic debates sometimes duplicate exactly earlier debates in the Soviet Union, Poland, Hungary and other places[1]. Is history, after all, able to repeat itself?

The purpose of this essay is not a comparison between Soviet/East European and Chinese economic debates, nor shall I attempt conclusions about the changing orientation of economic policy. My purpose is to take a look at the fact that the various 'schools' and trends in Chinese 'political economy' are all based on this or that interpretation of Marxism, a Marxism[2] which is in a constant process of absorption and transformation by the elite, but nevertheless very much alive as framework and structuring element. It is probably in this context of the ongoing sinification of Marxism and the changes in the functions of ideology that the peculiar aspects - if any - of China's economic thinking can best be demonstrated.

Why bother about Chinese Marxism, one might ask, since apparently the Chinese are busy 'liberating' themselves from a lot of it? The point is, Chinese Marxism is an economic paradigm and no mere formality. It provides economists with a framework, a world outlook, basic methodology, biases - much like Keynesianism or monetarism in the West. What is more, in China the ideology of the economists is far more than just an economic paradigm, it is also the central ideological code, vital to the elite in its struggle to provide legitimacy and self-identification.

This is not to suggest that there is fundamental unity in China's economic thinking; the elite has its internal struggles, too, and in the sphere of economic thinking they have been quite acute at times. Today one finds very different approaches, from 'market socialism' to technocratic plan reform to Stalinist orthodoxy, etc. But the various trends and interests all have to express themselves in terms of this or that interpretation of Marxism; and the ongoing debate among these trends is intelligible only in the light of this framework.

The case of Xue Muqiao might serve as an illustration. Xue is a leading economic ideologue in the post-Mao era, his articles are generally given the most prominent position in the Party and economic journals, and his latest book has even been translated into English in full (Xue Muqiao, 1981). In China - and outside China as well - he is usually seen as the main spokesman of the 'market reformers'. Since the middle 1950's he has been associated with the Chen Yun group[3], consistently arguing a relaxation of the planning structure and the high level of accumulation. He is a 'liberal'. But he is more than that: looking back at his writing in the transition years of 1976-78, one is struck by the fact that Xue in those not so distant times actually defended certain elements of late Maoist orthodoxy, apparently fighting against great pressure. As late as 1978 he stuck to Maoist concepts like 'to limit the negative effects of the law of value', 'restricting bourgeois rights', 'criticizing new-bourgeois elements' and the like [4], at a time when these concepts were rapidly going out of circulation. So perhaps he is a 'left dogmatist', too?

How do these two characteristics fit in with each other? Does he have a clear opinion at all, it might be asked. Of course Xue, being authoritative, cannot be very consistent, since he often acts as a spokesman of the leadership as a whole rather as an individual. But the clue to this apparently blatant contradiction lies in his interpretation of Engels' Anti-Dühring, with its identification of socialism with the dying away of commodity production and the law of value, Xue's point being that in the case of China this should be a very long process. In contrast, Xue's main ideological opponent throughout the last few decades, Sun Yefang, has based himself on an interpretation of Marx's ideas on 'time economy' as they are formulated in certain passages of Capital, with very different implications for the concept of the law of value (we shall return to these gentlemen in a short while).

Both Xue Muqiao and Sun Yefang perform political roles, they represent different strategies and interests. But these roles are performed in a universe of Marxist scholastics, which is not just an outer shell. Somehow, it is reality to these men.

The Stage

In the period immediately following the downfall of the 'Gang of Four' the efforts of the political-economic ideologues were concentrated on refuting the political economy of the 'Shanghai school' (see P.M. Christensen's contribution to this collection) and restoring pre-gang orthodoxy. But what exactly was that? How far back to go?

In the ideologically very authoritarian period of 1977 and early 1978, libraries and book stores were systematically purged of economic literature that could be associated with 'Gang' viewpoints. Altogether about two dozen books, published in Shanghai, Tianjin and Beijing in the years 1973-76, were taken out of circulation. The operation left very little on the shelves: the 'Gang' had had its authoritarian periods, too.

In universities and schools, time-honoured textbooks of political economy from before the Cultural Revolution were reintroduced. But what did these generally quite formalistic texts have to offer to the solution of the economic and social problems of the post-Mao era? In the search for a

usable ideology in the field of economic theory,
the ideological functionaries were painfully remin-
ded of the fact that before the Cultural Revolution
quite different approaches had been in existence
beneath the surface of ideological unity. So the
search went ever further back in time. For a time
in 1977, the economic thinking of late Stalinism
was promoted. The anachronism of this project must
have been apparent to everybody.

The very concept of 'ideological unity' had to
be reformed, if the economic theoreticians were to
have any function to perform. The outcome was a
kind of controlled diversification of the economic-
theoretical discourse, or 'hundred flowers' as the
Chinese prefer to call it. To a large extent the
'great debates' in the field of economic theory in
the years of 1957-63 were restaged in the years
1978-80, very often with the same people performing
the same roles, having been rehabilitated to their
old jobs. A wave of publishing started in late
1978.

But getting rid of 20 years of Maoist infil-
tration of the political-economic discourse cannot
be an easy job; one might expect the Chinese ideo-
logists to encounter even greater difficulties than
did Khruschev in his 'half revolution' against
Stalinism. Let us take a look at these difficulties
in a simple case study, the debate on the commodity
or non-commodity status of the means of production.

The Status of the Means of Production

In an economy such as China's, there are different
forms of transfer and circulation of goods. As for
the transfer of means of production, typically from
one state-owned enterprise to another, the theoretical question facing the Chinese economists is:
what is the nature of such transactions? To put it
more exactly: do these transactions have the nature of commodity exchange or not? This question
has been the subject of extensive discussion in
China in the last few years. Obviously, the answer
to the question has a lot of implications for the
practical economic strategy to be adopted, particularly to the strategy of 'market reform'. Within
the general paradigm of Chinese Marxism, it is a
focal question.

Chinese debates on this subject do not take
place in an historical void. Looking back at the
whole tradition of 'the political economy of socialism', it has been a central issue of economic

56

debates at one time or another in most state socialist countries. Also in China, it is not an altogether new question.

The point of departure for Chinese debates on
this question is Stalin's Economic Problems of
 ocialism in the USSR from 1952 and the official
Soviet textbook of political economy from 1954,
which was a follow-up of Stalin's book. These two
texts came to play an enormous role in the formation of Chinese economic thinking in the People's
Republic, filling up a theoretical vacuum: in the
Chinese context, there was very little else to
build on at the time.

In a way, that was true also of the Soviet
Union at the time, since Stalin's little book marked the end of a two-decade-long period of 'everything quiet on the theoretical front'. After the
conclusion of the great economic debates of the 20's
and the establishment of Stalinism, the Soviet
Union was in fact left without any general economic
theory, not to mention debates. The purpose of
Economic Problems ... was to put an end to this
situation.

Stalin's vision of socialism was that of
smoothly functioning clockwork; socialism was seen
as an independent mode of production based on public ownership of the means of production, governed
by a number of 'objective economic laws'. Among
these, the 'law of value' was reintroduced after
decades of banishment. It was a 'law of value'
very different from the one operative in capitalist
societies, a tame 'law of value', viewed as a useful instrument for the planners, whose job was seen
as that of interpreting 'objective economic laws'
and putting them to good use.

Basically, Stalin's contemplations on the
theoretical problems of value remained faithful to
the general consensus of the early economic debates
of the 1920's. Despite numerous contradictions
(viz. the Bukharin-Preobrazhensky debate) the generally accepted idea was that of an irreconcilable
conflict between capitalist value and elements of
socialist economy. In Stalin's version, too, value
was seen fundamentally as an alien element in the
socialist economy, but unavoidable due to the fact
that there was not yet a single state ownership comprising all sectors of the economy. There still
had to be exchange between the collective and the
state sector. But on the other hand, with planning
supreme, '... the law of value has no regulating
function in our socialist production' (Stalin, 1972:

19), its influence being restricted to the sphere
of circulation. Particularly in relation to exchange within the state sector, the 'law of value'
was thus seen as an <u>outer shell</u>, in contrast to the
essentially socialist nature of the economic functions.

In China, these ideas of Stalin were introduced
as infallible dogma and applied to a very different
reality, the reality of the gradual transformation
of private industry into state industry and private
farming into collectives. Liberating the regulation of production from the 'law of value' became
a practical task. As expressed by Xue Muqiao in
1953 - already then a leading spokesman - 'The
sphere of influence of the law of value (<u>jiazhi</u>
<u>guilu qi zuoyong fanwei</u>) has already without doubt
been somewhat restricted, and in the future it shall
be restricted even more' [5].

In connection with the general crisis of the
Soviet bloc in 1956 (and for a number of other
reasons, not to be discussed here), the Chinese
leadership began to drift away from the mainstream
of development in the state socialist countries.
It became possible, even mandatory, to find one's
own feet, also in the context of economic theory.
The first expression of this fact was Mao's famous
speech on <u>Ten Major Relationships</u>, and in the following years some aspects of Stalinist dogma came
to be challenged in China - from both the Left and
the Right.

To mention the latter first, Sun Yefang - the
<u>enfant terrible</u> of Chinese economic theory - had
opened up the attack already in late 1956, suggesting that planning and statistical work should
actually be <u>based</u> on the law of value [6] rather
than restricting or negating it. In the following
years Sun developed this notion into a full-fledged
theory of value under conditions of a socialist
economy, particularly in his major work on value
from 1959 [7]. From a slightly different point of
departure, Gu Zhun in 1957 advocated making fuller
use of the law of value to activate the powers of
self-interest in the service of production [8].
Both of these approaches are very much alive in
Chinese economic debates today.

As for the first-mentioned challenge, the one
from the Left, 1958 saw a renaissance of what was
essentially classic Bolshevik thinking (a prime
example of which is Preobrazhensky's economic
thought): Socialism was perceived as the ongoing
struggle against remnants of capitalism, among

which was the 'law of value'. Arguments in this
direction were put forward by people like Chen Boda,
Zhang Chunqiao [9], and, notably, Mao Zedong, in
his 'Reading Notes on the Soviet textbook of
"Political Economy"', a lengthy commentary on the
first full Chinese translation of the above mentioned official Soviet textbook, written by Mao
around 1960 [10]. The Leftists did not, however,
tackle the question of the status of the means of
production in any concrete or precise way. An indication of Mao's line of thought in those years
was offered at a symposium on economic theory in
Suzhou in 1979, when it was revealed that Mao had
opposed Stalin's axiom of the non-commodity status
of transfers within the state sector, reportedly
with the argument that this axiom was an expression
of 'lack of trust in the peasants' [11].
    The first few years following the debâcle of the
Great Leap Forward saw a lively debate on questions
of economic theory; it was in fact the First
Golden Age of Chinese economic thinking, and most
of what is now the stock of economic thought was
developed in those few years in the early 1960's.
But when a new ideological Ice Age came around in
1963-64, Stalin's value concept emerged unharmed.
And this situation remained unchanged for about a
decade.
    The Cultural Revolution did not produce much in
terms of economic theory, apart from a heap of vicious attacks on Sun Yefang and other unorthodox thin-
kers (these criticisms were in fact not very substantial from a theoretical point of view...). It
was left to the Shanghai school, headed by Zhang
Chunqiao, to formulate theoretically the experience
of the Cultural Revolution, shaping an economic
platform of the Left. In a number of publications
appearing in 1975 and 1976, Stalin's above-mentioned
axiom on the non-commodity status of the means of
production was finally challenged once again. The
message was: the means of production are in fact -
in a certain sense - commodities, submitted to the
regulation of the law of value, since even within
the state sector each enterprise functions as a
relatively independent unit, with its own profit-
and-loss calculations, etc. There was a political
point behind this theoretical operation: since in
the theoretical edifice of the Shanghai school the
law of value was seen as the general basis of
'bourgeois rights', 'restoration of capitalism',
etc., the operation aimed at opening everybody's
eyes to the danger of a restoration of capitalism.

Look how widespread the law of value is! Not even
in the state sector can we feel safe!

Of course this heterodoxy of the Shanghai school
was duly criticized after the downfall of the 'Gang
of Four', and the criticism went hand in hand with
a new orthodoxy of what can be characterized as the
authoritarian current of 1977. The general trend
was one of strengthening the central organs and
institutions in relation to local ones, re-
establishing confidence in those kinds of people
that the Shanghai school had designated as (potential or real) capitalist-roaders.

But re-centralization turned out to be a short-
lived approach. The overheating of the economy in
1978 and the ever more serious sectoral imbalances
paved the way for the triumphant ascendancy to
power of the market reformers, and very quickly the
orthodoxy which had been only recently re-
established turned out to be more of a problem and
a liability. The need for deep-going reform was
urgent, not least so in the state sector, where the
plan system of material allocation became ever more
inadequate, with supplies of certain goods piling
up in the storehouses, while other, needed, equipment was unavailable.

It was entrusted to the top ideologue Hu Qiaomu
- a historian by trade - to present the new official line. In a speech to the State Council in the
summer of 1978 he introduced the slogan of 'running
the economy by economic mechanisms' (rather than by
administrative means). Essential to this new
approach was the notion that the law of value does
in fact 'regulate' production, even within the
state sector. Or, in other words, the means of
production are 'in a way' commodities, too [12].
Finally the Stalin dogma had been overcome, with
full official backing! Ironically, the new gospel
was just a repetition of what Zhang Chunqiao & co
of the Shanghai school had been saying earlier on,
and with the very same argument (the relative independence of the economic units). But basically it
was a reform of Stalin 'from the right': the law
of value is not inferior to the other economic laws
of socialism (- and soon a number of people started arguing that it was in fact superior....).

Hu Qiaomu's speech was presented to the public
in such a way that there was no doubt about the ob-
ligatory nature of this new axiom. And everybody -
with very few and rather insignificant exceptions
[13] - quickly tuned in. Throughout 1979 and 1980,
the ideological establishment was busy building up a

theoretical foundation to the new line. The arguments vary somewhat, some people finding the <u>division of labour</u> behind it all; or the quantitative and qualitative differences in human labour (Fan Jigang, 1980); or rather 'the unique relation of material interests in the period of socialism' [14]. But behind the subtleties of the various Marxist exegeses, one perceives rather deep differences. To simplify matters, let us return to Xue Muqiao and Sun Yefang as representatives of different approaches to the question of value. It will be demonstrated that these two gentlemen differ significantly in their use of economic categories, and that these differences are not just a matter of academic nicety but a reflection of diverging economic strategies.

As for Xue Muqiao, his long career has always been based on a combination of theoretical and practical work (particularly in the field of price policy). As was mentioned above, he is associated with Chen Yun, China's economic strongman after the Third Plenum of the 11th Central Committee of the Chinese Communist Party in December 1978. But Xue has never been very partisan, and his career shows remarkable stability; he was never really in disgrace. In his own words, his views throughout the times are 'to a certain degree representative' of the mainstream of Chinese economic thinking (Xue Muqiao, 1978:1).

Xue started out on the 'liberal' reformation of Stalin's value concept in 1957. Putting aside his earlier contempt for the 'law of value', he suggested that even though this law did not <u>regulate</u> production, it did have an 'enormous influence' (<u>juda yingxiang</u>) on it (Xue Muqiao, 1978:24). The historical background for this reformulation was the decentralization measures of 1957. As a matter of fact, these measures in the last analysis did not take on the form advocated by Chen Yun and Xue Muqiao: rather than a combination of sectoral and territorial decentralization, with emphasis on greater freedom to the enterprises, the leadership decided on territorial decentralization, giving more power to the local Party organizations (Schurmann, 1968:196ff.).

In the post-Mao era we once again find Xue Muqiao among those advocating more freedom of action to the enterprises, and correspondingly making better use of the 'law of value'. Why, then, was it entrusted to the generalist Hu Qiaomu rather than the expert Xue Muqiao to deliver the new for-

mula on the commodity status of the means of production in 1978? Xue's stubborn defence of certain
aspects of late Maoism in the 1976-78 period has
been mentioned, and even though there is no documen-
tation to it, he probably resisted the new formula.
No matter how flexible the man is, the new formula
must have been hard to stomach, since it implies a
value concept antagonistic to Xue's own.

Xue's 'making fuller use of the law of value'
is comparable to what the Soviet Union's New
Economic Policy was to Bukharin around 1925: a
necessary retreat, an attempt to establish a working relationship with the peasantry, a smoothing of
the economic structure. Certainly it is not the
abandoning of the long-term perspective nor the
idea of the ultimately contradictory nature of the
relation between (socialist) planning and (capitalist) law of value. The fundamental difference
between Bukharin and Preobrazhensky was that of the
time horizon of socialist construction, Bukharin
advocating a slow approach. In a very similar way,
Xue's basic point is that of the slow approach, the
necessity of retreat. In his view the state sector
and the planning system in China has taken on far
more than it can handle, and a good part of the
economy - above all the production of the means of
consumption (agriculture, light industry) - must be
delegated 'back' to the market. But no matter how
much is delegated, the commodity sector is still
conceived of as a temporary measure in Xue's theory.
In the last analysis it is supplementary to the
essentially socialist state sector.

The position of Xue Muqiao has been very nicely
summed up by Sun Yefang. In 1980 he wrote:

> 'They |Xue Muqiao and others| say that, since
> China's planning does not cover the making and
> selling of all products, certain minor sectors
> of the economy must be regulated by the law
> of value.... People holding such views actually
> divide a unified planned economy into two
> separate parts: planning and the market.
> On the one hand, they are not convinced that
> the market can be controlled by socialist
> planning; on the other, they think that
> once the role of the market is brought into
> play, planning has to be given up' (Sun,
> 1980:168).

Sun Yefang is even more of a veteran than Xue
Muqiao, his occupation with economic theory going

back to his time of study in Moscow in the late
1920's, where he became acquainted with the thinking of, among others, Leontiev. In the 1950's he
was associated with the Statistical Bureau, gradually moving into general theoretical work. Today
he is adviser to the Institute of Economic Research
under the Chinese Academy of Sciences. He is also
more of a victim than anybody else: in 1964 he was
branded as 'China's Liberman' and persecuted for
the next 14 years - out of which 7 years were spent
in jail under the harshest conditions.

In Sun's theory, the 'law of value' ought to be
the foundation of planning rather than a supplementary function. His value concept goes far beyond the distinction between value 'regulating' or
merely 'influencing' production, thus putting Sun
in a rather special position in relation to the
general course of development of economic debates.

The core of his theory is the 'essential value'
concept. This concept implies a clearcut distinction between 'essence' and 'form' of the law of
value, commodity production being only one specific
form or appearance (biaoxian) of the essential
value (zuowei shiti de jiazhi), and certainly not
the only possible form (Sun Yefang, 1979:11). The
classical view of the law of value as the general
economic law of commodity production has thus been
done away with. In fact, Sun's value theory implies that the law of value is only imperfectly
developed under capitalism, whereas socialism and
planning offers the opportunity for a far more perfect unfolding of the law of value, to develop con-
tinuously all the way into communism, where the law
of value is the only economic law, in the form of
a pure 'economy of time'.

The practical implications of this theory are:
organize production and circulation on the basis of
the categories associated with value. The price of
any product should be in conformity with its value
(i.e. the average socially necessary labour-time
involved in producing it), thus allowing enterprise
profit to perform as a rational criterion for eval-
uating enterprise performance. It was precisely
his insistence on profit as the sole criterion of
enterprise performance that cost Sun 14 years of
banishment.

Now Sun has been resurrected, even granted the
highest honours. At the Wuxian conference on 'the
relation between plan and market in the socialist
economy' in April 1979, Xue Muqiao - who in 1964
took part in the criticism of Sun Yefang - in his

inaugural speech cited Sun as a model in the field
of daring to stick to one's opinion. 'We should all
learn from his style of daring to uphold one's viewpoint', said Xue (1978:5). (I think that the irony
of the situation was not lost upon the audience...).

But no matter how high his prestige, Sun cannot
function as the guru of official economic theory,
either. His approach is consistent, but not very
practical. How does his magical 'law of value'
manifest itself? The cost price approach to the
exchange of products - which is the practical implication of his value theory - is in fact no novel-
ty in the history of state socialism, and it implies
a host of problems [15]. Since actual economic
proportions and production relations at any given
time are always the product of an historical and
political process and of previous planning priorities, how can the 'value norm' ever be truly established? And what about future priorities, how is
an economic strategy to be operated at all?

Particularly in relation to the contemporary
period, Sun's theory has serious shortcomings from
the viewpoint of the decision makers, since it more
or less ignores the practical problems of the market reform strategy. The commodity concept being
peripheral to Sun's value theory, it has little to
say about market reform, which makes enterprises
operate like commodity producers. Furthermore,
Sun has never occupied himself much with the 'material interest' aspect of the value approach, concerned with wages and other forms of reward for
labour, his theory being directed more towards an
internal reorganization of the state sector than
the complex problem of work incentives [16].

To sum up the differences between Xue Muqiao
and Sun Yefang: whereas to the former planning
should make use of the law of value, to the latter
it is exactly the other way round. In relation to
the new formula put forward by Hu Qiaomu in 1978,
they represent the two poles of possible interpretation of the value concept, Hu's formula being
somewhere in the middle, theoretically quite un-
decided.

The implications of these differences are
rather far-reaching. Behind the different concepts
of value are different visions of what socialism is
really like. Xue's vision is that of the Party's:
we have achieved this or that, and we won't give it
all up! In the long run - longer, perhaps, than we
imagined before - the last traces of the law of
value will disappear, the differences between

country and town, intellectual and manual labour,
etc., will be narrowed down, and we can march into
communism. Sun's vision, in contrast, is that of
modern, large-scale industry, complex economic
organization and technological advance, socialism
being essentially a system ensuring the maximum
rationality in the process of industrialization.

The different implications of these two approaches can also be demonstrated in relation to the
practical problems of the contemporary period,
price policy being a convenient case in point.

In the course of 1980, inflation, an unavoidable
side-effect of the programme of economic reform,
gradually developed into a social problem of prime
importance. In December 1980 the State Council
decided to take action - the events in Poland must
have been perceived as somehow instructive - and
declared war on inflation. In the press Xue Muqiao
came out in favour of the anti-inflationary measures
pushed from the Centre, and there seems to have been
widespread consensus among economists that inflation was becoming a threat to both economic and
social stability. But contradictions became apparent at a major economic conference in Shenyang,
convened in January 1981. In his speech to the
conference (delivered by a tape recorder, since
Sun himself is now too old and frail to take part
in such events), Sun Yefang stuck to his conviction,
putting a thorough price reform as No.1 priority
(Sun Yefang, 1980). In the minutes of the conference, the debate on price policy was summarized in
the following words:

> '...Some comrades maintained that there can
> be no change in the price structure, since
> with change there will be economic chaos.
> Other comrades argue that if you only
> worry about stability, there cannot be any
> effective readjustment of the economy,
> since irrational prices are a major factor
> causing the imbalances in the national
> economy...' (Jingji Yanjiu 2, 1980;35).

So much for the theoretical problems around the
redefining of the status of the means of production.
The purpose of the case study has been to demonstrate that there are quite different traditions of
economic thinking within the general paradigm of
official Chinese Marxism. There is an altogether
different dimension of the matter, which has not
been touched upon, namely the problem of making the

means of production, now officially defined as commodities, actually <u>function</u> as such. The difficulties in this respect are no smaller than the theoretical problems..

Politics or Economics?

The debate on the status of the means of production
is only one out of a long list of debates (and it
is not even typical, since in this field the room
for argument is quite narrow after Hu Qiaomu's 1978
speech); in fact the ideological apparatus is
being geared to a situation allowing for several
'lines' in contrast to the classical two-line concept (one correct and one wrong). Already in 1977
there were some efforts to overcome the two-line
trauma of former years, the discussion of various
issues sometimes being presented to the public in
the form of <u>three</u> lines (still with the notion of:
one correct and two questionable opinions). Nowadays, there are generally no restrictions of this
kind.
     A major and rather all-embracing issue to the
high priests of political economy is, of course,
the relation between politics and economics. It is
well known that in Deng Xiaoping's China economics
have been put in command, in contrast to Mao's
slogan of 'politics in command'. Now, the Deng
Xiaoping slogan is a political utterance just as
much as is Mao's, and besides, the relation between
politics and economics cannot be dictated by this
or that leader at all. But nevertheless the course
of events has forced the political economists to
consider the question of what they serve, the Party
or the economy?
     To Xue Muqiao there cannot be any doubt. In
terms of methodology he is orthodox, so to him political economy is the key to the general Marxist
analysis and guidance of society, that is, Party
leadership. His definition of the object of the
study of political economy is classical:

> 'The object of political economy is the
> relations of production, but these cannot
> be analysed in isolation from the study of
> the forces of production and the super-
> structure; the laws of motion in the
> development of the production relations
> must be studied in relation to the dia-
> lectical, contradictory development of the
> relation between production relations

and the forces of production, and between
superstructure and economic base' (Xue
Muqiao, 1979:9).

In practical terms this dictum implies that economic theory is basically Party property; how could
economists working independently grasp all these
dialectical relationships?

Once again Sun Yefang can be used to demonstrate the other view. In recent years he has been
busy criticizing the classical definition of the
'relations of production'. Stalin defined these as
comprising the following three sub-categories:
property relations, relations in the sphere of production, and matters relating to distribution; this
is still the most generally accepted definition in
China. In Sun's view, this should be redefined to
'the conditions and forms of production, exchange
and distribution' (Jingji Yanjiu 8, 1979); the
property category, essentially a historical and
political category, is thus removed from the object
of study of political economy. Sun's message is
evident: let the political economists concentrate
on economic problems!

The mainstream of economic theory in China,
however, continues to discuss the relation between
politics and economics on the basis of Lenin's
definition of politics as 'the concentrated expression of economics', with varying emphasis on the
one or the other [17].

Judging from the ongoing economic debates,
regularly summed up and presented to the public in
the form of 'surveys of current debates', the ideological apparatus is doing just fine. Apparently
it has survived the introduction of pluralism, even
benefited from it. But this impression should not
close the eyes of the observer to the fact that
there is a challenge to the ideological apparatus.

This challenge is manifest above all in the
ongoing 'branching out' of economic theory. Political economy is a comprehensive science by definition, no matter which approach you take to it. Of
course specialized studies should be possible within this framework, but compartamentalization is a
different matter, touching the vital core of political economy. Already in 1977 Chinese universities
started running courses in 'economics' alongside
the traditional courses in political economy.
'Economics' is a quite comprehensive concept, too,
but how does it fit in with political economy? Is
it simply 'political economy' without the

'political'?

The publication of <u>Jingji Yanjiu</u> ('Economic Research'), the traditional forum of the political economists, was resumed in 1978, soon to be followed by a new publication: <u>Jingji Guanli</u> ('Economic Management'), the purpose of which is to cover the 'objective science' of the rational organization of production, particularly at the micro-level, i.e. enterprise management. This new development was logically followed in 1979 by the setting up of an Institute of Technical Economics (<u>Jishu Jingji</u>) under the leadership of Yu Guangyuan, who defines the object of this new science as the rational development and organization of the forces of production (Baark, 1980:43). Technical economics offers its services to the leadership as <u>the</u> science of rational planning, particularly at <u>the</u> macro-level. Since then a whole host of new economic sciences have been set up, each of them complete with an institute, a journal, and, generally, with Yu Guangyuan as the leader: Economics of Education, Land Economics, Labour Economics, etc.

With 'pure economics' branching out, and both the micro and the macro level being taken care of by experts, how much is left for the political economists, bred in the tradition of official Marxism? The long term perspective of this development is the reduction of political economy to a purely apologetic function, letting the theoreticians look for the right quotations from the Scriptures each time policy changes, and having rather trivial debates among themselves. In contrast, the new branches of economic science will be characterized by a non-political, strictly scientific atmosphere, based as they are on the study of 'objective economic laws'. It should be noted, however, that so far this is mainly a projection, since the new branches of economic science are only in the process of formation and getting established.

The Crisis of Ideology

The political economists, a group of Party functionaries who were generally autodidacts (or Party-didacts) in the field of economic theory, established their leadership over general economic work during the period of the First Five-Year Plan (1953-57), pushing aside the small number of Western-educated economic specialists or relegating them to secondary positions. They were able to do this because they promised to fulfill two basic

functions in the structure as a whole, integrating
the fulfillment of these functions in their work:
1. the task of producing an adequate conceptual
framework in the field of economics and propagating
it to the population with the authority of Marxist
expertise; 2. the task of supplying the leadership
with information and analysis as a basis for practical economical policy formulation.

The carrying out of these two tasks sometimes
involves specific contradictions, and the duality
of the function of official Marxism may even produce something like a vicious circle. This appears
to have been the case in the period of the Great
Leap Forward in 1958-60, and once again, in what
critics inside China have ironically coined 'The
Foreign Leap Forward' in 1978. In their role as
ideological high priests, the political economists
were sometimes forced (or encouraged) to produce an
unrealistic image of the economic situation, which
then encouraged the decision makers to push on with an
unrealistic economic policy even more energetically,
etc., in the long run undermining the credibility
of the theoreticians, both in the eyes of the population and within the elite. It would be wrong,
however, to put the blame for the mistakes of the
two 'Leaps' on the political economists. The 'Leap'
concept appears to be the product of a specific
system, and the political economists are only the
functionaries of that system, not the masters of it.

It should be pointed out that of the two above-
mentioned functions of political economy, the latter
is the primary one. Articles by the kind of people
that have been mentioned above, Hu Qiaomu, Xue
Muqiao, Yu Guangyuan, are regularly given spacious
coverage in the People's Daily, usually not less
than half a page each time and often a lot more.
But it is difficult to imagine that these articles
are actually read by any large number of people.
(But then again, that could be said also of other
kinds of articles in the People's Daily.) The
Shanghai school tried to 'take political economy
to the people' in a mass campaign to 'study the
theory of the dictatorship of the proletariat' in
1975-76. But it appears that a large number of
ordinary people probably found it hard to forgive
the cadres for the loss of precious free time which
took place on account of this campaign.

It is in any case above all in the internal
struggles of the elite that these theoretical articles acquire relevance. The divisions of thought
among the political economists generally reflect

the political divisions within the top Party elite, in the form of a 'Godfather' pattern. Each theoretician usually has his favourite 'Godfather' in the leadership. The affiliation between Xue Muqiao and Chen Yun has already been mentioned. As for Sun Yefang, he preferably quotes from his old friend Liu Shaoqi. It is not just a question of personal ties: the theoretical line of Sun Yefang is clearly associated with the centralist approach of Liuist politics. As for the technocrat Yu Guangyuan, his is a special case, since so far there is hardly any representative of the technocratic approach in the top Party leadership. But the political economists do more than just reflect existing divisions in the Party. In their own small way, they also take part in forming the various lines and in the working out of ideological compromises, helping the Party to shape a useable understanding of itself.

However, this whole setup, with the twin functions of political economy, is rapidly changing. In a very short time China has experienced a development which in the Soviet Union and Eastern Europe took about a decade following the death of Stalin: the emergence of a new concept of economic expertise, which allows the economist to base himself on knowledge and ideas that are beyond the command of the Party. The 'objective economic laws' that Stalin introduced proved to be a double-edged sword. Stalin's immediate purpose was that of supplying Party economic politics with a scientific aura; the 'objective economic laws' were, in the words of Wlodzimierz Brus, 'an instrument for presenting everything that exists as sensible' (Brus, 1977:128). But to some economists, there was another side of the argument. To quote Brus once again: '... if economic laws have an objective nature, then there is also the possibility of confronting politics with something that lies beyond politics and which may serve as an independent norm' (ibid:18).

But even though the concept of 'objective economic laws' may serve as a basis for more independent, even critical, economic thinking, it still manifests itself as a heavy ideological burden; somehow parts of the old problem are transplanted into the 'modern age' of Chines economic thinking. The Chinese (and Soviet, etc.) 'law' concept is a problem in itself.

The 'law' concept of official Chinese Marxism has its origins in Marx's analysis of the 'laws of motion' of capitalist society as presented, above all, in the three volumes of Capital. Marx quite correctly pointed out that these laws of motion take on the appearance of natural laws; but this does not mean that they are natural laws. In the last analysis the laws of motion of capitalist society are the product of economic and social alienation, in the sense that society under capitalism is not able to regulate itself consciously and freely.

This Marxist concept of laws of motion cannot be transferred to other, non-capitalist, social formations (and whatever China is, it is not capitalist). However, that is precisely what official Marxism - even in its 'reformed', 'modernized' version - does. And because the translation is not theoretically valid in terms of (genuine) Marxism, the notion of 'objective economic laws' degenerates into an idea of natural economic laws. This is the fundamental 'theoretical mistake' - what a polite term! - of Stalinism, a 'mistake' which is very much alive in any version of official Chinese Marxism.

The theoretical impotence of Stalin's 'law' concept is evident. In Economic Problems of Socialism in the USSR he argued that the 'law of value' implied exchange of equal values between the collective and the state sector. Well then, let us pretend for a while there is actually a law of value in operation in Soviet-type societies. What effect has it had? The economic relations between agriculture and industry had been grossly unequal, to put it mildly, during the whole period of Stalin's rule, as well as afterwards.

Nowadays Chinese theoreticians are arguing among themselves whether this or that economic law is primary. Of course, their debates somehow reflect real problems and policy options; but the 'law' concept draws a curtain of idealism over the whole affair. One of the currently most esteemed 'laws' is that of 'the balanced and proportionate development of the economy', even though no Chinese economist would deny the fact that the course of economic development in the People's Republic of China so far has been characterized to a high degree by imbalances and disproportionate development.

In fact, the phenomenon of economic disequilibrium in China has been alarmingly regular so far. Is it really a 'law'? What were the moving forces behind, for example, the Great Leap Forward in 1958-59? In my opinion there are two sets of explanations, both of them relevant. First, there

are the problems relating to 'taking off' from a
situation of economic underdevelopment. The weaker
the foundation, the greater the social overheads and
capital costs. From a strictly economic point of
view, forced accumulation never makes sense, but,
as Alex Nove has pointed out, 'if the objective is
the most rapid industrialization, the investment
choices in any developing country are bound to be
based on principles quite different to those which
would minimize unemployment or economize scarce
capital in the short term, (Nove, 1969:133). Second,
there are the problems relating to the rapid changes
of the social structure. The Great Leap Forward
was also the context of the 'Partification' of
society, with Party committees taking on leadership
in every enterprise, every economic unit. With this
development, it became ever more difficult to distinguish between economic phenomena as such and the
'Needs of Power'.

But if these two sets of explanation are true,
they are still of a quite different nature than the
'objective economic laws' of official Chinese
Marxism.

It may be noted in this context that Mao
Zedong's above-mentioned 'Reading Notes' struck a
refreshing chord in terms of the question of objective economic laws. He soundly criticized the
scholastic approach of the official Soviet textbook
of political economy: 'Quite without foundation
the book offers a series of laws, laws which are
not discovered and verified through analysis of
concrete historical development. Laws cannot be
self-explanatory...' (Mao, 1979:108). Mao's criticism was unable to penetrate the core of Stalinism,
however, and his sound, common-sense approach to
economic laws does not appear to have made much of
an impression on official Chinese Marxism.

Status and Prospects

The fundamental raison d'etre of Chinese Marxism
18   is that of introducing the twin concepts of
Development and Progress. Marxism presented itself
as the only way for China to achieve genuine independence and social change leading to ultimate Progress. The Party introduced the concept of the
inevitability of Progress, and in the name of Progress the Party ruled society ever more uninhibi-
tedly.

Nowadays there is no way of preventing the
Chinese from asking: what happened to Progress?

Doubts in this respect cannot but touch the vital core of official Marxism.

China is now experiencing the emergence of a marginal, critical intelligentsia, which dares to challenge official Marxism, some of them even trying to turn Marxism into a critical weapon against the establishment. With roots back in the Cultural Revolution, it has expressed itself above all in the Democracy Movement of the years 1978-80. The social system of China appears to have greater difficulties in absorbing, assimilating and controlling its intelligentsia than do the other Soviet-type societies. The Cultural Revolution was, among other things, also an indication of these specific difficulties. In the long run, the capacity for survival of official Marxism is closely related to the question of establishing new and more efficient mechanisms for integrating the intelligentsia within the elite.

THE SHANGHAI SCHOOL AND ITS REJECTION

Peer Møller Christensen

From 1971 to 1976 a Chinese conception of the political economy of socialism was formulated, based upon a repudiation of the Soviet theories of socialism and upon the practical experiences of the Cultural Revolution in China.

It was a radical conception underlining the incomplete socialist transformation of Chinese social relations and describing it as a society which was to a high degree ruled by a 'new bourgeoisie'. This conception was developed by a group of economists from Shanghai, many of them from the Institute of Political Economy at Fudan University. Zhang Chunqiao and Yao Wenyuan – half of the 'Gang of Four' – played important roles in the Group, and a smaller group from Tianjin was also attached.[1]

I have chosen to call this entire group 'The Shanghai School' because their conception had its specific features and because their work was centred around Shanghai.[2]

When the 'Gang of Four' was 'smashed' in 1976, the theories of the Shanghai school also came under attack. During the following years, one of the important tasks for the new rulers and their economists was to 'smash' the Shanghai school's theories and establish a new frame for understanding the political economy of socialism.

In the first period after Mao's death and the purge of the 'Gang of Four' – from October 1976 to December 1978 – economic policy was optimistic. The 'smashing' of the 'Gang of Four' was supposed to make way for a new 'Great Leap Forward' towards the realization of the '4 modernizations'. Theoretically this policy was supported by a return to the policies and doctrines of Maoism from before the Cultural Revolution and by a critical attitude towards the Cultural Revolution itself. The debates

were still characterized by a strong belief in the
superiority of socialism compared to the capitalist
system.

After 1978, when this policy had failed, the
new Great Leap Forward was also criticized, and the
Chinese economists started to turn towards non-
Chinese models for inspiration, market-socialism and
the like. The superiority of Chinese socialism was
down-graded and Mao's idea of 'underdeveloped socialism' was revived. Like Mao and the Shanghai
school, the economists now emphasize the incomplete
nature of Chinese socialism, but with completely
different solutions to the problems. The underdeveloped nature of Chinese socialism is now used as
the explanation for the use of methods which would
otherwise be politically tabu.

All these discussions took place within the
frame of the 'political economy of socialism'.

The Political Economy of Socialism

The 'political economy of socialism' seems to be a
misconception. Marx called his work on capitalism
a 'critique of political economy' and identified the
term 'political economy' closely with the system of
capitalism. Accordingly, some of the Bolshevik
Marxists of the October revolution in Russia expected the need for a political economy to disappear
very soon after the revolution. Socialism was supposed to mean the abolition of classes and class
struggles, and, furthermore, that commodity production with its autonomous laws would be replaced by
planned production. All this should rule out the
necessity for a specific discipline called political
economy.

But in reality, commodities, money and wages
continued to play important roles in the Soviet
economy. Therefore Soviet politicians and economists had to draw one of two conclusions: either
the Soviet Union could not be called socialist; or
Soviet socialism would need its own political economy, a political economy of socialism. Stalin and
his supporters chose the latter.

Ever since, the 'political economy of socialism' has been the frame within which economy and
economic policies are discussed in 'socialist' countries. Indeed, a lot of the contents of this discipline is pure ideology; but on the other hand
this frame implies that economy and economic policy
are always perceived and discussed in connection
with their broader social implications - ultimately

75

implications for development towards communism and
the abolition of classes. This is the common frame
of reference for economic discussions in 'socialist'
countries. A theory of pure economic growth can
tear itself away from this political grip only with
great difficulty.

The Soviet tradition of political economy of
socialism which was transferred to China alongside
economic assistance, was only fully established as
late as the fifties with the publication of Stalin's
Economic Problems of Socialism in USSR (in 1952) and
the Political Economy Textbook (from 1954).

In these books socialism was defined as a relatively coherent system characterized first and foremost by the state's expropriation of the means of
production from private ownership. The socialist
system determines the character of economic mechanisms and individual parts of society. Commodities,
money and wages may seem to be almost identical with
capitalist ones, but in fact they are socialist because they exist in a socialist society. Classes
and class struggles no longer play any important
role under socialism, and the relations of production accordingly will need no major changes; after
a continuous development of the productive forces
the socialist society will develop smoothly into
communism.

The Political Economy Textbook was translated
into Chinese in the late fifties and gave rise to
a heated debate within the Communist Party of
China. In this connection Mao made his personal remarks, or 'Reading Notes', both on Stalin's Economic
Problems , and on the Political Economy Textbook,
(Mao Tsetung, 1977). His comments were used as reference material for broad discussions throughout the
party, and provided the starting point for the
Shanghai school's elaboration of its theory in the
1970s.

Mao's Critique of the Soviet Theory

Mao's ideas about socialism and socialist development differed in important respects from the Soviet
theory. In earlier writings Mao had already underlined the continued existence of classes and class
struggle under socialism. In the 'Reading Notes'
he further criticized the concept of socialism as
developed by the Soviet tradition.

Mao stressed the primacy of the relations of
production in relation to the productive forces,
stating that a major development of the productive

forces generally <u>follows</u> a change in the relations
of production. He saw these changes as the major
driving force behind historical development, thus
underlining the need for conscious political change.

He emphasized the limitations of planning. The
planning system, he stated, although important and
necessary, cannot provide a balanced development of
society, as the Soviet theorists had claimed. The
task of the planning system is, according to Mao,
mainly to re-establish balance between the inevitably occurring imbalances. Imbalance is the rule,
balance the exception.

Mao did not believe that a balanced development
could be secured by following the law of value
either. The law of value has, according to Mao, a
certain influence on socialist economy, but, he
stated, political priorities often run in other directions than the law of value. The Great Leap
Forward was, according to Mao, an example of political priorities being contrary to what the law of
value would imply for economic development.

As for the ownership system, Mao emphasized the
necessity for a gradual but not too slow transformation of the collectively owned units into state
ownership. A protracted consolidation period was
what, in Mao's opinion, had been the case in the
Soviet Union. It would, in his view, result in
economic problems and stagnation.

Mao's overall view of socialism was thus basically different from that of the Soviet tradition.
Where the Soviet writers saw socialism as a stable,
classless and coherent system developing by its own
laws and gradually - following these laws of development - moving towards communism, Mao saw socialism
as a transitional system full of contradictions,
class struggles and with a development consciously
shaped by political factors and priorities.

Shortly after the publication and discussions
of Mao's 'Reading Notes', a Chinese manual on the
political economy of socialism was published in
Shanghai.[3] This manual was influenced by Mao's
critique of the Soviet tradition and may be seen as
the first attempt to write a genuinely Chinese, comprehensive textbook on the political economy of socialism. After its publication, however, nothing
further seems to have happened in this respect,
before the Shanghai school started its theoretical
work in the 1970s - presumably on the basis of both
Mao's critical 'Reading Notes' and the Shanghai
manual.

The Shanghai School And Its Rejection

The Shanghai School

The Shanghai school was part of the 'cultural revolutionary' wing of the CCP. This wing had actually been on the retreat since very soon after the beginning of the Cultural Revolution. From 1967 and onwards the reforms and political movements of the early Cultural Revolution were gradually brought to a standstill. The wave of rehabilitation of criticized cadres after the fall of Lin Biao in 1971 drove the 'radicals' on the defensive.

However, they still had strongholds in the media and within the educational system, the battlegrounds of theory and ideology. These strongholds could be used to strengthen their overall position.

The Shanghai school, therefore, tried to maintain the theoretical perspectives of the Cultural Revolution by making a theoretical summary of the practical experiences gained in this and earlier Maoist campaigns. This took the form of writing a manual, Political Economy of Socialism. The actual work on this book started in June 1971 when Zhang Chunqiao approved the plan for the book, and from 1971 to 1976 five drafts were written.[4]

From draft to draft the theory was clarified and the original self-contradictions contained in the theory were gradually solved, so that in 1976 a fairly consistent and comprehensive book was ready for publication. It was never published. In October 1976, Hua Guofeng and his supporters staged their coup d'état, the 'Gang of Four' - and presumably also the members of the Shanghai school - were arrested and the manuscript for the book was confiscated.

After the purge of the 'Gang of Four' this book was, however, criticized in a great number of articles in newspapers and magazines, which carried a lot of quotations from the book and a parallel book written by the Tianjin group. Through these articles and quotations it is possible to gain a picture of their theories.

The starting point of the Shanghai school was the acceptance and incorporation of Mao's critique of the Soviet tradition into a comprehensive understanding of socialism. But one important self-contradiction made this conception of socialism inconsistent.

The Shanghai school claimed that a 'restoration of capitalism' was possible in a socialist country and that a 'new bourgeoisie' would develop, which might be the agents of a restoration, similar to the

Soviet one. But on the other hand the Shanghai
school accepted the idea, inherited from the Soviet
tradition, that the socialist system determines the
economic mechanisms and components of society making
them very different from capitalism.

How could this basically socialist economy then
be transformed into a 'restored' capitalist economy?
If the economic categories of socialism were so different from their capitalist counterparts how could
they be active factors in capitalist economic processes? The first two manuscripts, finished in 1972
and 1973, did not solve this self-contradiction.
But in 1975 a new quotation by Mao was published,
which seemed to provide an answer.[5]

The quotation which was called 'The latest instruction by Chairman Mao' read:

> In a word, China is a socialist country.
> Before liberation she was much the same as
> capitalism. Even now she practices an eight-
> grade wage-system, distribution to each accord-
> ing to his work and exchange by means of money,
> which are scarcely different from those in the
> old society. What is different is that the
> system of ownership has changed. ... Our coun-
> try at present practices a commodity system,
> and the wage-system is unequal too, there being
> the eight-grade wage-system, etc. These can
> only be restricted under the dictatorship of
> the proletariat. Thus it would be quite easy
> for people like Lin Biao to push the capitalist
> system, if they came to power. (my italics)
> (Beijing Review, 14 Feb. 1975.)

According to Mao, socialist economic categories
such as commodity, money and wages are not very different from commodity, money and wages under capitalism. They could, therefore, with no great effort
be made functional in a capitalist production process.

A great obstacle for the development of a consistent and comprehensive radical theory of socialism had been removed with Mao's instruction. After
solving a few more self-contradictions in the third
and fourth manuscripts, the final theory could be
outlined by the Shanghai school.

According to the Shanghai school's 'Political
Economy of Socialism', socialism is a transitional
society composed of communist as well as capitalist
elements and factors, existing simultaneously within socialist relations of production. The

capitalist factors are incompletely transformed
structures within socialist society such as commodity, money wage relations, exchange at equal values
as a regulatory principle in the economy, and the
division of labour inherited from the old society.

The existence of the capitalist factors and
elements within socialist relations of production
form the material base for the constant production
and reproduction of capitalism as well as a 'new
bourgeoisie' in socialist society. This new bourgeoisie emerges within the ranks of the working
people and especially inside the communist party.

The division of labour leads to the development
of an 'intellectual aristocracy' which deprives the
workers of the real (in contradiction to formal)
right of leadership of the economic units, that is
the real ownership of the means of production.
Within the enterprises there will emerge a system of
intellectual workers ruling over manual workers.
The Shanghai school goes so far as to state that
such a system has already - to a certain degree -
developed in China. This means that the proletariat
is being ruled over and exploited by the new bourgeoisie.

The class struggle between the proletariat and
the new bourgeoisie will, therefore, be the most
important contradiction in socialist society, and
this class struggle will first and foremost be a
struggle for the extension or the limitation of the
capitalist factors and elements within the socialist
relations of production.

Capitalist Elements - 'Bourgeois Right'

According to the Shanghai school, the collectively
owned economy is an incompletely transformed structure within the public ownership system. The means
of production as well as the results of production
are private property owned by individual collective
units; in that sense production is private production.

Furthermore, the question of the leadership of
the collective units as well as within the state-
owned sector plays a very important role, the key
problem being which class really controls the means
of production. If the power structure within the
leadership of an enterprise is changed so that the
workers are deprived of the right to run their enterprise or collective unit, socialist enterprises
may actually become the property of the new bourgeoisie, not formally but in reality.

When the new bourgeoisie controls the means of production it will be able further to promote a capitalist production process, as capitalist factors and elements already exist in all spheres of socialist production. For example, production and circulation of commodities and the 'law of value' springing from this are hardly different from capitalist society. The same goes for the wage-system following the principle 'to each according to his labour'.

By letting the law of value regulate production the new bourgeoisie can subordinate production of use-values to production of values. When using money and prices, the price of a commodity may, for certain reasons, be higher than its value; production of this kind of commodity would then earn a bigger profit than the average, and therefore it may be attractive for some enterprises to maximize their profit by producing these profitable commodities rather than less profitable ones. Production aimed at realizing surplus-value may thus distort planning and the allocation of resources in socialist society. The law of value, not the plan, would then regulate production.

The ideological form of a 'restoration of capitalism' in China could well be, according to the Shanghai school, 'the theory of the productive forces' and 'the 4 modernizations', both of which express the ideology of 'the dying out of class struggle under socialism'.

To prevent a 'restoration of capitalism' it would, the Shanghai school claims, be necessary to stage many 'cultural revolutions', gradually limiting and finally eliminating capitalist factors within the relations of production including the old division of labour. The influence of the law of value on production must gradually be minimized, in order to facilitate planning in accordance with 'use value' criteria.

The worker's control within the enterprises must be secured by the workers taking part in the management of the enterprises. Intellectual workers on the other hand, must be forced to take part in manual labour. The material privileges of the new bourgeoisie must be eliminated, material incentives, piece-rate wages and bonuses abolished, and a more even distribution of wages established.

In this way the material basis for the existing privileged class would be eliminated and with it the basis for its re-emergence.

The Shanghai School And Its Rejection

The Critique of the Shanghai School

Shortly after the purge of the 'Gang of Four', a campaign for criticizing them and their supporters was started. At the beginning the campaign was directed mainly at the 'subversive' activities of the 'Gang' and their plans for seizing political power. But soon it was announced that one of the topics of the campaign would be the 'distortions of political economy' made by the gang and their followers.

The process of criticizing the Shanghai school was thus planned and well prepared, and did not start until more than a year after the arrest of the 'Gang of Four'.

The criticisms started on the 24th of November 1977 with an article written by Dong Fureng[6] and Tang Zongkan and published in the People's Daily. Through 1978 this article was followed by a number of other articles written by different people and published in newspapers as well as the magazine Jingji Yanjiu (Economic Research). The critics basically agreed in their criticisms, but, nevertheless, important disagreements among them were evident in the articles.

During most of 1979 there was a pause and in September that year the repudiation of the Shanghai school was apparently finished and rounded off and the disagreements among the critics settled by one final article written by Dong Fureng.

The first article written by Dong Fureng and Tang Zongkan, in People's Daily (24 Nov. 1977), stated that the Shanghai school confused socialist with capitalist relations of production. According to Dong and Tang, the Shanghai school did not take into consideration that the property relations had been changed. In his 1975 instruction Mao said that China was socialist because the property relations were transformed. Thereby he, in their view, accentuated the fundamental difference between capitalism and China's socialist system.

The idea of 'capitalist factors' within the socialist relations of production was heavily criticized. In a later article Tang Zongkan claimed that what the Shanghai school called 'capitalist factors' - the collective ownership system, commodity exchange and 'distribution according to labour' - are actually all negations of the class-exploitation based upon private property. They all have a historically advanced character, (Jingji Yanjiu 8, 1978).

A capitalist element or factor, stated two other critics, Zhang Chaozun and Hu Naiwu in

People's Daily (5 April 1978), is necessarily connected with bourgeois relations of exploitation or
relations of private property. Within socialist
relations of production there is no suppression or
exploitation as there is in capitalist society. No
relations of production containing class exploitation or class antagonism can, in their view, be
called socialist.

Any society in history, claimed Hu Ruiliang
(Jingji Yanjiu 2, 1978) carries with it elements
from the preceding society. This does not, however,
indicate that, for example, feudalist remnants within capitalist society are not capitalist. Division
of labour, contradiction between intellectual and
manual labour, the commodity system and the principle of exchange of equal values cannot - as the
Shanghai school did - be called capitalist, he
stated. They are all remnants of the old society,
but they are also much older than capitalism. They
first appeared when humanity entered slave society.
You cannot, for example, say that commodities in
socialist society have a capitalist character. You
might just as well say that they have a feudal
character. A commodity connected with the socialist
mode of production is a socialist commodity, as
economic categories are bound to and determined by
the society in which they exist.

The critics claimed that the socialist wage
system, i.e. the system of 'distribution according
to labour', is also fundamentally different from the
capitalist wage system.

Socialist and capitalist wages are basically
different categories, Wu Junglian, Zhou Shulian and
Wang Haibo (Jingji Yanjiu 9, 1978) stated. Capitalist wages express the price of labour power, while
socialist wages indicate that the workers receive
part of the total social product. The two wage
forms have different social effects as well. The
capitalist wage system indicates exploitation of
the workers, while the socialist wage system promotes the development of the productive forces in
combining the individual interest of the worker with
that of society. According to these authors, the
use of material incentives and piece-rate wages is
in full harmony with the principle of 'distribution
according to labour'. Of course, they admit, piece-
rate wages have some negative effects, but if material incentives are combined with political ones
(which they claim to be the most important type of
incentives) the link between labour and reward is
best established. The same goes for bonuses. Even

though the basic principle of 'distribution according to labour' is followed, the wages may not express precisely the work efforts of the worker. Therefore bonuses are necessary tools for making this distribution as closely linked to the work effort as possible.

The phrase 'the bourgeoisie inside the party' so extensively used by the Shanghai school was also criticized. Hu Ruiliang claimed (Jingji Yanjiu 2, 1978) that this concept was invented by the Shanghai school without any basis in reality. The communist party is the vanguard of the proletariat; therefore, he stated, quoting the Communist Manifesto, 'the communists have no interest differing from the interests of the proletariat as a whole'. This means that a bourgeoisie cannot exist inside the communist party. If the supreme leadership of the party is usurped by 'revisionists walking the capitalist road', the party has already changed its character and become a bourgeois party.

Following a similar line of reasoning Dong Fureng stated (Jingji Yanjiu 3, 1978) that if a few new bourgeois elements arise among the working people, these elements no longer belong to the working people and the relations between them and the working people will therefore not be an internal relationship, not a relationship within the relations of production.

Following Mao's idea from the 'Reading Notes' the Shanghai school considered changes in the relations of production to be the main force in the development of history. This idea was criticized, too. The Shanghai school was accused of turning historical materialism upside down by Yang Shengming and Guan Bei (Jingji Yanjiu 8, 1978). The relations of production, they claimed, are not the decisive factor. On the contrary, the most important factor in social development is the productive forces. Of course it is necessary to develop the relations of production so that they correspond to the level of development of the productive forces; but it is dangerous to do this too quickly, they stated emphatically.

It is obvious, stated Dong Fureng (Jingji Yanjiu 3, 1978) that any change of the relations of production has a development of the productive forces as its material base. Therefore, in the present stage of China's development, the main task is to promote the productive forces. This is the material base for all other tasks.

The Shanghai School And Its Rejection

Disagreements Among the Critics

So far there seems to have been basic agreement
among the critics of the Shanghai school. But on
the fundamental questions concerning the importance
of class relations in socialist society and the
possibility of a 'capitalist restoration', disagreements were evident.

Some of the critics argued that a 'capitalist
restoration' in a country like China is impossible.
Dong Fureng claimed (ibid.) that the fact that socialist relations of production carry some capitalist
traditions and birthmarks does not indicate that
these traditions and marks can cause a 'capitalist
restoration'. They are, he argued, expressions of
the immature nature of relations of production under
socialism, but will not pull society away from the
development towards communism.

Li Guangzi is even more explicit (Guangming
Ribao, 29 May 1978). The pre-requisite for circulation of capital, he stated, is the existence of
labour power as a commodity. In a socialist economy
labour power is no longer a commodity. How then can
money be transformed into capital and how can surplus value be extracted? When there is neither capital nor surplus value, where then should capitalism
and a bourgeoisie arise?

Other critics did, however, oppose these views,
accentuating the possibility of a 'capitalist restoration'. Among these were Hu Ruiliang (Jingji
Yanjiu 2, 1978). It is true that the relations
under socialism cannot themselves engender capitalism, he admitted, but this does not mean that there
are no pre-requisites for the development of capitalism in the socialist phase, where the productive
forces have not yet reached a high level of development. It is evident, he continued, that socialist
society uses the economic categories commodity and
money circulation, which are the fundamental pre-
requisites for a 'capitalist restoration'. But it
is also necessary to bear in mind that these pre-
conditions for the formation of capital do not
amount to capitalism itself. Commodity production
and money circulation are not a priori capital.

Zhang Wenxiao (ibid.) also underlined that
commodity production and money relations make a
'capitalist restoration' possible. His description
of the negative consequences of commodity production under socialism come very close to the theories
of the Shanghai school. Socialist commodity production, he claimed, is - like all commodity production

- ruled by the principle of exchange of equal values.
This may have negative effects on the relations between state and units of production and between units
of production themselves. It can lead to particul-
arism so that some units of production neglect the
fulfilment of state plans and the interests of the
state. Furthermore, the use of value as a yard-
stick will lead to differences of income and living
standard among producers in different units of production. But where the Shanghai school saw the solution to these problems in restricting the scope of
commodity production, Zhang Wenxiao stated that only
by developing the scope of socialist commodity production can the spontaneous tendencies towards capitalism springing from small-scale production, illegal capitalist factories and black-market trade,
be dealt with. Commodity and money relations make a
'capitalist restoration' possible, but only possible, he wrote, not necessary as the Shanhai school
claim. A firm proletarian policy will keep these
risks in check.

In the Political Economy of Socialism the
Shanghai school stated that the contradiction between the proletariat and the bourgeoisie was the
concentrated expression of the fundamental contradiction under socialism. Wang Qingbao criticized
this (Jingji Yanjiu 4, 1978), stating that the fundamental contradiction in socialism - the contradiction between relations of production and productive forces, and between economic base and superstructure - is non-antagonistic. Therefore, its
expression in the relations among the people must be
non-antagonistic too. The relations among people
under socialism are, according to him, relations of
equality and cooperation among brothers.

Hu Ruiliang, Zhao Renwei and Duan Ruofei agree
with Wang Qingbao (ibid.). The contradiction between the proletariat and the bourgeoisie, they
claimed, is the most important contradiction of capitalism, but not under socialism. To claim so would
be to blur the difference between socialism and capitalism. By the expropriation of the means of production owned by the bourgeoisie, the contradiction
between the proletariat and the bourgeoisie has been
basically solved.

Jiang Zhong explicitly criticized the views of
Wang Qingbao (Jingji Yanjiu 7, 1978). In the whole
historical epoch of socialism, he stated, class
struggles exist and express the basic contradiction
of society. He quoted Hua Guofeng as saying[7] that
the basic contradiction under socialism still has a

class nature, and that the struggle between the
proletariat and the bourgeoisie still exists in the
relations of production and within the superstructure indicating a risk of 'capitalist restoration'.
   According to Zhou Shulian (Jingji Yanjiu 5,
1978) the most important contradiction of socialism
is the one between the proletariat and the bourgeoisie. But this does not mean that this contradiction exists within the relations of production,
as the Shanghai school (and Hua Guofeng in the
above-mentioned article) said. Socialist society
and the socialist relations of production are
different categories. In socialist society, he
stated, the bourgeoisie can still - by means of an
economic, political and ideological offensive -
change the socialist enterprises into capitalist
ones. But if this happens their relations of production will already have changed into capitalist
relations of production.

Finishing the Critique

After a pause lasting for almost one year an
article written by Dong Fureng (Jingji Yanjiu 9,
1979) was published. In this rounding-off article,
he systematically repeated the criticisms of the
Shanghai school and apparently settled the disagreement among the critics concerning class conditions in socialist society. He criticized the
theory advocated by the Shanghai school that in
socialist society classes exist from the beginning
to the end. It is true, he admitted, that during
the transitional phase from capitalism to socialism
different economic elements exist and the most
important contradiction of society is that between
the proletariat and the bourgeoisie. But in the
present stage of China's development class struggles
are no longer the most important problem of society.
   This article appeared as part of a new debate
in Chinese economic circles concerning the very
nature of Chinese socialism. Through the discussions around the criticisms of the Shanghai
school the pre-cultural-revolutionary Maoism had to
a certain degree been reestablished - but not incorporating Mao's critique of the Soviet tradition.
It was agreed upon and officially recognized that
the socialist system - first of all the socialist
transformation of property relations - determines
the individual factors of society, implying that
these are socialist too. But apparently the diversified and incomplete nature of the Chinese socia-

list system and the underdeveloped character of the
economy together with the failure of Maoist Great
Leap Forward policies, made it difficult for the
economists and theoreticians to escape the crucial
and dangerous question: Is China socialist at all?
    Does China in its present state represent what
Marx and Lenin identified as 'the lower stage of
communism' (socialism)?
    This question was raised by Su Shaozhi and Feng
Langrui in an article in the May issue of Jingji
Yanjiu 1979. The question actually sounds more
radical than it is. In the minds of the authors
there is no doubt that the road towards socialism
is guaranteed and the transition period over. If
they seem to be more radical than do the Shanghai
school, this is mainly because they have a different
definition of socialism than the Shanghai school
had.
    Where the latter saw the development as running
through capitalism - transitional phase (socialism)
- communism, Su and Feng see the development as
capitalism - transition - socialism - communism,
with still further divisions of the socialist phase.
But if the question raised by Su and Feng is not as
radical as it sounds, the mere expression of it
must have been a severe challenge to the Chinese
political system as a whole.
    Su Shaozhi and Feng Langrui criticize the
viewpoint of the Shanghai school that socialist
society is a transitional phase between capitalism
and communism, a phase which covers a whole historical period and which cannot be divided further
into stages. They revive the division of socialism
described by Mao in the 'Reading Notes'. In this
text Mao divided the transition from capitalism to
communism into two stages:
1.   The transition from capitalism to socialism, a
      stage he calls underdeveloped socialism.
2.   The transition from socialism to communism,
      which he calls developed socialism.[8]
    Working from this concept, Su and Feng argue
that the transition from capitalism to communism
can be divided into the following stages:
1.   The transition from capitalism to socialism.
This again can be divided further:
      a) The period from the victory of the pro-
         letarian revolution to the basic trans-
         formation of the ownership of the means
         of production. In this period different
         economic elements co-exist and sharp class
         struggle still exists.

b) After the basic transformation of the property relations society enters the stage of underdeveloped socialism.
c) Developed socialism follows, being the transition from socialism to communism.

Underdeveloped socialism has the following characteristics:

The two forms of property relations, state ownership and collective ownership, still exist and so does commodity production and circulation. The bourgeoisie has been basically extinguished but capitalist traditions, bourgeois elements and even feudal traditions exist. Small-scale production is still very important. Class differences between workers and farmers still exist because of their different relations to the means of production and because of the uneven development of the productive forces. Class struggles involving great mass campaigns and great struggles are no longer necessary, but class struggle still exists and the dictatorship of the proletariat is still necessary.

All these characteristics fit China and this means that the Chinese society of today cannot be identical with what Marx and Lenin called the first stage of communism (socialism). Because of the incomplete nature of the Chinese socialist system, it can, according to Su and Feng, only be called underdeveloped socialism.

Although this view was criticized in later articles written by Zhu Shuixian (Jingji Yanjiu 5, 1979) and by Liu Jianxing and Zheng Kai (Jingji Yanjiu 11, 1979) it seems to have been accepted as the proper classification of the Chinese socialist system. At any rate the definition of Chinese socialism in Xue Muqiao's latest book (1981) is very close to that of Su and Feng.

As mentioned before, there is a close connection between abstract discussions on the political economy of socialism and practical economic policy. The theory of the Shanghai school had its ties to the practical policies of the 'cultural revolutionary' wing of the CCP. Therefore, it had to be rejected. The rejection went through discussions and disagreements, but ended up with a view of Chinese socialism as a society which had finished the transition to socialism but remained in an incomplete and underdeveloped state.

Because of the underdeveloped character of the society almost any means that can develop the Chinese economy are acceptable to the new leaders and economists in China, and because the transition period is considered to be over, none of these means, however 'capitalist' they may seem, are considered to endanger the system as such - it is believed to remain socialist.

Therefore the concept of socialism now broadly accepted by the Chinese leaders and economists may well be represented by the words of Deng Xiaoping: 'It does not matter whether the cat is black or white, as long as it catches mice.'

3

ECONOMIC REFORMS IN EASTERN EUROPE AND THEIR RELEVANCE TO CHINA

Athar Hussain

Since the middle of the 1960s all Eastern European
countries have tried to reform the structure of
their economies in their own particular ways. Just
when the projects of economic reforms were being
aired in these countries, the Sino-Soviet split happened; and China distanced itself politically and,
to a lesser degree, economically from the Soviet
Union and from other Eastern European countries.
Following that with the unleashing of the Cultural
Revolution, China seemed to set out on a path of
socialist development of its own. Loosely speaking,
if Eastern European countries opted for a 'technocratic' restructuring through the deployment of
material incentives to managers of enterprises and
to workers, then the Chinese denounced material incentives and profit as the indicator enterprise
performance as capitalist. Instead, they set out to
revolutionize their economy by mobilizing the masses
with the lofty aim of producing a man fit for a socialist economy. Given this divergence, perhaps more
marked in rhetoric than in practice, the experience
of economic reforms in Eastern Europe seemed irrelevant to the assessment and analysis of the Chinese
economy during the decade 1966-76. During the
last few years since the overthrow of the so called
Gang of Four, the official stance towards the

* I am grateful to Stephan Feuchtwang and
Paul Hare for comments. This article draws on the
work which I did at the Institute of Industrial
Economics of the Hungarian Academy of Sciences in
1979. I am grateful to the British Council for the
visit to Hungary.

economy has undergone a fundamental change. The
pilot economic reforms in industry which have been
introduced in China since 1978 bear a striking resemblance to the ones introduced earlier in East
European countries, and the Chinese officials are
now well disposed to learning from the experience of
some of the Eastern European countries: Romania,
Hungary and even from Yugoslavia. This makes an
account of the economic reforms in Eastern Europe
relevant to the analysis of the Chinese economy.

It is, however, necessary to indicate what
precisely this relevance consists in. First, the
economic reforms which are at issue here concern
industry alone, by and large the reform of agriculture preceded them. At the time of the introduction of economic reforms, the Eastern European economies, perhaps with the exception of Romania and
Bulgaria, were already highly industrialized: most
of the labour force was employed in industry and the
service sector. With 75% of its labour force
employed in agricultural communes, the same is not
true for the China of today.[1] The implication is
that it is the reform of the rural sector which is
central to the Chinese economy. Indeed, Chinese
leaders have taken some preliminary steps to alter
the relations between production teams, production
brigades and communes. But the point is that the
structure of the Chinese rural economy is sui
generis; hence, the experience of agrarian reform
in Eastern Europe is of little relevance to China.

Secondly, the political and economic context
in which current Chinese reforms are being introduced is in some crucial respects very different
from the context in which economic reforms were
introduced in Eastern Europe. The economic reforms
in Eastern Europe were a series of different attempts to steer out of a planning system which tried,
albeit without a great success, to control all
details of economic activity. From what one can
gather from Chinese accounts, during the period
1966-76 there was neither much planning nor much by
way of a detailed control of the enterprises in the
state sector. Paradoxically, the grant of autonomy
to 6,600 or so enterprises in the state sector has
been coupled with the affirmation of the primacy of
governmental institutions, the strengthening of the
chains of command from the government to enterprises
and the re-affirmation of the hegemony of the central organs of the party. Therefore, as the Chinese
themselves point out, the recent changes in the
stance of authorities towards the economy consists

of a paradoxical mixture of a tighter centralised control, and a cautious policy of granting autonomy to a number of selected industrial enterprises.[2]

One needs also to keep in view the differences among the East European countries. Generally speaking, one may distinguish between the two strands of the economic reforms. On the one hand, in Hungary the economic reforms have radically altered the nature of planning and of the structure of the economy: it has led to the emergence of autonomous enterprises which, formally, no longer receive binding directives from central authorities, and to the substitution of administrative measures by economic instruments of control like the tax and the credit policy. While in the GDR and the Soviet Union (the conservative reformers) economic reforms have done no more than to refine the traditional planning system. In all, economic reforms have been a process of differentiation among East European economies.

Thus, what an account of the economic reforms in Eastern Europe offers is a guide to the possible variants of reform in economies built around centralised planning by administrative methods – a method of planning which the Soviet Union pioneered, and which was emulated by all socialist economies initially. The subsequent discussion is divided into the following sections:

(1) An Outline of Economic Reforms in Eastern Europe.

(2) An Overview of the Effects of Economic Reforms.

(3) The Politics and Economics of Reforms.

An Outline of Economic Reforms in Eastern Europe

At a general level a striking feature of the reforms is that they have not been restricted to any particular type of country; both the 'radical' and the 'conservative' economies have tried out reforms. In fact the frequency of reforms has been greater in the latter than in the former. Leaving aside Yugoslavia which was excommunicated from the ranks of socialist countries in 1948, Hungary, the most radical of East European economies, has contented itself with one major economic reform in 1968. Another notable feature of the economic reforms has been their reversibility. In a number of East European countries reforms were introduced only to

be reversed later, at least in part. The regional-
isation of economic planning in the Soviet Union and
then in Bulgaria and in East Germany in 1960-62 is
one example.[3] Here too Hungary is an exception;
aside from periodic lapses into the administrative
control of the economy, it has adhered to and built
on the main tenets of the 1968 reforms.

China has had its fair share of the cycles of
reforms. In 1958 a large number of enterprises were
put in charge of regional authorities only to be
taken away from them in 1959-1961. In 1970 there
was yet another transfer of enterprises to provincial authorities.[4] Generally speaking, there are
two reasons for the reversibility of economic reforms. Given the control of the economy by the
state, economic reforms in planned economies are
immediately political, and hence political vicissitudes have an immediate impact on the stance towards the management of the economy. In China, for
example, the cycle of reforms can well be described
in terms of the rise and fall of various political
personalities. Correlatively, the continuity of
economic reforms in Hungary - and also in Yugoslavia
- is in large measure due to the continuity of the
top leadership of the party. Aside from this there
is a structural reason for periodic reversions back
to the traditional-style planning: the continuity
of the personnel in the departments of government
and in enterprises before and after the reforms.
Further, it seems that the usual response of East
European authorities to adverse circumstances is to
revert back to the administrative methods of controlling the economy - which admittedly do have the
merit of achieving desired results: a balance in
the foreign trade account - more quickly than indirect economic measures.

The analysis of economic reforms both in the
East and West has been conducted mainly in terms
of the introduction of market relationships, and the
use of profit to assess the performance of state
enterprises. The same is true of the discussion of
recent economic reforms in China. Indeed, both
these are among the central features of the economic
reforms, but the importance accorded to them has as
much to do with economic ideology. Having characterised markets and profit as hallmarks of capitalism, socialist countries could not introduce them
without first going through the travail of christen-
ing them as socialist. Similarly, in Western countries planning has usually been identified with planning in terms of physical quantities (traditional

Soviet planning), and the market and profit with an economy without a central plan. Thus the introduction of market and profit has often been seen as a retreat from planning and a move in the direction of capitalism. However, mathematical economists – Western as well as East European – have for long pointed out that planning in terms of physical quantities does not exclude prices, on the contrary it makes an implicit reference to idealised markets and prices.[5]

The general thesis which underlies this chapter is that the analysis of the economic reforms exclusively in terms of the market and the plan deflects away from some of the central features of the changes which have taken place in Eastern Europe. Instead the economic reforms should be treated as a series of changes strung along a number of different axes. And these changes are seen here as modifications of the planning mechanism. This indeed is the perspective adopted by leading Hungarian economists, who also are the staunch advocates of the market and profit oriented reforms.[6] This perspective has, undoubtedly, an element of public relations: it makes it possible to sell such reforms as being in consonance with socialist principles. But that does not detract from its considerable analytical merits.

One important reason for adopting this perspective is that apart from Yugoslavia, none of the East European economies (including Hungary) has jettisoned a centralised planning of the major sectors of the economy. There is not much of this kind of planning left in Yugoslavia. Thus, despite the enthusiasm of the Chinese to learn from Yugoslavia, it has less relevance for China than, for example, Hungary, or indeed the Soviet Union.

In order to structure this account of the economic reforms a general characterisation of a centrally planned socialist economy is in order here. The principal feature of such an economy is the regulation of the major sectors of the economy by means of a wide variety of possible instruments. Whatever its detailed physiognomy such an economy would have the following:

(1) A set of institutions of economic management.

(2) A set of enterprises in social ownership.

(3) A set of instruments which the former can wield to regulate the activities of the latter.

95

Economic Reforms in Eastern Europe

The subsequent discussion of economic reforms is
organised around these three. They do not provide
for a comprehensive coverage of a planned socialist
economy: the two important areas which are left out
are: (1) international economic relations and
(2) the determination of wages and salaries and the
distribution of income. Wherever pertinent I shall
refer to these.

Organs of Economic Management. Organs of economic
management refer to institutions principally concerned with the supervision and direction of economic activities - unproductive institutions in the
terminology employed in socialist countries. Subsequent to the reforms these can be either governmental or non-governmental institutions. Schematically they are as follows:

Governmental	Non-Governmental
(a) Planning commission	Multi-divisional conglom-
(b) Production branch	erates
ministries (central	(a) Horizontal conglom-
or Federal and	erates of units within
regional)	the same branch
(c) Divisions and sub-	(b) Vertical conglomerates
divisions of branch	
ministries (Glavki)	
(d) Regional government	
organisations	

The governmental organs pre-date reforms and,
mutatis mutandis, they are the same as in China.
While the latter, which have different names in different countries, are for the most part the products
of the economic reforms.

    An incessant re-patterning of the governmental
organs and the redistribution of responsibilities
between them seems to be a permanent feature of socialist economies. In the Soviet Union such changes
pre-date the economic reforms of the '60s; the '20s
and the '30s saw a frequent recasting of enterprises
and the structure of economic management. In fact,
such changes are a necessary concomitant of the
planning of major sectors of the economy. For such
a planning entails a partitioning of the economy
into administrative domains; and with the growth of
the economy the range of products increases and
their composition changes, which in turn

necessitates a recasting of organs of economic management. However, such changes by themselves do not imply a radical change in the nature of planning.

Besides, the penchant to control the minutiae of economic activities during the period of traditional planning found expression in the proliferation of managerial institutions. Prior to the economic reforms in the early '60s in the Soviet Union, the enterprises were covered over by as many as six to seven layers of organs of economic management.[7] They are now down to three: Branch ministry --- Industrial Association or Glavki --- Production Association --- Enterprises. A similar reduction in the links of the chain of economic command has taken place in other East European countries, though in different institutional forms: through the emergence of the VVB and Kombinat in the GDR, the Centrale in Romania, the WOG in Poland and industrial trusts in Hungary.

Contrary to its supposed purpose the proliferation of organs of management did not lead to more effective planning; rather it created new problems. As is often the case, administrative organs do more than administer according to a central plan: they render their respective domains of administration semi-autonomous with parochial interests of their own. They, as Nove (1978:Chapter 3) has emphasised in his analyses of the Soviet Union, turn what is formally meant to be central planning into an oligarchic bargaining between organs of management. This produces what is termed a split in the centre of decision-making with concomitant problems of a lack of coherence in the formulation of plans and of coordination in their implementation. The economic reforms have not eliminated these problems but they have rationalised the chains of economic command.

The creation of non-governmental organs of management has been one of the principal ways in which the economic reforms have reduced the tiers of economic management. These organs are conglomerates of enterprises and they are financially autonomous. Structurally - but not necessarily in their operation - they are similar to a multi-divisional firm in a capitalist economy. Their emergence has significantly cut down the number of economic units with which branch ministries have to deal. Since the functions performed by horizontal conglomerates of enterprises within the same branch are almost identical to the ones performed by sub-division of branch ministries (Glavki) in the pre-reform period, they are, in fact, Glavki under a different guise.

97

However, vertical conglomerates of enterprises from different branches of production is an institutional innovation. 'To what extent are horizontal conglomerates an improvement upon Glavki?' is a moot question. Their emergence has probably led to some improvement in the quality and the quantity of information about the productive capacity of enterprises. Secondly, there is some evidence that the horizontal conglomerates make a greater use of economic criteria in assigning the targets of assortment of products to enterprises than the pre-reform Glavki. As a result enterprises are now more specialised than before. Thirdly, by putting together the supplier and the user under one aegis, vertical conglomerates may have improved the supply situation, and provided for a better quality control in production. A number of vertical conglomerates have research and development institutions attached to them, and they are supposed to furnish a more hospitable environment for product innovation. East European countries have set great hopes on conglomerates as the institutional device for eliminating technical inefficiencies and speeding up technical innovation.[8] It is, however, too optimistic to assume that a mere institutional rearrangement can bring about an immediate radical transformation in the mode of functioning of planned economies.

There has been a massive merger and conglomeration of enterprises in Eastern Europe, and in some countries - e.g. Hungary - it predates the reforms.[9] As a result, some of the Eastern European countries - Romania, Hungary and Czechoslovakia - have industrial structures among the most concentrated in the world. Lenin in his famous pamphlet Imperialism the Highest Stage of Capitalism argued that the development of monopolies and trusts at the turn of the century had ushered capitalism into the era of monopoly capitalism. Following Lenin one could perhaps say that the socialist economies of Eastern Europe entered 'the monopoly stage of socialism' during the mid '60s and the '70s. The merger and conglomeration of enterprises may have rationalised the institutional structure, but in one respect they go against the grain of the economic reforms. For by decreasing the scope of potential competition they attenuate the disciplinary force of the market on which the projects of reforms rely to further efficiency and the quality of products.

The industrial structure in China is not concentrated as in other socialist and advanced capitalist countries. In fact between 1958-78 the share

of small and medium enterprises in industrial production went up. Since 1976 in Beijing, Shanghai and
Tianjin some medium and small enterprises have been
merged, and there is a shift towards a greater specialisation among small and medium enterprises.
Moreover, some Chinese economists have argued for a
further merger and conglomeration of enterprises in
certain branches of production.[10]

Changes in the Status of Enterprises. Formally,
under traditional planning the enterprises in the
state sector - enterprises under the ownership of
the whole population - were no more than the loci of
implementation of directives addressed to them by
higher organs of management. The status assigned to
enterprises cast them in a particular mould, which,
in fact, has turned out to be a significant barrier
to the devolution of planning decisions to them. In
addition it also affected the character of planning
itself.
      In keeping with their status, the enterprises
confined themselves to the immediate problems of
drawing up a schedule of production to hit the targets addressed to them. As a consequence their
planning horizon was short, often a month - the
usual period of time for which they received production targets, and they still do in, for example,
the Soviet Union[11] Brus (1973:26) has singled out
this induced myopia of enterprise managers as a
major hindrance to the introduction of new products.
For that requires a longer planning horizon. Moreover, as loci of implementation of directives, the
enterprises did not need to face up to the financial
consequences of their activities. The higher organs
of management supplied enterprises with the necessary funds to carry out current production and investment. Thus they got used to a state of affairs
where financial constraints were hardly ever binding
- a phenomenon which Kornai (1980:Chapter 13) has
identified as a major impediment to the regulation
of enterprise activities by financial means, on which
the projects of economic reforms have relied so
much.
      The shortage of means of production was - and
still is - perhaps the only effective constraint
which the enterprises faced. And they reacted to
that constraint by asking for more means of production than needed, by arranging supplies through informal channels and by reducing their dependence on
outside suppliers. The last, for example, took the
form of enterprises establishing their own workshops

to turn out the needed spare parts. Here, one may note an irony. For Marx and other fathers of socialism the superiority of a planned economy consisted in the elimination of the waste implicit in a competitive duplication of activities. This has not happened in practice; on the contrary the attempts towards self-sufficiency on the part of enterprises often implies a waste of resources through duplication of activities. The argument, in all, is that the type of enterprise which evolved under traditional planning was not conducive to the implementation of the projects of reform, which for their success depended on enterprises looking beyond the immediate problems of production to the introduction of new products, and for whom the financial constraint would be binding. The implementation of reforms, therefore, crucially depended on a radical transformation in the nature of enterprises - a process which is slow and disparate by its very nature.

The targets addressed to enterprises, as well as being a programme of activities, functioned as norms for their assessment. They were meant to be not only met but possibly exceeded. The built-in bias in favour of exceeding the target - in particular the production target - had a crucial impact on the character of planning. The enterprises tried to get easy targets in order to exceed them and hence earn a bonus for over-performance. The organs of management, aware of this, set high targets and revised them upwards whenever an enterprise exceeded its target by a wide margin. As a consequence, rather than a hierarchical relation of super-ordination and sub-ordination the relationship between the organs of management and the enterprises was one of bargaining. The end-result of plan bargaining, as it has been termed in Eastern Europe, and the premium placed on exceeding production targets was an incoherent and inconsistent plan.

Enterprises got not one but a large variety of targets: of output, its assortment, of the utilisation of labour and means of production etc.[12] Inconsistent as these targets often were, they could not be simultaneously realised. Enterprises exploited this lacuna by selecting the targets to satisfy. Thus, paradoxically, the very attempt to control the activities of enterprises in detail by addressing to them a multiplicity of targets provided the enterprises with room for manoeuvre.[13] The net result was a system of planning which was

centralised de jure but oligarchic de facto, and
one in which nominally powerless enterprises had a
significant capacity to set their own 'plans' by
doctoring the information they supplied to higher
organs, and by working around the cracks around targets. Mutatis mutandis, the situation after the reforms is not radically different from this.

However, the economic reforms have brought
about an important change in the de jure status of
the enterprises in the state sector. Following the
reforms most of such enterprises have become separate accounting units with revenue and expenditure
accounts of their own - a status commonly described
by the Russian word khozraschet. The same has
happened to the 6,600 state enterprises included in
the pilot economic reforms in China. The notion of
khozraschet is, however, not new; it was applied to
branch ministries in the Soviet Union in the 1930s
and the 1950s.

Though the literature on the reforms pays a lot
of attention to khozraschet, it on its own means
nothing more than that the institution in question has
a budget of its own. In relation to enterprises it
has acquired a significance only because it has been
complemented by the following:

(1) The description of the activity of the
enterprise in terms of its revenue rather
than the volume of production.

(2) The assessment of the performance of
enterprises in terms of profit or another
related measure.

(3) The grant of partial control to enterprises over their sales and purchases.

(4) The grant of a restricted right to enterprises to utilise their profit for
investment, wage and salary premia and
social services.

The extent of autonomy which has been granted
to enterprises varies between East European economies. With the exception of Hungary, enterprises
elsewhere in Eastern Europe still receive binding
targets, and indeed so do the pilot enterprises in
China. However, the actual practice in Hungary is
not always in keeping with the formal rule.[14]
In general, throughout Eastern Europe enterprises have less autonomy than granted to them

formally. This is so for two reasons. First, is the existence of informal instructions and pressures from organs of economic management. This, however, is secondary and is to be expected. The more important reason is that the general situation in the economy does not leave much room for the exercise of autonomy which enterprises formally have. The grant of the right to dispose of their earned revenue to enterprises - the most important component of autonomy granted to them - provides an apt example.

Despite the development of market relationships which has taken place in East European economies, they still remain, as Berliner (1976:63) has termed them, documentary economies. To acquire means of production an enterprise not only needs funds but also the relevant document - which could be an informal understanding with the appropriate authority. The document is essential because those economies seem to be permanently characterised by an excess demand for commodities, which necessitates rationing and thus a resort to an administrative allocation of scarce means of production. Moreover, since foreign trade in those economies still remains subject to administrative regulation an enterprise cannot turn to a foreign supplier without an administrative licence. The general argument, then, is that the effective significance of the grant of right to enter into market relationships and to use their revenue for investment to enterprises crucially depends on whether or not markets function, which often they do not because of the administrative rationing of scarce commodities. Autonomy cannot be granted to enterprises simply by a judicial fiat; it in addition requires a change in the general situation of supply and demand for commodities.

In the projects of economic reforms the grant of financial autonomy was meant to be complemented by market competition, but that has not happened because of the general scarcity of commodities and hence the ability of enterprises to dispose of their products without any competition. In addition to that,the conglomeration and merging of enterprises which has taken place in Eastern Europe has further reduced the scope of potential competition. In the smaller East European economies(e.g.Hungary)there are no more than a few enterprises in many branches of production; therefore foreign trade seems to be the only source of competition in those economies. In all the implication of these arguments for China is that the actual result of the grant of financial autonomy to a selected group of enterprises

and the emphasis on market relationships will crucially depend on the general situation of the demand
for commodities in the economy. And it would be
more like a change in the criteria by which organs
of management administer enterprises than a devolution of planning decision to the enterprises.

As in China, in East European economies side by
side with the state enterprises, supposedly under
the ownership of the whole population, there existed
cooperatives in agriculture and in the service
sector, supposedly under the ownership of a collective. Aside from that some East European countries
have had economic units in private ownership:
e.g. family farms in Poland. Traditionally, the
ownership of the whole population was regarded as
superior to the collective ownership. Indeed this
is still so in China.[15] The ideological ranking of
the forms of ownership manifested itself in a more
favourable treatment of the allocation of supplies
and investment to state enterprises. The economic
reforms have led to a loosening of the ranking, and
has resulted in a more favourable treatment of co-
operatives. Further, a number of East European
countries have overcome aversion to joint marketing
and production agreements between enterprises and
capitalist firms. And in certain sectors they have
allowed direct foreign investment in certain industries: in the hotel industry, for example.

A similar trend has been in evidence in China
since 1976. However, the collective and private
sector is much larger in China than in East European
countries, perhaps with the exception of Poland,
which has a large private sector in agriculture. In
the pre-1976 era in China the evolution in agriculture was to take the form of a shift from the production to the brigade team and then to the commune
as the unit of production. But recently this path
of evolution has come under question; the official
policy now is to allow for a diversity in the pattern of organisational development in agriculture.
Moreover, the collective - and indeed the private -
sector in agriculture has been singled out for expansion.[16]

Instruments of Economic Control. Traditionally,
central planning in Eastern Europe - and indeed in
China - has been synonymous with the issue of targets to enterprises. Such targets, as indicated
earlier, came in a large variety of forms. Among
them the output target was primary. It could be
argued that the aim of the traditional central

planning was to maximise output without much regard
for technical efficiency. Moreover, it was based on
the naive idea that the non-realisation of plans was
principally due to gaps in the control of the economy. As a result, organs of economic management
tended to respond to economic problems by issuing
yet more targets and instructions to enterprises.
A number of East European economists have pointed
out that the non-realisation of plans had much to
do with the nature of the plan and instructions addressed to enterprises. Plans were, to start with,
unrealistically ambitious and often inconsistent.

The targets and instructions issued to enterprises were legally binding, and non-compliance with
them was an economic crime. However, legal coercion
though employed was not the only and often not the
principal instrument for securing compliance with
the plan. Though they acquired a special prominence
following the economic reforms, material incentives
were widely employed during the period of traditional planning. This needs emphasis because in China
during the period of the Cultural Revolution the
economic reforms were attacked for their reliance
on economic incentives.[17] During the period of
traditional planning, apart from medals and honor-
ofic titles, the overfulfilment of targets was
rewarded by a bonus. There was, however, an important asymmetry: pro rata, the penalty for under-
fulfilling the target was less than the reward for
over-fulfilling them. Such an asymmetry still
exists. Apart from bonuses, one may note, differentiation of salaries and wages has always existed
in Eastern Europe, and that too is a part of material incentive for the implementation of the plan.
For, in part, that differentiation has been graded
according to the apportionment of responsibility for
carrying out directives addressed to enterprises.

Generally speaking the economic reforms have
not completely transformed either the nature of
planning or of instruments to secure the implementation of the plan. In most countries what they
have done is to refine the traditional instruments
of control.

With the exception of Hungary, enterprises
elsewhere are still issued binding production targets, though different from the ones prior to the
reforms. Production targets in physical terms have
been replaced by sales targets for specific commodities in order to discourage enterprises from producing sub-standard or unwanted products. As indicated above, the impact of this shift, which

crucially depends on the choice available to users of commodities,is attenuated by the general scarc-- ity of commodities, and the concomitant allocation of means of production by administrative means. Further, though Hungarian enterprises do not form- ally receive production targets, informally at least some of them do. In fact it can be argued that so long as there is central planning of the major sectors of the economy, the implementation of the plan would involve the issue of some form of produc- tion targets to the enterprises in the key sectors of the economy. In Hungary, for example, the high concentration of industrial structure implies that there are often no more than a few enterprises in most sectors of the economy; in such a situation any attempt by central authorities to plan the key sectors of the economy is tantamount to drawing up a plan addressed to the enterprises in those sectors.

However, it is not so much whether enterprises receive targets but, first, how much say they have in the formulation of targets and, second, what con- siderations enter into the formulation of targets which are of central importance. Since targets have to be based on the information supplied by them, enterprises always had at least some say in their formulation. There is some evidence that the re- forms have granted the enterprises a formal power to bargain about the targets addressed to them. In addition to that, as compared to the pre-reform per- iod, following the reforms plans have become less ambitious and planning methods more refined; there- fore, the divergence between the aims of central authorities and the capabilities of enterprises has become narrower. However, despite all the changes which have taken place in the techniques of planning, East European economies still go for a taut plan — a plan which is far from easy to realise.

Following the reforms, profit and an increase in profit - or a monetary measure like value added - have become the indices of efficiency in production in all Eastern European economies. Formally, these indices have replaced the traditional targets of efficiency in terms of the rate of utilisation of means of production and labour, thus their charac- terisation as synthetic targets in East European literature. However, pre-reform efficiency direct- ives did not have much operational significance; they were either meaningless as targets of effic- iency or neglected by enterprises. The main change brought about by the reforms is not so much the introduction of synthetic targets but a greater

weight placed on targets of efficiency in production
Arguably, the pre-reform planning was single target
planning, and that target was to maximise the gross
output of enterprises.

The main argument in favour of profit (or value
added) is that central organs of management do not
have either accurate or sufficient information to
formulate meaningful quantitative indices of efficiency for each enterprise. Therefore, they should
relegate the task of the efficient utilisation of
labour and means of production to enterprises, and
restrict themselves to broad synthetic measures of
efficiency. The main problem with profit as an
index of efficiency is that its significance crucially depends on the nature of prices which rule in
the economy. Thus the operational significance of
profit as an index of efficiency depends heavily on
the mechanism by which prices are determined in
planned economies.

Though the economic reforms have brought them
into prominence, prices and markets - at least
for consumer goods and labour - have always existed
in planned economies. Prior to the reforms, the
prices assigned to means of production were means
of accounting and an instrument of control: to
express the quantities of disparate means of production in aggregative terms and to provide an economic method for keeping a check on the input and
output of enterprises. For prices to perform these
functions they need only to be stable, and it does
not matter what they are. The grant of financial
autonomy to enterprises and the selection of profit
as the principal index of efficiency, and thus the
dependence of wages and salaries on profit, assigned
prices new tasks. To perform these functions efficiently prices need to change with economic circumstances, and they have to have a particular configuration. The important point then is that the type
of prices required by the two sets of functions are
not the same.[18]

Prior to the economic reforms prices were set
by organs of economic management, and once set they
had a long life. This method of determination of
prices did suit the performance of the accounting
and control function by prices. In all East
European countries an overhaul of prices was acknowledged to be one of the essential conditions of the
economic reforms. And that did happen in nearly all
the economies. The general formula for the determination of prices which finally came to be adopted
was that for means of production they should be

equal to a reference cost of production of the commodity (including the cost of fixed capital) plus a
mark-up for profit. To calculate such prices, organs
of economic management need cost of production data
from enterprises - who would have an interest in
inflating their cost and which they do indeed. Any
centralised determination of prices by its very
nature has to be a slow and a complex procedure.

In East European economies prices are still
determined by administrative organs of management.
In Hungary, the reforms of 1968 devolved the determination of prices of a large range of commodities -
but not all - to enterprises. The determination of
prices by administrative means has a number of important implications. First, to determine prices
organs of economic management need as much information as they do to set detailed production targets
for enterprises. Therefore, the former encounters
exactly the same problems which the latter does.
Second, as one would expect, political and social
considerations cast a long shadow on administratively
determined prices. Third, given that they are cumbersome and costly to revise, administered prices
have a built-in inertia. The net result of administered prices is that profits of enterprises depend
not only on their technical efficiency but also on
the price decisions of the organs of management.
Moreover, the prevailing prices are often out of
alignment with the prevailing economic conditions.
The former weakens the significance of profit as an
index of efficiency; while the latter implies that
ruling prices do not always provide a reliable guide
about the desired direction of technical efficiency
to enterprises. In all, what the grant of financial
autonomy to enterprises and the use of profit as the
main indicator of efficiency have done is to trans-
pose many of the problems which dogged traditional planning to the sphere of the determination
of prices.

Logically, the implementation of the projects
of economic reforms requires that organs of management confine themselves to setting out the rules for
determination of prices, and let enterprises determine prices in accordance with those rules. This
had not happened because of the justified fears of
unleashing a spiral of inflation on the part of
governments in East European countries. Kornai
(1980) has pointed out that because of the general
scarcity of commodities - and the monopolistic
position which enterprises enjoy, one may add -
there is a built-in potential for a cumulative price

inflation in those economies. East European economies, unlike capitalist countries, are not geared
to inflation; the events in Poland point out that
an upward revision in the prices of consumer goods
can be politically explosive. During the last two
years the Chinese authorities have also learnt that
the devolution of price determination can lead to
the politically embarrassing phenomenon of price
inflation.

The general argument, then, is that the system
of price determination in East European economies -
as indeed in capitalist economies - is subject to
disparate and inconsistent requirements. Johansen
(1977:Chapter 5.9) has drawn attention to the fact
that one set of prices - one price for each commodity - cannot perform all the functions which it is
supposed to perform. East European economies try to
reconcile disparate and inconsistent requirements by
a hybrid system of determination of prices. The
prices of 'sensitive' commodities - consumer goods
and the basic industrial inputs - are fixed by
administrative fiat. As for the rest, enterprises
are either informally or formally - in the form of
a specified band - allowed to vary prices within
limits. Apart from these there are some prices
which are allowed to vary freely. The range of free
prices is understandably wider in Hungary than elsewhere. The same three sets of prices exist in
China.[19] The western literature on the economic
reforms is often based on the implicit assumption
that a 'rational' price system would solve all the
major problems of socialist economies. But the
problem is that there is no unique set of rational
prices, and that the implementation of a set of
prices rational for a particular purpose often involves significant economic and social costs. The
latter needs to be taken into account as well as
the gain implied by a rational set of prices.

Prior to the economic reforms investment was
financed by grants from the state budget, and the
use of credit to finance investment and, correlatively, the inclusion of the cost of capital in the
cost of product was regarded as non-socialist. In
all East European economies the economic reforms
have changed the ideologically ingrained habit of
excluding the cost of capital from the cost of
enterprises. That change has paved the way for a
shift from grants to loans to finance investment.
Concomitantly, banks have started to play a more
active role in the provision of investment funds,
rather than just being a cloak-room of funds. In

general, there are three principal sources of
investment funds now: loans and grants from the
government and banks and the internal fund of enterprises. For obvious reasons, the last did not exist
during the period of traditional planning, when enterprises did not have financial autonomy. But it
now accounts for a significant proportion of investment funds; that proportion, for example, is around
a half in Hungary.[20]
   The important implication of the increase in
the share of internally financed investment is that
it constitutes a change in the configuration of
allocation of investment funds to enterprises. For
it implies the use of profitability as an investment
criterion, a role which it did not have during the
period of traditional planning. Allowing enterprises to employ a part of their revenue for investment is, one may note, tantamount to discriminating
between enterprises in the allocation of investment
funds. For, prima facie, the rate of profit would
vary between enterprises, and, consequently, the
more profitable an enterprise the higher its share
of investment funds. In addition, central authorities may well be influenced by the profitability of
enterprises in the allocation of funds under their
control to enterprises. None the less, profit can
only play a limited role as an investment criterion
in centrally planned economies for, generally speaking, two reasons. First, the rate of profit because
of the nature of ruling prices is an inaccurate
measure of return from investment. Second, there
are investment criteria other than the rate of
profit on investment. Among them one would include
not only political and social considerations but
also the fact that authorities in socialist economies want the economies to have a particular sectoral
composition. The traditional bias in favour of the
development of capital goods industries - which the
economic reforms have not eliminated - is an example
of the latter.
   When analysing instruments by which organs of
management exercise control over enterprises it is
useful to distinguish between direct and indirect
controls. The former take the form of directives
specifying the action to be taken; targets handed
down by organs of management to enterprises come
under this category. Control by issuing directives
is, one may note, not peculiar to socialist economies; it is usual within capitalist firms. In
contrast, indirect controls operate by laying down
the framework for decision making: rules for

computing costs and prices, and setting constraints
on the range of decisions ; restrictions on the
pattern of use of enterprise funds; and the require
ment that enterprises should at least breakeven.
The dividing line between the two is blurred, but,
in general terms, it consists of the following.
While direct controls, which take the form of directives addressed to a particular enterprise, do not
leave much room for decision making to enterprises,
indirect controls, which take the form of general
rules, allow enterprises freedom of choice and
thus allow them to set and follow their own objectives within constraints. The former unlike the
latter may require the controlling authority to have
more information about the capacity of enterprises.
Moreover, both direct and indirect controls can be
either formal or informal.

Though the economic reforms have not eliminated
the direct controls, they have brought some instruments of indirect control into prominence. Of them
the inclusion of the cost of capital in the cost of
production, the charging of interest on investment
funds and the levying of taxes are among the most
important. With the grant of financial autonomy to
enterprises the taxation of their income has become
at least a potential instrument of control. There
is, obviously, no place for the taxation of enterprise income when their receipts and payments are a
part of the state budget. Enterprise income is now
taxed in all socialist economies. With the exception of Hungary the pattern of use of income at the
disposal of enterprises for bonuses and premia, provision of social services and investment is controlled by a general regulation rather than by means
which penalise , for example, the use of funds for
bonuses and premia.

In their projects of reforms East European
economists argued for a radical shift from direct to
indirect controls. The point which needs to be
emphasised is that this shift from direct centralisation to indirect centralisation, as it has been
termed in the Soviet Union, cannot come about
without a concomitant change in the method of formulation of the objectives of the plan. For there is
no guarantee that indirect methods of control would
always help realise the objectives of central organs
of management. The general argument is that there
has to be some correspondence between the type of
planning and the instruments of control; a radical
reform of either is not possible without a radical
reform of the other. A radical shift towards

indirect controls would entail enterprises playing a central role in the formulation of the objectives of the plan. As a result planning would take more the form of forecasting than of the laying down of targets based on the preference of the leadership.

An Overview of Economic Reforms

A general assessment of the economic reforms can take the following forms:

> (1) a comparison of the actual changes brought about by the reforms with their blueprints, both of which vary from one country to another, and

> (2) an assessment of the likely effects of the realised reforms on the performance of East European economies.

Generally speaking the objective of the reform was to increase the potential rate of growth of the economy and to provide for a better satisfaction of the consumer demand for more and a wider range of consumer goods. These objectives were to be achieved by granting enterprises more decision-making power as well as financial autonomy, by enlarging the scope of market relationships and by recasting the price system, by encouraging a more efficient utilisation of resources by means of the adoption of profit in place of volume of production as the indicator of efficiency, by a greater reliance on material incentives, by a refinement of planning methods and procedures for calculating the costs of production and of investment and, finally, by accelerating the introduction of new products and new production processes.

The actual changes though significant fall well short of the blueprints of the reforms. Further, the problems which the reforms sought to eliminate – technical inefficiency in production, the production of sub-standard goods and the slow rate of introduction of new goods – have not entirely disappeared. The gap between actual reforms and their blueprints is however not something peculiar to East European economies. Further, the proponents of the reforms did not see them as a once-for-all overhaul to the system, but as a series of piecemeal changes distributed in time. What is of main interest is not so much the gap between blueprints and realisation but sources of resistance to the implementation of the types of changes envisaged by the reforms.

It might seem that since their central feature
is the devolution of decision making-power to enterprises, party officials and bureaucrats in organs of
management would be against and enterprise managers
for them. But such a line-up is based on the assumption that the relations between the two groups are
always antagonistic, and that they compete against
each other for decision-making power – a mistaken
assumption according to Hough (1980:Chapter 7).
The relations between the two groups can be either
collaborative or one of rivalry. Alternatively, one
should not assume that the two groups are locked
into a zero-sum game, where the prize is the decision-making power. In assessing those relations one
needs to take into account that not only are most
enterprise managers party members, but also that
they belong to the same occupational class as bureaucrats in organs of management. There is a two-
way mobility between them. Moreover, not all managers are against the traditional style of managing
the economy. The traditional command economy, one
may note, did indeed relegate the enterprise management to a subordinate position, but, as a correlate
of that, it also absolved them of responsibility for
economic decisions. Moreover, it had built into it
the possibility of accommodation and bargaining between enterprise managers and bureaucrats. In contrast, the economic reforms sought to shift the responsibility for decision-making to enterprise managers, and thus leave them open to risks to which
they were not accustomed. It was argued above that
the traditional planning geared enterprises to pursue short-term production targets without any worry
about the sale of their products and the availability of funds. In all, the general argument, then,
is that the division for and against the reforms
cuts across the bureaucracy and the enterprise management.

The resistance to the economic reforms comes
not only from 'conservative' managers and bureaucrats but also from workers themselves. Except in
welfare matters directly relevant to them, workers in
East European economies never had much say in economic management. In this particular respect China
has been different; it, since the early 1950s, has
tried to involve workers in the management of enterprises in various institutional forms. Thus the
interest of workers in the economic reforms principally lies in what they have to offer by way of
increase in wages and social services, and indeed,

the extra supply of consumer goods. As elsewhere,
the attitude of workers to performance-related payments (bonuses and premia) is asymmetric: the
better performers, obviously, like the link between
performance and wages but the same is not true for
the poor performers. The end-result is a compromise
between the aim of rewarding the better performers
with bonuses and premia and the more general aim of
guaranteeing a basic wage to all regardless of performance and to maintain within bounds the inequality of incomes. The compromise takes the form of
subsidies to loss-making enterprises, and thus a
dilution of the principle of financial autonomy.
The general point is that complete financial autonomy is not possible unless governments of East
European countries are willing to let a large number
of enterprises go bankrupt and to see the emergence
of large inter-enterprise differences in wages and
salaries, which for understandable social and political reasons they do not.
    The lack of labour discipline - variable among
different countries - is an important cause of technical inefficiency in Eastern Europe. The workers'
states of Eastern Europe may not have granted their
workers with decision-making power, but they did
provide them with an almost cast-iron guarantee of
remaining employed at the existing place of work.
To the extent that economic reforms are dependent on
a better work discipline, they have come up against
the ingrained inefficient work and employment practices. Here, it is interesting to note that the
right to employment has come under question in
China.21 However, it is difficult for socialist
economies, who have always prided themselves on being free from the problem of unemployment, to use
dismissals as an instrument for extracting efficiency out of workers.
    It was argued above that for profit to function
as the indicator of efficiency and for markets to
perform the task of rationing scarce commodities, an
overhaul of the method of determination of prices is
necessary. At the outset it has to be accepted that
organs of management are no more competent to set
prices of commodities according to some algorithm
than they are to lay down the targets of production
of those commodities according to some objectives.
Thus the argument in favour of letting enterprises
set prices is as strong as that in favour of letting
them draw their production plans. The main problem,
however, is that a complete devolution of the setting of prices to enterprises and use of prices as

a device to ration scarce commodities would, given the general scarcity of commodities in East European economies, unleash an inflationary spiral.

The correlate of the scarcity of commodities is their rationing, through either an increase in their prices or a 'lottery' - usually in the form of queues and sporadic supplies - or administrative allocations. All three are and have been used to ration consumption goods, while it is mainly the last which is used to ration means of production. Consumers in Eastern Europe understandably dislike queues and shortages; but there is no clear evidence that they prefer rationing through the market to non-market rationing. The events in Poland point to the contrary. However, during the last few years Hungary has succeeded in raising the prices of a wide range of consumer goods.

The general argument, then, is that the reform of the method of determining prices, an essential component of reforms, was not possible without cost in the form of inflation and the resistance of consumers to an increase in the prices of consumer goods. It could not but be a slow process. Among East European economies, Hungary is the only one to have radically altered the price regime.

The implementation and the success of the reforms has depended not only on the extent to which its different components were accepted by different categories of economic agents but also on the prevailing macroeconomic conditions in the economy: the balance between the supply and demand for commodities in particular. Take, for instance, the grant of financial autonomy to enterprises, a central component of the economic reforms. It was to make enterprises sensitive to costs of production, and provide them with an incentive to economise on resources of production, and to tailor their products to the requirements of users. The grant of financial autonomy was meant, in all, radically to alter the behaviour of enterprises. However, whether it does so crucially depends on the extent to which the financial constraint is binding on the enterprise.

A number of East European economists, in particular Kornai, have argued that the financial constraint is still not much of a constraint on the behaviour of enterprises. First, the grant of subsidies to loss-making enterprises to enable them to carry on production and to pay wages - and to increase them in line with the national norm - robs the financial constraint of some - but not all - of its disciplinary power. Second, the general shortage of commodities implies that enterprises have a guaranteed market for their products. So long as that remains the case there is not much incentive for enterprises to pay much heed to the needs of users of commodities and to introduce new products.

Following Brus, one could argue that an elimination of the shortage of commodities - which admittedly has decreased over time - is necessary for the implementation of some of the central measures of the reforms, and for them to have the intended effects. In fact there is a two-way connection between traditional planning and the shortage of commodities. Traditional planning, with its accent on output maximisation without much regard for technical efficiency, with its bias towards investment and its disregard of the balance between the money income of households and the supply of consumer goods, perpetually created a general shortage of commodities. That shortage of commodities, in turn, necessitated an administrative allocation of means of production, which has always been a central feature of traditional central planning. In time, it is consumer resistance to the shortage of commodities which has put brakes on this, what may be termed, 'cumulative causation'. The economic reforms by their reliance on material incentives - tantamount to an increase in household incomes - have introduced an additional brake on shortages of commodities. However, some of the features which characterised traditional planning, in particular the bias towards investment, have not entirely disappeared. One may note a paradox here: while the capitalist economies of the 1970s have found it difficult to invest enough to maintain the level needed to sustain a high rate of employment, the East European economies find it difficult to restrain investment and thus dampen the shortage of commodities and of labour.

I turn now to the effects of whatever reforms have been introduced in Eastern Europe. Generally speaking, the projects of economic reform were a technical response to the problems which East European economies started to encounter from the mid '50s onwards: a slow-down in the rate of growth despite massive rates of investment. Traditional planning, though technically crude and administratively ineffective, did manage to produce spectacular rates of growth in all East European economies, but only because of the following two factors:

(1) the ability of the governments to channel massive volumes of investment into a few selected branches of production, in particular the capital goods industries, and

(2) the reservoir of surplus labour in the countryside and among women, which could easily be tapped.

The massive rates of investment and the resultant expansion in industrial employment quickly drained the reservoir of surplus labour. Moreover, the initial burst of industrialisation enlarged the range of capital goods produced and required in the economy, and thus complicated the task of administering the economy. On the other hand, the rise in household incomes - concomitant of an increase in employment - brought about a qualitative and a quantitative increase in the demand for consumer goods. The general argument is that the traditional development strategy in time destroyed the pre-conditions for its own success, and thus it could not but be transitory. The span of time over which the strategy could work was inversely related to the level of industrialisation of the economy.

Eventually, improvement in labour productivity, a better match between the supply and demand for commodities and quality control in production came to the fore as pressing problems. Not that these problems did not exist before, but initially they did not act as brakes on the rate of growth of the economy. There is indeed a link between the gravity of these tasks and the stage of development; they have been more pressing in the highly industrialised economies of Czechoslovakia and the GDR than in the less industrialised economies of Bulgaria and Romania. These problems shifted the focus onto the management of enterprises, their institutional structure and the ability of organs of management to control their functioning. During the phase of what is termed in Eastern Europe 'extensive development', where the growth rate was maximised by the maximisation of investment in a few selected sectors of the economy, the restructuring of agriculture and the supply of good to the cities were the central problems. The latter is still a problem in some - but not all - East European economies.

The argument now is that however meagre the economic reforms have been, they have improved the functioning of East European economies. It is true that the pre-reform economies did initially produce

rates of growth which, by and large, have not been
matched in the post-reform period. But, as argued
above, those rates of growth could not have been
repeated; and there was, one may note, a rapid
deceleration in the rates of growth before the reforms. Moreover, the problems of inefficiency
which East European economies exhibit today are not
an effect of the reforms but a result of the continuation of the traditional ways of managing the
economy. [22]

The general thesis put forward here has an
important implication for China. Since the Chinese
economy has an immense reservoir of surplus labour
the traditional economic strategy based on the maximisation of investment still has a long lease of
life there. By way of an indirect support for this
argument one may point out that the two less industrialised countries of Eastern Europe, Bulgaria and
Romania, though still managed according to the traditional style, grow at rates which are high both by
East European and wider international standards.

It is necessary to specify the exact significance of this argument. It is not that efficiency-
oriented reforms cautiously being attempted in China
are not necessary. Indeed the success of these reforms will improve the performance of the economy,
especially if reforms in training and allocation can
relieve shortages of skilled industrial labour and
channel surplus labour to places where shortage
might occur with expansion. Rather, the argument is
that because of its high rate of investment the
Chinese economy will still show a creditable economic performance even if the reforms do not completely succeed. Correlatively, the other part of
this argument is that one has to take care not to
attribute the improvement in the performance of the
Chinese economy with respect to that during the
decade 1966-76 solely to the economic reforms
which have started to be implemented since 1978.
A part of the improvement in performance between
1978 and now is simply due to the end of political
uncertainty and the restoration of the chains of
economic command.

The Politics and Economics of Reforms

The essential feature of socialist economies is the
intertwining of political administration and economic management. And the economic reforms in
Eastern Europe have not disengaged the two. Leaving
aside the doctrinal disputes, the social ownership

of the means of production has been equated with
the political control of enterprises - Yugoslavia
is an exception here. As a result the enterprise
is both an economic and a political unit. To a degree
the party organisation in Eastern Europe has always
been anchored in the enterprise: the party organisation at the level of the enterprise has been and
still is basic among grass root organisations of the
party. And it plays an essential role in the running
of enterprises. By and large the leadership of the
party at the enterprise level and the enterprise
management consist of the same personnel. Not only
are most enterprise managers in Eastern Europe party
members but also a managerial position is often a
stepping stone on to higher reaches of the party and
governmental organisations. Most enterprise managers
in Eastern Europe got to their present position by
being good party members.

Given the permeation of the state by the party
at all levels, enterprises are linked to their respective branch ministries and other organs of management through two and not just one channel. The
first channel is the administrative link between
enterprises and organs of economic management; one
may term this the economic and administrative link.
The second link is through the party. Since the
occupation of responsible positions is often contingent on membership of the party, the two links are
inextricably intertwined. In fact, the party provides
links between institutions which are not linked to
each other by a direct administrative channel.

It is, however, only the administrative and
economic link between the enterprises and the organs
of economic management, and the status of the enterprises which have been the targets of economic
reforms. The link between the enterprises and the
state apparatus through the party has been left
untouched. This has had a significant effect on the
course of the economic reforms. Political considerations continue to exercise a powerful influence on
policy towards enterprises. The link through the
party provides a possibility for enterprise managers
to get special dispensations and to arrive at informal understanding with branch ministries, hence to
contravening the spirit of the reforms. This has some
relevance for China. Unlike Mao and the Gang of Four,
the present leadership in China may want to put economics in command in place of politics. But that
cannot happen so easily; for even if the top party
leadership is in favour of reforms the same is not
true for all other sections of the party.

The economic reforms in Eastern Europe have left the internal organisation of enterprises - the relations between the management and workers, and the respective positions of the party committee, the trade union committee and the management - unchanged. In Yugoslavia economic reforms took the form of the introduction of workers' control, but elsewhere in Eastern Europe workers' control has not been on the agenda, except for a short period of time in Czechoslovakia and perhaps in Poland in future. Brus (1973 & 75) has rightly pointed out that the autonomy of the enterprise is a necessary precondition for the introduction of workers' control. But in addition to that a political change is necessary. For the party and the trade union have traditionally claimed to be the representatives of the workers. The introduction of workers' control may well entail a devaluation in the position of these two organisations. One may, however, note that in Yugoslavia self-management has not affected the primacy of the party. But there the party took the lead in introducing the system, while in other East European countries workers' participation, if introduced, would be forced on the party.

Apart from Yugoslavia, among socialist countries China has had the longest experience of the participation of workers in the running of enterprises. Following the downfall of the Gang of Four, the revolutionary committees which had sprung up in enterprises during the Cultural Revolution were dismantled. But during the last two years workers' participation in management has been resuscitated, albeit under the name of workers' congresses, traced to similar organisations which were introduced in 1957. The basic issue which concerns such organisations is the range of their competence. Generally speaking, their competence can extend to three areas: economic activities of the enterprise, questions of welfare and work-discipline and the determination of wages and salaries.

Centralised planning and making the manager responsible for the running of the enterprise puts the former outside the range of competence of the representative organisations of workers. The second has been the domain of trade union activity in Eastern Europe. As for the third, the wage and salary scales and so too the regulations concerning bonuses and premia are national in China as well as in Eastern Europe. Yugoslavia, in contrast, does not have such national scales.

The determination of wages and salaries in Eastern Europe raises an important political problem. Traditionally, the maxim 'to each according to his work' was equated with national wage scales, similar to the 'eight grade wage scale' in China. National wage scale has provided the authorities with an instrument to keep the inequality of wages within certain bounds. In principle, the dependence of wages on the performance of enterprises introduces a radically new element. For the differences in the profitability of enterprises will imply a differentiation of wages according to the place of employment as well as occupation. This indeed has happened in Yugoslavia where inter-enterprise wages differences can be wide. This to a small degree has also happened in other East European countries. There the basic wage and salary - and increases in them - are guaranteed independently of performance. Moreover, only a small part of profit can be paid out as bonuses and premia; and the latter do not increase pro rata with the former. In addition the dependence of total earnings on performance varies according to the position of the personnel: it is closer for management than for workers.[23] Here one may note a contrast: in capitalist economies it is the workers who get performance-related wages, while the management gets fixed salaries. At a more general level one may note that to regulate wages and salaries is to control personal income. In this connection it is interesting to point out that the system of personal taxation - of income taxation in particular - is rudimentary in Eastern Europe, and in China as well. What this means is that the authorities in those economies can only control personal incomes through a direct regulation of wage scales and performance-related payments, rather than by taxes.

To conclude then, the grant of autonomy to enterprises which has been central to the economic reforms in Eastern Europe and in China is constrained by political as well as economic factors. Important among the latter are: the centralised planning of the economy, the allocation of scarce means of production by administrative means, the retention of price determination by the authorities and the government control over investment. That the enterprise is a crucial node in the political network implies that political considerations cannot but have an important bearing on the relations between enterprises and organs of management.

4

JAPAN AND CHINA

Craig Littler

By 1980 Japan's economic output was equal to the
combined output of Britain, France and Italy; it
produced 50% more than West Germany, and roughly
equalled the economic performance of the Soviet
Union. Moreover, the Japanese income per head of
the population was also equal to that of the United
States - a country enriched by vastly more resources
of land and mineral deposits. Given,then, the stag-
gering industrial development of Japan from insul-
ated feudal economy, to radioactive rubble heaps and
on to the world's second largest economy, what are
the parallels and lessons for China?

During the 1960's the Japanese experience was
dismissed as irrelevant to Chinese socialist development, but since 1976 Japan has been put forward
by the new Chinese leadership as an example to be
carefully studied (Schram, 1981:408). Perhaps the
naive optimism surrounding the new vision of Japan

* This paper has benefitted from the help of numerous people. In particular I would like to thank
Ronald Dore, who over the years has taught me about
the complexities of Japanese society; Martin Lockett
for his extensive and meticulous knowledge of the
Chinese economy; and Peter Abell for stimulating discussions whilst walking the streets of Peking. The
Chinese research trip in September/October 1981 was
made possible by the British Academy, the S.S.R.C.
and the Chinese Academy of Social Sciences. I am
grateful to these institutions collectively, but in
addition I would like to single out Alison Cooper
for her quiet and efficient administration and
Gao Jinyuan for his good humoured interpreting.

at the end of the 1970's is best epitomized by the amazing (to Maoist eyes) film "Sakura". Produced in 1979 in Beijing, this personifies Japanese technology as a beautiful female engineer come to regenerate and modernize Chinese industry for entirely noble motives. Only political turbulence and economic U-turns frustrate the onward march of technological progress!

This chapter attempts to look briefly at the pattern of Japanese modernization,focusing on the development of industrial work organization. Subsequently I will draw out some comparisons and contrasts with China and then discuss the impact of recent trade links and transfer of technology.

Pattern of Modernization

From the Chinese perspective the Japanese path of development has a number of interesting features, especially the relative self-sufficiency of economic modernization, the role of the State and the dual structure of the economy. I will discuss each of these characteristics.

One critical variable in modern development is the distinction between dependent and independent industrialization. Thus one mode of industrialization is by formal or informal colonization, with the industrializing process carried out by the bourgeoisies of other societies (Clark Kerr, ed; 1973: 67-70; Kumar, 1978:130; B. Turner, 1975:97-100). Japan does not fit into this category. Japan was fortunate in that it not only resisted submission to colonial rule, but was able to separate and control the three crucial levers of economic domination: technology, imports and capital (Halliday, 1975: XXlll). In contrast, China was forced to give territorial concessions and commercial privileges to the Western powers and became 'hyper-colony - exploited by all, but the responsibility of none' (Kunio, 1979:89).

The self-sufficiency of Japanese modernization is tied in with the role of the State. The conventional starting-point for discussing Japanese industrialization is the Meiji Restoration of 1868. After the Meiji revolution there was a concentrated effort by the new Japanese rulers to achieve economic equality with the West as soon as possible. Thus, between 1868-1880 the primary initiative in promoting industrialization was taken by the State. Industrial policy was twofold: one programme was direct government investment to establish a core of industries to serve military needs (e.g. steel, shipbuilding and armaments). Many of the present-day heavy industries originated in this way (Smith, 1955). The second aspect of industrial policy was to stimulate export-oriented consumer industries via the encouragement of joint-stock companies. The earliest companies in Meiji Japan were set up in 1869: they were financial and trading organizations established in eight trading centres under government auspices but with capital and staff provided, with varying degrees of reluctance, by merchant houses (Westney, 1980:145). These companies failed, and it was not until the 1890's that a general understanding of Western-style joint-stock companies permeated through the Japanese elite. The spread of the company form is indicated by the fact that the number of Western-type companies increased eighteen-fold to 23,028 over the period 1885-1918. This indicates the eventual success of the Meiji leadership in creating the organizational base for capitalist machine production as opposed to the traditional basis of manual production consisting of family units or fictive kinship relations (Horie, 1965:202; Yoshino, 1968:12-13).

It is important to realize that limited liability companies were not a grassroots economic development, but could only develop with government encouragement and government assistance. A capitalist class had to be created in Japan. Moreover from the standpoint of the government leadership neither Western economic thinking nor capitalism per se were objects of policy. Capitalism came to Japan overlaid by a fervent nationalism (Horie, 1965:199; Hazama, 1981:4).

Thus the early industrialization process depended on state support and privileged relations between government and entrepreneurs. In general it was the State which mobilized capital for industrial investment, and the government share of investment activity continued to be predominant through to the 1930s. Overall the government's share of investment activity was larger in Japan than in any other industrializing society in Europe or North America (Rosovsky, 1961). This vigorous mobilization of capital meant that Japan was able to resist borrowing foreign money until the early 1900's. From the Meiji Restoration until the Russo-Japanese War the only major foreign loan was 5 million yen borrowed in 1870 to build the railway from Tokyo to Yokohama. In general the Japanese government was very reluctant to accept foreign capital (except during the

Russo-Japanese War of 1904-5) or to countenance
direct foreign investment. Although by the 1930's
a few multi-nationals (including Siemens, General
Electric, Westinghouse, Shell and I.B.M.) had set up
operations in Japan, their total investment was min-
iscule (Lockwood, 1968:322-3). This policy persis-
ted after World War II, and until 1964 the Japanese
policy was to prohibit direct foreign investment.

Given the above prohibitions what, then, of
technology transfer? The Japanese approach was to
'unpack' the complex of capital, technology, managerial skills and market control offered by foreign
multi-nationals and utilize the technology by means
of licensing agreements. This policy was pursued
both before and after World War II. In general,
this approach can work only if the domestic capital
market can raise adequate flows of funds and there
is a pool of managerial skills. Thus, faced with
conservative merchants and the lack of a capitalist
class at the beginning of industrialization, the
State was crucial in mobilizing capital (largely
from a new land tax) in order to build up industries
(Brugger, 1976:31).

Given the rapid rise of petty commodity production, the spread of market relations, and the
Western impact after the 1850's, Japan would probably have developed a capitalist mode of production
anyway. But without state intervention and particularly if the state had actively tried to maintain
pre-capitalist modes of production (as occurred in
China at certain periods) the transition would have
been much slower. And with few natural resources
Japan would have ended up like some of the poorest
and most dependent Third World societies today -
tied into the world capitalist system, but with an
extremely underdeveloped internal capitalism.

So far I have argued that the role of the new
Meiji state in solving the problems of capital
supply and, over time, of an adequate organisational
form for machine-based industry was vital to a
relatively independent process of Japanese modernization. However the role of the State had other
consequences which have received wide attention in
the economic literature on Japan: namely the creation of a 'dual economic structure'. "Dualism" is
not a very precise concept. Generally it means the
division of an economy into two separate spheres
with limited economic interactions. The notion has
been applied to developing societies in which there
is an export-oriented industrial and urban enclave
co-existing with a vast agricultural and peasant

hinterland barely touched by the modern sector's
market economy (Hirschman, 1958). Other associated
features are large income and productivity dispari-
ties.
    This model of sectoral relations does not apply
to Japan. Nevertheless, there has been a fundamental economic divide between Japanese large, capital-intensive firms with high productivity and
small, under-capitalized companies subject to much
greater economic insecurities. But, unlike many
Asian societies, large modern enterprises and traditional medium/small enterprises exist in a complementary relation. The latter have a symbiotic subcontracting relationship with the former and the
large enterprises use the cheap labour products of
medium and small enterprises and regard them as a
buffer against business fluctuations. Essentially,
Japan has succeeded in integrating the premodern and
modern sectors into a national economy (Miyazawa,
1964).
    It is worth noting that the vast majority of
the Japanese manufacturing labour force work is in
small/medium enterprises, (see Table below).

Table 4.1

Distribution of Japanese and British Labour Forces by size of Establishment, (manufacturing).

% of Labour Force in Establishments with:-

		1 - 9	10 - 99	100 - 999	1000 +
Japan	(1970)	16.4	35.2	29.9	17.5
U.K.	(1968)	2.1	16.7	46.1	35.2

(Source: Boltho, 1975:26. Boltho's figures are
          wrong as printed and have been corrected.)

It is worth noting the distribution of the Japanese
labour force because of the sharp contrast with the
U.K., as a comparable, capitalist economy and because most of the English literature on Japanese
industry and work organisation refers to the minority (i.e. 17.5%) in the large corporations. Generally the existing literature neglects the family-
based small/medium enterprises. The sharpness of
wage differentials between the two is shown in Table
2. It can be seen from Table 2 that these wage
differentials have been shrinking: in the early

1950's the wage costs of large firms were four times those of small firms, since then they have narrowed to slightly over double. Nevertheless the differentials are still large by international standards. Similarly there are large productivity differentials between the large and small firm sectors.

Table 4.2

Japanese Wage Differentials in Manufacturing (Enterprises employing 500 + = 100).

	500+	100-499	30-99	5-25
1960	100	70.7	58.9	46.3
1965	100	80.9	71.0	63.2
1970	100	81.4	69.9	61.8
1975	100	82.9	68.7	60.2

(Source: Nakamura, 1981:164).

Why does this dual structure exist and persist? In brief, it is caused by the interaction between features of the Japanese labour market and capital market. Japanese, as well as Chinese, development has been marked by severe shortages of capital and by an unequal distribution of capital accessibility. At the same time there has until recently been a large number of people seeking jobs such that only a small percentage could find work in the modern sector. Abundant supplies of labour and low wages are likely to result in labour-intensive methods of production, but in the Japanese case this was overlaid by the government's active encouragement of modern, technologically-advanced, large-scale production both before and after World War II. This policy meant that preferential loans were extended to mainly large companies leading to the adoption of capital-intensive production. For example, if we go back to the Meiji period (1868-1914), then we can see the beginnings of this type of policy.

During the 1870's the Japanese government set up and operated model factories in such industries as textiles, silk-reeling, cement, glass, etc. in order to demonstrate Western factory design and production methods. In 1880 the government decided to sell off all but a few of its model factories to private interests, but they were not sold on the basis of public shareholdings; instead a few selected families were allowed to buy the model factories and mines, often at only a fraction of the cost.

These favoured few were the origin of the zaibatsu
groups in Japan (E.H. Norman, 1940). The zaibatsu
were a unique form of structure and economic power,
and provide an interesting contrast to Western
organizational conglomerates. They entailed cent-
ralized control by one family which extended its
power through strategically-arranged marriages and
personal patronage relationships. Secondly they
were based on their own commercial banks which were
used as the leverage to extend control across several industries. In other words they were 'monopolies of capital' rather than market monopolies.
Thirdly they were organized around holding companies
and controlled the affiliated firms by means of
interlocking directorships and mutual stockholdings
(Yamamura, 1964:539-40; Halliday, 1975:57-61).
With government protection and support the zaibatsu
groups grew through the World War I boom and even
the recession of the 1920's. Thus by 1933 the
Mitsui empire consisted of 150 firms, and Mitsubishi
controlled nearly 200 companies (Yamamura 1975:167 &
169). After World War II, there was an American
Occupation policy to break up the zaibatsu. In
practice, the U.S. policy was short-lived, though
there were some structural effects. Essentially,
the single-family domination of the zaibatsu was
eradicated. However, by the mid-1950s the central
economic importance of the zaibatsu groups was re-
established in a new form. Today, the Japanese
economy continues to be marked by a very high degree
of economic concentration. There are now six
zaibatsu groups - Mitsubishi, Mitsui, Sumitomo,
Fuyo, Dai-IchiKangyo and Sanwa. All these groups
are organized around their own banks, and also control insurance firms, trading companies, transport
and storage, construction and property firms as well
as industrial corporations.
    The resurgence of the zaibatsu group in the
1950's has depended on the continuation of an unequal distribution of capital accessibility. The
linkage of the Japanese corporations to their own
bank allows a ratio of capital to debt which is un-
heard of in Britain. For example, Mitsui, one of
the big six, was capitalized at only 23 billion yen
in 1972, but it had long-term debts of 400 billion
yen, nearly 20 times its capitalization and the
grand total of its loans amounted to 1,000 billion
yen - or about 50 times its capitalization
(Halliday, 1975:273). Nor do Japanese corporations
have to achieve a high rate of return in order to
attract capital. The willingness of Japanese banks

to lend to companies with a high capital-to-debt
ratio and a relatively low return on capital employed reflects an implicit promise of support from the
central government in the event of a crisis. The
government has certainly not extended this promise
to small businesses who have faced higher interest
rates than the large corporations and the possibility that when money became tight the banks would
call in loans to small firms (Miyazawa, 1964:33-47;
Nakamura, 1981:175).

The zaibatsu groups have traditionally boosted
profits by subcontracting work to the small firm
sector. This practice started during World War I,
became a general practice in the 1920's and accelerated in the 1950's. For large corporations, subcontracting offered cheap labour and flexibility.
When business was poor the zaibatsu corporations
would drop the subcontractors and postpone payment
on accounts. This forced many small firms into
bankruptcy during economic downturns, especially as
many firms have a symbiotic relationship with one,
or possibly two, parent corporations. As Nakamura
points out, 'the bulk of small and medium manufacturing was carried out via subcontracting relationships, which was the mode of production for approximately 70% of small and medium size businesses in
textile, electric machinery, machinery, clothing ...
and steel industries'. (Nakamura, 1981:175-6).

As overall labour costs have risen in Japan
arising from an increasing labour shortage, especially of young workers, so the cheap labour advantage of the Japanese small firm sector has been
eroded. As a result the Japanese economy has reacted in two ways. Firstly, many firms have shifted
from labour-intensive methods of production to more
capital-intensive methods and introduced labour-
saving plant and equipment. This process has been
partly helped by government counter-measures to the
dualism problem: for example the 1956 Law to Assure
Prompt Payment to Subcontractors and the 1963 Small
Business Modernization Law. The latter provided
government support for the introduction of new technology, rationalization and co-operation between
small firms.

However, a second strategy has been to establish production facilities, especially for standard-
ized assembly work, in neighbouring low-wage countries, notably Taiwan, Hong Kong, Korea and now mainland China. A distinctive feature of Japanese
foreign investment has been the involvement, often
coordinated by major trading companies, of small or

medium sized firms (Yoshino, 1974).

Overall, dualism in the Japanese context should be seen as a process of state-induced and state-backed industrial development being super-imposed on a traditional mode of production and work organization. Almost uniquely these two sectors came together in a complementary and exploitative relationship via the mechanism of subcontracting. Now the picture is changing rapidly and the earlier pattern of economic relations is being transposed outwards to occupy the Pacific Basin.

Segmentation of the Labour Market

In the previous section I have examined economic dualism largely in terms of the role of the state and capital accessibility. In this section I wish to look at the labour market aspects of dualism and the further segmentation of the labour force within the enterprise.

Not only the Chinese but also Europeans and Americans have been impressed by the performance of the Japanese economic machine. For example Bill Hayden, vice-president of Ford Europe visited Japanese car firms in 1980 and returned full of admiration. In an internal Ford report he wrote:

> The Japanese have a strong family tradition and this is fostered by their policy of employment for life, effective worker participation in the business through quality circle organisations, incentive schemes, sport and social facilities, housing and housing loans, assistance and encouragement in further educational training and the treatment of everyone as equals. The attitude was expressed as centring daily life around work. (Quoted in New Statesman, 28 Nov. 1980).

This quotation neatly encapsulates modern Western perceptions of Japanese industry. At a different level much of the Western academic literature concludes that the essential elements of Japanese work organisations are the lifetime employment system, wages determined by length of service rather than type of work and the ideological concept of the firm as a community. However most of these perceptions and conclusions are half-truths. It is helpful to untangle Japanese realities by starting with the general description of a dual labour market. This concept put together several employer and

production system characteristics into a simple
framework. Firstly it is hypothesised that there
are primary enterprises which are large, oligopol-
istic and capital intensive, able to pay high wages
and to offer considerable job security. Such corporations exercise control over the product market
and help to structure the labour market itself. In
addition training and job advancement systems are
incorporated within the body of the enterprise such
that an internal labour market is formed. Thus most
jobs in an organisation, especially the higher,
better-paid jobs are shielded from the direct influence of competitive forces in the external labour
market. Instead positions are filled by the promotion and transfer of workers who have already gained
entry to the firm. The internal labour market con-
nects to the external market by certain job positions which constitute points of entry into the
organisation.

Distinct from the primary sector are secondary
enterprises which are smaller, more labour-intensive
and with jobs which tend to be low paying with
poorer working conditions. In organising production
these enterprises have to face frequent instabil-
ities in the product market and, consequently, there
is considerable instability of jobs, little training
or prospect of advancement and a high turnover among
the labour force. In the secondary sector the
external labour market is the major job allocator
(Doeringer & Piore, 1971; Piore, 1977; **Gordon, 1972;**
Friedman, 1977; Edwards, 1979). It is also recognised that the secondary enterprises frequently
function as subcontractors for the primary sector
(Friedman, 1977).

If we take the concepts of 'primary' and
'secondary' as referring to the firm-level characteristics of scale, market position and capital
intensity, then it is possible to relate them to
the job-level characteristic of linkage to an internal or external labour market. This results in the
four sector model (see Figure 4.1).

Figure 4.1 enables us to see beyond the standard
Western descriptions of the Japanese employment
system. Most Western reports focus exclusively on
the standard workers in large companies, i.e. box A.
However large companies cannot be understood unless
the secondary sector is understood too.

Figure 4.1

Segmented Employment Structure

JOB LEVEL

FIRM LEVEL	Linked to internal labour market	Linked to external labour market
Primary firm sector	A) Joyo workers in large corporations	B) Rinji-ko or temporary workers
Secondary firm sector	C) Key workers in small firms	D) Old & female workers in small firms

The 'joyo' employees are the permanent labour force in large firms working under lifetime employment and seniority wage systems. The first thing to note is that lifetime employment is not for life. Even in the largest corporations men have to retire early at 55 or thereabouts. Most old workers take other jobs, but in the current recession there are few jobs for them. As Clark points out, 'Large Japanese companies take the best and most productive years of the employees' lives, and then leave them to look after themselves in the period of decline' (Clark, 1979:174).

Nevertheless, from 25-55 this category of workers is a privileged group. Ideally they are recruited direct from school or college and in return for job security stay with the same corporation until retirement age. Though starting salaries are low, they move towards high pay levels through the seniority pay system and the semi-annual bonuses. In addition the non-wage benefits include housing and welfare facilities. Most crucially the internal labour market is structured in terms of seniority not functional merit: workers are promised comparatively equal advancement regardless of differences in ability (Dore, 1979:32-6).

What proportions of the Japanese labour force benefit from the permanent employment system (P.E.S.)? Unfortunately data on the extent of lifetime employment are difficult to obtain. In general the system only applies to large firms and the public sector. One estimate is that about 40% of wage labour and only about 25% of the total labour force fall within the scope of the P.E.S. (Levine & Kawada 1980:308; Boltho, 1975:34-5). However, there is no consensual view and some estimates are as low as 20% of wage labour (Cole, 1971:114-5; Cole, 1979:60-1).

Given that lifetime employment is not for life, is it any realistic guarantee against dismissal or, on the other hand, high rates of staff turnover? Though dismissals certainly occur in Japan (usually surreptitiously as enforced resignations), many authors have argued that the ideal of lifetime employment constrains employer behaviour (e.g. Clark 1979). Assuming that lifetime employment does offer substantial protection against dismissal, then this, of course, creates a crucial problem of fixed labour costs. Indeed for the employer the situation is worse than this: given the pay-by-age wage system there is a direct correlation between wage costs and growth, such that a static or slow-moving company is faced with accelerating wage costs because it contains a higher percentage of older and more expensive workers. Essentially there is an organizational dynamic towards economic expansion. The employment system depends on rapid growth because continued expansion underwrites the guarantee of lifetime employment: 'Expansion meant that there was substantial annual intake of new workers at the bottom of the wage scale so that the commitment to annual wage increments with length of service did not result in too much rise in average wage costs' (Crawcour, 1978:243; Halliday, 1975:397). Therefore, come the downturn in the business cycle, such as 1973-5 or 1980-1, large firms resort not to direct dismissals but to 'dispatching' of workers to major subcontractors in order to reduce costs. Usually, though not always, dispatching is done in consultation with the company union. Some Japanese economists expect dispatching to become more common in the 1980's.

The only detailed study of Japanese and Western labour markets (Yokohama and Detroit) confirmed the view that inter-firms job changing in Japan was only half that of the USA, but the survey also produced some unexpected results. Firstly, both inter-and intra-firm mobility were significantly lower in the

Japanese sample, such that there was little evidence
to support the common view that internal labour markets operate with distinctive strength in Japanese
firms. Secondly there was little difference between
the proportion of dismissals in Yokohama and Detroit.
Moreover the proportion of involuntary dismissals
was highest in the largest Japanese firms and lowest
in the smallest firms.

These results raise large questions about the
structural significance of lifetime employment in
Japan. 'Dismissals' in the study were defined so as
to include workers transferred to another company,
and this suggests that dismissals and dispatching
were running at such a level in the 1970's as to
approximate the notorious hire-'n-fire levels of
Detroit.

Dispatching is not the only means used by
Japanese firms to reduce the burden of fixed labour
costs. In both large and small firms there are a
considerable number of temporary workers and day
labourers with limited employment contracts. These
'rinji-ko' workers are paid about half the wages of
permanent workers and suffer far worse working conditions. Most crucially the temporary workers have
no job security; they can be dismissed at a day's
notice, thus providing a convenient flexibility to
the employer in relation to demand oscillations.
Temporary workers were willing to accept their dis-
criminatory job positions, partly because they had
no choice, and partly with the hope of a better job
future. Until the 1960's there was a large excess
labour supply, and temporary workers were kept out
of the enterprise unions which blocked the development of any collective strength. Additionally most
temporary workers lived in the hope of being promoted to the status of a permanent employee.

The use of temporary and other forms of non-
committed labour varies greatly between sectors and
firms. Generally, large corporations employ the
most temporary workers. Throughout the 1950's temporary workers amounted to about 7% of the labour
force in manufacturing with a concentration in the
car industry and with firms such as Toyota classi-
fying 52% of all its workers as 'temporary'
(Halliday, 1975:226).

With the labour shortages of the 1960's many
workers saw their economic chance and moved on in
the search for more favourable employment opportunities. Some were indeed promoted to the status of
permanent worker. Throughout the 1960's the number
of temporary workers went on declining to the point

where they no longer provided a buffer against business fluctuations. Japanese industry adapted by mobilizing female labour, especially the over-35's, as part-time workers. These replaced the temporary and day labourers in the essential role of providing some labour flexibility to the rigid cost structures of large Japanese corporations (Nakamura, 1981:169-70).

The use of low-wage, female labour has always been central to Japanese industrialization. During the early period of industrialization at least half of the labour force were women and even in the 1970's they accounted for 38% of all factory workers (Whitehill & Takezawa, 1968:73 & 417; Statistical Handbook of Japan, 1980:103. Traditionally women workers have been aged between 14-25, i.e. they were young, unmarried and were expected to leave after marriage. This pattern still persists with the difference that employers now re-hire older women as cheap, flexible labour.

Though there are many women workers in large Japanese corporations, there are also concentrations of women, especially older women, in small firms in the secondary sector (i.e. Box D in Figure 4.1). Typically they receive less than 50% of the wages of a large firm's permanent employee and have to face considerable job insecurities. Generally such workers are at the bottom of the Japanese job hierarchy. Finally, there is some extension of job security to key technical workers and white-collar staff plus, of course, family members in a family-based enterprise, in the small firm sector (i.e. Box C in Figure 4.1).However this status does not necessarily include the considerable bonuses and non-wage benefits which accrue to joyo employees in large corporations.

In the interwar years lifetime employment and the seniority wage system applied to only an inner circle of elite workers - managers and skilled employees. Since the war the pattern has spread outwards to cover many semi-skilled workers, which has occurred partly because of the shifting power balance. After World War II there was a rapid burst of unionisation which, after a struggle, the employers were able to confine into limited forms. The Japan Federation of Employers'Associations was able to prevent the formation of horizontal combinations of workers across industries or firms. Instead another characteristic feature of the modern Japanese employment system was added, namely company (or enterprise) unions. However these unions were

not toothless creatures, and attempts by employers
to dismiss workers in the late 1940's were met frequently by long and bitter strikes. The upshot was
some curtailment of the right of employers to dismiss workers. In general, many of the paternal-
istic practices of pre-war Japan have become institutionalised as a matter of right, such that we can
see the crystallisation of a new model of capitalist
work organisation, namely bureaucratic paternalism.

Japan and China: Comparisons and Contrasts

The Japanese modernization experience since 1868
raises questions for China. In this section I wish
to look at some of the parallels and differences of
development, especially in relation to industrial
work organization.
      The most interesting feature to emerge from a
glance at the economic starting points of Japan and
China is the similarities in many significant areas.
Though with hindsight we can point to certain
characteristics such as a lower literacy rate (literacy facilitating the learning of new roles and the
processes of innovation), or, perhaps, higher internal transport costs in China, none of these factors
fit into an adequate theoretical framework. In many
ways the most important characteristic of Chinese
development was the dependent nature of that development up to 1949. The continuing foreign domination of the industrial sector of the economy is indicated by the fact that as late as 1936 42% of industrial capital in China was owned by foreigners.
They also controlled 61% of total coal production,
88% of steel, 76% of electric power and 54% of textile spindles, (Chen & Galenson, 1969:20). I have
already noted Japan's fierce determination to resist
colonial rule and to control the levers of its own
economy.
      Beyond the broad comparison of Japanese and
Chinese development remain several questions of industrial policy for the Chinese leadership which are
posed sharply by the Japanese experience. Firstly,
most developing economies lack the capital accumulation to provide high productivity employment for
all workers. Therefore there is an important choice
to be made between allowing a dualistic structure to
develop, or following an egalitarian approach by
introducing, for example, regulations against dis-
crepancies in wages, or by enforcing strict minimum
wage regulations (Okita, 1980). Given the poverty
of the Chinese economy and the perennial lack of

capital resources, does China have any choice about
this? Secondly, can China avoid a permanently seg-
mented labour force with permanent, temporary and
casual factory workers? This was a significant
issue during the Cultural Revolution. In the rest
of this section I will consider the issues of dualism and labour segmentation in the Chinese context.
In 1949 the CCP was faced with unifying at least
two industrial economies. Because of the long
period of foreign domination the bulk of industrial
capital was concentrated in light and especially
consumer industries. Many of these industrial units
were in the treaty ports along the coast. Shanghai
alone accounted for 54% of the number of factories
and a similar proportion of the industrial labour
force (Chen & Galenson, 1969:21). As Rawski points
out, 'Features shared by most of these plants included moderate size, a lengthy and varied industrial
history that often includes repair work as well as
manufacturing, and a substantial proportion of
equipment that is old, self-manufactured, or both'
(Rawski, 1979:58). Such plants were skill-intensive
rather than capital-intensive. The accuracy of the
final product depended on the skill and experience
of each individual operator. In contrast to these
industrial enterprises, the Northeast of China was
a heavy industrial base created largely by the
Japanese in what had been an underdeveloped area.
It was this area which in 1949 had suffered most
from war damage plus the fact that the Soviet occupation had removed more than half of the capital
equipment.

Because of the war damage and the unbalanced
nature of the Republican economy it is understandable that the investment programme of the First Five
Year Plan (1953-57) emphasized heavy industry. In
the event 154 Soviet-aided projects were built.
These were massive, capital-intensive plants (such
as the Wuhan steel works which now employs 100,000
people) often on greenfield inland sites. They represented a discontinuous leap in technology for the
Chinese economy requiring new skills and new technical training schemes. They had, at least in the
1950's, complete State support and a high priority
in China's investment policy. The outcome of the
First Five Year Plan policy of creating and supporting large industrial units to realize rapid economic
growth was a large gap in management and capital
intensity at the end of the 1950's: a revolutionary
dualism described by Andors in terms of the
'Shanghai system of management' on the one hand

and the Soviet model of 'One-Man Management' on the other. The Shanghai system involved a major role for the collective leadership of the Party Committee and significant de facto shop-floor worker participation arising from the residues of the old gang-boss system. The Soviet model was essentially bureaucratic and entailed job-definitions, job hierarchies and the widespread use of incentive systems, (Andors, 1977:50-62).

In many ways the basic divide in the Chinese industrial economy is between the State sector and the collective sector; between two systems of ownership. The origins of the collective sector lie in the handicraft workshops inherited from the pre-revolutionary period. According to Xue Muqiao, in 1949 'handicraft workshops and household handicrafts accounted for about 20% of the country's gross industrial output' (Xue Muqiao, 1981:39). During the 1950's the handicrafts sector was reorganized into cooperatives, until by the late 1950's the socialist transformation of this sector was completed. During the Great Leap Forward the existing producer cooperatives were reorganized and placed more under State control, but at the same time many new co-operatives and collectives sprang up as neighbourhood workshops, often utilizing unemployed or under-employed women (Lockett, 1981:20). This pattern - the rise of a great number of neighbourhood enterprises in the cities - was repeated in the 1970's (Xue Muqiao, 1981:62). Many of the non-handicraft cooperatives and collectives are involved in sub-contracting work for larger enterprises.

Generally the Chinese collectives sector displays many of the characteristics of the small-firm sector in Japan: there are sharp differences between the State and collective sectors in terms of capital equipment, productivity, size, wages and working conditions. If we take the last point first then a visit by a British trade union delegation to China provides a more blunt Western reaction to the conditions in part of this industrial sector than the over-polite responses of academics. In 1980 a National Union of Mineworkers delegation visited a small, neighbourhood factory in Hangchow employing 30 people. It was set up a few years before by ten women who had sought technical advice about extruding copper wire in order to make electronic components for a State factory. The group records that 'Our first reaction to the most unsafe practices, high speed unguarded belts on all machines, "Heath Robinson" design of all equipment, was that the place should be closed down'. Having made this point to their Chinese hosts they were partly persuaded that 'economic reality and job provision were paramount'. The trade unionists go on to record that a certain dilemma occurred when at the house they visited they were received by a women with her arm in a sling, she having been injured when her hand was trapped in a machine (NUM, 1980:10-11).

Apart from working conditions and safety, the differences in the average size of enterprises according to the system of ownership are set out below.

Table 4.3

The Structure of Chinese Industry (1978)

	State-Owned	Collective/ Cooperative Ownership	Total
No. of Enterprises	84,000	264,000	348,000
No. of Employees	74.51m.	20.48m.	94.9m.
Total Wage Bill	Y46.9 bill.	Y10.0 bill.	Y56.9 bill.
Mean Size of Enterprises (employees)	887	78	

Y: **Chinese Currency**
(Source: Lockett, 1981, Table 7).

There are no reliable figures on difference in capital intensity between the two sectors but most indications are that capital employed in the collective sector is a small fraction of that used in the State-owned plants. For example, 1975 figures show that gross output per collective worker was only 28% of that of the State worker (Rawski, 1979:43, Table 3.1). Finally, in relation to wage differentials, in 1980 the average earnings in the State sector were Y 803 compared to Y 624 in the collective sector (Lockett, 1981, Table 8). These wage differentials are not, of course, the product of unmediated market forces. Thus Xue records that 'In some cities it was stipulated that members of neighbourhood enterprises under collective ownership should get lower pay and fewer benefits than the workers and staff of the enterprises under ownership by the whole people' (Xue Muqiao, 1981:62; also 41).

The differences in the wage and non-wage benefits between the two industrial sectors of China's
economy is given a vague, but nevertheless real,
justification in terms of the notion that ownership
by the whole people is a higher form of socialist
ownership, whereas collective ownership is a less
mature form of ownership (Xue Muqiao, 1981:45-6).
It used to be a widely promulgated precept that
lower forms of ownership would be transformed into
higher forms. However this view is now under question in China. At a policy level, the State has
begun to promote the collective sector as an important supplier of consumer goods and as a means of
job creation (Lockett, 1981; Research Trip, 1981).
This has been a major switch of emphasis since the
1979 Readjustment Policy.

Japan and China: Trade Links and Technology Transfer

Since 1949 there have been large variations in
Chinese imports of machinery and equipment. During
the 1950's there were large imports of machinery and
complete plants from the USSR and East Europe.
During the 1960's, following the Sino-Soviet split,
there was little import of technology. Indeed in
the early 60's the import of complete plants was
halted entirely. During 1963-66 imports were
resumed on a small scale and more than 50 complete
plants were purchased from Japan and West Europe.
During 1966-72 complete plant imports ceased again.
Then in 1972 a decision was taken to give some
priority to complete plant purchases and between
1973-78 more than 70 plants were ordered from overseas. In 1978 contracts were signed for another
70 or more plants in a single year (Barett, 1981:
188-96).

In general, 1977/early 1978 is a watershed in
Chinese trade policy and trade links changed
rapidly. In 1978 China signed a long term trade
agreement with Japan. This was revised in March
1979. Some of the details of the agreement are set
out in Table 4.4.

Following the Four Modernizations policy and
the 1978 trade agreements, China went on a plant
purchasing spree and imports of Japanese machinery
and capital equipment rose by nearly 200% between
1977 and 1979. Some of the effects of the 1978
trade agreement can be seen in Table 4.5.

Table 4.4

China/Japan Long-term Trade Agreement

	Feb. 1978 Version	Mar. 1979 Version
Period of Agreement	1978 - 85	Extended to 1990
Value	$ 20 billion in two-way trade	$ 40 - 60 billion
Items	China to export coal and oil	Unchanged
	Japan to export plant, technology and construction materials	To be decided

(Source: China Business Review, Vol. 6, No.2, March/April 1979).

Table 4.5

Japan's Trade with China 1962 - 1979 (1962 = 100)

Year	Total Trade Index	Imports from Japan
1962	100	100
1963	162	162
1964	368	397
1965	556	637
1966	735	819
1967	660	749
1968	651	845
1969	740	1015
1970	974	1478
1971	1067	1503
1972	1303	1584
1973	2386	2706
1974	3890	5151
1975	4482	5865
1976	3596	4327
1977	4125	5036
1978	6011	7919
1979	7882	9636

(Source: compiled by the author) - continued

(Total trade = Imports + Exports. The figures are rounded. 1962 was the year of the Liu - Takasaki Agreement which was the first agreement for regular trade between the two countries).

During 1978 the Japanese expectation was that if the Chinese modernization programme went ahead, then its imports should grow faster than its exports and that foreign trade should expand twice as fast as the rest of the economy. Japan was particularly attracted by the fact that Chinese plans called for just those imports (steel and machinery) which are in over-production in Japan. Moreover the Japanese have a low opinion of Chinese management and industry and do not expect China to become a serious competitor even by the turn of the century.

The wild hopes of 1977 and 1978 were damped down by the announcement of the 1979 Readjustment Policy. The Chinese became alarmed at the deteriorating trade balance, the costs of investment in heavy industry and the long periods needed to bring new equipment into production. The problems were exacerbated by bottlenecks and energy shortages. The so-called Readjustment Policy envisaged cutting back on imports of plant and machinery and the redirection of investment into agriculture and light industry. Light industry was expected to provide the quickest returns in terms of job creation and the expansion of exports. Many capital projects were cancelled and this caused serious problems in Japan. Despite the Readjustment Policy the new burst of China/Japan trade flows have been constricted not choked off. Indeed it is still not clear what is the extent to which there has been a fundamental change of policy concerning modernization, foreign trade and technology imports. What does seem clear is that there has been a continuing debate within the CCP leadership concerning how to pay for technology imports. This debate has centred on capital self-sufficiency. As Barnett points out, the Chinese had proudly claimed that from the mid-1960's on they had no foreign debts and, as a matter of principle attempted to balance their commodity trade each year, paying most of the cost of imports by exports (Barnett, 1981:143-4). This rigid policy of avoidance of large-scale foreign indebtedness parallels the similar policy of Japan. The ironic thing is that from 1977 on the country pushing low-interest long-term foreign loans has been, of course, Japan. Certainly the long-maintained policy of capital self-sufficiency seemed to be crumbling during

1977-79 and by the end of 1979 China had concluded
agreements giving it access to between $20-30
billion of foreign credits up to 1985. The largest
percentage of these loans were Japanese.

Apart from foreign loans the Readjustment
Policy has meant that the Chinese have been stimu-
lated to explore and develop new types of trade and
industrial relationships with foreign business. In
particular there has been an emphasis on cooperative
arrangements and joint ventures. There are several
types of cooperative manufacturing ventures. First,
there are processing or assembly deals in which the
foreign company supplies raw materials and components which are processed by the Chinese for a fee.
Secondly, there is direct compensation trade in
which the foreign firm supplies capital equipment,
the cost of which is re-paid by the products made
with the capital equipment. For example, Itoman, a
Japanese trading concern, has signed a deal whereby
it supplied 100 modern sewing machines and 15 technicians to a Shanghai clothing factory in return for
300,000 suits of pyjamas every year for five years.
The necessary cotton is purchased in China and the
garments are sold under Itoman's brand name. Significantly, the Chinese production replaces part of
Itoman's supplies previously obtained from Taiwan
and South Korea. (Financial Times, 20 Aug. 1979).
Thirdly, there is indirect compensation trade in
which the imported capital equipment is paid for by
other goods, such as coal, which the foreign company
needs or is prepared to accept. Recently (1980/81)
the Chinese have favoured this kind of barter trade,
a trade which serves to advantage the Japanese and
disadvantage European and American firms. This is
because the Japanese sogo shosha, or general trading
companies, provide the essential organizational
framework for barter trade, whereas Western corporations tend to be more industry-specific and do not
know what to do with one million tons of lychees!

Finally, there are 'joint ventures' strictly
defined, which involve an equity interest and direct
foreign investment. One such venture is the agreement with Sanyo Electric to set up a factory in
Shanghai to produce compressors for refrigerators.
Capitalization is set at 500 million yen (about £1
million) with capital inputs being 75% Japanese and
25% Chinese. The president of the company is
Japanese with a six to four ratio in favour of the
Japanese on the board of directors. In principle
the company will be able to remit freely all profits
royalty payments and dividends to Japan (Financial

<u>Times</u>, 11 Jan. 1980). The original intention was to
set up a plant to produce 500,000 compressors with a
starting date in mid-1981 and with 50% of the output
being exported. However the starting date has been
put back to mid-1982. To facilitate joint ventures
a Joint Venture Law was published in February 1979.
This proved to be surprisingly vague. It did not
preclude 100% foreign ownership and displayed very
little concern about national sovereignty (Brugger,
1981:233; <u>Financial Times</u>, 21 March, 1979, 10 July,
1979, 20 Aug. 1979, 21 April, 1980 and 1 Oct. 1980).
    The Joint Venture law is only indicative of the
fact that the Chinese have displayed considerable
naïveté about potential integration into the world
capitalist system and the international division of
labour and, so far, have exerted less control over
these economic processes than did capitalist Japan
in the 1880's - a century before (Halliday, 1980).
    A number of Japanese firms including Matsushita,
Honda, Sanyo, Hitachi, Toshiba, and Canon, have been
involved in cooperative contracts in China. In
general the pattern is the expected one of the devolution to China of subcontracting work involving
the assembly of components despatched from Japan
with the completed article being marketed in both
China and abroad. China is beginning to be a valuable source of low-cost labour for Japanese and
Western manufacturers. For the Chinese leadership
the objectives of cooperative arrangements and the
'Special Economic Zones' (such as Shenzhen) are
threefold: first, to use China's cheap labour to
earn foreign exchange and to speed modernization;
secondly, to help cure the problem of urban unemployment with limited capital inputs from China; thirdly, to assist the transfer of technology, including
managerial expertise, and to broaden the industrial
base. In the remainder of this section I wish to
focus on the last objective - the transfer of technology and managerial skills-and consider the extent
to which this is occurring and its effects in China.
It is still early days in this process and I can
only make some suggestions on the basis of a recent
research trip.
    One example of technology transfer is the
Beijing Television Factory which was set up in 1973
after some preparation in the preceding year. It
was a focal point of State investment with an initial capital funding of 10 million yuan, and a capacity to produce 50,000 sets a year. After two
years negotiation with Matsushita a contract was
signed in 1979 for the importation of a colour

production line. In addition an agreement was signed with JVC in 1980 and with Telefunken in 1981.
Clearly the Chinese did not in this case wish to become dependent on any one supplier and have endeav-
oured to gain access to varying production technologies, though in the case of televisions there is
the complication that the PAL colour system used by
the Japanese is controlled by Telefunken.

The end result of these technology transfer
agreements was (in 1981) three production lines: a
black and white line using components produced elsewhere in China with a capacity of 100,000 sets
annually. Second, a Matsushita colour production
line with a capacity of 150,000 sets; and, thirdly,
another colour line with a capacity so far of
60,000 sets using components from Telefunken, JVC
and, also, Toshiba. Both the colour production
lines are based entirely on the assembly of foreign
components. Moreover the Beijing plant has nowhere
reached its theoretical capacity. Because of start-
up problems (the Telefunken line only started in
July 1981) plus technical and, one suspects, managerial problems the 1981 production was only 44% of
the theoretical capacity.

The agreements with foreign suppliers run for a
period of seven years and involve the Chinese paying
for the basic manufacturing process plus a premium
on each set sold. There is also an advanced technology clause, such that Telefunken and the Japanese
corporations must inform the Chinese about new technical developments. There are some restrictions on
exports, but they do not yet affect the Beijing
plant because at present exports are negligible and
the output goes to satisfy a rapidly swelling home
market.

In relation to quality control, the agreement
specifies that both sides must guarantee quality,
which is not seen as a serious problem at the moment
because all components are brought in. The plant is
basically an assembly plant. In the long term the
Beijing management want to make all their own components. Interestingly, quality-control circles
modelled on Japanese practices have been transferred
to the Beijing shop-floor. Generally, techniques of
management have been learnt from Japan. The present
factory director and some other senior managers have
visited Japan, and Matsushita sent over a core of
technical experts to install the production line and
teach techniques.

With the wholesale transfer of Japanese capitalist technology and management techniques, the

question arises of compatibility with democratic
management and, indeed, Chinese culture. The response of factory managers was that there was no in-
trinsic incompatibility between what was called
'scientific management' and democratic management.
Essentially 'scientific management' was formalistic,
'it only tells people how to organize', whilst democratic management was political and mobilized human
initiative within the technical framework laid out
by 'scientific management'. Despite this view,
Japanese companies were seen as having mobilized
workers and 'in some fields they do even better than
we do' (Research Trip, 1981).

The setting up and financing of plants such as
the Beijing T.V. factory clearly mark the abandon-
ment of a do-it-yourself approach to modernization.
As Barnett points out, reverse engineering, involving the copying of imported machinery, is slow and
difficult. One prototype reveals little about the
production technology behind it (Barnett, 1981:199).
Equally the purchase of whole Western plants is not
a ready-made solution to technological and economic
backwardness. There are several barriers to technology absorption, particularly lack of skills, lack
of training, and lack of economic infrastructure.
The problems of the Chinese steel industry are notorious. For example, the Wuhan Iron and Steel Works
has acquired a German rolling mill and a Japanese
hot strip mill, but both foreign-supplied plants are
working at only 45% of potential capacity because of
technical problems and power shortages (Financial
Times, 14 Dec. 1981). Similarly the Wuhan No.2
Truck Plant started in 1964 with Western equipment
and technology was designed with a capacity of
100,000 trucks per year. However, it has never
achieved this output. It did not produce its first
truck until 1977, and is still operating at about
one-seventh of its capacity (Barnett, 1981:205).
These problems and the experience of the 150 large-
scale Soviet-aided industrial projects in the 1950's
suggest that there are sharp limits to the Chinese
ability to absorb foreign technology and managerial
methods, at least in the short term, over and beyond
the political debate concerning foreign technology
and self-sufficiency.

In the early part of 1981 there was a spate of
cancelled plant orders as China's capital construction budget was cut by 40%. This threw the
Japanese/Chinese trade links into confusion and some
hostility. Nevertheless, Japan still has a huge
commercial stake in China's modernization programme:

in 1980 China was Japan's second largest export market. China, for its part, is tied more closely to
Japan than to any of its other trading partners.
Japanese capitalism does not want to see Deng usurped nor China retreat into a new economic isolation-
ism. At the height of the hostility caused by the
arbitrary cancellation of contracts totalling more
than 200 billion yen, the Japanese Stock Exchange
Journal ran an editorial which concluded that 'Japan
owes it to China to be as helpful as possible under
the circumstances. Asia needs above all a stable
China and Vice Premier Deng and his colleagues need
all the help they can get in their formidable task
of providing a decent living for a billion people'
(Japanese Stock Exchange Journal, Mar. 1981).

Conclusions

There are many similarities between the industrial
development of China and Japan. The major difference is the independent modernization of Japan in
contrast with the dependent, foreign-dominated development of China up to 1949. That difference was
ultimately the spur to different political frame-
works. Despite that gulf, both economies industrialized within a state-guided mould, and faced the fundamental problem of severe capital shortages and an
abundance of unskilled labour leading to a dualistic
economic structure and divisions within the working
class based on job status. But we must be wary of a
premature Asian convergence theory, particularly as
the reactions to these economic outcomes were different in the two societies. In Japan the business
elite attempted to exploit these differences in an
ideologically-buttressed industrial hierarchy cul-
minating in a form of bureaucratic paternalism. In
China ideologies of egalitarianism have spasmodic-
ally washed up against the industrial inequalities
of differing labour status, fuelled by a belief that
'contradictions' can be solved. The results have
been mixed: there has not been sufficient awareness
of the gulf between the State and the collective
sector, largely because efforts to upgrade neighbourhood enterprises to the level of 'big collectives' have been periodically overwhelmed by fears of
mass unemployment (as now) and low-wage, unsafe
working conditions are tolerated for their job
creation benefits. China does not have the resources to provide high productivity employment for all
its vast population.
    The post-Mao economic development strategy has

sucked in Japanese technology and Japanese management ideas but their eventual effects are hard to
discern. Clearly there have been similarities between the Chinese work organization, with its job
security, largely seniority-based payment system,
factory housing, and enterprise-related welfare benefits, and the bureaucratic paternalism of Japan.
But some of the present economic reform policies,
particularly the stress on piece-work, merit bonuses
and different promotion systems are pushing away
from the Japanese model of work organization. On
the other hand, there does seem a clear tendency for
a greater integration of the activities of large,
capital-intensive enterprises and the small collectives.
　　China's ability to absorb Japanese technology
is another barrier to overnight 'Japanization'. A
comparison between the Baoshan fiasco, the wrong
plant in the wrong place using imported iron ore,
and the Japanese Fukuyama plant - a meticulously-
planned integrated steel works which produces more
steel with 30,000 men than the entire British Steel
Corporation - shows the gulf between the two industrial cultures. That this comparison is made at all
however, indicates the distance we have travelled
down the road of a different development strategy
from that of Mao.

PART 2

THE REFORMS IN PRACTICE

CHINA'S NEW AGRICULTURAL REVOLUTION

Jack Gray
Maisie Gray

Maoism

Collectivised agriculture in China has now run the
whole gamut of the possibilities of socialist farming, producing a richer variety of experience than
in any other Communist country. China has moved
from the mutual-aid teams and service co-operatives
of 1951-53, to the abruptly enforced Soviet kolkhoz
style of collective of 1956-57, to the communes of
1958-59, to the 'three-level ownership' of commune,
brigade and team in 1960, to the looser experiments
of 1962-65, to the reassertion of commune-style
collectivism in the movement to follow Dazhai models
of raising the level of ownership, and now to the
'production responsibility system' which replaces
direct collective management of labour by a system
of contracts between the collective as planning
centre and the members of the production team as
groups or individuals.[1]
    Ideological conviction has played a part in all
these changes, but in the last analysis they have
been concerned with the practical problems of the
conduct of collective agriculture.
    These problems are common to all Communist
collective agriculture. Farming has proved almost
everywhere to be the Achilles heel of Marxist socialism; in only one country, the German Democratic
Republic, do the levels of production in agriculture
compare remotely with those of advanced capitalist
agriculture of the British kind, and this is largely
because of the high levels of efficiency inherited
there. Nor do these levels compare well with those
of modernised peasant agriculture in Western Europe.
In the Far East, China's agricultural record, though
respectable, is much inferior to that of Japan,
Taiwan or South Korea. Ironically, throughout the
Communist world, although collectivisation remains
theoretically a shibboleth of socialism it has

almost become a bad word.

There is no inherent illogicality in the idea of collective agricultural production, especially as a means of rapidly eliminating the problems of pre-modern agrarian societies where development is inhibited by gross economic and social inequalities and an adverse class structure. But the particular tradition which the Soviet Union created and propagated and which, although eroded in places by piece-meal change, still remains dominant in most Communist countries, involves an inheritance of misapprehensions which have plagued socialist agriculture since its inception.

The first is Lenin's naive idea that American agriculture alone represented the farming of the future. In fact, prairie agriculture was based on almost unlimited land, plentiful capital, and scarce and expensive labour - factor proportions which existed nowhere else except Canada and Australia. High outputs per worker are got at the sacrifice of high yields per unit area; none of the Communist countries - least of all China - could adequately feed its population at present American yields per acre.

The second assumption, one which has grimly distorted agriculture, is that industry can only be built up at the sacrifice of peasant incomes. This is based on Marx's theory that the main driving force of the original British industrialisation was 'primitive capital accumulation' at the expense of the peasantry. This, as research historians now recognise, is a myth; the industrial revolution thrived not on the destitution of the masses but on the rapidity with which mass purchasing power was increasing. Wiser heads in Russia in the 'twenties, although they could not be aware that Marx had been wrong about history, saw well enough that the increase of mass (in Russia's case, peasant) purchasing power, not ruthless accumulation at the expense of the poor, was the key to rapid development; but Stalin over-ruled them.

The third assumption was that collectivism had some sort of moral socialist value for its own sake, instead of being merely a possible means to socialist ends: the increase of production, the improvement of incomes, the diffusion of new technology, the accumulation of capital, the elimination of exploitation and the extension of equality. And derived from this was the assumption that the collectivisation of production was the sine qua non of socialist agriculture, irrespective of whether the state of technology in relation to increased yields per acre justified it or not; but hundreds of peasants milling around on large areas of land, doing only what they would have been doing individually on small plots, is not socialist agriculture; nor does it become any more socialist just because the same crudity is operated by tractors.

If one adds to this the minimisation of incentives by the pillaging of agriculture to feed industrial investment, it is not difficult to account for the relatively poor performance of the collective farms. Such a system is not capable of creating the only conditions in which collective farming can ever become a stable part of a socialist system: the establishment of a technology which compels cooperative working, while producing such substantial increases in production and incomes that no peasant in his senses would want to revert to household farming.

The result is to produce a deep contradiction in the system: while the state sees collective agriculture primarily as a means to maximise the marketable surplus of grain and other staples, the members of the collective see their work simply as a means of ensuring subsistence supplies of grain before devoting their remaining energies to more profitable forms of labour. The private-plot concession does not resolve this contradiction; on the contrary, it condones and institutionalises it.

The political framework within which collective agriculture operates is in itself inimical to economic efficiency. In theory the collective is a self-managing, democratically-governed, voluntary association. In fact, it is a state enterprise - with the important proviso that unlike either state enterprises it remains responsible for its own losses. Politically, the collective is the lowest rung of the state-party hierarchy, the members of which are only responsible - and responsive - to the higher levels of the organisation; and these higher levels constantly interfere blindly in the conduct of farming simply because there is no power to prevent them from doing so.

The result, it is not too much to say, has been and is an alienated labour force, and the resort to piecework which is always a sign of such alienation. And in agriculture, in which quality of work and a sense of responsibility towards the whole process of cultivation are vital, piecework is useless for anything more complicated than picking strawberries. The piecework system deals - and deals ineffectively

- only with the symptoms of the disease.

Finally, the notion of agriculture as a sort of factory mass-production, the scarcity of efficient management, the difficulty of maintaining adequate supplies of grain, and the necessity of conceding private plots, all combined to create a bias towards one-crop farming with the emphasis on grain. This has tended to make socialist farming inferior from an ecological point of view to the peasant system it replaced, with less rotation of crops, reduced supplies of manure, and a threat therefore to the maintenance of the organic content of the soil.

In the last two decades the Soviet Union and the East European Communist regimes have made massive investments in agriculture, and as a result there has been a substantial improvement in performance; but the return to capital has remained very low. Investment alone has not proved sufficient to overcome the problems of the system.

China broke more quickly and more drastically with the orthodox collective system than any other Communist country except Yugoslavia. The breach came with the Great Leap Forward and the commune system of 1958 which represented Mao's alternative to the Stalinism-plus-revisionism system in the Soviet Union. The policies of 1958, in this their first application, were a dramatic and demoralising failure, but the Leap launched ideas which outlasted the event itself. Some of these have come to be so widely accepted in China that they are now scarcely questioned. Indeed, their Maoist origin is scarcely recognised; ironically, while most Chinese think of Mao as having had no economic theories, they continue to accept and operate the economic strategy which he alone created.

Mao condemned Soviet squeezing of agriculture to finance industrialisation. He condemned the idea that the development of heavy industry must have absolute priority in investment, and insisted that agriculture must come first, then light industry, believing that the increase of peasant purchasing power was the real key to development. He accused Stalin of neglecting individual incentives and overstressing collective incentives. He accused him of having eliminated the masses from economic decision-making. He repudiated Stalin's insistence that socialist society is without conflict, argued that conflict was the necessary motive force of change and accepted that there were conflicts of interest between state and collective and between collective and individual. He argued that in China's economic

conditions the market must play a greater role than
in the Soviet Union and that producers' goods as
well as consumers' goods must be bought and sold
rather than allocated. He insisted on the importance of the diversification of agriculture and of
the rural economy, and he saw the development of
rural industries as the main means of accumulating
the capital necessary to transform agriculture. He
was the first to see that the original large-scale
commune of 1958, which brought rich and poor villages into a single unit of account and distribution,
was unacceptable to the more prosperous villages;
hence the creation of the three-level system with
the small production team as the main unit of ownership. He roundly condemned the coercive allocation
of peasant resources by county and commune cadres in
the Great Leap, and defended peasant resistance to
this 'banditry'. He insisted that agricultural planning should be indicative, not authoritative, so
that grass-roots economic decision-making would become a reality. He asked for, but never got, proper
and regular election of commune, brigade and team
cadres (Gray and White, 1982:293).

Every point in this has been accepted by Mao's
successors; indeed it could be argued that on these
issues Deng Xiaoping and his supporters are better
Maoists than some of the Maoists were. This is the
strategic background of the new agricultural policies.

Production Responsibility Systems

The fulcrum of the agricultural changes of the past
two years lies in the 'production responsibility
systems'. The plural serves to emphasise their variety and the flexibility with which they are meant
to be applied, but the central thrust is clear. It
is the replacement of the relation of subordination
of the commune members to the leadership in day-to-
day farming operations, by the relation of contract.
Groups, households or individuals enter into output
contracts with the team; it should be stressed that
these are not contracts to plough or hoe so much
land, or to perform other partial tasks; they are
for the final output. Such contract systems, however, are only the middle range of the spectrum of
new forms of organisation of labour. The choice
depends, in theory at least, on the level of existing development of each team. In developed
Liaoning, one prosperous area has actually gone over
to a system of weekly wages - the antithesis of the

responsibility systems, which aim to link rewards to labour via individual or small-group output. This is of course wholly exceptional. The norm for more prosperous and developed teams is the use of a labour, as opposed to an output, contract system, essentially the retention of a piecework system. At the other end of the spectrum, especially in areas of scattered farms or in very poor areas which - it is now decided - cannot sustain the overheads of collective organisation, the land and means of production have been allocated to the farming families on condition simply that they pay the state grain tax, meet their procurement obligations, and meet whatever charges the team agrees should be allocated for welfare and other common purposes. Beyond this, the households can keep and dispose of all surplus. As, typically, in such areas the grain tax has commonly been reduced (and in extreme cases even waived entirely), state procurement norms have been cut down, and little or no public accumulation by the collective is at present contemplated, the autonomy of the farming household is very considerable and its state and communal obligations minimal. There is little or no team income to distribute.

More commonly, however, the return to smaller scale farming operations takes a less drastic form. The farming household, or a group of households, contracts for a given output; any surplus over the contracted amount is divided between the farm family and the collective in proportions agreed in the contract. All production is subject to unified distribution by the team or brigade leadership, though in conformity with the contract. Although the labour involved in meeting the contractual obligation is often initially calculated in work-points, the value of the work-point no longer varies as formerly with the total production of the collective; the calculation is simply the preliminary means of arriving at an equitable contract, to ensure for example that the family working full time on raising rabbits for export does not earn unconscionably more for an hour's labour than the family growing grain.

Two and a half years of experiment in China's endlessly differing local conditions has produced a perplexing variety of arrangements and combinations, and the distinctions among them are not always clear. Beyond the broad distinctions made above, interpretation becomes difficult. In justice to the reader, it is necessary to quote directly from Chinese materials some of the descriptions given, so that he can form his own judgment of the differences.

On the 9th April 1980, an article by Wu Xiangan and Zhang Guangyu in People's Daily made the following distinctions:

'(i)   fixed output quotas assigned to work groups, with work-points calculated on output

(ii)   contracts with work groups for fixed output

(iii)   work-group responsibility for task until completion

(iv)   individual responsibility for task.'

The assignment of responsibility to households is not listed here (although the article goes on to defend it in special cases), and the idea of individual responsibility is not elaborated. Perhaps People's Daily was foot-dragging, and this accounts for the concentration of attention on work groups. However, it makes clear in the case of work groups the varying levels of autonomy in production now occurring, levels equally applicable to households and (within technical limits) to individual labourers.

In October 1980, Henan reported two forms of responsibility system in use, noting that few teams had chosen to make use of work groups but had preferred direct remuneration of the individual labourer:

(i)   short-term work contracts with fixed remuneration

(ii)   'The four unified (planning, farming, investment, allocation and use of tools and animals) and five fixed (manpower, tasks, output, investment, work-points)' system.

The second form had proved the more popular, with 65% of teams having chosen to adopt it as against 21% for the alternative, and the Henan authorities stipulated that this minority of teams should be encouraged to progress to the more widely accepted form.[2]

On the same day, a provincial conference on responsibility systems in Jilin (whose First Secretary Wang Enmao showed greater reluctance than any

other provincial leader to implement the new responsibility systems), while continuing to stress the
now fading work-group idea, commented on alternative
modes of payment similar to those described for
Henan. Short-term labour agreements were favourable
to the unity of the collective, but because they did
not satisfactorily link remuneration to output they
led to 'less than full enthusiasm'. On the other
hand, contracting with work groups for a given output, while it 'often results in increased production
and incomes', has a tendency to prejudice the unity
of production, diversification, farmland capital
construction and long-term investment in general.
The conference reluctantly adopted the second form,
but laid down rules to limit the damage to the int-
egrity of the collective.[3]
    The next month, People's Daily stated that 'the
masses have instituted over ten different forms of
responsibility system', but it listed only five,
presumably as general categories:

    (i)   contracts for specialised production

    (ii)   fixing quotas for individuals 'in field
            management'

    (iii)   mixing collective with individual con-
            tracts

    (iv)   fixing output quotas for households

    (v)   full responsibility for households.

    In April 1981, the First Secretary of Anhui,
Zhang Jingfu, approved three systems:

    (i)   for the poorest teams dependent on state
            subsidies, output quotas to households

    (ii)   for medium teams, unified management with
            rewards according to labour

    (iii)   for the best teams 'production-task
            contracts'.[5]

    The second category is a vague one; but in
another recommendation ten days later the First
Secretary of Jiangxi, Jiang Weiqing, also stated
that medium teams 'may experiment with and popularise the system of pay according to work and output
under unified management'.[6] The reference here to

work <u>and</u> output makes this statement even more ambiguous than the last; but Jiang Weiqing went on to
add that in this case, steps must be taken to maintain public ownership of the means of production;
and this can only mean that the system he had in
mind involves small group or family farming under
contract. Otherwise his warning against prejudice
to the collective system would not be necessary.

At about the same time, the Shandong authorities listed five types of responsibility systems:

   (i)   Collective administration with management
       of norms and with rewards for output in
       excess of targets

  (ii)   Farm output quotas for households

 (iii)   Contracts with specialist production
       households, with rewards and penalties,
       for overfulfilment and underfulfilment

  (iv)   Individual ownership and management, with
       output owned by the individual (this pre-
       sumably applies to sideline production
       and not to agriculture, except for the
       private plot and is strictly speaking
       not part of the responsibility systems)

   (v)   Joint management with output shared among
       the parties concerned (again, this prob-
       ably applies only to non-arable produc-
       tion).[9]

   <u>Shaanxi Ribao</u>, reporting from the minutes of a
meeting of the provincial party's 'economic work
leadership group', puts a little meat on these bare
bones, distinguishing five different systems:

   (i)   Contracts for specialised production, run
       in a unified way, with teams dividing up
       the work: the teams assign to every
       group, labourer and household the respon-
       sibility for farming, forestry, etc., and
       for industrial and commercial work. 50%
       of Shaanxi teams had implemented this
       system.

  (ii)   Unified management with assignment of res-
       ponsibility to every labourer; this, it
       was said, is especially good for teams
       with 'mediocre' management. It involves

'five fixed items and one reward': man-power, tasks, output, investment and work-points - with reward for overfulfilment.

(iii) Output quotas for households (for poor teams dependent on the state).

(iv) Full responsibility for households (for remote and scattered farms).

(v) Assigning sectional or seasonal tasks.[8]

People's Daily on 21st July 1981 gave a more elaborate breakdown:

(i) Specialised contracting to teams, groups, households and individual workers. This is explained as follows: 'Under unified management by production teams, the division of labour and co-operation is practised, with agriculture, forestry, husbandry, etc., contracted out according to the skills and specialities of workers.' This is known as the 'four specialisations and one unification' system.

(ii) Contracting production to work groups, with land, tools, manure and seeds allocated to each group, and sown areas and output targets specified. Accounting and distribution remain unified. People's Daily adds that as this system merely reduces the scale of confusion without eliminating it, it is being phased out.

(iii) 'Linking remuneration to output for each worker under unified leadership'. This is the system of 'three constants and four unifications' (collective ownership, basic accounting unit, unified distribution of income; planning, farming, investment, allocation of use of tools and animals). Land and production are assigned 'according to labour force', or 'a proportion of total population to labour force', and distribution is calculated according to output, with rewards and penalties.

(iv) Output quotas for households. In this case, teams sign a contract with the household, including the specification of output, output value, work points and consumption, with rewards and penalties.

(v)   Full responsibility to households. 'The masses', People's Daily comments, 'like this form'.9

The following day an article in Shaanxi Daily added some information which throws a little more light on these imperfect distinctions. Asserting that fixing output quotas for households (originally contemplated only for very poor teams) could also be suitable for both 'intermediate and fast-developing teams', it comments that such teams 'are using the strong points of this system with modification', ending up with output quotas for each labourer and the signing of contracts for specialised work. This is called 'the pupil outdoing his teacher'. These two forms have in common that 'they both involve the efforts of the whole household'. The weak point of the household quota system, however, is that it involves maintaining fewer items under unified management and specialist contracting.10

In the spring of 1981 a group from the Central Committee Party School visited five provinces (Anhui, Zhejiang, Jiangxi, Jiangsu and Henan) to look at responsibility systems. They were satisfied that all the systems in operation increased production, personal incomes and the marketed surplus. They found four main forms:

(i)   Assignment of output quotas to households.

(ii)   Full responsibility to households. In this case land is allotted, and the means of production either allotted or sold to the household, which meets all costs of production. There is no unified distribution of the product.

(iii) Unified management with responsibility assigned to labourers. The framework is that of the three constants (collectivisation, the team as the unit of ownership, responsibility systems), the four unifications and the five fixed things and one reward. The virtue of this system is that it makes it easier to maintain collective operations and long-term projects. Its faults are that it 'fails to

bring personal enthusiasm into play', and
it leaves unsolved the difficult problems
of quality control.

(iv) Assuming full responsibility for specialised tasks: for example, a team in Hunan
which is divided into six groups - farming.
vegetable growing, forestry, animal husbandry, sidelines and manure collection.
This the Party School group identified
with the best and most diversified collectives. They quite clearly favoured it for
its several advantages - that it integ-
rates centralised management with specialised division of labour; makes full use
of resources; promotes enthusiasm for
innovation; strengthens economic accounting; and promotes the training of cadres.
It is not clear, however, precisely how
these groups are rewarded except that
'remuneration is linked to output'. Presumably they operate on output quotas.[11]

The problems of interpretation are due partly
to the variety and flexibility of the new experimental systems, but also to a certain ambiguity resulting from their controversial nature, and - not
least - from anxiety over the strong pressures towards individual farming, which these chronolog-
ically arranged excerpts reveal. The very phrase
used for the particular form of responsibility which
most fully restores peasant independence - 'full
responsibility for task until completion' - is
clearly a deliberate piece of obfuscation. No 'task'
is involved, and little or no 'responsibility' -
merely the obligation on an individual peasant farm-
er to meet state and communal levies and sell a
stipulated amount of grain (and/or oil) to the
state; and such responsibilities are compatible
with a completely non-collective system.
    In order to make sense of what is now going on
in Chinese agriculture, and to understand the information made available, it is necessary to analyse
the various lines of distinction involved in the
responsibility systems.
    First, there is a distinction between arable
farming on the one hand, and other tasks - 'diversification items', which the peasant traditionally
called fu ye - on the other. These include care of
animals and poultry, vegetable farming, forestry,
fish raising, handicrafts. To encourage diversifi-

cation and increase local crafts and industries in
order to reduce surplus rural labour and to maximise
peasant incomes, a division of labour is now seen to
be necessary. Also, to increase labour productivity
a degree of specialisation is needed. Hence there
is a move away from the idea that every labourer,
whatever else he may do, must devote his normal
working day to participation in the growing of grain.
It is now acceptable that some may spend their full
time in some other line of production. The contract
system was therefore applied first to activities
other than arable farming. Subsequently in some
areas it was applied also to grain growing; for
once it is accepted that some members of the collective can specialise in raising poultry or taking
care of the team's orchard, it is difficult to resist the idea that grain also might be advantage-
ously grown by 'specialist' groups or households in
the same way. The distinction, however, still remains, as our sources show in their references to
systems which use contracts for <u>fu ye</u> but maintain
some degree of direct collective management in arable farming.

Second, there is the obvious distinction as to
the unit rewarded for labour or output - the production team (specialised within a brigade), the work
group, the household and the individual labourer.

Third, there is the basis of remuneration -
fixed remuneration for an assigned task; remuneration for an assigned task with rewards and penalties for over or under-fulfilment; remuneration for
contracted output; profit sharing; and individual
enterprise subject only to taxes, levies and procurement.

Fourth, and related to the last, there is the
task for the performance of which remuneration is
given: piecework, target, quota, contract, or
(virtually) the payment of 'rent' and taxes.

Fifth - and perhaps the most critical for the
future of collective agriculture - there are distinctions in the way in which the product of team members is distributed: unified accounting and distribution of the whole product (except for that of
private plots and private sidelines); unified distribution of quota production; unified distribution
of communal levies on and profits from contractors;
and in the case of the system of 'full responsibility to the household for tasks until completion',
little or no communal distribution except in the
form of the social wage represented by welfare,
health and cultural services where such exist or

continue to exist.

Sixth, there is the division of teams into poor, middling and successful. In the first stages of the introduction of the responsibility systems this distinction was critical. It was argued that in successful teams relatively little change in the organisation of production and the remuneration of labour was necessary, except to slough off the Dazhai inheritance, although it was admitted even then that these were mostly confined to a few places - Jiangsu, Zhejiang and the Northeastern provinces. It was argued that the poorest teams, in which (ironically) collectivisation had proved to be a source of burdens rather than of benefits, a return to some form of family farming was appropriate. Middling teams had the choice of a range of intermediate possibilities, mostly involving group, household or individual quotas or contracts. The distinction has now worn rather thin. In the successful teams, because prosperity and the degree of diversification tend to be related, there is actually the maximum scope for specialised contracting, in which arable farming soon becomes involved. And at every level, the strong desire of the majority of peasants - or, to be more cautious, of at least a minority strong enough to enforce the desired changes - to maximise their independence as producers has had an impact on the results. The various forms of individual and household cultivation have clearly grown far beyond the original 1979 idea that such an unsocialist mode of production was permissible only for a few remote and scattered farms, which had probably never in practice operated as a part of the collectives in any case.

Facing the Practical Problems

It might seem, at least at first sight, as if collectivised agriculture in China is well on the way to near-total collapse. It would also seem, again at least at first sight, that the new system (if it is indeed a system) is at virtually all points in contrast to the Maoist inheritance. To reach a conclusion on these issues, it is necessary to begin with the reasons given by Deng Xiaoping and his supporters for undertaking this sweeping, revolutionary (or perhaps counter-revolutionary) transformation.

It is not unreasonable that the Party and Government of China should be discontented with the progress so far of Chinese agriculture. Although production has increased at a commendable rate over-

all and has somewhat more than kept pace with the
growth of population, the situation is still far
from acceptable.

The scarcity of grain is still a tight constraint both on development and on the increase of
welfare. Growth has been erratic, and the present
leaders of China point to the fact that the worst
periods from this point of view have been those in
which the Left was in power and put its egalitarian
policies into operation. In 1960 after the Great
Leap Forward, writes Yu Guoyao in Red Flag, (5th
Mar. 1980) grain output was less than in 1951 when
the reorganisation and development of agriculture
had scarcely begun. Recovery was slow until 1962,
when output was still less than that of 1957, the
last year before the Great Leap Forward. With the
relaxed policies of 1962-65 (comparable in many ways
to those now being implemented), grain production
increased at 6.7% per annum, the fastest rate on
record, and on the eve of the Cultural Revolution
production once more surpassed 1957. Then the Left
returned to power, and the rate of growth slowed
down to 4.5%; while this is a respectable enough
figure, Yu asserts that the more rapid rate of
growth in grain output from 1962 to 1965 was accompanied by an even more rapid development of the production of non-grain agricultural staples (edible
oils, cotton, sugar cane and sugar beet, pork, tea
and aquatic products). However, the subsequent
slower rate of growth in grain was actually accompanied by rates of growth in most other key agricultural products even lower than that of grain. The
conclusion drawn is that left-wing policies actually
minimised growth in agriculture, and that in particular the disincentive effects of insistence on giving absolute priority to grain and neglecting - or
even condemning - diversification was counter-productive even from the point of view of grain production itself.

This counter-productive effect is ascribed to
two causes. First, by depriving peasants of alternative sources of income from other crops and commodities, the incentive to work was reduced, collective labour discredited and grain production adversely affected. Second, concentration on grain pre-
judiced the ecology of farming, in particular by
limiting supplies of manure. Third, the policy
limited agricultural profits derived from non-grain
production, which could have increased investment in
agriculture. In 1978, states Yu, arable agriculture
accounted for 67.8% of total agricultural output

value, and of that proportion 66% was accounted for
by grain. Animal husbandry, forestry, fish culture
and aquatic products play a far smaller part in the
Chinese rural economy than in, for example, Japan,
and very much smaller as a total proportion of output value than is the case in advanced countries.

These charges against the Left are somewhat
overstrained. They certainly do not apply to Mao
himself: peasant that he was, he showed himself
second to none in his persistent calls for diversification. And observers in China during the decade
of the Cultural Revolution (the author included) saw
communes - show places no doubt, but show places
precisely because they were examples of proper implementation of current policy - which exhibited
their all-round development with pride. The fact is
that the Cultural Revolution was the first period in
which the diversification of agriculture was taken
seriously. Mao's slogan that grain should be taken
as the key link in a process of diversification was
the first breach in China in the orthodox Communist
obsession with grain supplies as the raison d'être
of collective agriculture. The true criticism of
the policies of the Cultural Revolution in this
respect was that while it proved easy to ensure by
political pressure that grain was made the key link,
it proved far more difficult to induce local cadres
to apply new rotations and new farming ecologies.
If their ability and experience were strained enough
in conducting a simple monocrop system, then how
much more strained would they be in attempting to
manage the complexities of mixed farming.

To some extent, the leaders and the cadres of
the Cultural Revolution years have been made whipp-
ing boys for deficiencies in Chinese agriculture
which are centuries old. China has not had, at
least in her later history, the symbiosis between
hill and plain, upland pasture and lowland arable,
so typical of European agriculture and so central to
the agricultural revolution of the eighteenth century. Her neglected mountains, it is now realised,
may be her greatest untapped agricultural resource;
and the new responsibility systems are partly inspired by the perception of these possibilities and
the need to re-deploy agricultural labour to exploit
them.

One must distinguish, however, between the new
regime's stress on the use of hill land, and their
other policies with respect to the relations between
grain-growing and diversified farming. As far as
regional agricultural specialisation is concerned,

the new regime's policies do not now differ very
sharply from those of their predecessors, in spite
of the rhetoric. Their first somewhat uncritical
commitment to regional comparative advantage ended
with the famine in Hubei and Hebei, which followed
and was exacerbated by the reduction in grain acreage of over five million hectares between 1979 and
1980. It is now realised that the tightness of
grain supplies and the uncertainties of China's mon-
soon climate leave less room for manoeuvre than had
been hoped. It is stressed that the acreage of
grain cannot be further reduced, and that diversification can only take place on the assumption that
grain output is given priority and that its output
increases. They are back to Mao's original slogan.
The means of achieving both higher grain output and
greater diversification, Li Erzhong, First Secretary
of Hebei, proposed,[12] is to use dialectics to find
'mutual stimuli' between grain and other agricultural crops and products.

Another cause for discontent is the very great
differences in yields between one area and another.
This is both a problem and a challenge. In 1981 it
was reported from Liaoning (an agriculturally developed province) that the grain yields of the best and
worst counties varied in the ratio of three to one;
of the best and worst communes, six to one; and of
the best and worst teams, ten to one.[13] Similar
figures were quoted from Hubei.[14] Some of these
differences have natural causes in soil and climate,
but it is now accepted that there are enormous potentialities here. Yet there is a contradiction between this idea on the one hand, and on the other
the opposing idea (for which much evidence could
certainly be produced) that China's total grain output could be best maximised not by concentrating resources on improving the worst yields, but by concentrating them on the best grain land where yields
are already highest.

A further cause for condemnation of past policies is the disappointing results of the vast campaigns which have since 1949 more than doubled the
area of irrigated land. In Guangming Daily in May
1980, Zhan Wu, Director of the Agricultural Economics Institute of the Chinese Academy of Social
Science, stated that, 'due to failure to link up
projects and to poor management', the water utilisation rate was under 50%.[15] Responsibility systems
for the management of water distribution are now
being introduced.

Also, in spite of heroic and partially

successful efforts to create effective defences
against flood as well as drought, China remains
vulnerable to natural disasters, as the recent
famine tragically showed. The uncertainties of the
Chinese climate can still play havoc with the har-
vest and put millions of lives at risk. For this
reason alone the marketable surplus of agriculture
must be vastly increased to provide buffer stocks
adequate for any probable emergency.

Finally, the new regime, while conceding that
agricultural production continued to rise - though
more slowly - during the period of the Cultural
Revolution, point out that peasant incomes failed to
rise in proportion, and in some areas even decreased
in spite of the increases in production. People's
Daily calculated that among one hundred million
peasants collectivisation had failed to raise production significantly during a period when population
as a whole had doubled.[16] Average rural incomes remained far below average urban incomes; the rural
80% of the population received only 20% of national
income. In an editorial on 14th May 1980, People's
Daily stated:

> 'Some localities have not had one good year
> since agricultural co-operativisation; and
> others have never recovered from the Three Bad
> Years'.[17]

In such places - reckoned at one in six of China's
two thousand or so counties - the peasants had 'lost
faith in the collective', and where this was so, it
was necessary to allow them to return, for the
present, to family farming.

The present diagnosis of past failure can be
summarised as follows:

(1) Unrealistically high levels of investment
in attempts at improvement of agriculture, but with
poor results. We have referred to Zhan Wu's statement that irrigation works were less than 50% effective; and he added that while from 1965 to 1977 the
capital invested in farm machinery had increased
over 8-fold and chemical fertiliser supplies had
grown by almost two and a half times in the same
years, and while farm costs had increased 130%, production had only risen by 80%. This relative failure - costly in terms of peasant incomes - was due,
he asserted, to 'an irrational economic structure
and low levels of management', and he emphasised the
point that 'increased investment is not the only way
to speed up development'. People's Daily added:

'Some units think you must increase expenditure to increase production ... the more chemical fertilisers, the larger the scale of a project, the more mechanisation the better', but management and especially financial management, is the key.[19]

(2) The level of management ability among many rural cadres is very low.[20] Their notion of management is 'to ring the bell and count heads'. Proper accounting is scarce. Some teams have no accountants; some leaders have worked for ten years without even an account book. Others combine the posts of team leader, accountant, work-point recorder and store-keeper. Thus many teams do not know what they have spent in materials, money and labour, and have no means of judging the return on expenditure. There is little or no democratic discussion of expenditures, or of the accounts. 'Loss and waste of collective property and funds is appalling', and there is every opportunity for privilege and peculation because cadres need not make any distinction between their public business and their private interests. Rural cadres also have little knowledge of modern scientific methods: 'today's cadres are yesterday's peasants'. They were mostly recruited in the days of land reform and collectivisation, they are ageing rapidly, and there is little prospect of their being replaced by younger men with greater knowledge and new ideas because there are too few graduates in agriculture, and too few of such graduates are willing to serve in the villages. The cadres are largely incapable of taking decisions for themselves, and the institutional framework - in which commune-level cadres are salaried servants of the state - actually discourages initiative: the safest course is to obey orders. Many of them are ignorant of simple local market possibilities which, with the help of state trading organs and the supply and marketing co-operatives, could rapidly increase both incomes and accumulation of capital.

(3) The burdens imposed on the peasants are heavy, unpredictable and counter-productive.[21] In some cases the total handed over to the team, brigade, commune and state in taxes, levies, accumulation, etc., is over 50% of gross production, and in this respect the poorer teams - less able to support this wasteful superstructure - suffer most and suffer grievously. If those who now oppose change, writes one prefectural party secretary, 'had starved as the peasants have starved', they would take a different attitude.[22]

The first burden is the wasteful and

uncontrolled investment already alluded to. The
second is the swollen administration, the number of
cadres supported by 'subsidies' and enjoying from
this source incomes often two or three times as high
as those of the peasants. The third burden arises
from the abuse of the state monopoly of trade: procurement norms are raised in good years or prices
reduced[23] so that 'the more enthusiastic you have
been, the greater your burden'. Supply and marketing co-operatives play the same game of forcing
prices down in times of plenty, while the peasants
are not allowed to seek an alternative buyer. Not
only the team leadership but the higher levels also
put in their claims: 'Commune and brigade enterprises are in debt. The phenomenon of state enterprises and units and state cadres owing money to
teams is universal.'[24]

It is in fact normal for over 30% of gross production to be siphoned off before any distribution
of the product is made to the peasants; this is
about the same proportion of total farm incomes as
was taken by the landlords from their tenants before
the revolution.

(4) The authorities re-allocate peasant resources with no respect for the rights of ownership
of individuals or of teams. According to People's
Daily, 'in violation of exchange at equal value,
some state organs, enterprises, departments and
units transfer the resources of teams, and appropriate labour, grain, funds and materials'.[25] So
widespread is this problem that several proposals
have been made to disband the communes entirely in
order to prevent these abuses, and an experiment of
this kind is now under way.

(5) The problem of 'to each according to his
labour' has never been solved. The piecework and
job contract system which was used in imitation of
traditional Soviet methods was not satisfactory;
quality of work could not be controlled. The free
supply system of the Great Leap Forward, however,
was far worse: the labourer received much the same
income whether he worked hard or not. The Dazhai
system was similar. The self-assessment system was
equally unsuccessful:

> 'we recorded stereotyped work-points which
> only related to the previous, not the current,
> state of the labour done by each individual.
> People came to think that they would get the
> same whether they worked hard or not. The
> system of work-points combined with work

assessment was tried in some places, but it proved very difficult to assess promptly and accurately the quality of the performance of a farm task involving so many people, because for most of the year farm tasks cannot be expressed in terms of output. So work assessment usually became a formality'.[26]

Many times it has been pointed out that productivity on the private plot, where incentives are not impaired, is much higher than on the collective fields, and represents the intensive and meticulous cultivation which China must achieve on all her farmland.

(6) The suppression of private plots, rural fairs and family sideline occupations severely limited peasant incomes. The obsession with growing grain prevented the team or the brigade from pursuing similar sources of profit collectively. These restrictions, by reducing incomes, also reduced the possibilities of accumulation; this in turn limited the improvement of arable farming; this was reflected in the failure of incomes to rise substantially; and the result was to depress incentives still further: 'who wants to do unprofitable work?' said the peasants. 'The women made sandals, the men loafed ... those with nothing to eat stood about waiting for state relief'.[27] Peasants deserted the collective farm for itinerant peddling or craft work. National figures for overall increases in agricultural output conceal the near total failure of some areas to improve production while population continued to rise.

The responsibility systems are believed to be the cure. They must be seen in the context of more general changes in agricultural policy. These include the recent increases in procurement prices and decreases in the price of farm inputs; the enlargement of private plots and the provision, in addition to them and according to circumstances, of fodder plots, grain ration plots, hill plots for the growing of timber, fuel, fruit and tea; the partial freeing of rural markets; the encouragement (in place of the repression) of individual and family sideline production; measures to increase investment in light industries in order to increase the flow of incentive goods; increased investment in agriculture, especially investment by local authorities; diversification of agricultural and rural production; and - last but not least - the democratisation of collective management.

Behind this range of policies lie certain

assumptions about the strategy of rural growth:
that increased peasant purchasing power is a major -
if not the major - driving force of national economic development; that therefore priority in state
investment should be given to agriculture; that all
the potentialities of each local community must be
exploited in order to increase income and so increase the possibility of local investment; that in
this last process, local collective industrialisation has a key role to play as the major means of
raising capital for the transformation of agriculture; and that local potentialities can be fully
developed only if the process is a democratic one,
in which the grass-root communities and their individual members are given the maximum freedom of decision-making compatible with general - and largely
indicative - socialist planning.

These assumptions are all, as we have seen,
derived from the thought of Mao Zedong. The strategy has not changed. What has changed is organisation, and the main reason for this change is the
conviction that the system, more especially as it
was applied by the left wing, unnecessarily minimised incentives. The new regime is often regarded
abroad as 'pragmatic'. This, however, is to do them
an injustice. True, the agonies of the Cultural
Revolution struggle induced a process of re-thinking
about the nature of socialist organisation, in the
course of which some hitherto sacrosanct assumptions were rejected. Mao dropped some of the ideological baggage and his successors have dropped some
more. But they also have a positive theory. They
deny that there is something intrinsically socialist
in collectivising everything, and in doing so on the
largest possible scale. Scale alone does not create
economies if there is no division of labour and no
specialisation and co-operation in any meaningful
sense. Such a system incurs the inevitable wastes
of large-scale production while offering none of its
advantages. As the Chinese put it, to allow production relations to outrun the development of productive forces is positively counter-productive.

Second, they affirm that it is the content of
collectivisation, not the mere fact of it, which
matters, and to allow collectivisation to outrun the
development of management ability, accounting skills,
technology, the willingness of prosperous communities to share with adjacent poorer communities, and
political consciousness generally is also positively
counter-productive. Mao's speedy collectivisation
in 1955 and 1956 is now condemned as a 'strategic

failure'; the 1958 destruction of the marginal
economic independence left to the peasants in the
form of private plots and rural fairs is denounced
as an excess; the merging of rich and poor teams in
single units of account and distribution is rejected;
and the ideological identification of collectivism
with one particular form of labour organisation -
large-scale direct management by the collective
leadership - is repudiated: 'Socialist mass production does not mean, as usually understood, merely
"mass participation", but the production of commodities through highly developed co-ordination of
specialised production departments on the basis of
mechanisation. It will be a long time before the
rural areas reach such a level'.[28]

The responsibility system aims, among other
things, to substitute temporarily for this ideal and
final type of socialist mass production a pattern of
specialisation based on existing, largely manual,
technology through the system of contracts. It is
argued that this is not a retreat but an advance,
because divisions of labour will stimulate technical
change. The case of 'full responsibility to households', however, is frankly admitted to be a case of
'reculer pour mieux sauter'; as Guangming Daily
admits, such full responsibility 'is not a Communist
aspiration'.[29]

The new system (or the various systems grouped
round the idea of contract) is seen as a single, key
change which can solve many problems of collectivisation. The specialisation and division of labour
provide a form of organisation which can deal with
the urgent need for diversification. It improves
incentives in collective production. Where successful, it makes private plots unnecessary, thus eliminating a major conflict of interest. It minimises
managerial overheads and the effects of managerial
incompetence. It is simple and comprehensible. It
cuts down the need for collective accounting, and
reduces the possibility of waste and peculation, by
ensuring that most of the accounting is done in
terms of the negotiation of contracts, during which
peasants as individuals and as a team can defend
their financial rights and interests. Finally, it
is democratic.

This last point - the political implications of
the responsibility systems - is one which is given
equal stress with the economic implications: 'The
reason why the responsibility systems are regarded
as the key link is that a suitable responsibility
system represents a way of practising democratic

management by members. It can encourage members to
increase their independence and their initiative,
and free cadres from their unnecessary task of
"disciplining" people'.[30] In another article:
'Each working group or labourer has to assume economic responsibility, and thus the scope of relations
among state, collective and individual has been enlarged and the number of those participating has
increased'.

An attempt is being made to create an effective
framework to protect the rights and interests of
teams against higher authorities, and of the members
against the team. Jiefang Daily reported in
October 1980 that the suburban communes round
Shanghai had begun the election of management committees, to give members 'the minimum necessary guarantee for exercising their democratic rights. In
future, members have the right to assess, criticise,
supervise and select cadres'.[31] Thus it is possible
that the proper and regular election of grass-roots
cadres for which Mao pleaded but which he could get
from neither left nor right, may at last become a
reality.

In May 1981, Hebei province laid down the following rules for the conduct of commune finances:

> 'No unit or person is permitted to force
> people's communes and production teams to make
> expenditures that are not included in their
> plans. Financial plans must be approved by
> mass meetings of commune members. Let the
> masses take part in democratic financial man-
> agement and regularly analyse economic activ-
> ities to find ways of cutting costs ... If the
> reserved grain is to be used, this must first
> be discussed by commune members, reported to
> the brigades, and approved by the commune ...
> No unit or individual is allowed to apportion,
> borrow, or retain the funds of people's comm-
> unes and production teams, who have the right
> to refuse ... Purchase of large-scale farm
> equipment and the setting up of collective
> welfare facilities must be discussed in full
> meetings of commune members or of their repre-
> sentatives ... cadres and members are not all-
> owed to borrow grain or money from production
> teams unless for particular reasons, in which
> case they must ... seek approval from full
> meetings of commune members or of their repre-
> sentatives ... Commune members have the right
> to investigate and question the publicised

> accounts, to criticise and to make suggestions
> ... Financial and accounting staff have the
> right to supervise the cadres of their units
> in implementing ... financial policies and
> laws ... higher organisations must severely
> punish those who retaliate ...'32

In these rules, and in many comments on the same
subject, can be seen the realisation that democratic
control is as important for the prevention of waste
and corruption and for the maintenance of efficiency
as for its more philosophical virtues.

Great stress is now put on the protection of
the autonomous decision-making powers of the team.
County plans for sown areas are to be only 'for reference' and not mandatory, and the only specific
obligations laid on teams by the state are the fulfilment of procurement quotas of main crops (these
quotas being fixed for four years or five depending
on the province), and the payment of the agricultural tax.

In the choice and implementation of responsibility systems, it has been repeatedly and univers-
ally stressed that the decision lies with the team
members; they should be guided but not coerced.
The First Secretary of Gansu, Feng Jixin, said:
'We have entrusted to the masses the power to choose
the right system for their conditions. We must not
wrangle with them nor promote "rectification of dev-
iations".'33 Cases have been widely publicised
where the team Party committee has been severely
reprimanded by higher Party authority for attempting
to force a particular system on its members. This
insistence on a democratic decision has been taken
to the point of accepting that even a majority decision of the team's members should not necessarily
be imposed on a dissenting minority; it is permissible for teams to use different responsibility systems at the same time, so that members can enter into any reasonable relationship with the collective.

The sanctity of contracts under the responsibility system is also stressed, and the number and
variety of comments on this are a startling illustration of the power which cadres have hitherto
enjoyed to make arbitrary changes of all kinds. The
National People's Congress has demanded the provision of an adequate law of contract, which is now
said to be in preparation.

The responsibility system itself, however, is
held to be the keystone of this new and more democratic structure, designed, as the new slogan puts

it, to guarantee the 'power, responsibilities and interests' of the peasants.

The most interesting feature of the whole movement is, indeed, the admission that the operation of rural economic life by a party hierarchy whose members owed no responsibility to anyone except their hierarchical seniors, has been not only politically dangerous but economically counter-productive. In agriculture as in industry, China now seeks to replace central party direction by a combination of controls - indicative planning, market discipline and democratic control from below.

Even the commune system itself has been under fire as essentially anti-democratic. An article in Jingji Guanli (Economic Management) makes the case against it.[34] The original unitary commune system was an expression of the 'communist wind' of 1958, and the result of the ideas enshrined in the slogan 'large in size and collective in nature', which manifested itself in the 'communisation' of all property, in over-accumulation, in uncontrolled and wasteful use of resources, and in bringing the prosperous down to the same level as the poor; and so production was undermined. Mao roundly condemned this, and in 1960 the communes were articulated into commune, brigade and team, with the team as the basic level of ownership. 'But this system was still related to the "two transformations" system of ownership (from small collective to big collective, and from big collective to full public ownership) so that it still left room for pursuing leftist tendencies'. Rights of ownership and the disposal of resources and of manpower were left undefined and subject to abuse. 'It is inevitable that the commune and the brigade will carry out egalitarianism and transfer of resources because they are "building up from nothing".' They are 'empty frames', unrelated to economic needs, which have thrived only on 'artificial and compulsory "escalation" of ownership'. And this, too, has undermined the productive forces.

One result, says Jingji Guanli, is that teams were given no right to pursue their own diversification plans or to develop their own industries. And most of the net income from commune and brigade industry remains with communes and brigades; it is treated as a source of accumulation, not of increased peasant incomes, although it is the teams which have to provide the labour force and the resources.

Commune (as opposed to brigade and team) cadres are paid by the state: 'they are only responsible to ... the higher level ... so it is easy for them to issue instructions blindly'. 'It has been proposed to respect the right of the production team to act on its own; but this problem cannot be fundamentally solved if the system of three-level ownership ... is not changed'. The author proposes the abolition of three-level ownership, and the vesting of full ownership rights in teams, somewhat enlarged to give them a greater capacity for diversification. Teams might come together voluntarily for certain economic purposes, and may even voluntarily form agriculture-commerce-industry integrated enterprises. No state-salaried personnel would be involved.

The operation of the commune system tended, said Guangming Daily, 'to put everything in the hands of the county secretary'; it was time, Guangming argued, to separate the commune from the state.35 The First Secretary of Shaanxi, Ma Wenrui, about the same time said that 'the practice of integrating government administration with commune management is not conducive to the running of the three-level economic organisation of the commune as a normal enterprise'.36 By late 1981, the experiment was under way in Fengyang xian (county), Anhui, of abolishing the commune and brigade, virtually turning the teams back into the old Agricultural Producers' Co-operatives, restoring the xiang (district) government, and setting up under it three companies to undertake industrial, commercial and agricultural business. No further details were given.37

The communes, therefore, may very soon be abolished; the most famous institution of Chinese socialism may disappear. If so, there would be losses as well as gains, and perhaps a more considered diagnosis of their failings would recognise that the fault lay not in the commune system itself but in the undemocratic domination of the three levels by the state-party hierarchy; and the consequent change of the three levels of communal ownership (a concept quite compatible with democratic control) into three further levels of the centralised hierarchy.

Local reports of the operation of the responsibility systems show striking increases of production and incomes. Caution is needed, however. We had no lack of striking examples of success from the communes of 1958 and from Dazhai and its imitators in the '70s, examples which were no doubt true but not necessarily typical. Widespread resistance to the new system obliges its supporters to redouble their propaganda. Moreover it should never be forgotten that in China's climatic conditions it is difficult to judge the effects of any agricultural policy over less than a period of ten years; and so far none of China's successive policies has ever been allowed to run unchanged for so long. More convincing, perhaps, than selective accounts of dramatic success is the report of a crash programme in Anhui to build extra grain-storage capacity, after two years of the responsibility systems.[38] Significant, too, is the unprecedented boom in rural housebuilding. Such information gives some credence to the reports of striking increases in almost all branches of agriculture, in rural incomes, and in the amount of grain marketed, from eleven provinces; from poor Gansu to prosperous Jiangsu, and from Guangdong's region of intensive rice culture to Jilin's extensive and partly mechanised farming. National production figures also suggest that agriculture has progressed at a sharply increased pace, although the information is not such as to make it possible to give any one part of the complex of new policies the greatest credit.

The local examples of success express the expectation that not only will grain production increase more rapidly, but also, and even more rapidly, the production of 'diversification items'; not only production, but incomes; and not only the incomes of those already prosperous, but the incomes of the poorest, and perhaps these will increase faster. Examples are already being given of the increased ability to face famine of those teams which have most successfully diversified production via the responsibility system.

There has been, nevertheless, and continues to be, much resistance to the new policies. The picture one gets is of reluctant middle and lower rural cadres being squeezed between the upper millstone of a leadership determined on change, and the lower millstone of peasant communities only too ready to accept it. In July 1981, Feng Jixin, First Secretary of Gansu, looking back on the two-year campaign, said, 'We met with obstacles every step we took'.[39] And it was admitted that a majority of rural cadres were still opposed to the changes.[40] Red Flag (Dec. 1979) put the chief blame on 'comrades (including leading comrades) engaged in rural work'. In May 1980, People's Daily complained that 'many local authorities are stubbornly hanging on to their power to plan sowing and planting and to handle and process products. They fear being unable

to "exercise control".'[41] At the provincial level,
Wang Enmao in Jilin and Liao Zhigao in Fujian were
conspicuous foot-draggers. Liberation Army Daily
mostly maintained an ominous silence. The resistance at lower levels was partly the expression of
vested interests. Some cadres, it was said, although they understood the policies and knew they
were good, resisted implementing them because 'there
was nothing in it for them'.[42] Banyuetan (Fortnightly Talks) attributed resistance to the fact
that basic-level cadres, as well as some peasants,
opposed because 'they gained certain privileges from
egalitarianism.'[43] One cadre, talking to the Party
Secretary of his prefecture, frankly said: 'If you
assign households full responsibility for task completion ... what am I going to eat?'[44]

People's Daily itself admitted that the new
system had its dangers to socialism, and listed ten
of them.[45] They were dangers to

- (i) purchase, use, maintenance, repair and
  management of large machines and tools

- (ii) unified and rational use of water resources

- (iii) care of draft animals

- (iv) prevention of pests and diseases

- (v) popularisation of scientific farming

- (vi) defence against natural disasters

- (vii) farmland capital construction

- (viii) commune and brigade enterprise and diversification

- (ix) water and soil conservation

- (x) care of the needy.

The author of the article might well have added a
few more to the list: danger to the implementation
of family planning, to the maintenance of rural
employment, and most significant of all, to the very
continued existence of collectivised farming.

With the proponents of change in full control
of the media, one can scarcely expect a great deal
of evidence to be published at this point showing

that the fears expressed in People's Daily were real. Inevitably, the tendency has been to give examples showing that such fears are illusory, that, as the People's Daily author himself concluded, these problems were not inherent in the responsibility system, and would be solved by good administration.

Examples are given to show that mechanisation has not suffered, that in fact peasants holding contracts have persuaded their teams to buy, or have themselves bought, or have joined others in buying, hand tractors and equipment on an unprecedented scale. One xian (county) in Anhui has just reported that by these means its farming is now basically mechanised.46

The system of control of irrigation water in China is little discussed, and we know remarkably little about it, but one article47 describes the application of the responsibility system in this field, suggesting that payment by results for those in charge will actually improve the effective use of water. The change in the organisation of farming will in any case scarcely affect large and medium catchment areas, but only small village networks.

The effect on the care of draft animals cannot yet be estimated. Depending on the form of responsibility in operation, they may be allocated under unified management, hired out to the contracting peasants, allotted on long loan to contractors, or in some cases sold to households operating the full responsibility system. Contracts are expected to guarantee the care and protection of animals handed over, and if the contracts are sensibly drawn up care of animals might well improve.

A return to farming operated by individual families could jeopardise pest and disease control; but examples are given of household farming contractors forming organisations of neighbours to carry out spraying.

Innovation is being encouraged by contracts between teams, groups or households and the extension stations, by which the extension station will take the risks and share the profits. This arrangement, begun in Sichuan, is now being generalised, and the hope has been expressed that this will represent a vast improvement over the present state of things in which 'the peasants doze while the leaders shout themselves hoarse propagandising new techniques'.48 Examples are given to show that the peasants, with a measure of independence restored to them, are taking a keen interest in innovation.

Another of People's Daily's fears was that

defence against natural disasters would suffer.
This is to assume that such defence depends solely
on the ability to mobilise the necessary labour,
which may indeed be impaired by the greater independence both of teams and of their members; but defence depends in the long run as much on the increase
of production and so of reserves, on diversification
so that peasants do not have all their eggs in the
one basket, and on the capacity to accumulate funds
for irrigation and flood control which depends again
on increased production and incomes, all of which
(the supporters of change would argue) can be best
delivered by the responsibility systems.

On the danger to soil and water conservation,
it has been admitted that where peasants are uncertain whether the new dispensation will last or not,
there have been cases of over-exploitation of the
soil; but it is argued that this changes rapidly as
soon as farmers accept that the system is here to
stay; they then begin to show a far greater interest in good husbandry than under the old form of
collective. Some provinces have recommended rules
for compensating and rewarding contracting peasants
who create improvements, as judged by their fellow
team members.

The threat to the maintenance of social security services is serious enough for the State Council
to have issued a circular on the subject, warning
that 'five guarantee' families should not suffer.[49]
But there is plenty of evidence from the areas where
full responsibility to households is widespread that
there is some difficulty in inducing the peasants to
meet their social obligations, such as contributions
to the payment of teachers and barefoot doctors.
Those who favour the responsibility system argue
that as production and incomes increase so will the
ability of teams to accumulate, and those in dist-
ress can then be better provided for. Feng Jixin
dismissed the fear on these grounds, and added 'any
problems are not due to the system but to the personnel concerned'.[50] Guizhou has laid down (and no
doubt the other provinces have done so in some form
or another) that the contracts made with full-resp-
onsibility households will stipulate their share of
welfare funds, rational remuneration of brigade and
team cadres, funds for education, public health,
etc., and the costs of maintaining and improving the
infrastructure.[51]

In the end, the overcoming of such problems as
these depends on the successful maintenance of the
necessary degree of 'collective' control, which

could be exercised by the team or by a reconstituted local political authority, or by a division of
responsibilities between the two. The problem here
is primarily with the systems which give contracts
for arable farming to households, or give them full
responsibility. Here, there is a manifest danger,
amply illustrated in the records, that the peasants
will use their autonomy to resist their remaining
responsibilities. To speak first, however, of what
is intended by the leadership rather than what may
happen if they fail to stem the tide of peasant
individualism which the relaxation has released, it
is clear that the responsibility systems are not
regarded as a surrender to individualism but a re-
articulation of collective responsibilities. Ownership remains with the production team; land allotted to contractors is to be used only for the purposes specified in the contract, and it cannot be
bought, sold, pledged or rented out or in, nor can
it be built upon or used as a source of clay, sand
or minerals.[52] Normally, means of production such
as tools allotted for use are hired to the contractors or if allotted free are subject to the payment
of a depreciation charge. It is emphasised that
land must be distributed according to labour power,
with or without some modification to take account of
dependents, and it should on no account be allotted
according to the individual holdings of the post-
land-reform period.

Planning is expected to remain firmly in the
hands of the collective. The team is free to choose
what it sows, plants or manufactures, vis-à-vis
higher authorities, though subject to the state's
'reference plans'. The team members do not have
such freedom. The team plans production, and allocates responsibilities within this plan to groups,
households and individuals.

The collective is expected to continue the
process of accumulation of collective capital, although in the poorer areas it is accepted that
little or no accumulation can be expected in the
near future until the economic wounds of the past
have healed. With this exception - a large exception it must be said - it is laid down, though as an
expectation rather than a rule, that about 20% of
net income[53] will be accumulated for all purposes:
next year's production expenses, overhead costs,
welfare funds and funds for 'expanded reproduction'.
In all cases except that of the assignment of full
responsibility to households, all contracted or
quota products, the products of remaining collective

operations (such as handicraft workshops) and products from joint team-member shared-profit ventures,
are handed over to the collective for unitary distribution. In most cases of quota agreements (as
opposed to contracts) the whole product is handed
over.

Provincial and local stipulations on these questions vary a good deal, but this is the essential
position of the collective in the contract system.
The collective remains owner, planner, accumulator
and distributor, and although collectivism has been
relaxed it has by no means been destroyed.

The perspective of future change also remains
firmly socialist. The contract system, including
contracting to households, is regarded as a new and
better beginning for the gradual building up as
technology changes of a true system of socialist
division of labour and specialisation.

The assignment of full responsibility to households is clearly a different matter, and difficulties are already appearing. Offered the opportunity
of restored independence, peasants in many parts of
China have responded by returning collective property to individual ownership – even sometimes des-
troying what cannot be distributed.[54] Some are
stubbornly planting what they choose to plant, or
refusing to plant at all and taking up non-agricultural occupations.[55] They are refusing to contribute to the upkeep of cadres, teachers and paramedics.
Often rural cadres, caught between insistence from
above that the peasants must be allowed to choose
the responsibility system they want, and the determination of many peasant communities to choose whatever gives them the most independence, resign their
posts or cease to lead, leaving the way free for the
re-assertion of individual farming. The national
leadership has moved – or has been pushed – from the
concession of restored family farming only to remote
and scattered households, to consenting to its
extension to the poorest villages, to acceptance
that this would in fact involve 100,000,000 farming
households, to admission that full responsibility
'is the system preferred by the masses', to a point
at which collectivised agriculture, in any sense
recognised in the past, may well come to apply only
to a minority of China's peasants.

It may be that the new leadership is providing
a further illustration of that old political saw,
that the most dangerous time for an authoritarian
regime is when it starts to reform; it may have
aroused, in its attempts to replace collective

management by contract, expectations which it cannot control.

On the other hand, there may be more of deliberation in the process than is admitted. In October 1980 Red Flag [56] referred with admiration to the Danish agricultural system.[57] This was in a context which showed plainly that an analogy was perceived between the Danish system and the new responsibility system; and it was followed by the assertion that the latter could be the foundation of a Chinese style of socialist agriculture. The Danish system is one of independent agricultural producers operating within a framework of co-operative supply, processing, marketing, credit, and research and development, and linked to these co-operatives by contract.

Is this what Deng Xiaoping has in mind?

6

CHINA'S SYSTEM OF INDUSTRIAL ECONOMIC PLANNING

Paul Hare

In the early 1950s, China established an economic
planning system modelled quite closely on Soviet
practices and embarked on a programme of rapid industrialisation. Observers of the Chinese scene are
in agreement that overall growth rates in industry
averaged more than 10% per annum for the twenty-five
years after 1952, though with sharp falls in output
in the early 1960s (usually attributed to a combination of adverse natural conditions, and disloca-
tion and imbalances resulting from the Great Leap
Forward of 1959), and slowdowns in the mid-1960s
(Cultural Revolution) and again in the mid-1970s
(said to be due to inappropriate 'ultra left' policies pursued by the so-called 'Gang of Four') (see
Hidasi, 1979; Howe, 1978; Barnett, 1981:16-27).
Given a system capable of delivering such a
high average rate of growth over a sustained period,
however, it is initially somewhat surprising to find
that the Chinese are now actively studying possible
reforms in their economic planning procedures.

* This paper is based on a four-week visit to China
in June 1980, when I had the opportunity to interview a number of academic economists and economic
officials in Beijing, Jinan and Shanghai; I am
grateful to the Institute of World Economy, Beijing,
for supporting my visit and making the necessary
arrangements, as well as to the SSRC for generously
providing financial support (grant HR7054). Helpful comments on an earlier version were provided by
B. Fine, M. Fransman, Huang Teh-ming, M. Lockett,
S. Robertson and members of the London China seminar.
Remaining errors are my own.

Naturally, no-one yet knows where all this might lead, though as I explain later, I remain somewhat sceptical about the likelihood of really fundamental changes being introduced in the next few years.

Nevertheless, the interest in reforms is now being accompanied by a less ambitious and more cautious approach to economic planning and management. Following the downfall of the 'Gang of Four' in 1976, the new plan targets announced by the then Chairman Hua at the First Session of the Fifth National People's Congress (Feb. 1978) were still exceptionally ambitious, envisaging the construction by 1985 of 120 major projects, including 10 iron and steel works, 9 non-ferrous metallurgical works, 8 major coalmines, 10 mineral oil and natural gas production areas, 30 power stations and 6 new railway lines as well as 5 important ports (Hidasi, 1979 :176). When these targets were announced, there was very little mention of the need for any organisational changes in the planning system. But just over a year later, at the Second Session of the Congress (June 1979), although the above targets were not formally rescinded, Hua declared that the three-year period from 1979 to 1981 should be a period of 'readjusting, consolidating, restructuring and improving the national economy' (Klatt, 1979; Dernberger, 1979).[1,2]

Readjustment entails more realistic and better co-ordinated planning, which seeks to improve the balance between sectors. In particular, attention has to be paid to relieving bottlenecks in the areas of energy supplies, the supply of agricultural raw materials for industry, and in port and transport facilities. At the same time, construction activity needs to be concentrated and light industry should expand more rapidly than heavy industry so that living standards can be improved.

Restructuring refers to changes in the structure of economic management, urgently required because, (according to Main Documents: 28) the existing structure frequently neglects the law of value and the principle of payment 'to each according to his work'. Consolidation involves some re-organisation of existing enterprises: closing down certain very inefficient ones, encouraging some mergers and rearranging the production profiles of different enterprises to achieve more efficient forms of specialisation.

In order to understand the economic reforms being introduced in China, it seems essential to understand their context, namely the existing planning system. The available literature provides us with quite detailed accounts of plan formulation procedures in the mid-1950s (Lardy, 1978), and the organisation of the planning system following the 1958 decentralisation which transferred control over most enterprises to the Provinces (Donnithorne, 1967 ch.17). Since the Cultural Revolution, however, published accounts of Chinese planning are notable for their studied vagueness and ambiguity on points of organisational and procedural detail (see e.g. Lardy, 1975; Andors, 1977).

In this chapter I can hardly hope to fill such a major gap in our knowledge. However, I can make some progress in that direction by setting out my views about the way in which China's planning system currently functions, based on interview material, somewhat fragmentary published descriptions and my own extensive study of Eastern European and Soviet planning. My approach therefore presupposes that the latter provides a helpful framework within which to think about China.

Accordingly, the remainder of this chapter is structured in the following way: the following section outlines the organisational framework of Chinese planning, including the methods of plan formulation and execution. The third section discusses the economic problems which may be said to result from the present procedures, and then provides a brief account of the steps already taken to introduce a number of minor or experimental reforms into the planning system. To some extent, these measures involve granting greater autonomy to individual enterprises, and greater reliance on market forces and responses to smooth out inevitable imbalances in central plans. While not wholly misleading however, this is a distinctly one-sided picture of the recent changes, as I shall try to make clear. Finally, the concluding section summarises the preceding discussion by setting out some of the reforms in China's planning system that might be desirable, comparing these with the reforms which seem most likely to occur in the next few years. Of course, this kind of forecasting is always extremely hazardous; particularly as it is inevitably bound up with judgements about probable developments in the political sphere.

Organisation of the Planning System

The most important organisations participating in China's economic management are shown in Figure 6.1,

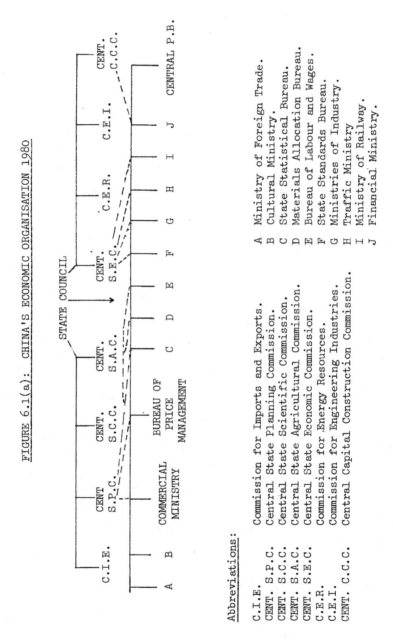

FIGURE 6.1(a): CHINA'S ECONOMIC ORGANISATION 1980

Abbreviations:

C.I.E.   Commission for Imports and Exports.
CENT. S.P.C.   Central State Planning Commission.
CENT. S.C.C.   Central State Scientific Commission.
CENT. S.A.C.   Central State Agricultural Commission.
CENT. S.E.C.   Central State Economic Commission.
C.E.R.   Commission for Energy Resources.
C.E.I.   Commission for Engineering Industries.
CENT. C.C.C.   Central Capital Construction Commission.

A   Ministry of Foreign Trade.
B   Cultural Ministry.
C   State Statistical Bureau.
D   Materials Allocation Bureau.
E   Bureau of Labour and Wages.
F   State Standards Bureau.
G   Ministries of Industry.
H   Traffic Ministry
I   Ministry of Railway.
J   Financial Ministry.

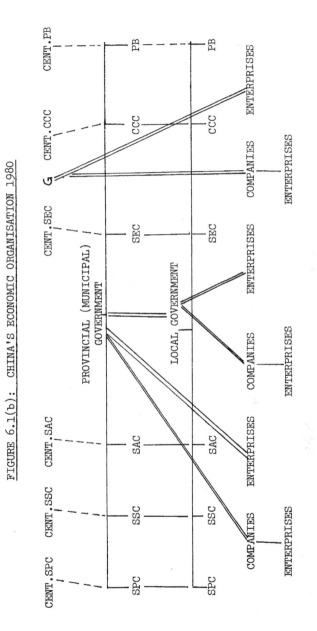

FIGURE 6.1(b): CHINA'S ECONOMIC ORGANISATION 1980

which also illustrates the main relationships between the different levels of the management hierarchy. (See figure 1.) Even from such a sketchy
figure, it is apparent that the structure is quite
complex; and in the present period of experiment-
ation and reform it seems likely to become more so,
at least until new operating rules, procedures and
organisational links have time to settle down. In
fact the present complexity (and at times confusion)
is one reason why reform is now under serious consideration. It is another question, however,
whether there is any feasible re-organisation of the
system which could actually reduce this complexity.

The state level of the management system com-
prises a number of functional agencies, namely the
various bureaux and commissions shown in Figure 6.1,
as well as agencies with general responsibility for
particular branches of the economy, namely the
industrial ministries, ministries dealing with
transport, communications and commerce, and the
State Agricultural Commission. These bodies are
directly responsible to the State Council. The
principal responsibility for co-ordinating the
economy falls to the State Planning Commission
(SPC). It has direct responsibility for plan formulation, and supervises the State Economic
Commission (SEC) which regulates plan execution.
Major roles in planning are also played by the
Capital Construction Commission (CCC) and the Bureau
for Materials Allocation (BMA) among the functional
agencies. The CCC is in charge of new capital construction, arranging for new projects by vetting
proposals, organising project design work and co-
ordinating the implementation of new investments.
But the SPC retains responsibility for the allocation of material and financial resources for investment. Similarly, the SPC also determines the framework of output targets and input requirements that
guide the work of the BMA. Finally, the branch
ministries elaborate and promote development plans
covering their own areas of responsibility.

Immediately below the state level come the
Provinces (including the three municipalities with
provincial status, Beijing, Tianjin and Shanghai).
Each provincial government supervises a set of functional and branch bureaux and commissions which
correspond fairly closely to the agencies operating
at the state level. These provincial organs receive
'professional guidance' from their state level
counterparts. Similar relationships operate between
provincial and local (i.e. prefectural and county)

level agencies.

The units directly engaged in production (including the provision of services) form the lowest
level of the management hierarchy, a level which
includes both enterprises and companies.[3] China has
about 350,000 enterprises, of which around 80,000
are state enterprises (i.e. units owned by the whole
people, to use the Chinese terminology) and the rest
are in collective ownership. A company seems to
correspond to what in most of Eastern Europe is now
called an association; it is a management organ
which supervises a number of enterprises, usually
confined to a fairly narrow range of products and a
definite area of the country. For example, the
Shanghai Plastic Products Company has responsibility
for one research institute and 38 enterprises; of
the latter, 24 are state enterprises and 14 are
collectively owned. This particular company has the
legal status of an administrative unit, but as explained more fully in the next section, some companies are now being transferred to khozraschet[4] so
that they will no longer be supported financially by
central and local budgets. As is clear from Figure
6.1, companies and enterprises may be supervised by
ministry, provincial or local levels of the management system. All co-operatives, however, are supervised by management units at the lower levels of the
system.

In order to make the following discussion
clearer, Figure 6.2 presents a simplified version of
part of Figure 6.1, drawing particular attention to
the organisations and relationships involved in the
process of plan formulation and execution. At this
point, it is useful to note how functional, branch
and regional responsibilities are assigned to the
various management organs which comprise China's
planning system. (See Figure 6.2.) We shall see
later on how this assignment gives rise to some of
the co-ordination problems faced by the system, and
comment on possible alternatives. Before considering such issues, however, it is important to explain
how plan formulation and execution are now being
carried out.

Plan formulation. Although China has completed its
fifth five-year plan (1976-80) and is now preparing
both a new five-year plan and a ten-year plan covering 1981-1990, there is really nothing of interest
to say about such medium and long term planning at
the moment. According to officials in China, in the
past these so-called plans have never been properly

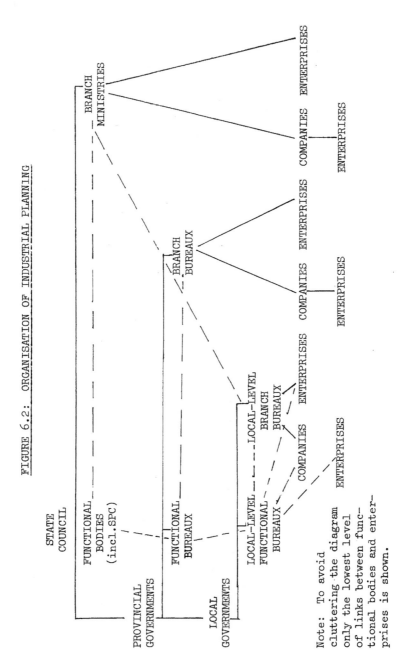

FIGURE 6.2: ORGANISATION OF INDUSTRIAL PLANNING

Note: To avoid cluttering the diagram only the lowest level of links between functional bodies and enterprises is shown.

co-ordinated and seem to have comprised little more than a collection of branch proposals brought together in the same document. Moreover, the published statistics on these plans are so highly aggregated that they could not possibly provide useful guidelines to help such agencies as the CCC in selecting and approving specific investment projects. Perhaps the sixth five-year plan (1981-85) will turn out to be more coherent and more detailed than its predecessors; in the meantime, our analysis must confine itself to the effective operational plan, which is the annual plan.

As in other socialist countries, plan formulation in China is accomplished over a period of several months, during which time massive volumes of information flow between the various levels of the system and initial plan conceptions may be revised several times. A complicating factor in the Chinese case is that for most types of plan information there are at least two information channels linking the state level authorities with enterprises. The first is the so-called general system, using the standard administrative bodies as intermediate links (i.e. counties, prefectures and provinces), while the second is the specialised system, in which the intermediate links are the branch ministries and the provincial and lower-level bureaux under their 'professional guidance'.

In principle, since most enterprises were placed under provincial or lower-level supervision following the decentralisation of 1958 (Lardy, 1978; Eckstein, 1977),[5] one might expect that communication via the general system would take priority over that via the specialised system in cases of conflict. However, this is not what happens in practice: planners in Shandong Province were quite convinced that the central authorities would attach greater weight to proposals coming up through the specialised system than to provincial proposals in preparing the national plan. Despite the formal decentralisation, therefore, this means that many enterprises are subject to a form of dual subordination.

The possible contradictions between regional and ministerial forms of organisation of the planning system are especially interesting when considered in the light of Soviet experience. The Soviet Union attempted to organise the whole of its planning system on a regional basis between 1957 and 1964. All the branch ministries were abolished, and over a hundred regional economic councils (sovnarkhozy) were established in their place.

Unfortunately, it rapidly transpired that in the promotion of reasonably well balanced and efficient economic development, links between enterprises in a given branch but in different regions turned out to have much more importance than links between different branches in a given region. Accordingly, embryonic ministries soon emerged again in Moscow, and gradually assumed the co-ordinating powers of the sovnarkhozy: this situation was formally recognised soon after the fall of Khruschev, when the status quo ante was restored. Only in the materials supply system were some elements of regional organisation preserved, and these still appear to work satisfactorily. It appears from this experience that, although both regional and ministerial autarky impose serious costs on the economy, tendencies towards the former which rapidly develop in a regionally based system are much less acceptable. (See Nove, 1977, ch.3.) From this point of view, complaints from provinces in China that their suggestions are taken less seriously than ministerial proposals may well be regarded as grounds for satisfaction with the present system, rather than as grounds for reform. Indeed, given the importance China attaches to inter-provincial financial and resource transfers (as emphasised repeatedly by Lardy; see especially Lardy (1975), it would, probably,be undesirable for greater autonomy in their economic management than they already possess to be conceded to the provinces, even apart from the efficiency argument mentioned above.

Let us now return to the process of plan formulation. Just as elsewhere, the first task of planning is to analyse economic performance in the recent past and to estimate, as far as possible, the main characteristics of the current position. The State Statistical Bureau (SSB) is responsible for assembling the relevant data, and for ensuring that it is prepared properly and at the time when it is needed. Naturally, special attention has to be paid to areas where the current plan is running into difficulties (e.g. the unexpected emergence of capacity limitations or other forms of bottleneck) since the study of such situations is an essential part of formulating the next plan. In this way, plan formulation and implementation are interrelated.

The preparation of an annual plan normally starts in September or October of the year before the plan year.[6] Thus at the beginning of the formulation period (as we may call it), data is available for the whole of the preceding year and for the first three quarters of the current year. On this basis, the SSB can estimate the likely performance for the whole of the current year, and identify the most significant trends; this information is reported to the SPC. Later on, when data for the current year becomes available, some minor adjustments to the annual plan might be required, but these are readily introduced in the course of its implementation. Using the available SSB reports, the SPC works out guidelines for the plan year, which would typically include growth rates of the major economic aggregates such as national income, consumption, investment, foreign trade volume and output of certain key industries and other branches of the economy, generally broken down by province.

These guidelines (called 'control figures' in the Soviet Union) are sent to all the branch ministries and the provincial SPCs for their consideration. In a manner similar to the national level procedure, the ministries and provinces have to analyse their current situation to identify factors which could influence plan fulfilment, such as changes in the financial position of important enterprises or revisions in material consumption or labour input norms. Then in consultation with the bureaux, companies and enterprises under their supervision, they formulate draft plans for the plan year, which are submitted to the SPC.

Since these initial drafts almost certainly fail to balance when combined at national level, the SPC, BMA and other central agencies have to propose adjustments in order to achieve balance. In practice, the BMA assumes principal responsibility for eliminating the most blatant imbalances, acting under instruction from the SPC: in doing so, it takes on a task of almost unimaginable complexity which no socialist country has ever solved to its own satisfaction. The balancing techniques used in China are quite conventional, though inevitably subject to more severe operational impediments than is usual in the smaller East European countries: in particular, appropriately trained workers are less readily available, and communications are much less well developed. Nevertheless, given information on capacities to produce various products and the demands for them in the draft plans, the BMA can employ the following balancing techniques:

(1) reduce consumption of major resources, by requiring some or all users to find some way of economising;

(2)   seek substitutes for products in short
      supply;
(3)   raise production of shortage goods;
(4)   lower certain output targets if essential
      inputs cannot be supplied;
(5)   make proposals for imports and exports.

Technique (1) is the simplest in that it has no
repercussions beyond the immediate adjustments made;
on the other hand, if the initial plan is already
rather taut, it may simply lead to a plan that is
feasible on paper but impossible to implement. The
other balancing techniques all require some associated adjustment in branches other than that where the
imbalance first arose; consequently, repeated
revisions are necessary until an acceptably balanced
plan is arrived at. Of course, a perfectly balanced
plan is impossible, for as Kornai (1975) has emphasised, there are too many inter-relationships to
take into account in too little time; and in any
case, the central authorities only have a very hazy
notion about the form of many economic relationships. In the Chinese case, although the BMA only
allocates on a national basis about 193 products and
product groups,7 the process of plan balancing concentrates on about 30 of the most significant products. Thus for most products, the finally approved
plan cannot be assumed to imply overall balance;
in general though, experience in operating the
system over a number of years should ensure that
errors are relatively small, since most established
economic links only need to change fairly slowly.
     After balancing, the plan is approved by the
State Council, and then returned to the branch ministries and provinces for implementation. When a
province receives its plan, it may add further tasks
before directives are issued to regional commissions
bureaux, prefectures and municipalities, which in
turn hand down directives to the enterprises under
them. Ministries also issue instructions to their
own enterprises, via provincial bureaux where relevant. At the same time, the BMA prepares the assignment plan, indicating the needs and supplies of
various materials and products, broken down by
branch and province, so that the necessary inter-
provincial and inter-branch transfers can be calculated. At state level, the BMA also organises the
supply of materials to those major enterprises
supervised directly by the ministries, while at
lower levels, provincial bureaux allocate the main
nationally distributed materials to their own

196

enterprises, as well as to prefectures and municipalities, and so on.[8] It should be borne in mind
that many materials are simply allocated locally,
without any central intervention or supervision at
all. In addition, because of the dual subordination
mentioned earlier, many enterprises will receive
supplies of nationally distributed materials both
from the province and directly from state level
(from the BMA, or from the appropriate branch ministry), since they will be seeking to fulfil tasks
assigned by both levels: in most cases, whoever
assigns a particular task has the responsibility to
supply the necessary materials.

Let us now consider the annual plan from the
point of view of an individual state enterprise.
Each enterprise (or company) receives eight main
targets or groups of targets, which are as follows:
volume of output, quality, product mix, consumption
of raw materials and energy, costs of production,
the wages and salaries bill, profits, and the permitted amount of working capital. At one of the
organisations I consulted, the Shanghai Plastic
Products Company, there was an additional plan target relating to scientific research and innovation,
which had been imposed by a scientific department in
the relevant ministry. Another Shanghai enterprise,
the Jia Feng Textile Factory, claimed that only four
targets were considered especially important in the
sense of being checked by superior authorities and
affecting bonuses for management and workers, namely
those concerned with the volume of output, quality,
product mix, and profits. Elsewhere, it was suggested that all eight targets had to be fulfilled:
most probably, the practice is not uniform throughout China.

Except for a small number of the most important
products, enterprise output targets and material
allocations are typically expressed in terms of
rather broad product groups. For this reason, meetings between producers and users of various products
are held in order to settle precise quantities,
specifications and delivery dates in the form of
contracts. These meetings are normally held twice
a year, though some enterprises I visited reported a
higher frequency (e.g. monthly). Interestingly, for
one enterprise the fulfilment of contracts was included among its plan targets, a practice which may
well spread.

The remaining aspect of plan formulation to be
dealt with here concerns capital construction.
Since the financial side of investment is discussed

below, I only explain here how individual projects become part of the annual plan. The formal procedure has varied somewhat over time, but the present position seems to be as follows. For small projects (accounting for about half the total volume of investment), local authorities and/or the enterprises concerned make proposals to the municipal or provincial planning commission; for large projects, a joint approach would normally be made to the SPC by the appropriate branch ministry and the Provincial Planning Commission for the area where the project would be located. Detailed design work is not normally set in train until the project has been approved in principle by the SPC at some level. Needless to say, this implies that project costs are hard to estimate at the time when the approval is being sought. Apparently costs were given greater weight in project selection in the 1950s, but more recently the SPC begins by asking whether the project is 'necessary' for the economy. Since almost anything can be claimed to be necessary, especially in a rapidly growing economy in which market signals provide only a very imperfect check on project claims, such an approach is clearly open to a great deal of manipulation. Aside from the question of necessity, the SPC also examines available resources, notably construction capacity and services such as transport, electricity and water. In principle, costs should also be considered at this stage, but it was already noted above that this is a weak point in current procedures.

After approval of the project and completion of the design work, it can be included in an annual plan; if it turns out to be more expensive than expected then the normal response before the present adjustment period was simply to amend the annual plans - either by assigning more resources to the project or by accepting that its construction period would be longer than expected. No-one was held responsible when projects turned out to be so inefficient, and since enterprises themselves paid nothing for their investment they too had no particular incentive to strive for efficiency. Reasonably enough, the CCC itself favours completing projects as rapidly as possible once they have been approved, implying that at any one time investment resources should ideally be concentrated on a relatively small number of projects. However, shortages of certain construction materials, especially steel, cement and wood, delay completions, while strong pressures from enterprises, ministries and provinces lead to an excessive number of starts being approved. The result is an investment process[9] that operates much less effectively than it should, with problems strikingly similar to those often encountered in Eastern Europe (see Hare, 1981).

Plan implementation. In order to fulfil a plan, it is never sufficient merely to issue detailed instructions to the basic producing units and then await results. All plans are imperfect and have to be carried out by agents whose interests may not be wholly concordant with those of the central authorities. Accordingly, it is essential for there to be some form of monitoring of economic activity as the plan unfolds, and desirable for the economic system to permit flexible adaptation to unforseen contingencies. In the Chinese system, both of these elements are present.

As far as monitoring is concerned, the principal responsibility inevitably falls to the SSB, though to a limited but undoubtedly increasing extent the People's Bank (PB) also has a part to play. For industry, the SSB assembles daily information on the output of 25 major products (for 10 of these, data are for the whole industry, while for the other 15, only the major enterprises are covered), which is reported to the State Council the following day. And each month, national figures on the gross value of industrial output (GVIO) and on the output of about 100 major products are compiled, being reported to the State Council by the fourth of the following month. This output data is supplemented, with about a month's delay, with reports of the degree of fulfilment of the eight standard plan targets in the major industrial enterprises. In the field of capital construction, monthly reports to the State Council cover the volume of investment, the number of large and medium projects under construction, increases in productive capacity and fixed assets and progress of certain major projects. Similar, though generally much less detailed, reporting occurs in other fields too, either reflecting the lower priorities assigned to them or the lack of opportunity for effective intervention during the plan period. The latter point would apply to agriculture, for example, where the lower frequency of reporting certainly cannot be assumed to be indicative of low priority for the sector. (For more detail on these statistical practices, see SSB, 1979.)

Each enterprise is assigned to a suitable branch of the PB, where its account is maintained and where its financial transactions can therefore be monitored. Thus the PB should only permit transactions consistent with the enterprise's approved plan and should investigate failures to meet plan targets insofar as these manifest themselves in the form of poor financial performance. While this approach to the question of financial discipline is quite standard in the planned economies, it is hard to avoid the suspicion that this discipline has been rather weak in China until recently.

Nevertheless, when the central or provincial authorities realise that some enterprise is in serious difficulty and cannot fulfil its plan without help there are several possible responses. Often the appropriate response will only be determined following a visit to the enterprise by an official investigation team, charged to identify, as far as possible, the source of the problem and suggest a remedy. In some cases, the enterprise might be experiencing supply difficulties through no fault of its own: then either its plan must be reduced for a time, or higher level intervention may succeed in arranging more regular deliveries. Alternatively the enterprise might be very badly managed: that is a harder problem to pin down, and so such an enterprise might have to perform badly for some years before the management would be changed. In other cases, resources could be provided from state reserves or through extra imports to allow an enterprise to continue in production,and new markets could be sought for products that are not selling well. In general, all this type of response seems to be analogous to what in the West is called 'management by exception': for China, this basically means that enterprises doing reasonably well are left alone, while various forms of intervention are concentrated on those not doing so well. Given China's shortages of skilled personnel, this procedure is also an effective means of economising on scarce managerial skills.

Another important aspect of plan implementation arises when an enterprise is able to produce more than the planned amount of output. Above-plan output normally requires extra materials from somewhere and also has to be marketed: recent changes have made the Chinese economy substantially more flexible in its treatment of these matters than it was before about 1978. Let us first consider how an enterprise might obtain additional materials.

Before an enterprise can obtain such materials, it must have completed the tasks laid down in its

plan; it must also be able to show that there is
additional demand for some or all of its products
and that it has some spare capacity. Then the
source of additional materials depends on the nature
of the products and the source of demand. In the
case of an important product in short supply (e.g.
some types of lathe), the enterprise would apply to
higher levels for materials, relying on reserves
held by the BMA or overfulfilment of output plans at
enterprises producing the required materials. If
the additional demand comes from a state body, then
that body normally has the task of finding and supplying the necessary materials. In other cases, materials may come from outside the formal planning
system, either from market sources or from enterprises not included in the normal planning arrangements
described above: this category seems to cover a
number of enterprises producing materials that only
have a local market. Factories may also make their
own arrangements to secure materials using informal
contacts that were previously not approved but are
now recognised. For example, enterprises which
find themselves in possession of excess amounts of
some material - either due to some error in the material supply system or a change in the enterprise's
product mix - were supposed to return it to the
supply authorities in the past (but they had no incentive to do so, of course) and could not simply
sell it: now they can. Some enterprises producing
materials like steel are now permitted to retain
part of their above-plan output in order to facilitate the development of such market-type transactions. Finally, and probably most commonly, the
needed materials come from savings achieved in the
process of fulfilling the original plan tasks.

Financial Aspects of Planning

If China's planning system really bears the close
resemblance to the Soviet system that is often
claimed, then we should expect financial matters to
be relatively unimportant as compared to plan targets referring to approved quantities of inputs and
outputs. Nevertheless, an increasing emphasis on
profitability at enterprise level means that we
cannot neglect finance altogether. So in this short
section,I will comment on price formation rules
within the sphere of production (i.e. producer prices) and the treatment of enterprise profits. In
principle, credit should also be treated here, but
since its use in an economically significant sense

is so recent it is best deferred until later.

The State Bureau of Price Management (BPM) and its lower level correlates have responsibility for fixing prices in China. For pricing purposes, there are three categories of product. At national level, the BPM fixes prices for the first category: this includes the main agricultural prices, the main consumer goods prices and the prices for transport and communication services (including local transport in cities); and also the prices of industrial goods assigned by the national level of the BMA or the industrial ministries, e.g. steel, coal, petroleum and timber. At Provincial level, second category prices such as the less important means of production, the charges for minor transport activities and the fees for access to cultural, educational and medical facilities are fixed. There are also BPMs at Prefectural level with responsibility for pricing third category products (everything not in categories one and two); and enterprises themselves often participate in price formation by submitting pricing proposals based on guidelines from the appropriate level of the BPM. The State level fixes prices relevant to about 70% of transactions, leaving about 30% to local levels.

In principle, whenever there are changes in production costs of any good, its price should be changed, since the usual rule is to set a price equal to costs of production (material costs, labour costs, depreciation of fixed capital, taxes) plus a mark-up, the latter varying from branch to branch.10 For many established and widely used products, however, price changes appear to be extremely infrequent. In practice, therefore, the formal rules probably have greatest influence in determining the prices of new products. Enterprises cannot sell such a product until a price has been approved. They submit detailed cost data plus a suggested price to the appropriate level of the BPM; the price office then compares the product with close substitutes to check that the proposed price is reasonable (in this way, demand considerations enter into the analysis, so that prices are not merely cost-plus), and query the cost estimates before approving a price. Then two cases may arise.

For a completely new product, costs are largely a matter for speculation, and in such cases a temporary price would be set in the first instance, this often depending to a considerable extent on the relative bargaining skills of the price office and the enterprise concerned. Later on (and this may be anything from a few months to several years) a permanent price would be determined on the basis of the relatively firm cost information then available. Apparently, during the mid-1970s price control became rather lax because price office staff were sometimes unwilling to accept responsibility for any errors they made. In these circumstances, some enterprises were able to make small product changes and use these as a pretext for proposing relatively large price increases to the relevant BPM. It is hard to estimate the extent and significance of this practice.

It should be emphasised that for any given product only one price should be established in the region supervised by the BPM office responsible for fixing the price. Thus prices fixed by the national BPM are valid nationwide, these prices being set on an ex-factory basis, with customers paying transport costs plus various fees imposed by the BMA and other supplying agencies.

Turning to the experience of the enterprises I visited, four of the six claimed that their prices were fixed by the state for long periods: to support this, only one product of one of these four had been revised since 1972. Of the other two, the Beijing Leather Products Factory had to consult the Municipal BPM about price changes: enterprise proposals based on costs plus a 15% margin were normally approved. In the Shanghai Plastic Products Company, factories reported costs for new products to the Company which then discussed pricing with the Municipal commerce department: agreed prices then had to be reported to the Municipal BPM. Typically, products to be sold to the agricultural sector were permitted a mark-up below 5%, those for industry about 10%, and products destined for immediate purchase by consumers about 15-20%.

Within the framework of a system of planned economic management, the price system is considered to play a number of distinct roles, some of which may be strengthened in reforms (see next section). Above all, price policy has the aim of stimulating enterprise production in general, and encouraging cost reduction. It can also serve to encourage proportional economic development, in particular by regulating the balance between agriculture and industry (e.g. in 1979 the price paid for agricultural products rose by 22% on average), and by stimulating each region to develop its own specialisms. At a more microeconomic level, the price mechanism may be used to encourage higher output of goods in short

supply and to discourage production of those in surplus: this is important, for example, in the production of medicines where there are literally thousands of distinct products, far too many to be listed separately in any central plan. Yet until price
policy began to be used more actively in this sphere
there were already three to five years' stocks of
certain medicines and severe shortages of others:
revised prices are starting to stimulate changes in
the pattern of output.

Using prices in this way may seem strange in a
country committed to planned economic development,
but in my view the complexity of the economy makes
such a practice unavoidable. It is important to
appreciate, however, that prices can only fulfil
their essential functions if enterprises themselves
have some incentive to respond to the resulting
price signals. To some extent, these incentives are
provided by the treatment of profits at enterprise
level, as we explain below.

It is not easy to gain a clear picture about
enterprise-level financial arrangements in China,
since the situation is undergoing rapid change involving several experimental schemes. Until 1978,
most enterprises kept almost none of their profits,
very little of their depreciation allowances (which
were in any case too low), and were only just beginning once again to pay bonuses to managers and workforce dependent on plan fulfilment. In addition, as
already mentioned, virtually all enterprises paid
sales tax based on the value of their output, the
effective rate varying considerably from product to
product. Thus, almost the entire surplus generated
by production was siphoned off to higher levels for
redistribution in accordance with state plans.
This practice no doubt still has its defenders, but
it is hardly conducive to the exercise of that initiative and independence in enterprise decisions
which is so crucial to successful economic development.

Under the new arrangements, enterprises are
increasingly being allowed to retain a portion of
their profits in order to form three enterprise
funds: these are the bonus fund, to finance the
payment of bonuses to management and workers; the
social welfare fund which finances such facilities
as workers' housing, some schools, and medical services; and the development fund providing resources
for enterprise investments. In most cases, 50% of
the enterprise's depreciation allowances is now
added to the development fund, and in certain

branches and/or localities the proportion is even higher. Thus in Shanghai, the Jia Feng Textile Factory reported that from 1980, it could retain 70% of its depreciation fund, this being the normal rate for the textile industry in Shanghai. In the case of the Shanghai Plastic Products Company, the individual factories keep 50% of their depreciation funds in respect of machinery and equipment, the Company keeps 20% and the remaining 30% is remitted to the Shanghai Handicrafts Bureau, which happens to be the relevant superior authority. In respect of buildings, the factories keep 100% of their depreciation funds. Also, in some smaller enterprises that have been starved of new investment for many years, 100% of the depreciation fund can sometimes be kept. These figures indicate an important shift in the financial position of many enterprises, though one should bear in mind that at present, the permitted depreciation rates are usually very low. The rates used to be 5% or less for most types of asset, though now some of the rates have been raised to 7% (possibly even higher in some branches).

The bonus fund usually amounts to about 12% of the enterprise's wages and salary bill, its precise size being contingent on fulfilment of the eight key plan targets, or in some cases a subset of these; thus the No.2 Cotton Mill, Jinan, had to fulfil the plans for output volume, quality and variety, and fulfil all contracts before bonuses could be paid. 50% of the bonus paid at the Jia Feng Textile Factory depended on meeting the quality target, the rest depending on the profit, output and output mix targets, while profit was the main bonus-forming indicator at the Plastics Company (along with quality, output and contracts). At the Jinan Petrochemicals Factory, 80% of any cost savings could also be added to the bonus fund. Bonuses paid to managers seem to be less than those paid to workers under the present system.

Despite the variety of rules that are operating now, it is at least clear that enterprises do have an interest in raising their profitability levels in order to accumulate larger enterprise funds. Some of the retention ratios may seem to be extraordinarily low, but before drawing such a conclusion one has to recall that in some branches of Chinese industry and in certain areas (e.g. light industry in Shanghai), profitability levels are extremely high. Since, as already observed, prices are adjusted very infrequently, and costs can be expected to fall as workers gain experience (learning by doing), with wage costs being a small fraction of costs for many individual enterprises, such high profits are not too surprising: consequently, even low retention ratios can generate substantial enterprise funds.

The Beginnings of Economic Reforms

In this section I begin by outlining some of the shortcomings of China's system of economic planning that have been identified by those currently seeking to introduce reforms: this account can be quite brief, since virtually all the problems have exact counterparts in the Eastern European experience for which there is already a voluminous literature. Some of China's initial moves towards economic reform are then discussed, including both measures associated with the present period of adjustment and consolidation and longer term but still experimental measures granting greater autonomy to enterprises.

Almost all the economists that one can speak to in China are in agreement about one fundamental point, namely that the economy is over-centralised and has an excessively complex bureaucracy to manage it. The division of rights, responsibilities and powers between various levels of the system is frequently unclear, and planning in practice tends to lack flexibility. One economically harmful consequence of this has been to encourage tendencies towards ministerial and enterprise autarky.

In both cases the result is a low level of specialisation of production between different production units, and poor co-operation between different branches and provinces. For example, at ministerial level, funds allocated to a particular ministry can normally only be used to develop products falling within the production profile of that branch. By-products may therefore be used very badly, if at all. Thus when funds are assigned to the coal ministry for survey work, anything other than coal that might be discovered is quite likely to be ignored. Similarly, the electricity supply industry concentrates attention on its main responsibility, generating electricity; dealing with the by-products of burning coal, that would be suitable for making building materials, are someone else's responsibility. It seems, also, that enterprises in the steel industry are sometimes only interested in producing enough of certain types of steel to meet the needs of other enterprises in their own ministry. Lastly, and to me very surprisingly, many ministries operate their own car factories to provide their own transport requirements, though it is hard to see how such production can be remotely efficient. At enterprise level, the situation has not been any better as indicated in some examples mentioned later.

The present disenchantment with over-centralisation has generated extensive debate about the appropriate division between administrative and economic approaches to economic management. The issues raised partly concern the choice of instruments to be employed in managing production, particularly the choice between issuing instructions and relying on market-type signals (price policy, tax and subsidy policy, credit policy, and so on) to elicit the desired behaviour. And partly, there is the question about autonomy for lower-level units in the system. Thus at present, most companies in the hierarchy are administrative units, while the enterprises that they supervise are at least notionally on khozraschet. Nevertheless, the companies generally have the right to redistribute resources (including both capital equipment and financial resources) between the enterprises under their control, while not themselves having clear financial/economic incentives to pursue efficiency and profitability. There are two obvious solutions to this kind of conflict: either turn the company into an economically independent unit with enterprise status (the original enterprises then become merely operating divisions), or limit the powers of the company to intervene in enterprise management in what must often appear to be a fairly arbitrary manner. As indicated below, Shanghai appears to be adopting the former of these solutions.

Capital construction has perhaps been the major source of economic problems in recent years. Persistent over-investment, associated with an excessive number of projects underway at any time, very long construction periods and totally inadequate control over project costs, have been the main symptoms of these problems. Pressures from enterprises (for whom investment is generally costless) and their supervising ministries for new investment have proved to be irresistible in the past, but the resulting levels of investment have exceeded the economy's absorptive capacity. The failure to provide enough resources for the construction materials industry has led to shortages of several important materials, though again this should only be regarded as another symptom of the wider problem. In the short run, some of these difficulties should be mitigated by the present adjustment period policies of reducing the volume of investment, though I doubt these can remain effective for long in the absence of significant institutional reforms.

The consequence of over-investment in China, combined with some mis-allocation between sectors (notably an overemphasis on heavy industry), was a tendency for returns to investment to be very poor. Capital-output ratios were frequently far too high and it is clear that substantial investment resources were quite simply wasted. An important indicator of the extent of this inefficiency is the fact that for most Chinese working people, living standards have only improved very slowly since the mid-1950s (e.g. see ch.8 by Bruce Reynolds, in Howe (1981)). Thus it is the desire to accelerate the growth in living standards which lies behind recent changes in the pattern of investment in favour of light industry and agriculture. But much remains to be done to improve the efficiency of individual investments.

Finally, the price system needs a mention in this list of shortcomings. Since enterprises inevitably use the prevailing prices as guides to some of their decisions, though perhaps only in limited fields, defects in the price system are bound to lead to some inefficiencies in resource allocation: either it will not be 'profitable' to produce certain products, so that high-level intervention will be needed to get them produced; or unsuitable materials might be used if relative prices fail to reflect real relative costs. Both of these cases are commonplace in China. From the planners' point of view, it is always highly convenient for prices to be very stable so that plans and outcomes are readily comparable; but that tends to produce a reluctance to revise prices even when costs of production change considerably. Also, even when prices are adjusted, they still contain no allowance for the costs of using fixed capital equipment - what are called, in Eastern Europe, capital charges - so that the prices of relatively capital intensive branches of industry tend to be too low, and the incentive for any enterprise to use capital efficiently must be somewhat weak. It seems, however, that although the advantages of a degree of price flexibility, and the proper accounting of capital costs, are recognised, a general price reform is considered to be a very difficult and complex exercise. Such reform is unlikely to be seen until several other reforms, to be mentioned below, have had a chance to take effect.

China's System of Industrial Economic Planning

Before examining reforms in general, let us survey the diverse views on the subject expressed by the enterprises I visited, presumably reflecting the very different branch/regional positions of the enterprises concerned.

1.   Beijing Leather Products Factory

This factory has changed its output mix during the present adjustment period, so that it now specialises much more than before on shoes and footballs. Part of its production has been transferred to other enterprises in Beijing, but some low technology production has been transferred to neighbouring communes. The management appears to give strong support to this kind of specialisation.

2.   No 2 Cotton Mill, Jinan

Here the managers would simply like more independent authority and simpler procedures when dealing with higher agencies.

3.   Diesel Engine Factory, Jinan

The 1980 plan was based on a study of market demand; the proposed output target was merely sent up to the ministry for approval. However, there was no corresponding change in the materials supply arrangements. As far as reform is concerned, managers were unhappy about the present self-sufficient organisation of the factory, that even included its own casting section. Proposals have now been sent to the Petroleum Ministry suggesting that the foundry should be hived off and reconstituted as a separate enterprise, perhaps also incorporating the foundry divisions of other local enterprises. Similarly, some spare parts manufacture could be transferred elsewhere. The general view here seemed to be that greater specialisation would result in higher efficiency, as managers are enabled to concentrate attention on a narrower product range.

4.   Jinan Petrochemicals Factory

The Municipality had selected this enterprise to become an experimental enterprise, but it was not keen to participate in the scheme

straightaway, apparently because it was currently engaged in completing a major construction project: the enterprise was unwilling to
undergo management changes at the same time.
Also, the managers were unhappy about the
present practice of selecting just a few enterprises in each area to be experimental while
most others continued to operate the old system.
Although they basically approved of some move
towards a form of self-management, they believed that a mixed management system would result in great confusion.

5.   Jia Feng Textile Factory

This enterprise has had experimental status
since 1979, but it would welcome still more
independence as well as opportunities for co-
operation with other enterprises, of the kind
now becoming possible. It also favours more
competition.

6.   Shanghai Plastic Products Company

On an experimental basis, the No 1 enterprise
under this company is to be given more independence, with the right to retain 20% of its
above-plan profits; the company will no longer
be able to redistribute these profits to other
enterprises under it. Within two or three
years, the company may well shift from being
an administrative unit to being an enterprise
in its own right; this would enable the company to use retained profits without consulting
higher bodies. It might also be able to economise on administrative staff and simplify some
of its procedures. Finally, it would like to
be able to handle its own marketing arrangements to lower costs and improve flexibility.

In the face of such diverse views and experiences, it is clearly not going to be easy to design
reforms that will please everyone; but let us now
consider the steps that have been taken so far.
Within a planning framework broadly similar to the
present one there is room for quite a number of lesser reforms. During the present adjustment period,
several changes are being made to help mitigate some
of the harmful effects of over-centralisation mentioned above. Most parts of the country are reorganising the production profiles of their enter-

prises in order to develop specialisation and
improve co-ordination. According to experience up
to the middle of 1979, the re-organisations were already making possible much higher levels of output.
A particularly striking case of this is provided by
the merger of 47 Shanghai television set plants into
a single company which led to a 96% increase in output in 1978 and was expected to yield a further 70%
increase in 1979. The mergers and formation of
companies are also improving the quality of output,
reducing production costs and lowering the consumption of raw materials in many cases (SWB, 15th
August 1979:A/1-3).   The First Ministry of Machine
Building is reorganising its own key enterprises
along similar lines, throughout the whole country.
The Ministry has laid down twelve requirements for
improving management and economic performance in its
enterprises, and by the end of 1979, more than half
of the 655 key enterprises were able to meet the
requirements (SWB, 20th February 1980:A/2-3).
Product quality was much improved, and while in 1976,
67 of the enterprises recorded deficits, this was
only the case for 4 of them in 1979. A related aspect of adjustment is that by early 1980, about
2000 inefficient enterprises had been closed down,
converted to other lines of production, or merged
with others (SWB, 23rd January 1980:A/1-2).
    Despite these gains re-organisation is not
without its problems. Apart from the natural resistance to any change in the structure of industrial
management the new arrangements require a number of
more concrete issues to be resolved. Firstly, there
is the question of subordination. If the factories
being combined are initially supervised by different
levels of the administrative hierarchy, then some
transfers of control are required before a company
can be formed. Secondly difficulties have arisen
with spare parts production: sometimes this has
been transferred to smaller factories either inside
or outside the proposed company, with some increase
in production costs resulting. If the problem is
not handled properly, other enterprises may be stim-
ulated to resume production of spare parts, contrary
to the planned specialisation. Thirdly, the nature
and rights of the new companies are still unclear.
The preferred solution is for them to assume the
status of state enterprises in their own right,
rather than remain as administrative units; but
progress so far is slow.
    Another field in which re-organisation is pro-
ceeding apace is that of capital construction. The

general aims are to reduce the overall share of capital accumulation in the national product, which
apparently reached the exceptionally high ratio of
36.6% in 1978 (Tian, 1980:18);   and to restructure
investment to give greater weight to light industry.
This is important because, according to a fascinat-
ing study by Lu (1980), over the period 1952-78 sur-
pluses generated by light industry provided the resources to finance 97% of China's investments in industrial capital construction. Yet over the period
1966-78, heavy industry received 55.5% and light industry 5.15% of the country's total capital investments. At the same time, the prevailing price structure means that investments in parts of light industry can actually recoup their initial costs within two years, whereas the corresponding figure for
much of heavy industry (e.g. iron and steel) is
about 16½ years. In the light of these figures, it
is not hard to understand the present restructuring.
     The investment effort is now being concentrated
on a smaller number of projects, in order to reduce
construction periods. As a result, 330 large or
medium sized capital construction projects were cancelled or postponed in 1980 (SWB, 23rd January 1980)
and the number started in 1979 was only 8.7% of the
number under construction ('Economic readjustment',
1980:19).   Nevertheless, there are still some problems of over-investment involving duplication of
capacity, in cases where individual projects may be
quite small. For example, it seems that in early
1979 there were already about 60 units in Shanghai
producing steel window frames, providing capacity
well in excess of demand; despite this, 11 more
units set up steel window workshops in the first
half of 1979 (SWB, 24th October 1979:A/7-8).
     The final new policy of the adjustment period
is the introduction of very limited price flexibility. Since the cutbacks in investment affect most
severely the demand for products of the First
Ministry of Machine Building, it is natural that
this reform should be introduced there. Certain of
the ministry's products now only have centrally
fixed upper limits to their prices, with individual
enterprises free to lower price by up to 20% in
order to attract more customers (SWB, 23rd January
1980:A/4-5).
     With a view to extending enterprise autonomy in
certain areas, and also to stimulate better economic
performance by enterprises, many enterprises are now
operating under a variety of so-called experimental
schemes. In essence all these arrangements confer

on the enterprise concerned the right to retain a
share of profits in order to form the three enterprise funds referred to earlier; thus these funds
no longer depend on instructions and permits from
higher bodies, but only on the performance of the
individual enterprise. Moreover, the significant
expansion of the development funds under all schemes
gives the enterprises involved far greater influence
over investment decisions than was possible previously.[11] In 1979, about 3300 enterprises took part
in one or other experimental management systems
('Economic readjustment', 1980:19), but by June 1980
this number had risen to 6600 (Beijing Review,
August 18th 1980:3), accounting for about 16% of the
total number of state-owned industrial enterprises.
This relatively small fraction of China's industrial
enterprises, however, accounted for around 60% of
the value of output and 70% of the profits in industry. Thus what began as a fairly small scale experiment in Sichuan Province is rapidly being extended
to the whole country, and the attribute 'experimental' is becoming less and less appropriate.

Indeed, the State Council itself sought to introduce some clarity into a somewhat confused situation by issuing, in July 1979, five policy documents
concerning the restructuring of enterprise administrative systems, following wide-ranging consulta-
tions. These regulations cover the following topics:
some regulations to expand the state-run industrial
enterprises' administrative authority; regulations
on the percentage of profits allowed to be retained
by the state-run enterprises; tentative regulation
on raising the depreciation rate of the state-run
enterprises' fixed assets and improving the methods
of spending the depreciation charge; tentative regulations on levying taxes on fixed assets of the
state-run industrial enterprises; and tentative regulations on extending full credit to the circulating
fund of the state-run industrial enterprises. The
State Economic Commission and the Ministry of
Finance have worked out detailed regulations to put
these measures into effect (SWB, 8th August 1979:
A/3-4), but full implementation is bound to take
several years.

The various experimental schemes that have been
introduced have been analysed by Xiang and Du (1980).
The State Council scheme (based on the regulations
just mentioned) permits participating enterprises to
retain a fraction of their total profits, this fraction remaining constant for a three year period. As
a result, the enterprise welfare, bonus and develop-

213

ment funds, instead of being determined by higher
authorities and then treated as part of enterprise
costs, are converted to fractions of profits. A
second scheme is that approved in Sichuan in
February 1979. This permits enterprises to retain a
share of planned profits (s_1), plus a share of
above-plan profits (s_2); it was envisaged that s_2
would be much larger than s_1, the precise numbers
depending on the branch concerned. On fulfilling
its plan, an enterprise could keep 5% of planned
profits for the enterprise development fund. Contributions to other funds would depend on profits as
indicated in the above formula, but would continue
to be treated as part of enterprise costs. In practice, Sichuan did not issue profits targets in 1979,
so actual profits in 1978 were taken as the basis
for applying the retention rules. Yet a third
arrangement has been adopted in Shanghai's metallurgical industry, with enterprises being permitted to
retain a share of the increase in profits achieved
over a specified base period. 1978 is being taken
as the base for the next five years, and enterprises (together with the metallurgical industry
bureau) can now keep 40% of increased profits, the
rest being remitted to higher levels, as before. Of
the retained profits, 70% is to be used for enterprise development funds, 15% for welfare funds and
15% for the payment of bonuses. All enterprise
funds will now be financed from profits, and not
from costs or state appropriations. There are a few
other schemes that do not require a detailed discussion here; for example, some Beijing enterprises
adopted an arrangement whereby they would keep a
share of total profits plus a share of increased
profit, while their supervising bureaux would keep a
share of above-plan profit.

Some early reports have suggested that economic
performance of these experimental enterprises has
improved rapidly, but it seems far too soon to
attempt a proper evaluation.[12] Moreover, if experience in the Soviet Union tells us anything, it is
that most economic experiments can appear successful, at least initially. For one thing, the enterprises that participate are usually those that were
already relatively well-run and successful. Consequently, their performance can tell us very little
about the likely effectiveness of the same measures
when extended to the whole economy. Nevertheless,
the experiments are of interest in indicating the
current direction of thinking about China's economic
management.

By increasing the size of enterprise development funds (both through retained profits and by
allowing enterprises to keep 50% of their depreciation allowances), the experiments give enterprises
increasing power over investment decisions, though
notionally only to the extent of facilitating simple
rather than expanded reproduction.[13] An increasing
number of enterprises is also eligible to receive
investment credits from the People's Bank, or from
the People's Bank for Construction, and these credits do allow production to be expanded. The
People's Bank supervises the day-to-day financial
operations of enterprises, but since 1979 has also
been able to provide short or medium term loans (up
to three years) for equipment and machinery (e.g. in
Shanghai's textiles industry) to aid renovation.
The Bank for Construction can provide finance for
longer terms and for larger projects than the
People's Bank, but the general rules and regulations
for granting credit are quite similar in the two
banks.
  The approach to economic reform being pursued
in the last two or three years in China involves a
number of elements, of which the above enterprise
experiments constitute just one; other important
elements include the following:

  (1) more cautious planning, associated with
       less centralised material allocation;
  (2) some use of competition and markets;
  (3) a tendency to restrict state-level
       responsibility to macroeconomic and
       investment-related issues, while extend-
       ing enterprise independence;
  (4) changing procedures for setting up new
       enterprises, and for dealing with un-
       successful ones.[14]

  To some extent, the increased caution in planning is covered by the above comments on China's
efforts to reduce the rate of capital accumulation.
But caution also entails making greater efforts to
make the plan for each production unit realistic, in
the sense that under normal conditions it should be
capable of fulfilment. This is really a precondition for reducing the degree of centralisation in
the material allocation process. At present, the
procedures for allocating materials operate very
slowly and inefficiently, but if the set of commodities for which demand falls somewhat short of the
potential supply can be extended, central allocation

215

could be abandoned in these areas.

Thus in Shanghai, for example, it might be possible to reduce central procedures to as few as 70 key materials, and the number of enterprises needing to apply to the BMA could be drastically reduced. If only 5% of factories had to apply to the BMA for their materials, this would account for about 80% of the main materials and produce most of the major products. Smaller enterprises could then obtain their materials in the market, and avoid complex administrative procedures altogether; clearly, that would entail accepting a greater role for the market. A factor often inhibiting the work of the BMA is the high levels of enterprise stocks of various materials, which can be hard to reallocate. In Shanghai, about 80% of material stocks are held by enterprises, and only about 20% by the BMA, so limiting the latter's ability to respond rapidly to meet new demands. A possible solution would be to reduce enterprises' permitted working capital allocations, but even better would be a diminution of the shortage conditions that stimulate excessive stock holding in the first place. Some enterprises are now free to sell excess stocks on the market, whereas until very recently this was prohibited: this change should help to eliminate some of the present imbalances.

Aside from improving material supplies, a more cautious approach to planning seems likely to be associated with stricter observance of the numerous rules and regulations concerning the operation of the planning system, that fell into abeyance during the mid-1970s. In some cases this will confer greater autonomy on enterprises by clarifying their rights and powers once more, and so inhibiting arbitrary and unlawful interventions by higher authorities. But the major effect should be the opposite of this: enterprises will no longer find it easy to get approval for unjustified price increases or hopelessly inefficient investment projects. To an important extent, therefore, following the rules amounts to a degree of recentralisation of economic management from the enterprises' point of view, only tempered by the fact that higher-level agencies should also be bound to follow their own rules as well.

It is now widely asserted that competition is essential in order to stimulate efficient production, even in a socialist economy. Precisely what is meant by competition, and how it should be exercised, are however matters for vigorous debate. Enter-

prises that have fulfilled the tasks set out in the
state plan are now increasingly free to offer other
products on the market, though the prices have to be
approved in the usual way. Such a manifestation of
competition has already given rise to problems.
Thus many enterprises have moved into the production
of electric fans and refrigerators, with the result
that positions of shortage have rapidly been transformed into excess supply. The problem has to be
seen as a typical effect of market adjustment in
circumstances where each enterprise's decision to
provide additional capacity has to be taken in the
face of highly imperfect information about their
competitors' decisions. Despite its practical importance, this problem has only received adequate attention in the Western literature from a very small
number of authors (see Loasby, 1976; and Richardson,
1960). Essentially, while competition can facilitate more flexible economic adjustments, it can also
give rise to new forms of imbalance or disequilibrium; for this reason I would expect its extension
in China's economic management to remain fairly
modest.

There is some suggestion that the higher levels
of the planning hierarchy should confine themselves
to macro-economic management and the regulation of
major investment decisions , although such an extreme position is unlikely to move beyond academic
debate into actual practice. To an increasing
extent, enterprises are now permitted to make their
own marketing arrangements in respect of above-plan
output (this does not apply to major, centrally
allocated commodities such as cotton cloth, of
course), and can also arrange their own material
supplies if the official agencies are unable to
help. A variety of co-operation arrangements between enterprises in different areas or of different
types is being encouraged; and enterprises can now
choose to offer products on the market that may not
even fall within the production profile of their
branch, provided that they have first fulfilled the
state plan and still have some spare capacity.
Moreover, there are many cases where the plan itself
depends on orders received from customers, so that
the formal plan does little more than ratify the
prevailing market signals.

All these possibilities serve to strengthen the
horizontal, market-type links in the economy at the
expense of the vertical links that predominate in
the traditional planning hierarchy, though it is
important to emphasise that so far the degree of

change has not been great. Nevertheless, the new
possibilities for market-type transactions are naturally expanding the role of economic contracts in
regulating exchanges between enterprises. As mentioned earlier, the fulfilment of such contracts is
sometimes added to the list of plan targets now, and
they are becoming increasingly relevant in connection with credit regulation, to which we now turn.
    Enterprise autonomy can only become effective
if enterprises are able to obtain the resources to
carry out at least some of their own decisions.
This point would be completely trivial and obvious,
were it not for the Eastern European experience indicating that talk about autonomy is rarely translated into the release of real resources by the
central planners. In the Chinese case, some reforms
in the credit system are giving enterprises greater
access to financial resources to implement small and
medium investment projects. Even when credits are
granted, however, the enterprise concerned must
apply to higher bodies for the required physical
equipment (and possibly construction), and one won-
ders whether in practice enterprise demand will be
accorded very high priority. At present, with state
investment being held back as a matter of policy,
the resources should be available to meet relatively
modest additional demands from enterprises.
    Early in 1980, 2000 million yuan in loans was
made available by the State Council, to be allocated
by the People's Bank for developments in light industry and textiles; this has given rise to about
2000 projects some of which were already producing
output by the end of 1980 (NCNA 21 Aug: 3) . The
success of this scheme should lead to its repetition
in future years. As far as possible, the People's
Bank seeks to allocate this and other funds to individual projects on the basis of their profitability.
Branches of the bank now have stronger incentives to
operate in this way because they are increasingly
being transferred to khozraschet, so that each
branch becomes an independent accounting unit. One
aspect of this is that any branch that secures or
attracts more deposits can offer more loans to
enterprises. Previously, credit would have to be
granted to an enterprise proposing to produce something specified in the state plan, but this condition is no longer sufficient. Instead, enterprises
wanting credit must show that they have a contract
or contracts to sell the product, in other words it
must be demonstrated to the bank that the proposed
output can actually be sold. Not only that, but

they must also demonstrate the ability to earn enough extra profits to repay the credit in the short period normally permitted (1-3 years). If poor pricing policy makes losses or low profits more or less inevitable, the bank will only grant a credit if the local or higher-level planning authority is prepared to give a subsidy to the enterprise concerned to improve its credit-worthiness. Should an enterprise be unable to repay a loan on time, then higher interest charges would be imposed and the enterprise would experience great difficulty in obtaining credit in the future. All these strict financial principles have frequently been enunciated in Eastern Europe, but the practice has tended to accord greater weight to the need for more output per se than to the observance of financial discipline; it will therefore be interesting to see how the Chinese practice compares with this.[15]

If the financial position of some enterprises becomes (or remains) very weak, then some form of re-organisation is needed. If the management is bad and the products are adequately supplied by other enterprises, then production may be halted altogether, and the workers transferred elsewhere - a form of socialist bankruptcy. Alternatively, as noted earlier, the enterprise may turn to the production of other goods or combine with other enterprises. This kind of adjustment is being pushed very forcefully during the present consolidation period. It is not clear as yet whether any changes are taking place to facilitate the start-up of new enterprises. The normal procedure is that the branch ministry concerned (or one of the lower level-bureaux under it) has to approve the establishment of any new enterprise while the ministry of finance provides the initial funds. Subsequently, the bureau supervises the production activities of the enterprise, while the local branch of the People's Bank supervises its financial operations. But this procedure is rather cumbersome, and makes it very difficult to establish new small firms in the state sector. For collectively owned units the procedures are apparently simpler, but such enterprises often fall outside the normal framework of planning regulations as these operate in the state sector. Thus although the need to encourage the formation of new producing units is widely discussed, any significant change might be seen as weakening the control of the central planners over the pattern of economic development.

Conclusions

What do all·these preliminary and distinctly tentative reforms amount to? Can the changes mentioned
above, if implemented throughout the whole economy,
lead to a fundamental transformation of China's
planning system? My own suspicion is that these
reforms will certainly improve the flexibility of
the existing system, but I doubt whether they can be
regarded as a fundamental change. Although it is
clear that enterprises will have more autonomy, this
will be autonomy within quite narrow limits, constrained by the vertical relationships of the traditional planning system that show no signs of breaking
down. Quite the contrary; there are signs that the
reassertion of formal rules and regulations will
effectively strengthen some elements of these relationships. So far, the reforms are more like attempts to improve the efficiency of the existing structure of planning, and are similar to corresponding
measures introduced in much of Eastern Europe, as I
have remarked from time to time. I see no reason to
regard China's reforms as a victory for market
socialism; they are instead a recognition that central planning has its limitations, while continuing
to be the main plank in China's economic management
system.
     The reforms involve some increase in enterprise
autonomy, including a limited role for market-type
transactions, with no change in the institutional
structure above enterprise level other than the
transfer of some companies to enterprise status. At
the same time, it seems that many formal procedures
and regulations that fell into abeyance during the
1970s are now being revived (e.g. the procedures for
approving investment projects, or for determining
producer prices), so that in some respects enterprises will find their activities more tightly controlled than in the recent past. On balance, there
is a definite gain in autonomy for efficiently
operating and hence profitable enterprises (actually the correspondence between efficiency and profitability is far from perfect because of defects in
the price system; but even allowing for these defects, any increase in profit must normally be associated with an increase in efficiency, a point that
may account for the form of some of the profit retention rules in experimental enterprises). For
loss-making enterprises and those not fulfilling
their plans, supervision by higher bodies will not
have changed appreciably as yet.

My reasons for expecting quite cautious reforms have to do with the strong vested interests in the existing institutional structure (the lack of serious discussion about possible institutional reforms is merely symptomatic), shortages of personnel capable of organising and putting into effect a major reform, and the ability to solve, at least temporarily, many of the problems referred to in section three within the framework of the present planning system.

As far as vested interests are concerned, one can expect that staff in most bureaux, Ministries and state commissions would be opposed to reforms that might threaten their jobs. And although it is not hard to find entrepreneurially minded enterprise managers, I would also expect many managers at least to feel nervous about thorough-going reforms that might oblige them to study markets more assiduously and respond to their signals, rather than continue the easier life of fulfilling plan targets. Similarly, while some workers would undoubtedly benefit from the higher earning opportunities made possible by reform, many others might feel threatened or might resent their lack of success in the market. Consequently, it is far from obvious that far-reaching reforms could secure the wide support needed for successful implementation. Moreover, after nearly thirty years of operating the present system (the first five year-plan began in 1953), many people will have become familiar with its operating procedures, largely based on vertical relationships, and will not have experienced any other type of system. Because of this, the sheer inertia of large established organisations is bound to inhibit or slow down change. And the paucity of people in China with any knowledge or experience of other systems of economic management can only make such change even harder to bring about.

Despite these factors which may well slow down the pace of reform in the short run, there are some other reforms that I consider desirable, and which might even be feasible in the not too distant future.[16] For example, as suggested in the previous section, there is room for much improvement in the procedures for setting up new production units, especially where new types of product do not fit very well into the existing branch structure or where the existing structure proves to be unresponsive to new demands.[17] At present, the main source of initiative for the formation of new units rests with the branch authorities, but I would envisage a more flexible pattern, perhaps allowing the banks to set up holding companies of some kind, to supervise a group of new firms of which many could be producing a range of products that straddled the traditional and rather rigid ministerial boundaries. Such a proposal is certainly not new, since it has been put forward in some of the Hungarian debates on economic management (notably by Tardos), though it has not been implemented in any socialist country. In the short term, this sort of reform would make almost no appreciable difference to economic performance, but over the longer term it could turn out to be an important means of stimulating innovations.

Secondly, a reform of producer prices is long overdue. At present, prices bear very little relationship to costs, with the result that enterprise tax rates have to be strongly differentiated from branch to branch in order to ensure that branches with differing ratios between prices and costs are not permitted to retain disproportionate amounts of their profit. But if, as seems likely, market signals are to play a somewhat greater part in guiding the allocation of resources in China, then it is more important than in the past that these signals provide sensible information about relative costs in the economy. A price reform that ensured this would also permit substantial simplification and unification of the rules for enterprise taxation, and would eliminate much of the special pleading to which present arrangements must give rise.

Thirdly, there is the question of changing the institutional structure above enterprise level. It is hard to make definite suggestions here, other than the familiar observation that the existing organisational boundaries - whether in the province, prefecture, county hierarchy or in the one of ministry, bureau and enterprise can be justified much more readily for their administrative convenience than for their economic rationality. In particular, existing arrangements certainly do not facilitate the most efficient development of economic relationships and transactions over provincial or ministerial boundaries. It is important to remember that the present organisational framework was set up in the early 1950s, and presumably, therefore, it corresponded reasonably well to what were seen as the key economic relationships at that time. But after thirty years of development, it would be most surprising if the same organisational structure above enterprise level were still appropriate for the economy.

It will be interesting to see whether these issues attract the serious attention of Chinese economists in the near future, or whether they will confine themselves to studying and analysing the reforms now underway. As emphasised at the beginning of this chapter, much will depend on developments in the political sphere. The present Chinese leadership, under Central Committee Chairman Hu Yaobang and Premier Zhao Ziyang ,appear to be united in their determination to pursue the path of modest reform mapped out above. But they will need substantial support and co-operation from the state bureaucracy if reforms are to succeed, and their ability to elicit such support has only just begun to be tested.

7

ENTERPRISE MANAGEMENT – MOVES TOWARDS DEMOCRACY ?

Martin Lockett

Most of the discussion of Chinese economic reforms has been in terms of their impact on relations between enterprises themselves, and in terms of fairly narrowly defined criteria of economic performance. This chapter looks at a different aspect of the process of reform which has been taking place in China since 1978, that of enterprise management. In particular it analyses the reforms in terms of their democratic content; in other words, to what extent have economic reforms such as increased enterprise autonomy been associated with a process of democratisation of decision-making within enterprises? After an initial section which discusses in relatively abstract terms the implications of economic reforms for enterprise management, the main part of the chapter discusses the changes which have taken

* I am grateful for the assistance of the British Academy and SSRC in the UK, as well as the Chinese Academy of Social Sciences, in arranging a visit in September 1981 as part of their exchange agreement including myself, Craig Littler and Peter Abell. This included research in Beijing, Chengdu, Chongqing and Shanghai. Detailed arrangements were made by the Institute of Industrial Economics in Beijing, the Sichuan Academy of Social Sciences Institute of Economics, Chongqing Municipality Foreign Affairs Bureau, and the Shanghai Academy of Social Sciences Institute of Sectoral Economics, whose assistance was invaluable. Outside this formal research period, I also visited enterprises in Beijing, Datong, Wuxi, Suzhou and Hangzhou during July and August 1981.

place in three areas - the election of managers, the role of workers' congresses and Chinese trade unions Finally some conclusions are drawn.

This chapter concentrates on the state sector in industry for two reasons. The first is that the sector is predominant in terms of industrial output, employment and fixed assets as Table 7.1 shows. However its share of output and employment has been decreasing as its expansion since 1977 has been less rapid than that of the collective sector. For example, between 1979 and 1980 the gross output value of state industry increased by 6.2% while the collective sector growth was 17.8% (Zhongguo Baike Nianjian 1981:237). It should however be noted that the output figures usually given by the Chinese are gross ones (rather than net value added) and therefore may overstate the real share of the collective sector as its output value will include that of the materials in its production, which will often have been produced in the state sector.

The chapter is based on Chinese and other published sources, visits to over 20 enterprises in the summer of 1981 and discussions with Chinese economists, management experts, trade union cadres and officials from state economic organisations.[1]

Economic Reforms and Enterprise Management

At the heart of the economic reforms implemented so far in China is the idea of the enterprise as a relatively autonomous economic unit (Jiang Yiwei, 1980a; see also Lockett, 1981). On the one hand this idea implies that the main concern of management in industrial enterprises should be in the economic sphere, rather than in social, political or educational ones. On the other hand, it stresses the expansion of enterprise autonomy and the rights of those managing an enterprise to make decisions about what and how the enterprise should produce. In practice the implementation of reforms both expands the rights of enterprise management and imposes new constraints on what can be done with the increased autonomy.

Amongst the expanded rights which have implications for enterprise management are:

(i) greater choice of inputs: as direct negotiation between enterprises and other forms of market allocation replace planned allocation of materials, this increases the

TABLE 7:1: STATE AND URBAN COLLECTIVE SECTORS IN CHINA

	(1) No. of workers and staff (1979)	(2) Of which: industrial workers & staff[1] (1979)	(3) No. of industrial enterprises (1978)	(4) Proportion of gross industrial output value[2] (1980)	(5) Proportion of fixed assets (1973)	(6) Average earnings (1980)
STATE[3]	76.93m (77%)	31.09m (70%)	84,000	¥395.1 bn (79%)	97%	¥803
URBAN COLLECTIVE[3]	22.74m (23%)	13.28m (30%)	264,000	¥102.6 bn (21%)	3%	¥624
TOTAL	99.67m	44.37m	348,000			

Notes

1. This category excludes construction, transport, public utilities and various other categories, and so is a fairly narrow definition of industry. The exact definition used in column 3 may not be the same. Individual employment in urban areas was 0.32m in 1979, but has expanded rapidly. It was put at over 0.55m in March 1981 (He, 1982:43).

2. The figure for the collective sector given here may include industrial production by people's communes – the source does not make this clear.

3. 'State' industry refers to enterprises whose formal ownership is by the 'whole people'. In practice these are administered at levels down to county or equivalent in urban areas. 'Collective' industry is that in urban areas (rather than in communes) not formally owned by the 'whole people'; in practice some of this sector is administered in ways very similar to state enterprises whilst other, usually smaller, enterprises are administered by districts or neighbourhoods within a municipality. See note 2 above for the uncertain status of the state/collective division in column 4. These figures exclude those individually employed.

Sources

Columns (1) & (2) Zhongguo Jingji Nianjian 1981 (30–31)
        (3)   Xiang (1980:17)
        (4)   Zhongguo Baike Nianjian 1981 (236–237)
        (5)   Chang (1975:6)
        (6)   State Statistical Bureau (1981:20)

emphasis the management of an enterprise must
place on obtaining appropriate inputs, particularly in terms of quality and cost (in
areas where there is a degree of price flexibility).

(ii)   greater choice of outputs: where the planning system no longer specifies outputs in
detail, enterprise managers have to start
making decisions about the type and mix of
output in line with market demand and profitability. And where market allocation and
direct contracting exist, a new task of marketing faces managers. In practice, this
task of marketing is often a much more serious problem than that of supply in contrast to
the pre-reform situation. In sectors hit by
readjustment policies, such as machine-building, this may become particularly onerous.

(iii)   greater freedom to innovate: both in the
areas of products and production processes,
the rights of enterprise management to innovate have been increased. Rather than having to negotiate for funds with industrial
bureaus, enterprises now have access to funds
over which they have control, primarily from
retained profits but also potentially in the
form of bank loans. This combined with (ii)
above increases the need for enterprise level
planning.

(iv)   greater flexibility in labour management:
although this has so far been on a limited
scale in many respects, enterprises have been
given greater rights to appoint, promote and
demote both cadres and workers; to sack
workers on disciplinary grounds; and to determine their own pay and incentive schemes,
for example bonus schemes, various forms of
'subsidy' and overtime working.

All these imply both a greater range of possible decisions to be made within an enterprise and
the removal of previous constraints imposed by the
state primarily via 'administrative methods'. This
implies an increase in the range of decision-making
to be undertaken by managers. But there are also
additional constraints which have been created in
the process of economic reform. These include three
particularly important areas:

(i) increased economic constraints: through the operation of market forces to a limited degree, as well as other 'economic methods', the constraints on decision-making arising from economic performance have become much more prominent. Thus decisions must be based more on economic calculation of potential costs and benefits rather than on the bureaucratic and 'physical' calculation associated with meeting targets in a more rigidly planned system. At least in theory it implies that 'rational' calculation of economic effects and trade of commodities on economic criteria become more important than ability to manipulate within the planning and materials allocation bureaucracies, or the trading of goods or favours between individuals or organisations.[2]

(ii) changed state constraints: it is important to realise that when the Chinese talk about enterprise autonomy, it is only partial autonomy. Thus one must look at the constraints which the state and CCP place upon enterprises either through directives or administrative pressure. At present a key example of this is in the area of incentive payment schemes, as in their struggle to overcome 'egalitarianism' industrial bureaus are pressing enterprises to introduce highly individualised bonus schemes, based in particular on workers' output.[3]

(iii) constraints from the workforce: one cannot talk of enterprise management in purely technical or economic terms, for a large part of management work involves the workforce of an enterprise. The Cultural Revolution had a major impact on the Chinese working class. On the one hand it gave workers a limited say in some areas from which they had previously been excluded and led to the airing of many critical ideas as well as reducing managerial control in areas such as labour discipline, which has resulted in greater problems of managerial legitimacy than in many socialist countries, particularly amongst younger workers. On the other hand, the wages and other material benefits of workers broadly stayed the same for over 10 years (for example, average earnings in state enterprises were

¥ 595 in 1957 and ¥ 602 in 1977) reducing the
material incentives for better work at either
an individual or collective level. Thus dissatisfaction with wages and incentives, and
the problem of how to deal with the divisions
within the workforce over the fairness of new
material incentives posed constraints for
enterprise management.

Thus the process of economic reform poses a
number of problems for those managing an enterprise.
It requires a variety of new skills, notably in the
areas associated with determining inputs and outputs
(sales and marketing, and to a lesser degree buying)
economic calculation (eg accounting and enterprise
planning), and technology (especially in feasibility
and similar studies for innovation). It also implies changes in other areas of management, for example labour management. In short, according to
Wan Xiang (1980) it implies a transition 'from bureaucrat to manager', and poses major problems for
existing managerial personnel. In concrete terms
the educational and professional level of many
Chinese industrial managers is relatively low, as recent surveys have shown.[4] In addition the more
technically competent managerial and technical personnel may not be in senior positions within the
factory, as they tend to be younger and more recently trained. These problems are compounded by the
relatively centralised system of cadre allocation,
through which factories may find, say, technically
incompetent ex-PLA cadres put in fairly senior production management posts.
Thus the process of economic reform poses problems both of the level and type of managerial expertise at enterprise level, and the way in which managers are allocated to jobs. The great expansion of
enterprise management training for existing managers
since 1977, the formation of the Enterprise Management Association, the publishing of texts on management and the establishment of management courses in
higher education, are all attempts to raise the managerial and technical level of Chinese enterprise
management. Combined with increased attention to
workforce training these may contribute to reducing
the problems of shortage of qualified and experienced management personnel. However this shortage has
always existed, and it will be a relatively long
time before a significant impact can be made. In
the short term therefore economic reforms have exacerbated existing shortages of managerial skills by

both increasing demand for these skills and posing new and unfamiliar demands on enterprise management.

Thus a crucial part of the context of Chinese industrial management is a gap between the level and type of management skills available and those which economic reforms would 'ideally' require. A technocratic view of Chinese industrial management would see this gap combined with questions of appropriate forms of management organisation as the key to industrial progress. Whilst these are clearly important issues it is also vital to consider relations between managers and the workforce. For past Chinese policies, notably one man-management in the 1950's, by which one individual was responsible for and had power over all decisions in each production unit in a hierarchy of command ran into substantial resistance from the workforce, whilst reliance on material incentives in the form of bonuses in the early 1960's gave rise to a number of conflicts which were not easily resolved. For example, there were problems of differences in bonuses between factories and between workgroups which were often connected more to administrative rules than workers' effort or performance, as well as tendencies for bonus systems to become more and more complex in attempts to make them 'fairer' and more effective – with the result that they became less comprehensible to the workers they were supposed to be motivating. In addition the policies pursued during and after the Cultural Revolution called into question many aspects of relations between workers and managers; in particular some problems of labour discipline had developed. Absenteeism was relatively high in many factories, while 'over'-attention to production rather than politics had been heavily criticised by leftists during the 1970's leading to a reduction of material incentives for production. Combined with the lack of material incentives and more general political conflict, workforce motivation was low in many places. The subsequent re-introduction of bonus systems was designed to combat this, but this had adverse consequences as well as advantages for production. In industry bonuses did increase pay and rewarded extra skill and effort; they also created new inequalities within the workforce as a whole. So certain groups who did not receive bonuses, such as state employees and teachers, found their income going down, while in other places bonuses were financed by more or less disguised price rises. A more economistic attitude towards work was fostered, with workers wanting bonuses or extra pay for any extra

work. This was perceived as a problem by CCP leaders. So Deng Xiaoping, commenting on the situation
in 1979 (SWB, 6 March 1980), argued that 40% of the
¥ 5 billion (£1½ billion) paid out in bonuses had
been wasted, presumably because it was not related
to increased production.

Both for these reasons of management effectiveness and others relating to pressures for democracy,
both from within the CCP and state and outside it,
including the unofficial 'democracy movement', a
number of Chinese economists began to see the relations of managers and workers within enterprises as
important. It was argued that without greater commitment from the workforce economic reforms would not
succeed - or at least would be impeded. As a result,
reform of management systems of enterprises was
needed, posing both general questions of the relationship between the CCP and economic organisations
and the potential role of democratisation of enterprises.

Ling Chen (1979) saw 'democratic management' as
one of the five conditions for success in economic
reform. For, Ling argued (1979: 8),

> The expanded financial powers of the enter-
> prise ... must be based on an expansion of the
> democratic rights of the employees; otherwise
> petty bureaucratism will supplant big bureau-
> cratism, a command mentality on the part of
> factory heads and (Party) secretaries will re-
> place the command mentality on the part of the
> administrative leadership, and the system re-
> form will turn out to be a reform in name only.

Such views have been argued by other economists,
who have also noted trends to worker participation
in advanced capitalist economies (Wan Xiang, 1980;
Jiang Yiwei, 1980, and criticised Soviet industrial management for its lack of democracy (Wan
Xiang, 1980; Ma Hong, 1981). Democracy in management was also seen as a guarantee against the type
of degeneration of socialist enterprises which earlier Chinese criticisms of self-management argued
would occur (Jiang Yiwei, 1980 : 69-70, see also
Lockett, 1981). Thus in the conception of economic
reform held by a number of influential economists,
some form of democratisation of management was seen
both as a means of resolving problems and conflicts,
for instance in the area of labour discipline, and
as   realising socialist ideals of making workers
the 'masters of enterprises'. The question of the

methods by which this could be done was a complex
one, as well as being subject to the decision-making
structures of the CCP. In practice the approach
adopted was to a large degree a return to the policies of the mid-1950's, and were outlined in late
1978 by Deng Xiaoping.[5]
Speaking at the Ninth National Congress of the
All-China Federation of Trade Unions, Deng reaffir-
med the aim of increasing living standards and the
basic management system of factory directors responsible to an enterprise Party Committee. He went on:

> In order to achieve the four modernizations,
> all our enterprises, without exception, should
> have democratic management and this should be
> combined with centralized leadership. Work-
> shop directors, section chiefs and group heads
> in every enterprise must in the future be elec-
> ted by the workers in the unit. Major issues
> in an enterprise should be discussed by workers'
> congresses or general membership meetings, at
> which leading cadres of the enterprise must
> listen to the workers' views and accept their
> criticism and supervision. Such congresses and
> meetings have the right to suggest to higher
> levels that certain leading or managing person-
> nel be punished or replaced for serious negli-
> gence of duty or for a bad style of work. The
> trade union in an enterprise will be the func-
> tioning body between workers' congresses and
> general membership meetings. Therefore, it is
> no longer an unnecessary organization as some
> believed   (Deng, 1978:7).

This model of management (represented diagram-
matically in Figure 7.1) contained three main reforms.
The first was the election of managers by the workers they managed; the second the creation of elected workers' congresses with certain rights and
powers; and the third was a changed role for the
trade unions. These three reforms have formed the
basis of the changes in industrial enterprise management systems since 1978, and at least in theory
represent a move towards more democratic forms of
organisation. The next three sections therefore
discuss both what has happened in practice in these
areas, as well as the development of theoretical and
policy debate over how these reforms should be
developed.[6]

Enterprise Management - Moves Towards Democracy?

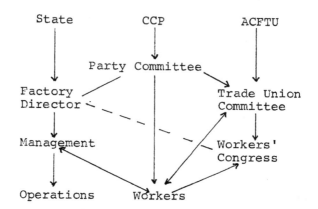

FIGURE 7.1 The management system advocated by
Deng Xiaoping (1978) - Party Committee
leadership with limited democracy

Notes to Figures 7.1 & 7.2

indicates a link of authority, in the sense
of hierarchical authority, election etc.

indicates reciprocal links of authority, as
in the case of the workforce electing
managers who then assume authority over the
workforce.

indicate similar links but of a weaker
kind, including those of supervision.

CCP   Chinese Communist Party

ACFTU   All-China Federation of Trade Unions

Source: Lockett (1982).

Electing Managers

From 1978 official CCP policy was therefore to start
a process of election of managers (below the level
of factory directors) and of workgroup leaders on a
much more systematic basis than had been attempted
before.[7] Whilst pressures for democratisation from
'below' and problems of workforce motivation were
two factors behind these moves, I would argue that
it was the desire of the top CCP and state leadership to improve the efficiency of management, and to
reform the cadre system, which was decisive. But

234

whilst the problems in this area have been outlined above, the question raised is why elections were advocated rather than an administrative process of assessment of managers.

A first reason is that from a technocratic view point the results of elections may be as good or better than administrative methods. For given the constraints on enterprises and the moves towards tying workers' incomes to economic performance, cadres with inadequate technical training and organisational ability are not going to be popular with the workers they manage. Such cadres, who would be difficult to remove or transfer under the existing cadre system, are likely to have strong tendencies towards 'bureaucratic' working styles - following rules in a formalistic way, restricting the flow of information and so on - unless they have a high level of organisational skills. In short, bureaucratic working styles are a cover for lack of competence. In such cases, the implication is not only poor performance in terms of economic criteria but also dissatisfaction among subordinates with this inefficient and bureaucratic management. Further, if workers' bonuses are dependent on economic performance which is adversely affected by such a manager, the motivational effects of bonuses will be reduced and dissatisfaction likely to increase. Thus on economic efficiency grounds, the main targets of an administrative shake-up of management will be hit by democratic elections.

This does not imply that administrative methods have not been used. For example, the Guangzhou railways organisation reviewed 104 heads and deputy-heads (the equivalent of station masters) of whom 10 were retired and 13 relieved of their posts as a result of their inadequate 'vocational and organisational skills' (Beijing Review, 10 Nov. 1980). Thus about a quarter of these managers were replaced. However such a process does have some problems which elections could avoid. The first is that, in practice, the use of existing hierarchies of authority may lead to different criteria from those intended by the top leadership, notably the settling of old scores and factional conflicts within the hierarchy. Also, cadres whose positions have been obtained by patronage and political manoeuvering rather than competence may well be able to resist removal by just these means. Another very important problem is that of the legitimacy of the removal of cadres and managers among the cadres themselves. Removal by any method is likely to be resented, particularly

if privileges are lost, and increases middle-level
opposition to the reform programme as a whole.
While significant resistance to elections certainly
exists, it may be more difficult to resist removal
by the workforce who in the official ideology of
the CCP are the 'masters of the enterprise'. As it
has been put, elections avoid 'making appointments
by favouritism' and 'will help avoid the tendency
that cadres are willing to accept leading posts but
unwilling to work at the grassroots later' (Beijing
Review, 5 May 1980).

A further major question is that of managers'
legitimacy among the workers they manage. Even if
many managers are re-elected to their previous
posts (as appears to be the case), the workforce has
some opportunity to influence the choice of managers. Managers will be able to use this to increase
their authority and justify their decisions. Thus
Renmin Ribao (4 July 1979, quoted in Xinhua, 4 July
1979) saw elections as both 'the practising of democratic rights by workers' and 'an effective measure
to improve enterprise management'. However it
should be noted that these elections of managers are
subject to approval by higher levels of management
or by Party committees.

So how does this system of elections work and
how far has it spread? The basic format of the elections appears similar to those used in the past,
including the Cultural Revolution period where at
times Revolutionary Committee members were elected.
An example is the best way to explain the procedure.
In the Beibei Glassware Factory, north of Chongqing
in Sichuan, elections had been held for two out of
three workshop directors starting in 1980. In one
of these workshops, the trade union first collected
opinions among the workers about who should be elected, coming out with a number of names. A period of
discussion of these 'nominations' followed, involving both workers and cadres at higher levels, after
which a list of 3 names remained. These were then
put to the vote at a public meeting of all the workers in the workshop, and the elected candidates
approved by the factory Party Committee. The
results of these elections were that in one workshop
the existing manager was re-elected but in the other
he was replaced by a skilled 'veteran' worker. The
previous manager, an ex-PLA man with limited knowledge of the technical processes, was transferred to
a job in the area of worker and staff education.

In practice the systems used vary from factory
to factory, with the equivalent of 'primary

elections' held in some cases, as well as secret
ballots rather than open meetings (eg Zhi, 1978).
Also the relative influence of workers versus higher
level managers and cadres will vary. At one extreme
is the manipulation of elections,which is by no
means unknown. For example in a Party Committee
election in the Tianjin Electronic Instrument Works,
the Secretary numbered the ballot papers. When he
failed to get all the votes, he was able to discover
who had not voted for him and attack them for 'non-
organisational activities' - but he was foiled as
his case made the pages of Renmin Ribao as a negative example (7 Sept. 1979, quoted in Beijing Review
26 Oct. 1979). But in cases where there is no clear
manipulation, higher level managers and Party committees may still have a major influence. Candidates
may not be nominated or voted for if it is known
that their election would not be approved. And
while the process of discussion involving higher
levels may be very useful in examining the suitabil-
ity of nominated candidates it can also be a means
of ensuring the election of 'approved' candidates
only. A further factor is workers' suspicion of the
fairness of elections and their suspicions of manipulation, which may reduce the interest they take in
them.
    The extent of elections for managers is signi-
ficant, though it still does not cover a majority
of enterprises. It was reported in early 1981 (SWB,
14 March 1981) based on 'incomplete statistics'
apparently collected in June 1980,[8] that elections
for some or all workshop heads had taken place in
over 11,000 enterprises; while at least some workgroup leaders and section heads had been elected in
33,200 enterprises. These figures represent 13% and
40% respectively of state enterprises. A broadly
similar picture was obtained in the factories visited in 1981, though in one case (the Chongqing Clock
and Watch Company) the election of workgroup leaders
had been abandoned after a trial in 1980 - according
to a senior factory cadre this was because those
elected found the work 'too troublesome' and gave up
after a couple of months. Instead 'those who like
to work harder' are appointed. More generally there
has been a significant degree of managerial opposition to elections - this is probably the main constraint on their extension (see, eg, Xinhua Ribao,
18 Aug. 1980). Objections to control from below are
disguised in terms of the supposed need for secrecy
in management work and the possibility that the
workforce will not make the 'right' choice. In this

context, the legacy of the Cultural Revolution in the area of work discipline is often used to justify opposition to elections.

As well as formal elections, there are a variety of processes of consultation practised in the appointment and appraisal of managers who are not subject to election, or whose jobs make direct election less appropriate, for example needs of factory-level administrative sections. There does not seem to be a standard method for this, and a number of techniques have been used. A few examples will show the range in use. In the Sichuan No. 1 Cotton Mill in Chengdu, workshop managers are not elected but the factory-level personnel section has meetings or discussions with workers about managers' performance, and also workers' congress representatives within the workshop present workers' views to the workers' congress (see below). More formalised methods such as questionnaires may be used, as in the Suzhou Forestry Machinery Factory (Xinhua, 16 May 1980) where one was used to assess (i) who should be promoted, and (ii) the competence of the eight top factory managers. After the poll of the '1000 odd' workers, decisions were made by the Party Committee on the basis of both the poll and an assessment of managers' technical expertise. One of the deputy directors had over 70% of the workers against him as he 'had done poor work', and a new younger group of six managers was appointed. There are also cases where such 'opinion polls' have been taken on a regular basis, sometimes at six-month intervals, with managers having to resign at once if they get less than 30% approval (Beijing Review, 11 Feb. 1980).

The extension of elections to top managers at factory level, in particular factory directors, is an issue which Deng's speech did not mention. Since 1979 there have been moves in this direction, though on a smaller scale than with lower-level managers and group leaders. The first case of an elected factory director was in the Tianjin Xinhe Shipyard in early 1979. This seemed to be a method for replacing a poor previous management as well as an extension of the elections of workshop managers a few months before. The exact procedure used was unclear but the Shipyard used an election to nominate eleven top managers, including the director, chief engineer and accountant, for approval by the relevant Ministry (Beijing Review, 23 March 1979; Tian Sansong, 1980:24-26). In mid-1980 the scope of these elections was limited to under 1,000 factories (SWB 12 June 1981; All China Federation of Trade Unions,

1981:3). Such an extension of elections for managers has been officially supported, for example by the head of the CCP Party School, Feng Wenbin (1981: 20) who argued that, 'conditions permitting, the electoral system should be extended to all fields, wherever it is essential, and it should gradually replace the appointment system'. In practice it seemed that during 1981 the scope of such elections was expanding as part of the functions of workers' congresses (see below) rather than in the form of direct elections. For example, in Beijing over 100 factory directors are said to have been elected by 1981. However development in Sichuan was much slower as it was stated that only one of the 400 odd experimental enterprises had an elected factory director.[9]

To sum up, it does appear that the election of managers may have begun to be applied in a fairly comprehensive way. Although the major motivation behind its adoption by the CCP is to improve the efficiency and legitimacy of management, it does represent a move towards greater democracy in industrial management. On the positive side, it seems that election systems are being institutionalised to a greater extent than before, making their degeneration less likely; for a major problem with the various elements of democracy in the Cultural Revolution period (1966-1976) was a lack of mechanisms for elections at regular intervals (see Lockett, 1982). However, while formal democratic procedures exist, the degree of worker influence in practice is probably rather less than it would appear. For not only do the CCP and higher-level management retain the right to veto elected managers; they can also exert a significant influence over the election process itself even if they do not clearly manipulate it. And, even where mechanisms for recall of managers exist, there is little or no evidence of their having been used. Elections also face significant problems of opposition from middle-level cadres, who see their power and privileges being challenged if they are subject to control from below. This resistance has been described as 'obstinate' in the Chinese press, and as Gongren Ribao stated in an editorial (6 Oct. 1980), the development of such forms of democracy 'depends on the workers and staff members waging an unremitting struggle against the remnants of feudal ideology, bureaucracy and a patriarchal style of work' (15-16).

Workers' Congresses

Workers' congresses, or rather 'representative congresses of workers and staff' (zhigong daibiao dahui)
have existed at various times in Chinese industry.
A particular attempt to popularise them was made
after 1956, but they were downgraded in importance
during the Great Leap Forward. Even when they were
re-emphasised in the early 1960's, they played a
fairly minor consultative role in industrial management. They were abandoned in the Cultural Revolution, although various types of representative bodies did play a significant role especially in the
late 1960's and early 1970's. However since 1978
they have been promoted much more systematically
than in the past and their powers significantly extended. In fact the extent to which this power
should be extended has become a major controversy:
in particular the question of whether they should in
future replace Party committees as the main policy-
making bodies in enterprises.
Workers' congresses are elected by the workers
and staff (including managers) of an enterprise,
usually on the basis of constituencies based on work
groups or workshops. Typically there is one representative for every 10 or 15 workers. Until mid-
1981 there was no formal national framework for
their operation, although it appears that more local
regulations were made. In June 1981 a set of
'Provisional Regulations Concerning Congresses of
Workers and Staff Members in State-owned Industrial
Enterprises' were issued by the CCP Central Committee and the State Council. While not all workers'
congresses which have existed fit in with the regulations, they do give some general principles of
their operation. According to these Regulations,
representatives are elected for a two-year term and
are subject to recall. Workers must make up at
least 60% of representatives with 'appropriate representation' guaranteed to technical and administrative personnel, young workers and women workers
(article 8). Meetings must be held at least every
six months, and also can be called by a third of the
representatives (article 12). The congress will
elect a 'praesidium' to run itself (article 11) and
may also set up working committees for investigation
work, collecting proposals and supervising the implementation of congress decisions (article 14). The
enterprise trade union committee looks after the
organisational work before and after a congress is
convened, and is its 'working organ' (article 16).

Finally the main powers of the workers' congress (article 5) are to:

(a) 'discuss and examine' the factory director's report, enterprise plans and budgets, major technical innovations and management issues;

(b) 'discuss and decide' on the use of labour protection, welfare, including housing allocation, and bonus funds; (in addition in 'trial' enterprises it has to approve the division of retained profits);

(c) 'discuss and adopt' changes in organisation, wages, training and 'important rules and regulations';

(d) 'supervise' cadres and managers in the enterprise;

(e) 'elect' leading cadres in line with 'the arrangements of the higher organ of the enterprise' and subject to its approval.

The formal power of workers' congresses is therefore quite wide-ranging and, although they are clearly under the leadership of enterprise Party committees, they do have a degree of independent authority in areas such as welfare. But in practice their development has been uneven and their performance does not necessarily correspond to the formal 'Provisional Regulations'.

The growth of workers' congresses, or their formalisation in cases where similar bodies already existed, has been fairly rapid since the introduction of the new management policies in late 1978. Partly this was a result of imitation of the types of workers' congress which had existed in the 1950's and 1960's. In March 1980 it was reported (Lin Pei, 1980) that only a fifth of enterprises had them, while a year later there were about 34,000 (about 41% of state enterprises; SWB, 9 June 1981). However they are unevenly spread, being concentrated in the larger cities and in medium and large size enterprises. For example the Beijing Municipal Trade Union Council gave figures for the end of 1980 of 88% of state enterprises, including 98.8% of large and medium ones; while in Sichuan Province as a whole only 60% of enterprises had workers' congresses, although in its biggest industrial centre,

241

Chongqing, there was a 90% coverage, of which 80% were in an 'active' state.[10]

Early reports of workers' congresses indicated that they were just consultative bodies and their influence low. For example in a fairly early case at the Wuqiao County Machinery Plant, Hebei, it was stated (FBIS, 7 Dec. 1978) that at the congress the factory director gave a report, the CCP branch presented a plan to implement the latest industrial policies and representatives expressed their views on 'enterprise management, production plans, personnel affairs and workers' wellbeing'. This lack of influence was reflected in Chinese criticisms of some of them being 'held ... only for the sake of formality' and so not gaining 'the wide attention of the masses of workers' (Lin, 1980:6 & 8), or as 'nothing but rubber-stamp organisations without real power' (Qian, 1980:16). Analyses by the trade unions in 1981 led to statements that only a quarter of workers' congresses were 'performing their job well', 60% were 'not so effective' and 15% were in a 'passive state' (SWB, 9 June 1981).[11] However two sets of developments have increased their power substantially, although at present only in a minority of enterprises. The first is the general process of economic reform in China, and the second a set of proposals designed to increase the power of the workers' congress which are now being used in a small-scale experiment.

As other articles in this book have outlined, the Chinese economic reforms have been applied both to all enterprises to a limited extent and to a much greater degree to a smaller number of trial enterprises (6600 in mid-1981). In general it was decided by the State Council in late 1978 that enterprises fulfilling over half of their plan targets would get additional funds for collective welfare and 'rewarding outstanding workers'.[12] The use of these funds had to be approved by the workers' congress. In the trial enterprises this type of power was extended so that the workers' congress had to approve the division of retained profits between (a) reinvestment in production, (b) collective welfare, such as housing and childcare facilities, and (c) bonuses. In practice this power is limited by regulations and guidelines made by higher-level bodies such as industrial bureaus as well as by State Council regulations on bonuses. This power in the trial enterprises seems to have given some stimulus to their workers' congresses, particularly given the link between enterprise performance and workers' pay and welfare in them. Reports from such enterprises indicate that in some of them the workers' congress has begun to be more independent and to exercise its formal authority. For example in one trial enterprise, the Chongqing Zhongnan Rubber Plant in Sichuan, the workers' congress not only discussed production and sales but also made 'more than thirty' criticisms of the management in two meetings and threw out a management plan for a new canteen in favour of more housing (Xinhua, 28 May 1980). In practice the funding and allocation of housing has been one of the main areas of workers' congress activities. In a number of cases they have taken over responsibility from management for the allocation of housing to workers, as the housing shortages in many areas make this a particularly contentious issue;for even if managers do not seek privileges in this (see below), the allocation among workers and staff is no easy task.

In some of the factories visited in 1981 it was stated that on a number of questions, mainly in the welfare area, discussions would first be held at the workers' congress and only after a decision was reached would the Party committee become involved. In others the workers' congress was much more likely to receive proposals from the factory director or Party committee for it to approve. There was also some diversity in the way workers' congresses operated. Meetings were held between once and four times a year, with some being half a day long and others up to five days. To take one of the more active congresses, that of the Chengdu Electric Wire Works in Sichuan, it was reformed in August 1979 and had 85% workers. As well as its meetings, it had elected a 'Democratic Management Committee' which met at least quarterly containing both factory leaders, trade union cadres and a majority (60%) of workers. Associated with this were four sub-committees (xiaozu) each responsible for supervising the work of one of the factory's four deputy-directors. And in the debates over housing, in 1980 the workers' congress idea of repairing old houses prevailed over the Party committee's preference for demolition followed by new building.

In some factories therefore, there is evidence that workers' congresses are rather more than 'rubber-stamp organisations'. For even if their influence is most evident in the area of collective welfare issues such as housing, these are often immediate and concrete issues for workers. But the activities of some congresses are not confined to this,

and they seem to be developing mechanisms to deal
with the complexity of other areas of managerial
decision-making and the supervision of managers.[13]
In addition congresses have in some cases pushed for
and organised the election of managers and group
leaders. Although there is no necessary connection
between economic reform and increased democracy, it
does seem that in the Chinese case the two have been
positively associated, in contrast to the views of
critics of self-management such as Bettelheim (see
below).

The second way in which workers' congresses may
be extended is through proposals for the congress
to replace the Party committee as the main policy-
making body within an enterprise - a move towards
the Yugoslav type of enterprise organisation. Within China this is a radical proposal for, since the
rejection of 'one-man management' in the mid-1950's,
Party committees have played this leading role
except for a few years during the Cultural Revolution. Such a move was implicit in the arguments of
Lin Pei in Renmin Ribao in early 1980 who argued
that workers' congresses should elect factory directors and also that it would be desirable if it
were 'the comrades of workers' congresses who hold
the real power over production and management of
enterprises' (1980:8). By early 1981 these arguments had been made explicit by a number of influential people arguing for a long-term policy of making
factory directors responsible to the workers' congress. The workers' congress would take over policy
making powers while the Party committee would concentrate on supervision, ie ensuring adherence to
overall state and CCP policies, and on ideological
and political issues, (see Figure 7.2).Amongst those
arguing for such a policy were Ma Hong (1980) and
Jiang Yiwei (1980(b)) of the Institute of Industrial
Economics of the Academy of Social Sciences, and
Feng Wenbin (1981), head of the Party School under
the CCP Central Committee. For example, Jiang Yiwei
(1980(b)) argued that there was a need to swap the
present role of the Party committee and workers'
congress in enterprises as shown in Table 7.2.

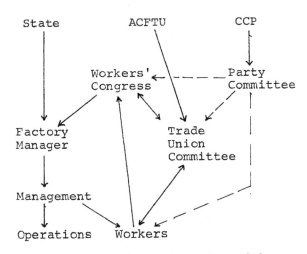

FIGURE 7.2: Experimental management system with workers' congresses as the main policy-making body (see Figure 1 for notes)

Table 7.2: Jiang Yiwei's analysis of present and improved enterprise management

	AREA OF MANAGEMENT		
	'Policy'	'Direction' (ie operational management	'Supervision'
PRESENT	PARTY COMMITTEE	FACTORY DIRECTOR	WORKERS' CONGRESS
IMPROVED	WORKERS' CONGRESS	FACTORY DIRECTOR	PARTY COMMITTEE

Advocates of such reforms argue that Party committees, especially the Party Secretary, are now much too involved in day-to-day management to effectively supervise the implementation of CCP and state policy. Factory directors should therefore have greater day-to-day authority over management issues

while workers should become more involved in policy-
making on both democratic and motivational grounds.
As a result of being freed from direct involvement
in management, the Party committee would have the
time and ability to supervise the enterprise as a
whole, and as a result could exercise more effective
leadership when necessary.[14] It is further argued
by Jiang Yiwei (1980(b)) that the need for Party
supervision is increased with the expansion of enterprise autonomy and the use of profit as a criterion
of performance.

The general need for reforms in the area of the
'enterprise leading system' has been argued by
Deng Xiaoping. In a speech in August 1980 he argued
strongly for reforms

> to free the Party committees from doing daily
> routines and to let them concentrate on doing
> a good job of providing ideological and polit-
> ical guidance as well as the work of organisa-
> tional supervision. This is not to weaken the
> Party's leadership, but rather to improve and
> strengthen it and to make it more effective.
> (1980:100).

However Deng and other state and CCP leaders have
not officially endorsed the proposals to make the
workers' congress the leading policy body within
enterprises. Instead Deng argued that after experiments, 'the systems of job responsibility will be
gradually placed under the leadership and supervision of factory management committees, company
boards of directors, and united economic bodies'
(1980:100), a rather ambiguous formulation. On the
other hand, the State Council did approve a small
number of experiments along the lines suggested by
the advocates of a leading role for workers' congresses, for which 44 enterprises were selected.

These experiments in the enterprise leading
system began in late 1980 in Beijing, Shanghai,
Liaoning, and elsewhere. For example, around
November 1980 an experiment began in five Beijing
factories with a 'factory director responsibility
system under the leadership of the congress of workers and staff' (SWB, 3 Nov. 1980). The results of
these experiments have not been publicised yet, but
it appears that some of the 44 factories involved
have suspended the experiment for a time, usually as
a result of wanting to concentrate on other aspects
of economic reform (such as profit and loss responsibility) or due to production problems resulting

from readjustment policies. In one of the factories in this experiment, the Beijing Leather Products Factory, visited in September 1981, the Party committee still seemed to play a major role in management but the workers' congress had a significant influence. The question of the division of retained profits in the enterprise illustrates this. According to the factory manager (who was confirmed in his post by an election in the workers' congress) he took his proposals for the division of profits for 1980 to the Party committee, which approved them. The proposals then went to the workers' congress which criticised them for not putting enough emphasis on workers' housing. After several months of discussion and costing of plans, the proportion of profits to be allocated to welfare was increased substantially from the factory director's proposed 30% to 44%, whilst that allocated to production was reduced (from 40% to 30%).

While it is too early to judge these experiments, the reform proposals have created a major controversy. As Jingji Guanli (Economic Management) stated in July 1981, 'Among the questions concerning the experiments in reform, the question of the leadership of the Party committee has been the most controversial one, and the one on which differences in view have been greatest' (CREA,170). Critics of the proposals argued that they wo ld undermine the position of the CCP in industrial enterprises, though the exact lines of criticism are not clear, as much of it was conducted inside the CCP. The result is that a rather ambiguous statement of principles has been agreed arguing that any new system must combine:

(1) overall CCP leadership through Party committees

(2) democratic management through workers' congresses

(3) administrative management rights for factory directors and managers.

This formulation has the merit of creating a degree of consensus but underneath it the differences of view remain over the emphasis on and precise roles of different bodies. As Ma Hong (1981:32) put it, 'Opinions are not yet completely identical as to what the responsibility system being in charge is'! To some extent, it is a terminological dispute but it does have major implications for the longer run emphasis of reforms in enterprise management, and the role of workers' congresses within a new system. For the moment, the emphasis of effort is on the establishment of workers' congresses in all enterprises in line with the 'Provisional Regulations' and their consolidation in the face of managerial opposition in some cases. This can be done without a firm commitment to making workers' congresses the leading policy body within enterprises, however important this may be in the long run. The result of current debates in this area will ultimately be decided by the CCP Central Committee, depending on the strength of the various groups involved, and could mean China moving towards a Yugoslav-style model of enterprise management though in the context of an economy with a greater degree of planning.

Changes in the Trade Unions

In the areas under its control before Liberation, and since 1949 throughout China, trade unions have been modelled on Soviet labour unions. They have played a major role in administering labour insurance, organising spare-time and welfare activities, and promoting the aims of the CCP both in the production area, for example through labour emulation campaigns, and more generally, eg in political education. Apart from a period in the Cultural Revolution (up to 1973), they have been a significant part of the organisation of Chinese enterprises, with the 'grass roots' trade union committees being part of the national structure of the All-China Federation of Trade Unions (A.C.F.T.U.). However they have also been in a continuing dilemma - to what extent should they be (i) a 'transmission belt' seeking to pass CCP policies on to their members and gain support for them, thereby acting more or less as an arm of management, or (ii) an organisation controlled from below by its members, seeking to represent the interests of workers even when they conflict with management or CCP policies.
    In practice the first of these roles has been dominant, but it has carried with it a persistent problem - that workers become alienated from the unions, seeing them as little different from management. While Chinese trade union leaders have never backed a role independent of the CCP, there have been times when they have tried to shift more towards the second view. The first was in 1951-52 when the All-China Federation of Labour (the

248

forerunner of ACFTU) led by Li Lisan began to press
for greater independence from the CCP and to push
workers' more immediate and material interests
rather than consistently siding with management. As
a result Li was ousted in 1952 and the trade unions
accused of 'economism' (see Harper, 1971). The second attempt was in 1956-57 when the ACFTU leader
Lai Ruoyu argued that unions should be more independent of management at factory level if they were
to regain the support of workers, arguing that while
'economism must be opposed ... The trade unions must
protect the material interests and democratic rights
of the workers and employees' (1956:240-241). The
ACFTU was also in favour of a significant role for
workers' congresses. This attempt was subverted by
the move towards strengthening Party committee control in enterprises, especially during the Great
Leap Forward. The lack of worker resistance to
their abolition during the Cultural Revolution also
indicates the alienation of many workers from trade
union organisation.

After 1973 when trade union work was restarted,
it seems that fairly orthodox policies were adopted,
with the trade unions absorbing various forms of
worker participation in management (Lockett, 1978).
As they were re-started in a series of provincial
congresses around 1973, it was stated for example by
a Guizhou CCP leader that unions should be 'under
the centralised leadership of the Party, to act as
good assistants to the Party', with the Guizhou
Ribao stressing that unions were 'the tether linking
the masses to the Party' and that Party committees
'must strengthen leadership over trade union work'
(SWB, 3 Jan. 1974). There were a number of disputes
over trade unions, particularly in 1974 to 1976 when
the 'Gang of Four' was accused of trying to sabotage
their work, restrict their membership to shopfloor
workers and release them from CCP leadership (FBIS,
10 Jan. 1978). However after 1976 their pro-manage-
ment and CCP-directed policies continued, with an
emphasis on boosting production through such methods
as emulation campaigns and the use of model workers.

The basic formal structure of the trade unions
which was re-established after 1973 is similar to
that of the past. At a national level there is the
ACFTU. Below this level there are both regional and
industrial organisations. Regional organisation is
through provincial, municipality or similar levels
down to the district, while the industrial organisation is through 17 national industrial unions. In
practice however the regional form of organisation

predominates at present, with the links between most national unions and lower levels apparently tenuous or non-existent. Thus from the trade union organisation in a state factory the upwards lines of responsibility would typically go through a corporation and/or bureau level based on current industrial administration to the municipal and/or provincial one. As a result the provincial and municipal (especially in the cases of Beijing, Tianjin and Shanghai) levels have a major role. Overall the unions in China have 61.2 million members, who are formed within enterprises into trade union groups (average size about 13 members, usually the union members within a workgroup). In practice nearly all workers in medium and large factories are members, for though membership is formally voluntary everyone joins.[15] Although members pay 0.5% of their monthly wages to the trade union, most of its finance comes from 2% of the enterprise wage fund which is allocated to them. Some of this is used to support higher-level trade union organisations, which also run such facilities as sanatoria and holiday homes for model workers. Within a factory there will be a number of full-time trade union cadres, maybe one for every 500 workers or so, who are responsible for the work of the union.

Since 1979, there has been much more stress than in the past on reducing the actual or potential alienation of workers from the unions. This has included both internal union democracy and the promotion of workers' interests even when they come into conflict with local management or CCP plans and policies. As well as pressure from below, the ACFTU has played a role in promoting these changes of emphasis. For example, Gongren Ribao (Workers' Daily), the ACFTU-run paper, has published readers' letters criticising unrepresentative unions and argued against unions blindly following orders from above rather than promoting workers' interests. As a result, unions are now urged not to allow health and safety to be ignored in order to meet production targets, and to push for the extension of democracy in enterprises through workers' congresses. In fact, it was stated in October 1981 by the ACFTU leader Ni Zhifu that 'the focal point of trade union work was to develop well the workers' congress system' (1981:5). However there has been no suggestion that they should be independent of CCP leadership.

In formal terms trade unions have been given a greater degree of autonomy from the CCP and management than in the past, combined with changes in

their structure intended to increase their represen-
tativeness. In practice these changes do appear to
have been reflected in the activities of the unions
at lower levels. There have been moves towards the
election rather than the appointment of trade union
cadres, though the factory management may have some
say in this. For example in the Beijing Leather
Products Factory the Chairman and Vice-Chairman of
the union were elected but other full-time cadres
appointed by the union in consultation with the factory director. Elected cadres may also be subject
to higher-level approval, by both higher-level union
organisations and/or enterprise Party committees.
However there are cases where pressure from enterprise management has been successfully resisted by
unions. For example, around 1980 in a small light
industrial enterprise in Shanghai, the trade union
chairman was 'very courageous in raising opinions
for the benefit of the workers', but too critical
for the liking of the Party branch secretary and
factory managers. The Party branch manipulated the
re-election, ensuring the union chairman was removed. He then wrote to the Municipal union federation who publicised the case. Eventually the Party
branch secretary made a self-criticism and the former union chairman was reinstated.

Unions have also intervened in a variety of
issues within enterprises. A major source of discontent has been manipulation of housing allocation
by cadres, notable in Tianjin (eg SWB, 13 Oct. 1981)
but also elsewhere. Municipal level trade unions
have backed complaints that enterprise cadres have
allocated new housing to themselves or their friends
rather than workers. Although in some cases such
complaints can be resolved within the enterprise,[16]
in others the backing of higher-level trade unions
has been crucial, for example at the Tianjin Eleva-
tor Factory in 1980 (Beijing Review, 15 Dec. 1980).
In other areas, unions have argued against the use
of unsafe chemicals and against factories changing
over workers' facilities for use as stores or workshops. In this bad publicity for factory managers
appears to be a weapon. In Shanghai, for example, a
cotton mill manager was persuaded not to convert
planned recreation space to production use when
threatened with publicity in the municipal union's
internal paper. So, while it is not possible to
judge to what extent unions have effective influence
on behalf of workers, the trend towards a more independent and assertive stance has been fairly clear.
This change has brought with it two kinds of

tension. The first is that between the two functions of trade unions outlined at the start of this
section; while the second is between enterprise-
based or other forms of sectional representation of
workers' interests on the one hand and an attempt to
represent the Chinese working class as a whole. In
the first area of tension, for example, Shu (1980:2)
argues that

> many union organisations have gradually lost
> their original prestige and role ... Union
> cadres have shown very little interest in the
> immediate interests of workers. Therefore the
> workers have never taken seriously things the
> unions did, such as "education" and "labour
> emulation". To gain the confidence of the
> workers, the union organisations must make
> great efforts to change themselves.

These concerns with lack of support for official
unions have existed for some time, particularly
given the history of independent workers' organisations in the form of factions during the Cultural
Revolution. The creation of 'Solidarity' in Poland
in 1980 has reinforced these concerns, and the
choice of CCP leaders to contain similar pressures
in China by a limited increase in trade union autonomy. Ji Pengfei, a vice-Premier, indicated the
degree of concern in the Chinese leadership when he
stated that 'events in Poland have been an important
lesson to us' (MacDougall, 1980).[17] In fact there
have been some isolated attempts to create independent unions in China (Guardian, 30 Jan. 1981; Hilton,
1981), although there is no evidence of any wider
movement.[18] The official attitude to such attempts
has been to prevent them, but commenting on their
promoters in central China one newspaper stated,
'These people are not acting out of ulterior motives
but simply represent the ultimate in ignorance' - a
fairly tolerant attitude by previous standards!
     Given the reality of CCP leaders' fears of the
outright rejection of official unions, the tension
between ensuring that unions are responsive to the
CCP and at the same time represent workers' interests will effectively make this a continual area of
debate. While it would be wrong to suggest that
this is necessarily an irresolvable contradiction in
all cases, there will be times when unions have to
choose between workers' interests and those of management and CCP bodies. Quite how this problem will
be resolved in future is unclear, but there are sure

to be pressures from more conservative cadres in the CCP who dislike the constraints which more independent trade unions can create for them.

The second area of tension in the role of trade unions is a result of their increased independence and responsiveness to workers' concerns. This is the question of the extent to which control over the trade unions from below should be based on enterprise trade union organisations. Given that economic reforms increase differences between enterprises in areas such as pay and welfare through profit retention, the interests of workers are tied more closely to their own enterprise. In addition, competition to some extent increases the conflict of interests between workers in different enterprises. The reforms in enterprise management have led to a situation where the enterprise level trade union organisations have a responsibility to its workers' congress, as its 'working organ' according to the 'Provisional Regulations' (article 16). The importance attached by trade unions to democratic management carries with it the problem of fragmentation of workers into groups with competing sectional interests which 'grassroots' trade union organisations will promote in order to maintain workers' support within the enterprise. As a result, the potential for trade unions to exercise influence on behalf of the working class as a whole will be reduced, especially in cases where this conflicts with the interests of particular factories. This might be the case with inequalities of pay and welfare between enterprises, especially as these are more closely tied to enterprises in China than in the West. Another area of concern would be redundancy if workers' congresses had the right to reduce an enterprise's labour force. Thus there is a tension in the form of representation of workers' interests through trade unions, which is reflected in controversies over the role of unions in China. It is interesting that a 'reformer' and advocate of democracy such as Jiang Yiwei also argues that on the whole unions should 'represent the interests of the working class as a whole', for while they should support workers' congresses in general they should not necessarily take the same position on particular issues.[19] In theoretical terms the logic of such a position is clear, but it remains to be seen if concrete forms of organisation can be found to achieve this without being in effect a return to a previous type of hierarchical CCP control, particularly if it is assumed that the CCP more or less automatically represents the 'interests of the working class as a whole'.

Conclusions

It can be seen that in the last few years, there have been real - but still limited - moves towards more democracy in Chinese industry. In particular it seems that there has been a positive association between economic reform in areas such as enterprise autonomy and increases in the influence of workers over decision-making. This stands in marked contrast to views of those such as Bettelheim who have seen a major contradiction in this area. However it is important to realise that the partial democratisation of enterprise management has taken place in particular conditions, and that democratisation has not necessarily been the prime objective of the moves towards democracy. So it is in the context both of inefficient and under-qualified management in many areas, and of problems of managerial legitimacy, that electing managers has been a relatively attractive option for CCP leaders. But this process of reform in enterprise management has raised opposition particularly from middle-level cadres whose positions and privileges may be threatened from two directions. The first is from the new demands placed on them as managers as a result of economic reforms. For example, some managers would rather not have the uncertainties of competitive pressures from the use of market forces, while longstanding CCP cadres without technical skills can no longer occupy important positions in enterprises in the same way as before. The second threat to the position of such cadres is the supervision from below as a result of democratisation. This has resulted in significant resistance to the spread of workers' congresses and elections by factory managers and other cadres on a reasonably wide scale. Politically there is evidence that these groups are attempting to slow down or stop further democratic reforms of enterprise management, notably the idea that workers' congresses should become the chief policy-making body within enterprises. The end result of these conflicts is by no means clear, and it is likely that it will be some time before there is a convincing resolution of the debates.

This analysis of the state sector is also relevant to the urban collective one. Enterprises within this are now being given greater autonomy, and it is argued that they have both been too rigidly controlled and not been controlled by the workers who in formal terms own them. In the case of 'large collective' (da jiti) enterprises, the process of reform has been broadly similar - if slower - than in the state sector. Small collective (xiao jiti) enterprises have also been given greater profit retention and autonomy rights, although most remain quite closely tied to local government organisations. Moves towards democracy have in many cases been rather slower. For example, I was told in Shanghai that, in 'large collective' enterprises, trials in electing managers had not yet begun although they were planned in enterprises which were involved in other economic reforms. So here again it appears that there are moves towards greater democracy associated with economic reforms, but that they are still on a rather limited scale.

Having criticised the formulation of Bettelheim on the link between economic reform and democratic enterprise management, it is also important to note the constraints upon democratic management which the economic reforms have created. The first constraint is clearly the impact of market competition. The 'trial' enterprises in China have been chosen according to specific criteria including relatively good management, large size and profitability (Lockett, 1981). As a result those which would be most adversely affected by competition have so far been excluded. Within these, the application of enterprise autonomy could result in strong pressures for intensification of labour as well as reduced pay and welfare provisions. So sections of the Chinese working class would suffer, and sectional divisions within it would be increased.[20] In such circumstances, democracy within the enterprise would have rather less relevance to the interests of workers.

Secondly, the use of bonus systems and other material incentives has had some adverse effects on the level of worker participation. For example, the worker participation involved in the 'responsible people' (dayuan) system within workgroups has been restricted in some factories, as it does not appear to fit in with fairly narrow criteria of individual productivity and measurement of performance. In the factories visited there had been tendencies towards restricting or abandoning this system, for instance by increasing the scope of the group leader's job. Some enterprises had overcome this by allocating a specific amount of time for the tasks involved, for example in the Shanghai High Pressure Oil Pump Factory which also had an elaborate system of bonuses and 'labour emulation'.[21] More generally if worker participation is not seen to be economically effective, these reforms will increase pressures for restriction of its scope.

Third, the concern with the division of labour and its transformation has been greatly reduced. While it was certainly the case that writers such as Bettelheim (1974) exaggerated the changes which took place in the Cultural Revolution, the stress which was placed on reducing the division of mental and manual labour and the sexual division of labour has more or less disappeared at least in public statements. Instead the merits of scientific management and the 'Taylor system' are expounded - though not always as uncritically as some critics of post-Mao China have argued;[22] and the position of women, such as the lack of them in leading management jobs, and possibly also on democratic bodies like workers' congresses, is no longer seen as a problem to be tackled in the short-term.[23] In particular the limits arising from the division of labour are insufficiently recognised, while the increasing complexity of managerial work arising from the economic reforms (see above) will increase the difficulty of effective worker influence over decision-making. However this can be offset to some extent by the potential for higher levels of training and qualification among the workforce.

To conclude, the economic reforms have not only created new demands for managerial skills but have also been associated with moves towards greater democracy in enterprise management. Although the actual development of such democratic decision-making lags behind the formal structures and is uneven, there have been some significant moves in the areas of (i) elections of managers, (ii) workers' congresses, and (iii) changes in the role of trade unions. These moves have led to opposition, especially from middle-level cadres, and remain clearly within a structure of CCP control. However advocates of further reforms are pressing for further moves towards democracy, notably more power for workers' congresses, along with the extension of other economic reforms, notably in the price system. Disputes and debates over enterprise management are likely to continue, and the outcome - more moves towards democracy or a strengthening of CCP and management control - are not certain.

8

URBAN EMPLOYMENT AND LABOUR ALLOCATION POLICIES

Gordon White

Among the backlog of problems faced by China's post-
Mao leadership in the late 1970s, questions of urban
employment and labour allocation were among the most
pressing and politically sensitive. They involved
complex and difficult issues: the quantitative
problem of providing enough jobs to keep pace with
the expanding urban population, particularly the
annual crop of middle school graduates; the qualitative problems of ensuring that jobs were productive rather than just make-work, of reducing the
high level of over-manning in state enterprises, and
of increasing the accuracy of the fit between skills
and training on the one hand and economic needs on
the other; the political problems of meeting the
aspirations of the younger generation and the demands of their parents.
     These problems were not new; successive lead-
erships had been wrestling with them since the Liberation in 1949 with only intermittent success.
They had given rise to widespread social tension and

* The author would like to thank Maisie Gray for
making available her invaluable research materials
which have contributed enormously to the analysis in
this paper. Thanks also to Julia Broomfield for her
assistance in preparing this manuscript.
     The author regrets the lack of materials which
would have been available from research access to
China. Though a research proposal on urban labour
allocation was submitted to the Britain-China
exchange programme and approved on the British side
(the British Academy), the project was rejected by
the Chinese Academy of Social Sciences.

political discontent, much of which found explosive expression in the Cultural Revolution (1966-69) and lingered on unresolved though muted into the mid-1970s.

As usual, current propaganda is overly negative about the Cultural Revolution decade (1966-76) and overly rosy about the situation before the Cultural Revolution. Radical Maoism did address labour problems and in distinctive ways – the encouragement of collective enterprises, expansion of the 'down to the countryside' (xia-xiang) movement to send urban graduates to rural production teams and various attempts to coordinate the educational and industrial systems (for example, through work-study programmes and 'open-door' schooling). Though certain progress was made, remaining problems were masked by propaganda and grew more acute. Urban unemployment appears to have mounted steadily in fact, even though in theory it was not supposed to exist. Deficiencies in the system of planned job allocation remained widespread and foreign visitors reported visible overemployment in state factories and offices.[1] Problems of 'efficient' labour allocation and utilisation were not tackled directly as a central concern of the radical Maoist project. Though there was much ad hoc adaptation in localities and basic units, political deadlock at the centre prevented policy debate and adaptation. At the intellectual level there appears to have been little systematic attempt to grapple with the complexity of labour and employment issues and develop an integrated programme of planning and policy. Where 'contradictions' arose, a dose of politics or 'persuasive education' (shuofu jiaoyu) was prescribed but political methods for rectifying planning inadequacies lost their effectiveness over time, leaving problems unsolved and discontent unabated even if unexpressed.

Thus the challenge to the post-Mao leadership was daunting. They had to confront two sets of problems. On the issue of employment they had to devise measures to reduce urban unemployment in the short run without resorting to programmes, such as xia-xiang, which had proven unpopular and very difficult to implement; in the long run they had to develop a coherent analysis of employment and labour issues and translate it into an effective planning strategy.

On the issue of labour allocation they had to design a system which would improve allocative efficiency at the macro level and encourage more

economical and flexible use of labour at the micro
level. The post-Mao leadership realised that success or failure in this endeavour would have considerable influence on the political viability and
economic effectiveness of their new development
strategy. The way they tackled the problem is of
interest to socialists everywhere given the crucial
socialist commitment to full employment and, in the
Marxian tradition at least, the ideological central-
ity of the labour allocation process. The freeing
of labour-power to be sold as a commodity in the
market to capitalists is one of the main definitive
characteristics of the capitalist mode of production.[2] Though formally free, the labourer is com-
pelled to sell his labour power since he is deprived
of the means of production and is subject to the
vicissitudes of the labour market. When employed he
is subject to the insecurity arising from the power
of the capitalist to render him redundant. To the
extent that these conditions have been introduced by
changes in the labour system of the post-Mao era,
they are one important touchstone for assessing
whether the new Chinese leaders are agents of 'capitalist restoration'.

Employment and the Readjustment Programme

Just how serious was the problem of urban unemployment at the time of Mao's death? The actual number
of unemployed in 1976-77 is unclear and estimates
vary widely. The precise figure is probably unknown
even to the Chinese authorities since statistical
services were weak or non-existent and many unemployed evaded official information nets. Unofficial
estimates put the total number of 'unemployed' at
the beginning of 1979 at about 20 million rising to
about 26 million by early 1981. Although these
figures were attributed to 'informed Chinese sources', their statistical basis is unclear, and they
may have been an overestimate to dramatise the
problem.[3] By contrast, an official source estimated
a total number of 13 million unemployed in 1980,
about 10% of the urban population and 1.3% of the
total population (Zhuang Qidong, et al, 1981).
Whatever the exact figures, clearly most of the unemployed were young and the problem was worse for
women (about 70% of unemployed youth in the late
1970s were female) (Manpower Bureau, 1980).
    To be more precise, urban unemployed fell into
four main categories in any one year between 1977
and 1981. First, there were two long-term 'backlog

groups': (i) young urban middle-school graduates who had been sent 'down to the countryside' between 1966 and 1976 - estimated to be about 17 million. As the xia-xiang programme was gradually scaled down towards the end of the decade after considerable official vacillation, most rusticated youth returned home to await urban postings, placing heavy pressures on municipal governments; (ii) peasants recruited formally or informally to work in the cities during the previous decade, estimated at 13 million (Beijing Review, 48, 1981:8) - where possible, they were to be returned to their home villages; (iii) there was in any year a short-term backlog group, composed of the previous or earlier years' graduates who were still waiting for assignment to jobs or were studying independently to repeat the exams for higher education - they were still economically dependent on their parents; (iv) there was the current crop of primary, junior and senior-middle school graduates available for employment.

As we shall see, the last two groups remained important into the 1980s, but it was the first two groups, forming an unemployment 'bulge', which posed the major problem for the new leadership during 1977-80. Inaction or complacency was difficult in view of the tremendous pressure on local governments from urban populations and the frequency of 'incidents' - sit-ins, riots and other sporadic violence. For example, in Chongqing, Sichuan province, in early 1979, groups of unemployed were reported to be paying 'collective visits' to the municipal labour bureau where 'they surround, attack and drag away' the reception personnel and leading cadres. In Shanghai, youth formerly sent to the countryside or Xinjiang province returned to the city, formed 'action groups' and organised petition parades, stopped trains, clogged traffic and attacked government offices. They demanded to be reunited with their families and assigned urban jobs.[4] Former xia-xiang youth also sent groups to petition the central authorities in Peking and contributed to a surge of (social and political) 'delinquency' in China's cities during 1978-79. They posed a challenge to the 'stability and unity' deemed necessary for the new course.

These problems prompted various stopgap measures by local authorities during 1977-79. For example, older factory workers were persuaded to retire early on the understanding that their children would be given jobs in their units. However, this method was unsatisfactory on various counts.

While it lowered productivity by replacing skilled
with unskilled workers, it did not appreciably
affect employment since many of the retired workers
were hired by other units and many of their children
had not really been 'unemployed' in any case - they
were still in school or working in the countryside
and used this as a welcome opportunity for transfer.
Clearly, there was a need for major rethinking of
employment and labour problems at the macro level.
    Serious public discussion of the issues began
in 1979 - particularly important was an intervention
by Xue Muqiao, an advisor to the State Planning
Commission, in July 1979 in which he criticised previous and current approaches to urban employment and
labour questions and called for policy changes
(Xue Muqiao, July 1979). The issues were discussed
(and to some extent actually debated) during 1979
and 1980 and new policies tried out in certain areas
with the North-East (especially Jilin province) and
the cities of Peking, Tianjin, Hangzhou, Zhengzhou
and Shanghai, taking a leading role.[5] Central ins-
pection teams were sent out to review local experiences and a National Labour and Employment Conference was convened in Peking in early August 1980
which reviewed the issues and announced a 'new employment policy'.[6] Over the next year, provincial
and municipal work conferences were held and new
policies were set in motion or expanded. The shift
in general economic strategy in early 1981, which
involved a prolongation of the readjustment process
and a (temporary) curtailing of economic management
reforms, changed the environment of labour issues.
The CCP Central Committee and the State Council
issued a set of decisions on employment and labour,
made public in November 1981, which reviewed the
experience of the previous year. These mostly reinforced the policy prescriptions made by the August
1980 conference, but, in line with the general climate of economic policy, the _reform_ as opposed to
readjustment component of the new policy was weak-
ened.[7]
    From the beginning of this process of policy
innovation, problems of employment and labour allocation were related to two main issues: first, the
overall strategy of economic development and the
consequent structure of the economy and, second, the
nature of the state labour allocation system. In
very broad terms, the policy responses in the former
area were embodied in the 'readjustment' programme
ratified at the Third Plenum in December 1978; the
latter was one target of the programme for reforming

or 'restructuring' the system of economic management,
also ratified at the Third Plenum. These two approaches to labour and employment issues were compatible to some extent, but, as we shall see later, in
the short run at least they were contradictory,re-
flecting competing political priorities and policy
objectives.

Let us first discuss the approach to employment
and labour problems embodied in the <u>readjustment</u>
programme begun in 1978. First, there was an effort
to develop a more integrated conception of the complex relations between different arenas of planning,
i.e. between employment and labour questions on the
one hand and the economic structure, social welfare
policy, the educational system and population growth
on the other; between urban problems on the one
hand and those of society as a whole on the other.[8]

Since these inter-relationships had been neglected in the past, critics argued, systematic imbalances and dislocations had developed. For example, since the educational and economic systems were
out of alignment, middle-school graduates could not
be accommodated and had to wait for employment,
often for several years. Even when employment was
provided, it often did not match individuals' skills
or aspirations, a situation which was particularly
costly in the case of technical and professional
manpower. Critics argued that the educational system as a whole should be expanded, educational out-
lays should be increased and middle-level technical
and vocational training should be increased; these
proposals appeared to be finding greater official
favour by late 1981.[9] Similarly, questions of rural
economy should be taken into account when assigning
urban labour: large-scale transfers of urban unemployed to the countryside were politically infeasible and economically unwise. In the longer
run, it was argued, a proportion of the rural population would have to be accommodated in the cities
(for example, through the creation of new small or
medium-sized cities).[10]

Second, certain central changes in the economic
structure were identified as essential to improve
the employment situation, in quantitative terms at
least. We can discuss these under two general head-
ings: first, the relationship between different
types of ownership and forms of production; second,
sectoral priorities between industry and agriculture
and within industry. It was maintained that the
balance between the three different types of ownership and forms of production - state, collective and

262

private - had to be changed to generate more job
opportunities. Collective enterprises absorbed more
labour than their state counterparts and thus
should receive greater ideological and practical
emphasis. One source estimated that collectives
required less than 2,000 yuan per worker while state
enterprises required an average of 9-10,000 yuan
(Feng Lanrui, 1981). The ideological definition of
the 'superiority' of state over collective and
collective over private production relations was
deemed to be inappropriate to China's material and
human endowments. The previous official position
had tended to define collective industry in the cities as a transitional expedient, a way-station on
the road to truly socialist (i.e. state) production
relations. Under 'ultra-leftist' influence, moreover, private businesses had been defined invidi-
ously as 'tails of capitalism' or 'capitalist loopholes'. Just as there had been premature 'transition in poverty' in agriculture - from private to
collective production and from lower-level to higher
level collectives (teams to brigades to communes) -
so in the cities private had been transformed into
collective, collective into state.[11] The
étatisation of urban collective enterprises had
either been through outright nationalisation or
through a more gradual escalation from 'small collectives' to 'big collectives' under tighter state
supervision. The early 1950s and early 1960s were
praised as periods when urban collectives were encouraged and employment problems eased; the
Cultural Revolution decade denigrated as a period
when collectives were restricted or ignored. Thus,
statistics were adduced to show that, between 1965
and 1976, the proportion of workers in collectives
dropped from 23.9% to 20.9% while that in state
enterprises rose from 72.8% to 78.9% (Feng Lanrui,
1981).

This picture of 1966-76 is somewhat exaggerated.
Certainly there was an effort after 1970 to encourage urban collectives, under the supervision of
neighbourhood committees. Xue Muqiao (1981:187)
acknowledges this fact but argues that 'they have
employed mostly housewives or people physically
unsuited for ordinary full-time jobs', an assertion
which he fails to support statistically. It should
also be noted, moreover, that a considerable amount
of collective (and private) economic activity had
been conducted outside formal channels in a 'second
economy'. However, it can be argued that the xia-
xiang programme absorbed surplus labour which could

have been organised into urban collectives to meet
mounting and unsatisfied consumer demand in the early and mid 1970s and invigorate the urban economy
generally. To the reformers of the late 1970s,
moreover, collective enterprises were economically
attractive not only because they absorbed labour,
but also because they could do certain things far
better than state enterprises (for example, catering,
consumer good production, transportation), they were
potentially more flexible in adapting to changing
market conditions and operated according to the
principle of independent responsibility for profit
and loss, a characteristic which the market reformers regarded as a <u>sine qua non</u> of enterprise initiative and economic efficiency.

The same type of arguments were applied to the
role of private (household or individual) economic
activity, which had been whittled away by premature
collectivisation, restriction or outright prohibition. It was reported that the number of 'individual labourers' in the cities had declined from 9
million in 1953 (50% of all urban workers and staff)
to a mere 150,000 by 1966   (Zhao Lukuan, 1980).
This had a damaging impact on the service, handicrafts and petty-trading sectors, clogged up suitable employment outlets and hampered the satisfaction of expanding urban consumer demands.
Xue Muqiao (July, 1979) argued, for example, that
in Shanghai individuals should take on short-dis-
tance transport with hand-carts, carry baggage, set
up laundries and small snack bars in alleys and repair shoes and clothes. To the extent that these
jobs had been done, it was often by suburban peasants, creating an anomalous situation whereby peasants took over urban jobs, often informally or ill-
egally, while urban unemployed were being shipped
out to the countryside.

Statistical evidence apart, this kind of argument seems plausible to anyone who, like the author,
visited China in the early 1970s (1972 and 1974)
when there was a clear and apparently indefensible
absence of (visible) individual enterprise. Fears
of 'capitalist restoration' did not seem to justify
such sweeping prohibitions. Employment considerations apart, moreover, one could argue not only that
the quality and convenience of urban life suffered
in consequence, but also that this situation was a
fertile breeding ground for the 'second economy'.

Because these two crucial outlets were restricted, argued the critics, there was great pressure on
the state sector to provide jobs which, in view of

264

its relative capital intensity, it was ill suited to meet. In consequence, excess labour was taken on and labour productivity suffered. There appears to be substantial merit in these criticisms, again based on the impressions of foreign visitors in the 1970s. Factory pay-rolls swelled through push and pull: the pull was the incentive within the planning system to overstock and hoard labour; the push was from the unemployed and their families transmitted through urban labour bureaux which pressurised enterprises to take on more labour. If this failed, people could either be taken on as children of workers in the same enterprise or through personal connections with enterprise officials. The pressure on the state sector was increased by the polarisation of urban employment options which emerged in the early and mid 1960s - either a state job or 'mobilisation' to the countryside. Many youth preferred to wait for several years after graduation in the hope of gaining a state job and avoid the rigours of xia-xiang.

This diagnosis of the ownership structure led to a set of policies designed to redress the balance. Individuals were encouraged to set up their own businesses in a wide variety of trades. Unemployed youth were encouraged to organise collective enterprises, as far as possible with their own funds; state enterprises could also set up their own collective enterprises, providing financial and technical support. Local governments were instructed to give material assistance to collective and individual enterprises through tax concessions, soft loans, access to material supplies, help with welfare benefits and grain rations, and were warned not to have 'negative attitudes' and engage in 'interference' and 'discrimination'. In the Central Committee and State Council decisions on employment in November, 1981, individual business-people were guaranteed the right to have 'two helpers and five apprentices'. Widespread publicity was given to individual 'entrepreneurs' who were expanding their businesses and taking on more help.[12] Political agencies were called on to accord individual and collective workers the same 'political treatment' and 'social status' as workers in state enterprises (for example, in terms of access to the Youth League and Party).

The other major component of 'readjustment' with major implications for urban employment was the rethinking of sectoral priorities in economic policy. The problems encountered in the xia-xiang programme over the previous fifteen years suggested that urban

employment problems could not be exported to the
countryside. Agricultural production in China
proper was already very labour-intensive and the
amount of land per capita was shrinking; with agricultural modernisation, surplus labour was growing
in the countryside and the 'down to the countryside'
movement caused antagonism among urbanites and farmers alike. Indeed, it was informally described as
'the sending down of contradictions'. In future,
only a small proportion of urban unemployed could be
placed in the rural areas and only then on a voluntary and usually temporary (contract) basis, and in
suburban areas and special units rather than the
'real' countryside.[13] For the time being, therefore,
the planned flow of labour either from or to the
cities is likely to be relatively minor though un-
planned flows to the cities will probably continue[14]

The decision to increase the importance of
agriculture vis-a-vis industry, most notably by
raising its share of state investment and increasing
procurement prices for agricultural commodities, has
employment implications. A faster pace of rural
development and rising farm incomes, it is hoped,
will stabilise the rural population, reducing the
incentive to migrate to the cities, and alleviate
urban unemployment by providing a growing market for
the products of labour-intensive urban light industries.

The efforts to readjust the structure of industry also have an employment objective. Within the
productive sector, shifts have been attempted in
favour of labour-intensive over capital-intensive,
small and medium scale over large-scale, light over
heavy industry - dichotomies which overlap to a
large extent. The question of factor composition -
labour vs. capital - is complex and linked with the
vexed issue of technology choice and debates over
foreign trade. Large-scale re-equipping with capital-intensive foreign technology has negative employment implications, in the short term at least,
and there has been a debate over the relationship
between technology and employment, seemingly unresolved as of the end of 1981. At least one author
(Yue Guangzhao, 1981) has suggested a 'dualist'
approach, i.e. key enterprises, civil and military,
should incorporate imported technology and strive to
reach 'advanced world standards' while other sectors
of industry should lay greater stress on expanding
employment. Scale is also important; in Shandong
province, for example, cited as a model for employment policy in 1981, relative success was attributed

partly to the high proportion of small enterprises.
At the end of 1980, the proportion was 0.2% 'large',
0.9% 'medium' and 98.9% 'small' with output value
proportions of 17.9%, 18.1% and 64% respectively
(the corresponding value proportions for all China
were 25%, 19% and 56%). Likewise 10,000 yuan of
fixed assets provided employment in the province for
0.6 people in large enterprises, 0.9 in medium and
1.3 in small (Zhuang Qidong et.al. 1981). The
conclusions for national policy were obvious. Similar arguments were made about the relationship between heavy and light industries. The previous industrial structure was condemned as irrationally
biassed towards heavy industry. It was estimated in
1981, for example, that between 1950 and 1980, China
had invested 374,220 million yuan in heavy industry
and only 39,430 million yuan in light industry. In
terms of expanding employment, it was argued, this
ratio was lopsided since, for every million yuan of
fixed assets, heavy industrial enterprises only provided 94 jobs, light industrial, 257 jobs (Feng
Lanrui, 1981).

Similar comparisons were made between the employment potentials of material production industries
on the one hand and the commerce and service sectors
on the other. The latter sectors had been allowed
to languish until the mid 1970s, allegedly under the
influence of the Gang of Four. This type of attri-
bution is unconvincing since the dominance of production over circulation and service is a common
feature of Stalinist or Soviet-type political economies generally. However, initial statistics appear
to support an expansion of these sectors on employment grounds: for every one million yuan of fixed
assets, they could provide 800-1,000 jobs. As we
shall see later, however, whether the urban unemployed - particularly recent middle-school graduates - can be persuaded to go into these trades in
significant numbers is a different question.

To the extent that the readjustment programme
succeeded in bringing about these structural changes
in the economy, it may well have eased urban unemployment - we shall assess the impact in a later section. It is important to remember, however, that
the strategy of readjustment also implied greater
unemployment, at least temporarily, for workers in
industries and enterprises falling victim to structural 'rationalisation'. A certain proportion of
factories producing goods in excess supply, or
chronically inefficient or unviable for other reasons (for example lack of adequate transport

facilities, power or raw materials) were to be closed and the workforce (eventually) reassigned.

(Attempted) Reforms in the Labour Allocation System

Let us now turn to the third crucial element of policy change, the effort to reform the state labour allocation system. This is a complex area of policy since it reflects the (partly incompatible) logics of 'readjustment' and 'reform' and the competing priorities of simultaneously increasing both employment and labour productivity. From the point of view of expanding employment, the previous system of labour allocation has been condemned as overly monopolistic, obstructing the emergence of alternative employment channels and stifling the initiative of the unemployed in seeking jobs for themselves, thus producing an attitude of 'dependence on the state'. But those calling for a reform of the labour allocation system had wider objectives, indeed they operated to some extent with a different set of premises and objectives. Let us examine the logic and practical impact of this 'reform' position.

The reform of the previous system of 'unified' labour allocation was one of a wider set of proposals put forward during 1979 and 1980, with the aim of restructuring the system of economic management.[15] Resurgent economists argued that, like the unemployment issue, analysis of the labour allocation system had been a forbidden zone for too long. Reconsideration and reform were needed with the following objectives in mind: (i) to improve allocative efficacy in two senses, technical and socio-political. From the technical point of view, it was important to have a system of labour allocation which could match available labour power with socio-economic needs both quantitatively and qualitatively, at both macro and micro levels. From the socio-political perspective, allocation methods should be such as to match job openings and careers with individual aspirations, maximise job satisfaction, reduce discontent and improve productivity; (ii) to encourage a certain degree of mobility of labour and flexibility in labour utilisation. This would allow enterprises to adapt more easily in the context of greater market pressures, and would encourage technical innovation and economical use of labour within the enterprise. This flexibility was seen as an essential precondition of greater macro and micro efficiency, on the principle that 'running water is never stale and a door hinge is never worm-eaten'; (Ye Ming,

August 1980); (iii) to the maximal extent compatible with the above two aims, to guarantee full employment and job security.

In the eyes of reform economists, the previous
system of labour allocation had not been successful
in achieving these goals. First, the previous system of direct control through 'unified employment
and assignment' had exercised a virtual monopoly
over the allocation of urban labour. As the economy
grew more complex it exceeded the regulative capacity of state agencies, central or local. The span
of state control was too broad and the machinery of
regulation too rigid.[16] Indeed, it was argued that,
of all aspects of allocation in the previous system
of economic management - human, financial and material - 'the allocation of labour resources is by far
the furthest from the market mechanism'(Liu Guoguang
and Zhao Renwei, 1979:63). Second, the system was
too 'top down', imposing 'plan' (or rather bureaucratic) priorities on individuals in initial job
allocation. After job assignment, moreover, the
individual found it very hard to move from his or
her original unit in the face of formidable bureaucratic obstacles in the personnel system itself
(inside and outside the enterprise) and by other
external controls, notably residence certificates
(hukou) and ration-tickets. The result was discontent, poor labour productivity and low morale, particularly costly among skilled workers and technical
staff.[17] The allocation system, it was argued, had
been partly responsible for the disappointing record of overall labour productivity in state industry
since 1949: while total industrial output value had
increased by 3,400%, labour productivity had only
risen by 300%, from 3,004 yuan per worker in 1949 to
12,031 yuan in 1980 (Yue Guangzhao, 1981).

Third, 'unified allocation' by state bureaux
had encouraged over-manning. State enterprises had
been allowed to develop extensively through additional labour, rather than encouraged to develop
intensively through technical innovation and greater
productivity: the example of one medium-sized plant
was cited where manpower had risen 120% between 1966
and 1977 but output by only 13.3%. Workshops,
branch plants and union plant all had their own repair and maintenance personnel and their own under-
utilised maintenance equipment - 'it was like supporting troops for a thousand days to use them just
once' (Ye Ming and Chan Guangzhen, 1979). There
was also inadequate provision for lateral mobility,
reassignment or dismissal, with the result that most

state workers and staff had life-time job tenure,
often in their original units, guaranteed regardless
of performance. This was the infamous 'iron rice-
bowl' (also called 'rubber rice-bowl')which in the
eyes of reformers, prevented the flexibility necessary for efficient enterprise behaviour.[18] Indeed,
there was a built-in tendency towards the <u>hereditary</u>
transmission of jobs within state enterprises. In
one admittedly extreme case of a factory in a remote
mountainous area (with 600-700 workers and staff),
retiring staff tended to be replaced by their children and the children tended to intermarry:

> As a result, husbands and wives, fathers and
> sons, fathers-in-law and sons-in-law, sisters-
> in-law and their husbands, sisters, sisters'
> husbands and brothers' wives were working in
> the same factory.

Not only did this have a bad effect on efficiency,
it was argued, but, if it continued, 'will our socialist enterprise not become a big feudal family?'
(Ye Ming, August 1980). Such 'regular' or 'fixed
workers' (<u>guding gongren</u>) eating out of their iron
bowls had a privileged position in the urban labour
force, as one commentator complained:

> (This system of the 'iron rice bowl') makes
> workers and staff members of collectively
> owned units and individual labourers in cities
> and towns restless at their jobs because they
> are always trying to find an 'iron rice bowl'.
> It creates contradictions between the workers
> and staff of several thousand units owned by
> the whole people on the one hand, and hundreds
> of millions of labourers on the other, and
> causes factors of instability among them.
> Therefore we simply must reform the system of
> "unified" employment and assignment
> (Zhao Lukuan, 1980).

Such criticisms of the labour allocation process tend to overstate the degree of <u>actual</u> state
control over urban labour under the previous system
- there was a gap between the way in which urban
labour bureaux were supposed to operate and the
often ineffectual way in which they actually did.
Nor were all workers in state enterprises 'regular';
'temporary' or 'contract' workers were still employed in the early and mid 1970s even though no formal
'two-track' system existed akin to that abortively

launched by Liu Shaoqi in the mid 1960s.[19] Yet the
argument about the gulf between 'fixed' state employees and other less secure, remunerated and pres-
tigious members of the urban work force is a valid
one.

The new policies, mooted in 1979-80, reflected
the logic of this critique. Policy proposals can be
grouped into two broad categories: first, improvements in the planning system and, second, a multi-
dimensional process of 'destatification' of the
system of labour allocation and utilisation, both
for initial job-placement and post-placement mobility. The latter category has received far more
attention and I shall concentrate on that. Planning
reforms parallel those put forward to deal with the
unemployment problem: more precise forecasting of
labour requirements and tighter integration of other
planning priorities - notably industrial investment
policy, educational policy, population control,
urbanisation - with labour plans. Destatification,
on the other hand, involves an attempt both to re-
define and diminish the role of direct state regulation of the labour force. For most analysts,
however, the planning principle remains supreme.
For example, Xue Muqiao has argued that 'the
nation's labour force should in principle be taken
care of by state planning', that is 'the state
should make overall arrangements', more precise
determinations being left to non-state agencies
(Xue Muqiao, 1981:216). Labour allocation was
ideally to become a 'three-in-one combination' between state agencies, enterprises (and other relatively independent economic organisations) and individuals.

Let us discuss the role envisaged for state
agencies. First, though the reformers envisage a
loosening of controls over all sectors of the urban
work force, certain distinctions inherent in the
previous system are to remain in force. Certain
'strategic' groups have been subject to tighter and
more centralised controls over initial job-placement
and later re-assignment, notably graduates of higher
educational institutions and technical middle
schools and demobilised army officers and men. This
arrangement remains, though it is urged that individuals in these categories should be given a say
about their assignment and more freedom to move in
mid-career. A second stratum, urban workers in the
state sector, are to stay under the 'supervision' of
urban labour bureaux though changes are envisaged in
the division of responsibility and initiative

between bureaux, enterprises and individuals. For urban workers in the non-state sector, formerly subject to regulation from labour bureaux and street committees, far greater freedom is envisaged. In essence, therefore, we have a three-level system of greater and lesser, more and less centralised or 'unified' state involvement.

Second, the role of labour bureaux in allocating non-strategic urban labour was to be redefined in several ways: (a) Bureaux were to continue with their overall planning of local labour requirements but their methods of regulation were to change. Rather than assigning workers to enterprises, they were to play more of a recommendatory or intermediary role; workers would apply to the bureau,which would forward their names to appropriate enterprises which would have the power of vetting, acceptance or rejection. The decision to recommend would ideally reflect both planning priorities and the labour demands put forward by individual enterprises. After deciding on the workers to be employed, the enterprise was to submit a list to the labour bureau for approval. (b) Labour bureaux were to hand over part of their functions to local non-state agencies, notably various kinds of collectively-owned 'labour service companies', under the supervision of street committees, state enterprises, even schools and offices.[20] These organisations would concentrate on arranging jobs in the collective and private sectors. Individuals and groups have also been encouraged to organise their own employment by setting up private or collective businesses without state administrative mediation or financial support. (c) Urban labour bureaux have been called on to extend their role in facilitating the mobility of labour between enterprises, and to act as a 'cushion' to ease the frictional unemployment which would be an inevitable outcome of the reform programme if implemented, since 'the market needs the labour force to change from time to time'. Labour bureaux would be responsible for receiving labour shed by enterprises, arranging interim welfare benefits and re-training and eventual reassignment to other units. One proposal suggested that such surplus personnel should continue to receive full or partial pay (half from the enterprise, half from the state) until they obtained new jobs and should receive supplementary benefits where appropriate from a social security fund to enable them to 'maintain a minimum standard of living'.[21] Vocational training institutions should also be expanded to meet this new task.

This decrease in state regulation was to be accompanied by a corresponding increase in the labour allocation power of enterprises, as part of the wider project of expanding the autonomy of basic units of production. Many reform proposals reduced the supervisory role of labour bureaux to a minimal level, the enterprises taking most of the major decisions on hiring and firing workers (though not necessarily technical and professional staff). Should they require more workers, they should be allowed to advertise, deal with applicants directly and establish their own recruitment methods and criteria. According to some reformers, moreover, they should also have the right to 'hire away' labour from other units, both skilled workers and technical staff, using their increased power to determine the shape of the wage system.[22] Even more crucial, argued the reformers, was enterprise power over firing - without this, the attempt to combine plan and market regulation would founder: overmanning would increase, technical innovation and labour productivity would flag and enterprises would not be able to adjust to changing market conditions. The rights of dismissed workers would be protected by involving enterprise workers' organisations, the trade unions and workers' congresses in the decision to dismiss, by the requirement that formal approval be sought from higher organs and by the special welfare provisions for their period of unemployment organised by state labour agencies.

The third major element of the redivision of power over labour allocation was the attempt to increase the choice available to individual workers and professional staff, particularly the latter (especially after their initial job posting) - an argument resting on a Marxian analysis that the individual worker in socialist society still retains ownership of his/her own labour power.[23] Xue Muqiao jokingly compared this to changes in marriage choice: 'If there were "freedom of love" instead of "parental command and the matchmaker's nice words" the problem (of employment) could be solved'. Xue laid particular stress on granting 'scientists, technicians and other people with special knowledge and skill ... the right to choose their jobs under certain conditions' (Xue Muqiao, 1981:217 and 1979). Other reformers went so far as to argue for allowing 'the free movement of qualified personnel and specialised cadre' (Zhou Xiuqiang, 1980). Greater freedom, it was argued, would increase the efficient

utilisation of scarce talent and skill and protect
specialised personnel against the arbitrary dictates
of administrative cadres in enterprises or state
organs. In such proposals, however, increased
choice and personal mobility was still seen as a
subsidiary method, a complement to the planned allocation of skilled labour in the state sector, rather
than as an alternative.

The reform position did not go without public
challenge and critique - indeed, the very publication of opposing positions testifies to the strength
of sentiment behind them. Xue Muqiao's initial
broadside on labour issues in the Peking Daily was
criticised in a signed article in the same newspaper
two months later.[24] The author, Liu Zizhen, argued
that the state should continue to allocate urban
jobs according to plan and workers should be guaranteed job security; if workers were given a 'mud
rice-bowl' this was hardly socialism. Indeed 'if a
worker can be kicked out because he is unfit, what's
the difference between this method and the capitalists?' The way to tackle the employment problems,
said Liu, was to shorten working hours and adopt a
system of 'low pay and more employment, five people
doing three people's work'. Clearly the proposed
power of dismissal concerned many workers, a sentiment which surfaced, for example, in the Workers'
Daily in a reader's letter in early 1981. The
letter stated that the masses, who are powerless,
are very worried about this power and they turn pale
at the mere mention of it.[25] The force of feeling
behind this letter is reflected in the fact that a
senior economist, Yu Guangyuan, was invited to write
a reply 'reassuring' the worried worker. Such public challenges have been few compared to the aval-
anche of reform literature, but this disparity con-
ceals the real magnitude of opposition to the reforms, as we shall see later.

The Impact of Readjustment and Reform on Employment and Labour Allocation

Employment: Achievements and trends. As the policy
proposals embodied in the readjustment and reform
programmes were, to varying degrees, put into practice during 1979-81, certain patterns emerge. Most
importantly, the political impetus behind the effort
to alleviate unemployment through economic readjustment has been greater than that to rationalise the
labour system through reform of the economic management system. As of the beginning of 1982, it is

impossible to assess the success of the employment
drive with any precision since official statistics
are inconsistent, statistical categories muddled and
figures mostly doled out in bits and pieces (like
the lamp-post and the drunk, for support rather than
illumination). Bare quantitative achievements certainly look impressive - it is claimed that, between
the beginning of 1977 and September 1981, 33.77
million people were given jobs (most of these were
probably urbanites but it is not clear what percentage). Within this, the backlog of 17 million urban
'educated youth' sent to the countryside between
1966 and 1976 had been assigned work, mostly in the
cities.[26] There appears to have been considerable
regional variation, with certain provinces such as
Jilin and Shandong being pace-setters with others
such as Shaanxi being slower off the mark. Of
course, one can doubt the reliability of these statistics, given the Centre's pressure on local governments to provide visible proof of their success in
providing jobs; one can also have doubts about the
stability of the jobs assigned. Even if one dis-
counts for doubt, however, these quantitative
achievements are considerable, especially if one
sets them against the total size of the urban work
force, which was about 75M.[27] (56% of urban population) at the end of 1979, and reflects the proportions of the urban unemployment problem which had
accumulated by 1976. The ratio of urban employed
to total urban population had also increased from
1:36 in 1952 to 1: 1.78 in 1981.[28] Notwith-
standing official Panglossian propaganda to the contrary, however, the problem was still severe as of
the end of 1981 and the immediate future highly
problematic. Even the most optimistic of official
statements could only claim that 'the employment
situation has gradually been eased', but only been
'solved basically in some cities and towns'
(Beijing Review 48, 1981:8). Although historical
backlogs appear to have been cleared, at least temporarily, the ranks of the unemployed were swelled
during 1980-81 by the addition of workers released
from enterprises declared redundant and closed as
part of the readjustment process and unable to be
reabsorbed because of cutbacks in the state's capital construction programme.[29] Moreover, the pressure of new job-seekers each year is unrelenting and
local governments are clearly having difficulty
coping. For example, while one authoritative source
estimated in mid 1981 that jobs would have to be
found for 10 million people in 1981 (Zhuang Qidong

and Sun Keliang, 1981), official statistics in late
1981 reported only 4.77 million job placements in
the first nine months and the average placement over
the previous four years only just over 7 million per
year. If one also considers that many of the new
jobs of the late 1970s may have been one-off opportunities opened up by the supply-side restrictions
and pent-up demand of the previous decade, and if
one takes into account the decision to restrain the
scale of capital construction in the early 1980s and
continuing population pressures, employment problems
may well remain acute over 1981-85, a period when an
estimated 30 million new urban jobs must be found.

The major policies of readjustment are reasonable and there is evidence that they are proving
effective, even if insufficient. For example, the
number of self-employed in China's cities rose to
800,000 in 1980 and exceeded one million in 1981, a
rapid increase but still small compared to a total
state payroll of over 100 million and an urban work
force of about 72 million. By 1980, individual and
collective enterprises were providing about one half
of new employment: of 6½ million people employed
in that year, 37% went to state enterprises, 43% to
collectives, 6% to individual enterprises and 14% to
'temporary work', figures which appear to represent
a significant shift in the pattern of urban employment (Feng Lanrui, 1981).

But readjustment measures cannot dispel the
problem of urban unemployment. One continuing problem is the weakness of labour planning: first, at
the intellectual level, there seems to have been
little progress so far in coming to grips systematically with the complex relationships involved,
though there was some movement in late 1981 and
early 1982; second, the implementation of planning
decisions is even weaker, particularly at the local
level. It is ironical that in this policy area, as
in many others, the last few years have seen great
effort to foster market regulation as a 'supplement'
to the planning system yet surprisingly little in
improving the efficiency of the planning system itself.

Turning to specific policy remedies, clearly
the employment potential of the labour-intensive
productive and service sectors is limited by movements in the economy as a whole, both industry and
agriculture.30 Many of the new individual and collective enterprises may lack the finance, technical
expertise or business know-how to remain viable,and
local governments (or state enterprises) may be

unable or unwilling to bail them out.[31] Moreover, private enterprises operate under strict ideological limits - if they are too successful financially or take on too many 'helpers', they run the risk of being classified as 'capitalist' and thus disbanded or collectivised.[32]

Even where collective enterprises thrive, the persistence of material and psychological differentials between the state and non-state (collective or private) sectors will maintain an intense pressure for jobs in the former, especially among young people emerging from a highly academic, competitive and elitist educational system. One should recall that in the early 1960s, when state jobs were scarce and urban collectives were encouraged, many urban youth refused assignments to collective units because of their tantalising hope for an 'iron rice-bowl' in the state sector and because they found jobs in services, transport and petty retailing irksome, demeaning, unremunerative and without a 'future' (qiantu).[33] It is not surprising, then, to hear the party secretary of Heilongjiang province complain in 1981 that 'some people think that only working in state enterprises is real employment, working in collective-run enterprises is semi-employment and engaging in private and household occupations is no employment at all'.[34]

Indeed, the very success of collective and private enterprises may bring conflict rather than complementarity with the state sector as state enterprises react against 'unfair' competition and state workers resist any erosion of differentials.[35] The influence of such state-based interests within the CCP is considerable, as is their ability to appeal to central ideological symbols: the superiority of state ownership, the notion of the skilled proletariat and warnings of incipient capitalism. From a socialist viewpoint, however, such claims can be contested: the 'proletariat' may be in effect a labour aristocracy, the top layer of a stratified working class; the social relations of production in collective enterprises might be considered 'superior' to those in state enterprises, since the former involve ownership and control by the work-force while the latter embody hierarchical control from (internal) managers and (external) bureaucrats.

Domestic constraints are thus considerable, but external outlets do not offer a solution. Employment in export industries and export of labour offers some relief - one source estimated that expanded exports of light industrial and handicraft

products could increase employment by one million
(Zhuang Qidong and Sun Keliang, 1981) - but it is
constrained (in the short run at least) by protec-
tionism or slack demand in the industrialised countries and competition from other Third World countries, notably the 'four tigers' of East Asia -
Hong Kong, Singapore, South Korea and Taiwan. In
overall terms, therefore, it is not surprising that
some officials, as the same source admitted, 'feel
that the problem is beyond us'. For the foreseeable
future, unemployment, particularly among young people, is likely to be a characteristic feature of
urban China, on a scale likely to cause continuing
social and political tension.

Labour allocation: achievements, trends and solutions. Though success in the area of employment
creation has been quite impressive, albeit overshad-
owed by the size and intractability of the problems
faced, the record of achievement in reforming the
system of labour allocation has been more modest
compared with initial proposals. In mid 1981,
Zhuang and Sun claimed that proposed reforms had had
little effect over the previous two years.[36] There
was some patchy progress in increasing the power of
state enterprises in selecting new workers: for
example, enterprises made increasing use of advert-
isements for job vacancies and examinations were
conducted, at the plant or municipality level, to
vet applicants.[37] But advertised openings were
still mainly directed at the jobless and the principle was not extended to attract those currently
employed, with a few exceptions. Moreover, labour
bureaux were still responsible for assigning labour
quotas and still exerted intense pressures on enterprises to accept recommended labour. Enterprises
were often forced to accept labour quotas above
their own estimated requirements because labour bureaux were desperately trying to expand employment.
In consequence, overmanning may have worsened and
productivity declined or stagnated. The tremendous
pressure of unemployment also retained and expanded
the practice of hiring the children of staff and
workers, either direct to the plant, or to new collective units attached to the mother plant. This
became official policy in most provinces during
1977-78 and attracted the understandable annoyance
of reform economists who saw it as an irrational
rigidification of the work-force (Shirk, 1981:577).
However, there has been some progress in diversifying channels of labour recruitment, largely

through the new 'labour service companies' which relieved labour bureaux of some of their burden by arranging jobs in collective enterprises.[38] But progress here was too slow for the reformers.

On the proposed power of dismissal, little progress seems to have been made, given ideological objections in the Party and strong resistance from workers and their representatives. An exception here is that of joint-venture companies in the south-east (for example, in the Shenzhen special zone in Guangdong province)[39] where management powers over hiring and firing are greater than elsewhere. The CCP and State Council decisions on employment in November 1981 confirmed the lack of progress in this area and called for a gradual move towards greater power over dismissals in future. But even this power would only seem to apply to workers who repeatedly violate labour discipline, relatively serious and infrequent cases. As such, the measure falls far short of the original reform ideas about the need to increase the fluidity of the work force.

To broaden our view, labour system reforms (like price reforms) have fared noticeably worse than other components of the reform programme.[40] Financial reforms have been carried farthest, notably various forms of profit retention by enterprises. As reform economists were complaining in 1981, however, the reforms are an integrated package which should not be introduced piecemeal or partially; failure in one policy area undermines success in others. Just as failure to change methods of labour allocation impeded the capacity of enterprises to raise labour productivity and adjust to market fluctuations, so slow progress in areas such as wage reforms impeded changes in the labour system. To the extent that the previous system of centralised planning remained unreformed, moreover, enterprise managers still had incentives to hoard labour to provide the reserves necessary to fulfill and exceed plan targets. Hopes for changes in labour policy were further dampened by the decision to slow down the general reform process in late 1980 and early 1981.

How do we account for this slow progress? One basic problem is the incompatibility between the priorities of increasing employment on the one hand and promoting labour productivity and flexibility on the other. In practice, the former priority has overwhelmed the latter, much to the chagrin of reform economists, who point to the impossibility of introducing economies in the use of labour while

labour bureaux are force-feeding already over-staff-
ed enterprises with unnecessary labour (Xue Muqiao,
June 1980). They argue that employment and labour
productivity are compatible in the long run
(Feng Lanrui 1981),but long run analysis makes more
sense in economic theory than political practice.
Since urban employment pressures are likely to continue at a high level through the 1980s, the kind of
breathing space needed to tackle labour reforms is
unlikely to be available.

Policy incompatibility aside, clearly the
political impetus behind the employment drive was
greater, and the political constraints less, than
that for reforms in the labour system. Demonstra-
tions of urban unemployed were still occurring in
1981. In Shanghai, for example, over 1000 jobless
demonstrated on April 13,the culmination of an earlier
series of smaller rallies, and the army and fire
brigade had to be called in to maintain order.41
Such incidents were not uncommon and caused acute
concern to central and local leaderships, a highly
visible index of the viability of their new strategy.
By contrast, the efficiency problems inherent in the
previous economic management system pinpointed by
the reformers did not provoke such immediate and
forceful political pressures. Clearly there was
some impetus from certain groups, notably from enterprise cadres who wanted a freer hand on labour
issues, but even they appear to have been ambivalent
as a group, some preferring the old system of
dirigiste allocation and labour immobility. Intell-
ectual-professional staff stood to gain insofar as
the reforms gave them greater leverage vis-à-vis
their managerial and administrative superiors.
Clearly, many professional staff in enterprises
keenly resented a system of labour allocation 'under
which a single word of a leading member often determines a (specialised) cadre's lifetime career'. As
one reformer put it, they should be able to say 'if
you don't find me useful here, I will go elsewhere'
(Zhou Xiuqiang 1980, Wu Lu 1980). The same logic
may apply to highly skilled manual workers.

Conversely, the employment drive met far less
opposition than the reforms. Though certain sectors
of the state economy did put up some resistance,
increased employment seemed a positive-sum policy
and with something - directly or indirectly - for
most sectors of urban society. By contrast, the
benefits of labour reforms were relatively invisible
while their potential costs caused considerable dis-
quiet. At the ideological level, calls for labour

flexibility and management power to sack workers touched a raw nerve - the prospect of labour power being transformed into a commodity, a process characteristic of the establishment of capitalist relations of production. This was a potentially powerful political weapon for opponents of the reforms: members of key urban groups who felt their interests threatened ; administrators in labour bureaux who faced the prospect of losing power to state enterprises; enterprise cadres (notably but not exclusively in personnel departments) who faced the prospect of losing control over their professional-technical staff; and workers in state enterprises who feared the loss of their iron rice-bowls and arbitrary dismissal by vindictive managers. Formal dismissal, of course, brought stigma and it would be particularly difficult for workers to obtain new jobs, even if they were dismissed because of 'rational' labour deployment. Moreover, given the gradual tendency for 'hereditary' recruitment within enterprises, an older worker faced with dismissal or redeployment was not merely losing his/her own job, but also a privileged position for acquiring jobs for his/her children. The strength of worker resistance to lay-offs can be gauged in the reaction to attempted closures of plants condemned as redundant in the campaign to rationalise the industrial structure in 1980-81. Reports in mid 1981 from at least two provinces depicted violent protests from redundant workers, who drove managers out of their offices and damaged expensive machinery.[42]

The debate between the 'worried worker' and reform economist Yu Guangyuan discussed earlier, is eloquent on this issue. The worker cited the following case to substantiate his concern:

> At present, to give the power of 'punishment' or 'dismissal' to enterprises at the basic level will surely bring new disturbances to our society which has just gained some sort of stability. In a certain unit, even before the power to 'punish' and 'dismiss' is implemented, 80 workers were fined, 21 were demoted and 14 were dismissed and put on reserve within a month merely to enforce the unit's 'labour discipline regulations.' Come to think of it: what kind of serious consequences would result if the enterprise's decision-making power on matters of 'punishment' and 'dismissal' were to be expanded? ... I hope that an extremely cautious attitude will be

adopted on this major matter which affects
tens of millions of workers.

Though Yu Guangyuan emphasised in his reply that
dismissals should only be made with the approval of
the enterprise's trade union and/or workers' congress, the 'worried worker' was not impressed:

> We must know that at present the organisation
> and establishment of workers' congresses have
> many defects. To a large extent, the cong-
> resses cannot really speak for the workers.
> In practice, it is still the leaders who have
> the say. Thus, expanding the enterprises'
> decision-making power is actually expanding
> some people's privileges. How can we blame
> the workers and masses for being worried?
> |emphasis added|.

From the point of view of many workers in
state enterprises, the new strategy of readjustment
and reform is not a good bargain.[43] On the one
hand, the emphasis on enterprises outside the state
sector threatens to erode the differentials between
relatively privileged state workers and the rest of
the urban work force; on the other hand, rationalisation and reform brings greater insecurity and
vulnerability to both the vagaries of the market and
the decisions of enterprise managers. At the same
time, there has been very little re-allocation of
power to organisations which represent their interests. We shall return to this issue in the conclusions.
    Reactions among the state work force not only
reflect 'horizontal' differences between managers
and workers but 'vertical' conflicts between
'factions', many of them a relic of the mass organisations and factional struggle of the Cultural
Revolution. These are networks which cut across
lines of authority and income, linking individual
cadres to groups of workers and staff on the basis
of personal ties. Thus the power of dismissal or
disciplining could be used as a potent weapon in
factional struggle.
    Clearly the divergent interests and unequal
power positions of the three main strata within
enterprises - managers, technical staff and workers
- and 'vertical' divisions between cliques and factions - provide a context which is inimical to a
thorough implementation of labour reforms. Intra-
enterprise divisions aside, however, enterprise

solidarity also poses problems. The stability and
security under attack from reformers reflects the
fact that state enterprises have tended to develop
as more than merely economic units, taking on their
own distinct social and political identities
vis-a-vis the outside world, reinforced by hereditary recruitment, particularistic networks, residen-
tial concentration (dormitories and other worker
housing) and welfare facilities such as clinics,
crêches, kindergartens and schools. Such
Gemeinschaft makes reforms based on Gesellschaft
assumptions rather problematic.[44]
  These political and economic constraints make
thorough-going reform of the labour allocation system in the state sector very difficult. Yet the
efficiency problems pinpointed by reform economists
are very real - much planned allocation is hit-or-
miss, many enterprises are overmanned and labour
mobility in the state sector is still constricted.
In the context of the new emphasis in the 1980s on
improving economic effects and shifting from extensive to intensive factor utilisation, labour reform
remains a desirable economic objective. Is there
any feasible way forward which can further the
objectives of efficiency in the allocation and utilisation of labour-power while being politically
feasible and compatible with socialist principles?
At the highest level of strategic allocation, any
argument for abandoning or radically weakening the
unified allocation of technical and professional
manpower, particularly tertiary graduates, would not
seem convincing given the desirability of allocating
scarce expertise according to plan and realising the
principles of redistribution embodies therein. If
significant freedom of personnel movement were introduced at this level, trends toward uneven development would be reinforced as 'talented people rush
towards big units and big cities with better conditions and the small units and remote areas face a
shortage of such people   (Zhou Xiuqiang, July
1980:18). One advocate of reform argued that such
concerns should not be paramount since one 'should
have faith in intellectuals' political consciousness. They have deep love for socialism and the
motherland and are dedicated to scientific undertakings regardless of conditions'. But most available evidence points to the naivety of such an
assumption. If the system of unified allocation is
retained, however, manpower planning needs to be
improved and certain elements of greater flexibility
built into it. There could be a more concerted

effort to open up the crucial process of initial job
allocation by granting more organisational independence to allocation authorities and making appeal and
review procedures available to individuals. This
might go some way towards reducing the impact of
'back-door' pressures, though the latter cannot be
eliminated. Moreover, political constraints on
inter-enterprise mobility by professional staff
could perhaps be eased through some form of state
compensation or incentive system for enterprises
shedding staff and by allowing staff greater access
to political agencies, such as unions or workers'
congresses, which could act as a counter-balance to
the secretive and often repressive system of personnel administration.

Turning to the second level of state labour
allocation - local assignment of skilled manual and
petty clerical labour to state enterprises - the
reformers' call for greater labour mobility and
greater power for enterprise managers to hire and
fire workers continues to face heavy economic and
political constraints,and the required changes pose
some problems when viewed from a socialist perspective. Particularly in a situation of labour surplus, the power of enterprise managers to hire and
fire workers would, by itself, raise the prospect of
transforming labour power into a commodity and increasing the power of managers over workers. Regardless of labels, such as 'state ownership' or 'the
hegemony the working class', such a system would go a
considerable way in real terms towards creating a
labour market and thus towards reproducing capitalist relations of production, as Chinese critics have
pointed out. Such real conditions of subordination,
powerlessness and insecurity would contradict reassuring assertions by reform economists to the
effect that 'in a socialist society, the means of
production are jointly owned by the labourers,
obviating any need for labour power to become a
commodity' (Xue Muqiao, 1981:73).

Reformers may argue that they do not intend to
push things so far, but such fears are reinforced by
the tendency of some reform economists to treat
labour as a mere factor of production to be manipulated, presumably now by 'experts' rather than state
cadres, rather than as human agents capable of controlling the economic process themselves. Here, the
parallel with bourgeois economics is sometimes dis-
turbingly close. Some of the proposals for labour
bureaux to provide 'a minimum standard of living'
for dismissed workers sound uncomfortably like a

socialist form of the dole. Small wonder that such
proposals have been resisted by workers and socialist cadres. One can agree with the logic of loosening the heavy grip of the state machine over labour
allocation and decentralising more power to the
enterprise, but basic questions remain: who comp-
rises the enterprise and who is to receive this increased power? The reform literature suffers from
ambiguity or unclarity over this question: sometimes the power structure of the enterprise is
treated as a black box and not scrutinised; at
other times, it is envisaged that macro-reforms will
be accompanied by tighter labour controls and more
'scientific' management in the enterprises; in some
cases (for example, in Yu Guangyuan's reply to the
'worried worker') there is a real effort to link the
questions of de-statification at the macro level
with democratisation within enterprises. A strong
argument could be made that the latter position is
both economically rational, politically advisable
and fully justifiable in terms of socialist aspirations. There may well be a greater prospect of
securing worker cooperation in reform proposals if
the workers themselves, through their unions and
worker congresses, are able to assume an increasing
role in enterprise management - determinative not
merely consultative, real not just formal. Hope-
fully, decisions about hiring and particularly dismissals and transfers would then have greater legitimacy and, if state labour bureaux provided a
guaranteed system of financial support, retraining
and reassignment and if some institutionalised
channels of appeal were set up in the judiciary, the
amount of labour flexibility, levels of labour productivity and rates of technical innovation could
gradually be increased.

In the short run, the conditions for such a
solution are not favourable. The capacity of local
governments to deal with frictional unemployment
seems to have improved only marginally. For all the
talk about democratic management and the powers of
workers' congresses, democratisation of enterprises
has only made limited progress. Given the continuing pressures of unemployment, moreover, democratisation of enterprises might just mean greater power
for state workers to protect their own jobs and
emoluments. The most realistic prognostication for
the first half of the 1980s, therefore, would seem
to be the following. First, very limited progress
in attaining higher levels of labour fluidity between, and labour utilisation within, state

enterprises; and the persistence of state enterprises operating according to the logic of solidarity and stability rather than 'efficiency' and
market - more like large Japanese corporations than
the 'rational' micro-economic models of reform economists. Here 'feudalism' and 'socialism' seem to be
mutually reinforcing rather than contradictory principles. Second, an increased role for enterprises
vis-a-vis local labour bureaux, the relationship
characterised by bargaining but with bureaux still
the dominant agency of allocation. Third, continued
tension surrounding each specific focus of initial
job allocation, whether this be at the point of
graduation from colleges, or urban middle schools,
or various forms of reallocation, notably attempts
at large-scale dismissals or transfers from state
enterprises, or conversely, stemming from constraints on the movement of (especially professional)
personnel seeking vertical or lateral mobility.
Fourth, the reinforcement of a 'dualist' urban economic structure in two senses: (a) within the state
sector, between entrenched 'fixed' workers on the
one hand and short-term contract workers or workers
in collective enterprises sponsored by state enterprises on the other hand, the latter groups supplying some degree of flexibility in labour disposal;
(b) between the state sector on the one hand and the
private and collective sectors on the other. The
latter two sectors operate according to different
principles: in the former, labour is still basically allocated, job tenure virtually guaranteed, and
labour mobility relatively low (except for contract
workers). Thus, in the state sector, it would not
be correct to talk of the resurrection of a labour
market and a consequent revitalisation of the law
of value; in the latter sector, one could say there
was much more of a labour market with far greater
freedom of entrance and exit, and lower job security.
Given a labour surplus, competitive pressures in
this sector may well keep wages low and the material
and psychological differentials between the two sectors are likely to persist and may also embody an
intensification of the gender division of labour.
Given the continued political dominance of the state
sector and its consequent prior claim on resources,
these differentials will remain and even where there
is some sign of a shifting balance (for example,
through burgeoning private enterprise or rich collective units), competition, conflict and 'colonisa-
tion' (i.e. the state taking over successful enterprises) are likely. The situation remains highly

volatile and it is important to remember that it was just such tensions and inequalities which stoked the furnaces of mass mobilization and conflict during the Cultural Revolution.

FOREIGN INVESTMENT AND TRADE; ORIGINS OF THE MODERNIZATION POLICY

Terry Cannon

The focus of this chapter is on changes in China's external economic relations and foreign trade, in the context of strategies of socialist development and the notion of self-reliance. It is important that these areas of China's economic development and changing strategies are related to the broader arena of political struggle. It will be shown that recent policies of new and increased external economic relations, which I am calling 'Open Door policies', are significant qualitatively much more than in quantitative terms. In fact, they represent some of the most significant changes to have occurred in China's external relations (economically and politically) since 1949. Along with other crucial changes in China's strategies, they mark out the period since Mao's death and in particular since 1978 and the return of Deng Xiaoping, as one involving crucial changes in the political economy.

What is meant by 'socialist strategy for development' and a policy of self-reliance is by no means as clear-cut as has appeared in the past. We now find a series of policies in China's external financial relations which resemble those of many Third World countries (foreign loans, World Bank involvement, export processing zones, rising food imports,

* My thanks to the following people for their helpful comments on earlier drafts of this paper: Stephan Feuchtwang, John Gittings, Janet Hadley, Martin Lockett and Alex Volkoff. An earlier, shorter version was published as 'Class Struggle and Foreign Trade' in both China Now No.91, 1980 and Economic and Political Weekly, 15:26, 28 June 1980.

compensatory trade, raw material exports, <u>inter alia</u>). Yet the term 'self-reliance' continues to be used to describe the basic policy - in very different circumstances from those of the late 1960's or mid 1970's. Could such a 'model' still be offered as an example to the rest of the Third World? In what way do such changes constitute a part of the economic reforms?

A word of caution is needed here: the period since 1976 can by no means be treated as a single phase, a period of common policy, a uni-directional 'de-Maoization' (witness the struggles involving Deng Xiaoping and the demoted Hua Guofeng). Nor is it possible to view the period of the Cultural Revolution (1966-1976) as a single phase. Precursors of some aspects of present trade policies are to be seen at certain times since 1971. Yet despite these qualifications, it is quite clear that since 1976 a very different political economy is being established; different, that is, from the dominant views of the Cultural Revolution. In my own view, neither period or set of views can be idealised, either for their political or economic achievements. Some attributes of present policies may be very necessary and politically 'correct'. But on the other hand, a great deal of the Cultural Revolution was beneficial to socialist transformation, and many respects of the present policies are, in my view, conducive to the restoration of capitalism.

China has undergone a socialist revolution and has, as a part of this process, embarked on a socialist transition which may lead to the establishment of a communist society. Yet one of the characteristics of such a phase of socialist transition is the continued existence of classes and various forms of capitalist and feudal social relations. Old exploiting classes may re-emerge, or reconstitute themselves in new forms. New classes or potential classes of exploiters may also emerge from within the political-economic system of the transition itself. Socialist transformation will therefore involve both changes in old social relations, and struggles against the potential emergence of new reactionary social relations. These are particularly a product of the exercise of Party power, and its authoritarian nature, especially where a Dictatorship of the Party has substituted itself for that of the Proletariat.[1] It is a characteristic of new exploiters who emerge from within the system that they continue to claim a revolutionary heritage, maintain the Party as an instrument of power (still

calling it 'communist'), and retain the term 'socialist' to describe policies and strategies which
are very different from those described by others or
their predecessors as socialist. Has this happened
in China's political economy? This chapter can explore the evidence for such a reversal only in terms
of international trade and finance, while a convincing thesis would require proper discussion of all
the areas in which economic policy has changed.
Such surveys as those of Bettelheim (1978) and
Tissier (1979) are not convincing in that they beg
the question of what socialism actually is (or
should be) during a transition period, and do not
give adequate consideration to the very real questions raised within China as to the role of planning, the need for acceptance of the law of value,
and the functioning of the market as a regulator of
production.

Alternatively, it can be argued that the present policies are a limited retreat, similar to the
Russian New Economic Policy (NEP) of 1920, and necessitated by the 'catastrophic' decade of the Cultural Revolution. It would be easy to agree with the
recent assessment by the Chinese Communist Party in
its Resolution that class struggle became extended
and widened in very damaging factional strife during
the Cultural Revolution.[2] But the fact that the
Resolution also concedes, in sharp contrast with the
previous assessment of the 'disastrous ten years',
that production was actually quite reasonable during
the Cultural Revolution, makes it difficult to
accept so easily arguments about the need for retreats.[3] I feel that problems in China's economy
may well have warranted retreat policies and readjustments. But the danger is that these Open Door
policies, which involve what one leading economist
has described as 'State Capitalism',[4] will have a
detrimental effect on social relations and can be
incorporated into a programme of capitalist restoration.

To call it a 'programme', with the implication
that it is planned as such, is perhaps too strong.
Certainly I believe there are Party leaders and ex-
capitalists who do plan it as such (some even
suggest that China ought to have gone through a
phase of capitalist development before attempting
socialism, and that it is not too late to make up
for it now!) Others genuinely believe the policies
are the best for socialism, so I do not feel it yet
amounts to a concerted effort. However, to a socialist there are also unhealthy signs visible in

relation especially to overseas Chinese capitalists and their increasing involvement, indeed integration, with the political-economic system, especially in South China. To a lesser extent, other foreign capital, in particular Japanese and Western, is providing a base for a renewed class of compradors amongst Chinese managers and Party officials. What requires study is the question of class formation, the potential and actual basis for the formation of new exploiting groups.

This chapter is limited to a discussion of foreign investment, foreign trade, technology acquisition and the international financial arrangements which have recently been made. The principal thesis is that changes in the policies affecting these areas, and hence alterations in the concept 'self-reliance', are much more important in terms of the potential for changes in the social relations than in the absolute amounts involved in, for instance, loans and trade. These qualitative changes involve in particular a series of political-economic retreats which are favoured by new and old exploiters within China and which also make China vulnerable to renewed exploitation from outside the country, in particular by overseas Chinese (and to a lesser extent Japanese and Western) capital. Much of the potential for capitalist restoration may arise not from a desire or programme for it amongst genuine reformers but from the increasingly decentralized and decreasingly planned nature of current policies, the 'laissez-faire' aspects of which will favour such class formation.

One method of examining the qualitative changes and the retreats and their potential for engendering capitalist restoration is by drawing a distinction between 'genuine' trade activities, and the forms of trade and financial relationships which are designed mainly to gain foreign exchange funds. The latter include the Special Economic Zones, the export of labour, compensatory trade, and foreign loans of various kinds. Other activities may overlap both categories, and are more complex. Such activities include raw material exports (especially of oil) and the joint ventures. We need to analyse the degree to which they are engaged in for the purpose of gaining foreign exchange, to the possible detriment of the domestic political economy. Particular attention is given to the 'non-genuine' investment and trade activities, and especially the role in them of the overseas Chinese. It is in these activities, and this group of people, that the graver threat to socialism can be said to exist, because the potential for producing and regenerating a capitalist class in power is strongest. Accordingly such activities are defined as 'non-socialist' to highlight the view that they are more than a component of a controlled retreat, indicating their role as part of a potential capitalist restoration.

Origins of the Modernization Policy

Modernization plans were publicized in 1977 under the tutelage of Hua Guofeng, then the new, and since demoted, Party Chairman. Since 1980, much less has been heard of these 'Four Modernizations' (in industry, agriculture, defence, and science and technology) and much more about the readjustments implemented in 1979 and 1981 to cut back capital expenditure and achieve balance between various sectors of the economy. Nevertheless, modernization is still the basic aim, and the readjustment is seen as a necessary phase for its more efficient implementation.

Modernization plans, including the import of foreign technology, have been propounded at other times. As far back as 1964, Zhou Enlai mentioned the four modernizations at the Third National Peoples' Congress. Rises in foreign trade and financial relations have, to some extent, been a reflection of the periods during which 'modernization policies' have enjoyed the support of the Party leadership. Perhaps rather surprisingly, the 1958-60 Great Leap Forward (despite the received wisdom of its strict emphasis on 'self-reliance') brought with it a massive rise in foreign trade, including more spending on complete plants than even in the first Five Year Plan (1953-57).[5]

That trade policies reflect struggles within the Party and changes in them correlate with different factions in power is confirmed by the experience of the Cultural Revolution.[6] Of particular interest is the period in the early 1970's, which saw a rapid expansion in trade, attaining the level of the Great Leap Forward once again. This phase, which also involved large-scale imports of modern plants, occurred after the demise and death of Lin Biao, an 'ultra-leftist'.

Debate on these issues during the Cultural Revolution was intense but 1971 seems to mark a turning point:

It was apparently decided that China would once

again pursue a more open foreign trade orientation and launch an active program of technological imports from abroad. At the same time, in order to minimise the vulnerabilities and risks of dependence, China would limit its reliance on any single source of supply and its overall financial or credit dependence on foreign countries. (A. Eckstein, 1977:240).

Eckstein estimates that between 1972 and 1974, a large number of complete plants were ordered from abroad, totalling in value some $2,500 millions. Thus the impact of widespread anti-foreign feeling which had dominated the early phase of the Cultural Revolution (1966-69) was reversed. Foreign trade, which had declined sharply, showed a rapid rise from 1970-71, as can be seen in Table 9:1, though the increase in value does not represent an equivalent actual volume of imports because of the rapid rise in inflation from the early 1970's. The Chinese themselves were very willing to acknowledge a new phase of expanded trade. In 1974, a new magazine, China's Foreign Trade, was launched. But Minister of Foreign Trade Li Qiang, while expressing China's desire to 'resume and expand trade', went on to condemn any notion of trying to attract foreign capital or engage in joint exploration of minerals.

By 1975 and 1976, however, trade policy seems to have undergone a reversal, and trade actually declined (Table 9:1). The period 1974-76 is now identified as the time of the 'Gang of Four's' greatest strength. In April 1976 they had succeeded in removing Deng Xiaoping from office for the second time, as an 'unrepentant capitalist roader'. The attitude of the time is reflected in a report carried by the Financial Times:

> The current political climate in Peking is unlikely to be conducive to the expansion of international banking activities. The pressure of the present campaign against the policies of the 'capitalist roaders' is all towards self-reliance in economic development ... Foreign trade may continue to increase but this will hardly see the striking growth that occurred in 1973 and 1974.[7]

A distinct shift had taken place in the policy on imports and the short-term credits which had been used for the previous expansion in trade.[8]

TABLE 9:1

CHINA'S FOREIGN TRADE, 1952-1981

(in Millions of U.S. Dollars)

Defi-cit Years	Year	In Current Prices[1]			In Constant 1963 prices[2] Total Turn-over
		Exports	Imports	Total Turn-over	
x	1952	875	1,015	1,890	1,800
x	1953	1,040	1,255	2,295	2,290
x	1954	1,060	1,290	2,350	2,275
x	1955	1,375	1,660	3,035	3,010
	1956	1,635	1,485	3,120	3,115
	1957	1,615	1,440	3,055	2,910
	1958	1,940	1,825	3,765	3,765
	1959	2,230	2,060	4,290	4,400
x	1960	1,960	2,030	3,990	3,990
	1961	1,525	1,490	3,015	3,060
	1962	1,525	1,150	2,675	2,765
	1963	1,570	1,200	2,770	2,770
	1964	1,750	1,470	3,220	3,120
	1965	2,035	1,845	3,880	3,790
	1966	2,210	2,035	4,245	4,070
	1967	1,960	1,955	3,915	3,770
	1968	1,960	1,825	3,785	3,655
	1969	2,060	1,835	3,895	3,655
x	1970	2,095	2,245	4,340	3,755
	1971	2,500	2,310	4,810	4,060
	1972	3,150	2,850	6,000	4,685
x	1973	5,075	5,225	10,300	5,886
x	1974	6,660	7,420	14,080	6,056
x	1975	7,180	7,395	14,575	–
	1976	7,250	6,005	13,255	–
	1977*	8,066	7,706	15,775	–
x	1978**	9,726	10,874	20,600	–
x	1979***	13,634	15,628	29,262	–
x	1980****	18,153	19,420	37,573	–
x	1981*****			39,827	

Sources

1. For the data in current prices, R.E. Batsavage and J.L. Davie in JEC (1980:733). (Continued).

2.   In constant prices up to 1974, calculations
            by A. Eckstein (1977:246).
*   Obtained from the percentage increase given
            for 1978 over the 1977 figures. (Source:
            Communique, State Statistical Bureau, Xinhua
            Weekly Issue, 5.7.79) converted at U.S.
            $ = 1.629 Yuan, based on Chinese figures for
            1978 exchange rate.
**   ibid.
***   Vice-minister of State Planning Commission,
            (Xinhua Weekly Issue, No.582, 10.4.80) con-
            verted at 1979 exchange rate, U.S.$ = 1.5549
            Yuan, given in Beijing Review 29, 1981:22.
****   Communique on Fulfilment of 1980 National
            Economic Plan. (Xinhua Weekly Issue No.638,
            7.5.81). At 1980 exchange rate given in
            Beijing Review 29, 1981:22: $ = 1.4984 Yuan
*****   1981 Plan figure (given in Xinhua Daily
            Bulletin 31.8.80: Yao Yilin's Report to 3rd
            Session of 5th NPC), plus 6% given as min-
            imum exceeding the quota at the end of 1981,
            in Xinhua Weekly Bulletin Issue 673, 7.1.82.
            Converted at 1980 exchange rate.

In short, the mushrooming growth in foreign
trade in 1973 and 1974 can be traced back to 1971
and the struggles which led to the fall of Lin Biao.
The slowdown and actual decline (especially in imports) which occurred in 1975-76 interrupted this
process. So the recent rise of imports and the modernization plans themselves cannot simply be attributed to a shift in policy resulting from a sudden
revisionist takeover. It is a policy over which
there has been a struggle for a good many years.
        Some of these conflicts over foreign trade and
finance were expressed by the arguments of some
leaders and theoreticians even into 1977. There
appears to have been strong opposition to the autarky supposedly fostered by the 'Gang of Four'.
Arguments strongly critical of the 'gang' and supporting trade were published. Yet one author also
said:

        Ours is an independent and sovereign socialist
        state. We have never allowed, nor will we ever
        allow, foreign capital to invest in our coun-
        try. We have never joined capitalist countries
        in exploring our national resources; nor will
        we explore other countries' resources. We
        never did, nor will we ever, embark on joint
        ventures with foreign capitalists. (Guo Maoyen,

                                                  295

1977).

Here we have a viewpoint highly critical of the
'ultra-leftism' of the Cultural Revolution, strongly
in favour of trade and learning from foreign countries and importing their technology, yet unequivo-
cally opposed to foreign investment, joint ventures
and mineral exploration.

It is these conflicts which suggest to me a
criterion based on Chinese conceptions for distinguishing between two forms of foreign trade and financial relationships. The first will be termed legitimate trade, the sort of trade normally engaged in
between countries and which does not lead to the
distortion of China's economy through necessitating
production of particular types of goods or materials, nor create extensive or long-term indebtedness
nor the acceptance of foreign capital or contracts
for the development of the economy and acquisition
of technology. The second form of investment policies and trade I have termed non-socialist. This
latter form involves the sort of policies which
Guo Maoyan clearly felt were non-socialist, but
which could be considered as retreats, valid under
certain circumstances. A crucial aspect of their
validity as a part of a socialist programme involving retreats is the acceptance by the Party and Government that they are indeed retreats, and a recognition of the dangers involved in terms of changes
in social relations and the potential for strengthening the forces favouring a restoration of capitalism. There is little to indicate that there is concern over these issues in the leadership, beyond
some recognition of the harmful influence of Western
ideas as contact increases and a need for education
to counter this. Such attitudes may be a sign not
of complacency but of an attitude that any changes
harmful to socialism are in fact what is intended,
at least by some of China's leaders.

Foreign Trade in China's Economy

It can be accepted that raising the level of productive forces is an aim of socialist construction, and
that as a result of production problems and lack of
investment during certain phases of the Cultural
Revolution, an intensive period of modernization is
now necessary. But we need to examine the role of
foreign technology, finance, and other external financial relations as part of this. It has long been
clear that the CCP had an established policy which

did not exclude learning from foreign countries in terms of science and technology, and which saw importation as a means of facilitating this. Equally, the policy opposed China becoming subservient to any foreign country, or depending on foreign technology entirely or even in the main. The aim has been to keep a balanced policy, based on self-reliance and letting 'foreign things serve China'.[9] Argument and conflict arises because 'self-reliance' can mean many different things, and interpretations of it will affect the level of imports, their nature, and hence the type of export policy and external financial arrangements. Do the new Open Door policies constitute a reversal of this policy and an opening up of China to exploitation and potential capitalist restoration?

Size of Foreign Trade

Although it is possible to show how the rise of imports of foreign technology since 1976 is a continuation of the growth since 1971 which was interrupted in 1974, there is no doubt that the present phase is a considerable expansion (Table 9:2). Because the level of exports has not risen as quickly, China has faced sizeable balance of payments deficits which are also likely in some future years (Table 9:1). The inflow of foreign currency from the growth of tourism cannot make up for the deficit; nor can other invisible earnings, including the sizeable remittances arriving from Overseas Chinese. Hence the crash programme to boost exports, the expanded trade which I suggest is 'non-socialist' in the sense that it constitutes a disguised balance of payments deficit and breaches self-reliance as a policy by distorting the domestic economy. The political price is not paid entirely in terms of deficits or indebtedness (as with many other Third World countries), but by covering up the deficits and avoiding indebtedness by means of various trade and investment retreats. However, it is difficult to suddenly and rapidly 'switch-on' a whole new export trade, and so China has also gone into debt and arranged some very large credit facilities from Japanese and Western sources.

Yet we should not get the trade expansion out of proportion. One way of assessing the effect of imports on self-reliance is to relate them to the overall economy. It soon becomes evident that China's trade was at such a low level proportionately that even rapid growth does not make it large

in relation to the total output. For example, in
1980 the value of all industrial and agricultural
production was 661,900 million Yuan. Imports of
all kinds (not only equipment and 'technology') were
valued at 29,100 million Yuan, and all foreign trade
was 56,300 million Yuan. Total trade was thus about
8.5 per cent of the value of industrial and agricultural output (Table 9:3). This is low in comparison with many Third World countries, even though
the figure is rising. The Chinese data are not comparable with conventional Gross National Product
(GNP) figures, but various calculations of the GNP
suggest similar, low proportions.[10]

TABLE 9:2

TRADE TOTAL AND PERCENTAGE RISE 1970-1981

(Data from Table 9:1)

Year	Deficit *	Trade Total $ in millions Current prices	% Rise over previous year **	Deficit or Surplus in millions $
1970	*	4,340	11.1	− 150
1971		4,810	10.8	+ 190
1972		6,000	24.7	+ 300
1973	*	10,300	71.7	− 150
1974	*	14,080	36.7	− 760
1975	*	14,575	3.5	− 215
1976		13,255	−9.1	+1,245
1977		15,775	19.0	+ 360
1978	*	20,600	30.6	−1,148
1979	*	29,262	42.0	−1,994
1980	*	37,573	28.4	−1,267
1981	*	39,827	6.0	− 465 first 6 months

(Sources: As in Table 9:1)

** N.B.   The rises here are much bigger than the
          actual value of the goods because of
          rapidly rising world inflation in the
          1970's.

TABLE 9:3

CHINA'S FOREIGN TRADE IN RELATION TO TOTAL
INDUSTRIAL AND AGRICULTURAL OUTPUT

IN MILLIONS OF YUAN

	1977**	1978	% Rise	1979	% Rise	1980	% Rise
AGRICULTURAL OUTPUT	134,000	145,900	8.9	158,300	***8.5	Ø162,700	2.8
INDUSTRIAL OUTPUT	372,700	423,100	13.5	459,100	8.5	499,200	8.7
TOTAL	506,700	569,000	12.3	617,400	8.5	661,900	7.2
IMPORTS	13,280	18,740	41.1	24,300	29.7	29,100	19.7
EXPORTS	13,900	16,760	20.0	21,200	26.5	27,200	28.3
TOTAL	27,185	35,500	30.6	45,500	28.2	56,300	23.7
TOURIST INCOME		*450		696	54	920	32
TRADE AS % OF INDUSTRIAL AND AGRICULTURAL OUTPUT	5.4	6.2		7.4		8.5	

*   Total 'invisible' trade was 2,100 million Yuan

**   Here, the base data for 1978, with percent increase over 1977, have been used to calculate approximate data for 1977.

***   These percentage increase figures based on the data here do not tally with those given by the Chinese, which were 7.3 per cent for agriculture, and 8.2 per cent for industry and agriculture combined.

⊕   For the first time it was stated that these figures are at constant 1970 prices.

Sources: 1977 and 1978: Communique, State Statistical Bureau on fulfil-ment of 1978 Plan, NPC. (Xinhua Weekly Issue 5.7.79)

        1979: Vice-Minister of State Planning Commission, (Xinhua Weekly Issue No. 582, 10.4.80)

        1980: Communique on Fulfilment of 1980 National Economic Plan, (Xinhua Weekly Issue, No. 638, 7.5.81)

TABLE 9:4

CHINA'S IMPORTS IN RELATION TO CAPITAL CONSTRUCTION

MILLIONS OF YUAN

ROW	CATEGORY	1977	1978	1979	1980
A	CAPITAL CONSTRUCTION: covered by the National budget	29,500	39,500	39,500	28,100
B	raised from the localities	7,000	8,400	10,500	25,000
C	TOTAL	36,500	47,900	50,000	53,900
D	Of this total, amount in Fixed Capital Investment	26,000	35,600	41,800	42,700
E	Non-productive uses (housing, welfare facilities)	10,500	12,300	8,200	11,200

F	IMPORTS: New Technology and complete units		1,478	1,847	3,754
G	Raw and Semi-finished materials for light and textile industry		1,900	4,180	7,071
H	Chemical Fertilizer and other rural means of production			1,434	2,124
I	Grain, food oils, consumer goods including TVs, cassettes, etc.		15,362	4,520	6,169
J	Remainder (including pig iron, steel, non-ferrous metals etc.)			12,320	9,982
K	TOTAL VALUE OF IMPORTS	13,280	18,740	24,300	29,100
L	*TOTAL STATE BUDGET EXPENDITURE	84,350	111,093	127,390	113,970
M	Imports as percent of State Budget	15.7%	16.9%	19%	25.5%

303

*SOURCES: STATE BUDGET

1977 & 1978: Speech of Zhang Jingfu at 2nd session of 5th NPC reported in Xinhua 30.6.79.

1979: Speech of Wang Bingqian at 3rd session of 5th NPC, Beijing Review No. 39, 29.9.80.

1980: Speech of Wang Bingqian at 4th session of 5th NPC, Xinhua Supplement 16.12.81.

SOURCES: CAPITAL CONSTRUCTION AND IMPORTS

1977: Figures for 1977 are derived from the percentage increases given for 1978.

1978: 'China's National Economy, 1978-79' Beijing Review 26, 1979. 'Communique on Fulfilment of 1978 National Economic Plan' Beijing Review 27, 1979.

1979: 'Communique on Fulfilment of 1979 National Economic Plan' Beijing Review 19 and 20, 1980.

1980: 'Communique on Fulfilment of 1980 National Economic Plan' Beijing Review 19 and 20, 1981.

1981: Provisional figures for 1981 were given by Wang Bingqian at the 4th session of the 5th NPC, Xinhua Weekly Issue, No. 668, 3.12.81 and Supplement, 16.12.81.

However, the disturbing factor is not simply the actual quantity of trade involved in the Open Door policy. On the export side this chapter explores the methods which are being used to create the foreign exchange needed, and the price involved in terms of the political and economic retreats. In terms of imports, a picture emerges of growing utilization of foreign equipment and technology in the country's capital construction, and of a large and growing proportion of the state's budget allocated to the purchase of imports in general.

The state budget is the annual allocation of central government funds to the various state-run sectors of the economy for their running costs and investment purposes. These sectors broadly are: existing enterprises; agriculture; education, health, science and culture; defence; and capital construction. In the last few years revenues have not kept pace with the budget expenditures, and the resulting deficits have been covered by reserves, by borrowing from the People's Bank of China, and more recently by the issuing of bonds. In addition, foreign borrowings have been made, especially to cover investments in capital construction.[11] As a proportion of the total state budget expenditures, imports have risen from 15.7 per cent in 1977 to over 25 per cent in 1980 (Table 9:4, rows L and M).

This indicator is too undifferentiated to show up the crucial area of the part played by foreign capital goods, 'technology', complete plants and other equipment. The categories used in China's published figures, for instance of imports and state budget spending (including capital construction), also present severe problems. For example, in the state budget, some imported equipment must be included under the heading for 'existing enterprises' and 'agriculture', and does not all appear under 'capital construction'. Likewise, of the categories of imports, the category of 'new technology and complete units' (Table 9:4, row F) has a figure for 1980 which is only half of what was borrowed abroad to cover investments in capital, construction, presumably to pay for imports. So the import categories may well conceal other aspects of imported technology and equipment. Using China's trade data as compiled by foreign organisations, Batsavage and Davis (1978:Table A8) suggest that in 1976 capital goods accounted for 30.6 per cent of imports. Even without taking any account of the increases since then, and taking the (unsatisfactory) heading of 'Fixed Capital Investment' (row D), in 1980 it would have included more than 20 per cent foreign equipment.

It must be said that China is in a position to resist the pressures from any single country or Multinational Company (MNC), and is able to play off one against the other to get favourable terms. This should be possible for as long as there is strong competition to get a share of the Chinese market, and provided that China maintains a careful balance between different suppliers rather than depending on a few, and has control over spares and the technology involved. The form in which China pays for such imports is crucial in these circumstances, and it is worrying to see that foreign loans are providing a larger proportion of the total spent in capital construction - 8000 million Yuan for 1981, or nearly 19 per cent of Fixed Capital Investment.[12]

Foreign Finance for Modernization

More important than the size of foreign trade are the qualitative issues, including the way in which the plans are being implemented, and in particular some of the methods being used to finance imports and cover the balance of payments deficit. Before moving to discuss the forms of 'expanded trade' which are used to do this, it is worth mentioning the more conventional mode of covering deficits by means of loans and credits. Since 1978, China has accepted a very wide spectrum of measures through which to borrow abroad. This represents another fundamental policy shift, as only a few years ago officials eschewed the notion of indebtedness and the government was proud of having no internal or external debts (Beijing Review 9, 1977).

China has been raising finance in a number of ways, including credits from banking and finance groups in Japan, Europe and the USA. Sometimes the credits are linked directly to particular import deals, so that the lenders deposit funds in a bank in the exporting country to pay the firm involved. The size of these credit deals varies, but there have been a number larger than $1,000 million. For instance, a Japanese consortium has been negotiating two loans for the Bank of China. One is a $2,000 million 4½ year loan, and the other a $6,000 short-term refinancing loan facility (International Herald Tribune, 25 May 1979). A group of British Banks are providing deposit facilities totalling $1,770 million, to finance U.K. exports (Financial Times, 7 Dec. 1978 and 6 April 1979). A French deal is reported to total some $7,000 million. Rates of

interest vary, with reports of some deals at the
7.25 per cent agreed internationally for developing
countries, and others at rates slightly above the
international base rate LIBOR (London International
Bank Offered Rate). These facilities are by no
means all being used, and after the prolonged nego-
tiations much of the credit offered is still sitting
waiting, especially as a result of the readjustments.
However, the Chinese authorities have been keen to
reassure overseas suppliers of their continued good
faith, and are maintaining an impressive panoply of
potential sources of credit. A report at the end of
1981 indicated that agreements had been signed with
40 international banks (Xinhua Weekly Bulletin 667,
26 Nov. 1981).

Interestingly, an array of new finance and
trade organizations has grown up in China, and often
important statements are made not by the Minister of
Trade (who is now Zhang Tuobin) but by officials of
the new organizations. Most prominent of these is
CITIC, the China International Trust and Investment
Corporation.[13]

Foreign governments are also acceptable now as
lenders. One of the first indications of an about-
turn on accepting foreign loans on a bilateral basis
was a statement by Li Qiang, who was eating his
words of 1974 (referred to above).[14] As yet, few
governmental loans have been arranged - by early
1981 a low interest loan from Japan and an interest-
free loan from Belgium had been announced (Xinhua
Weekly Issue 626, 12 Feb. 1981). A multilateral
approach has also gone ahead: China has re-established its membership of the IMF, and has joined the
World Bank. In 1981 the first credit was granted by
the latter body, together with the International
Development Association ($100 million each). This
is to establish better science and technology facilities in higher education (Times Higher Educational
Supplement, 14 Aug. 1981). The loan is small, and
as such may be a testing ground on both sides for
future involvement. The World Bank itself, in its
unpublished report (prepared in June 1981), clearly
sees China as a major world borrower, and recommends
that its debt should rise to $41 billion in 1990
(The Guardian, 24 Nov. 1981). The level in 1980 was
only $3.4 billion, and it remains to be seen how
strong or willing the Government is to stand by the
frequently stated position that China will only become indebted within the limits of its capacity to
repay.

One last and very significant means of

borrowing funds deserves mention. After a year or more of rumours, China arranged for the issue of bonds on the Japanese finance market, early in 1982. This issue of private placement notes totals 10,000 million Japanese Yen (approximately 80 million Yuan) and has been negotiated between CITIC and Nomura Securities Co. Ltd. (Xinhua Weekly Issue 667, 26 Nov. 1981). It is an arrangement which exemplifies the already close and growing financial links with Japan (See Table 4.5) long since China's major trading partner by a wide margin.

Trade and the Readjustments

Before considering 'expanded' trade in more detail, there are a few observations to be made on the way the post-1979 readjustments in the economy have affected trade. The readjustments, which began in early 1979 and were reinforced in 1981, aim at reducing the level of capital construction (Table 9:4, Rows A and C), and realigning the priorities in economic development to establish agriculture in first place, followed by light and textile industry, then heavy industry. Greater responsibility in economic management has been devolved to provinces and individual enterprises (as reflected in Row C of Table 9:4). There is also considerable emphasis nationally on infrastructure to serve the main sectors of the economy, especially in power generation (with rapid expansion of coal output) and in transport.[15]

As a result of the readjustments, there was considerable publicity about the suspension of projects, especially those in heavy industry involving foreign participation, like the Baoshan Steel Complex outside Shanghai.[16] Foreign business interests were also upset about the general slackening of orders and that the credit facilities which had been made available were not taken up.

Yet there is another aspect of the readjustments initiated in 1979 which, as well as the non-utilization of foreign credits, is closely linked to foreign trade. The emphasis on light and textile industries is not simply to generate funds for reinvestment in other sectors. Nor is it just to provide more consumer goods for the Chinese people. It is these industries whose rapid expansion can help pay for the imports which will provide modern technology and plant. Thus textiles, including garments, despite being in relatively short supply at home, are one of China's principle export commodities,

constituting 21% of total export value in 1979, and
17.1% in 1980. Some raw cotton is imported, mainly
from the U.S.A.[17]
    With the new priority on agriculture, there are
certain respects in which the new policies encourage
the production of a wider range of non-grain foodstuffs and agricultural raw materials, and the provision of cash-crops and commodities for export. In
some areas, new agro-industrial complexes are being
set up to produce, process and market foodstuffs for
sale within and outside China. Some of these involve overseas Chinese capital, and there are moves
to make Hainan Island a base for tropical cash crops
for export, using foreign capital. The provincial
government of Guangdong has announced that foreign
investors in Hainan will receive the same preferential treatment as in the Special Economic Zones, of
which more later.[18]
    Overall, the impact of the readjustment poli-
cies on foreign trade and investment appears to reduce the influence of major industrial nations and
MNC's to some extent, but at the same time reinfor-
ces the strength and penetration of overseas Chinese
capital which can operate rapidly in light and textile industries and in agricultural activities.

Joint Ventures

The 1979 National Peoples' Congress enacted a law
permitting the setting up of enterprises to be owned
jointly by Chinese and foreign capital. That a certain section of the means of production will be
owned by foreign capitalists, with some tax concessions and permitted repatriation of profits must represent a retreat politically and economically. Such
an economic base for the extraction of profit by
private capital is a danger, both in respect of
imperialism and the potential development of comp-
rador strata within China. Some economists while
playing down such dangers and stressing the high
degree of control retained by the Chinese Government
have recognised that such enterprises involve the
exploitation of Chinese labour by foreign capital
(Beijing Review 6, 1981:3). Certainly the increased
contact with foreign businesses has contributed to
an alarming rise (even for the Party) in corruption
and the acceptance of bribes.[19] Unfortunately, and
perhaps significantly, such activities are seen precisely as economic crimes, rather than as signifying

structural weaknesses and the propensity for social
relations to become increasingly capitalist.

When the joint venture law was first being discussed, it was understood that foreign holdings
would not be greater than 49 per cent and that gradually enterprises would become fully owned by the
Chinese State. It is now apparent and acknowledged
that 100 per cent foreign ownership is acceptable,
and that its presence is acknowledged on a long term
basis.

Regarding joint ventures and the readjustments,
again we find there is a strong desire to utilize
foreign capital to produce more goods for export.
The President of the Bank of China, Bu Ming, gave
the following principles for the use of foreign capital in China:

> Foreign capital should be used for the develop-
> ment of agriculture, light industry and heavy
> industry, in that order of precedence. It
> should also be used to strengthen the weak
> links and the national priority should be given
> to medium or small size export-oriented pro-
> jects which yield returns in a short time with
> very little investment. Financing should be
> given to tap the production potential of old
> factories rather than building new factories.
> (Xinhua Weekly Issue 632, 26 Mar. 1981).

By no means all of the joint ventures are in
light industry or export-oriented. For instance,
there are the oil prospecting consortiums in Bohai
Bay, the Guangdong Coast and elsewhere. But a large
proportion of them are likely to be small in scale,
and a very large proportion of them involve overseas Chinese capital, with Japanese next. At the
end of June 1981, approval had been granted for setting up 24 joint ventures, excluding compensation
trade and similar arrangements, dealt with below.
(Xinhua Weekly Issue 663, 29 Oct. 1981). It was
also stated that China 'is also in 30 joint ventures
in Hong Kong, Macao and abroad', though there has
been little explanation if any as to what these
might be. They may be related to the overseas contracts and 'export' of labour, discussed below.
Given that Joint Ventures are being encouraged in
weak areas of the economy, and to promote exports,
it is the potential for a high degree of integration
with foreign capital which causes most concern to
me. This is all the more so in the case of foreign
capital that is not really 'foreign', but controlled

by overseas Chinese.20 And despite the fact that foreign capital and joint ventures constitute a small percentage of the total capital invested in China, it is the potential for <u>political</u> integration of overseas Chinese capitalists with strata within China sympathetic to capitalist restoration that gives cause for concern. This may become clearer when the 'Special Economic Zones', compensatory trade, and processing deals are discussed below.

Overseas Chinese Capital

The role of overseas Chinese and their involvement in trade, and more significantly investment in China, requires particular attention. The Chinese authorities are especially keen to involve overseas Chinese in the investment projects which will generate growth in industrial and even agricultural output, especially in order to generate exports. There are indications that the recent overtures to Taiwan for reunification are in large measure related to Beijing's wishes to expand trade and make investment funds from Taiwan available to the mainland. In this way new technology and skilled manpower could also be made available for China's modernisation. The Bank of China has proposed ways of arranging financial deals between Taiwan and the mainland, if necessary via Hong Kong agencies for the time being. (Xinhua Weekly Issue 661, 15 Oct. 1981). Firm offers of trade co-operation have also been made by the Foreign Trade Minister (Zheng Tuobin), even including the export of coal and oil 'at preferential prices' (ibid).

The overtures to Taiwan and the strong desire for relations with other overseas Chinese appear to be seen as an aspect of the resurrected policy of the united front in China. This has even been referred to by Deng Xiaoping as the 'revolutionary and patriotic' united front, referring to an earlier period in China's revolutionary struggles when the goal was not immediately socialism, but independence, democracy and the defeat of the Japanese aggressors.

The return of such political concepts poses a number of questions. The 'united front' appears to have supplanted the 'dictatorship of the proletariat' as the form of state power, with little explanation or analysis. An important consequence of the shift in policy was the restoration, after 1979, of personal property, savings and posts to ex-landlords and patriotic capitalists who had been

expropriated during the Cultural Revolution. Such
a change in policy might be valid in the framework
of modernisation where their skills are of value,
and where they are deemed to have shown support for
socialism or to have reformed. But overseas Chinese
capitalists are not a part of the revolution,
nor are there opportunities for transforming them.
This particular use of the 'patriotic' united front
must throw doubt on the policy itself. In my opinion it represents a significant political as well as
an economic retreat into private ownership of part
of the means of production. It contains dangers of
the establishment of a new class of Chinese capitalists with a base both within and outside the country.

It may be useful to give a concrete illustration of the kind of formation within China which
heralds such a political integration with foreign
capital and especially overseas Chinese capitalists.
The example is taken entirely from an article in
China Reconstructs, April, 1980.

The article is called 'From Capitalist to
Leader in Socialist Trade!', and describes
Liu Jingji, who was a textile millionaire with several mills in and near Shanghai. He decided to stay
on in China after the Liberation of 1949, and demonstrated his patriotic bona fides by deciding to use
his capital and managerial skills in the development
of a new China. He handed over $2 million, together
with cotton stocks which he had been keeping in
Hong Kong, and new Swiss machinery for another mill
in Shanghai. From 1953, private businesses like his
began to be taken into joint state control pending
full state ownership in 1956. He was compensated
and got a salary, and himself agrees that this
income was higher and more stable than the profits
to be made at the time.

The united front policy has been applied to
him, and to thousands of other members of the national (i.e. patriotic) bourgeoisie, tens of thousands of the urban petty bourgeoisie (including intellectuals) and millions of landlords, since 1978.
The policy first emerged during the struggles
against Japanese aggression and the Guomindang re-
actionaries under Chiang Kaishek. It was designed
to unite the various patriotic elements, and was
continued after 1949 to enable them to integrate in
and be reformed by the emerging socialist system.
Quite obviously such reform and integration could
not be applied to Chinese who were already overseas
or who had fled from China for one reason or another.

Within China, the desire for unity expressed in the policy was formalized through the creation of the Chinese Peoples' Political Consultative Committee (CPPCC), which provided for political contact with the Government and Communist Party, and allowed for a continued role for various other political parties and other groups.

The ex-capitalists and others were, as a result of this policy, 'transformed from exploiters into working people over decades of struggle and education'. The article then quotes from a speech in 1979 by Hua Guofeng, who said that ' ... capitalists no longer exist as a class ... most members of this class who were able to work have been transformed into working people earning their own living in socialist society'.[21] However, the policy of keeping faith with the patriotic capitalists required and allowed a high degree of privilege for people like Liu Jingji, whose skills were to benefit the developing economy. After his companies came under state control, he received a salary of Yuan 600 per month, and was appointed manager of the Shanghai Cotton Textile Industry Company, described as a city-wide combine. (The current average monthly wage is around 60 Yuan per month He maintained his large house. It is not possible to calculate the money value of his assets, but the policy was to pay an annual 0.5 per cent interest on them for ten years. If we take the $2 million he had sent back in 1949 from Hong Kong, alone that would produce an income of $10,000 a year.

It is not surprising that such a contradiction between this privilege and his status as an ex-capitalist on one hand and the official attitude that he was reformed and an ordinary working person on the other should lead to conflict during the Cultural Revolution: China Reconstructs describes how he was persecuted and suffered, losing his salary and savings together with an end to the interest payments. His family home was taken over for use as a hospital for textile workers, an irony which has not been undone and has meant that he and his family have recently been given another big house and garden. In addition, he was recently appointed Chairman of the Shanghai Federation of Industry and Commerce, and is on the restored CPPCC. He is also now one of the leaders of CITIC and a vice-chairman of the All-China Federation of Industry and Commerce.[22] Some might argue that at the age of 80, his role in these posts may be purely token. But his own personal activity would indicate otherwise, and shows that the policy is doing more than just restoring the confidence of such people in the Party in order to involve them in the modernization plans.

Since the Cultural Revolution, his back salary, savings with interest, and frozen interest payments have been handed over as a lump sum (as they were to other ex-capitalists and landlords). What has he done with the money? A business has been formed, called the Shanghai Industrial and Commercial Patriotic Construction Company. Capital came from about seven hundred investors and totalled over Yuan 50 millions (about £14 millions). Dividends will be allowed at a rate equivalent to a medium-term savings account in the bank, that is about 5 per cent a year. One of the main activities of the company (which have to be approved by the state) is the construction of apartment blocks in Shanghai for sale to overseas Chinese. Land and labour will be allocated by the state, as will the raw materials, some of them imported if necessary. Other activities of the company will include foreign trade undertakings and some industries and services at the neighbourhood level.

China is short of building materials and skilled labour, and Shanghai is already crowded and short of land. There is a desperate housing shortage in Shanghai and other Chinese cities. Moreover, there are still restrictions on the movement of rural people to Shanghai and other cities, as part of a long-established policy of encouraging balanced growth between town and countryside. The only apparent benefit to China from such a construction company is the foreign exchange which will be earned by the presence of overseas Chinese in Shanghai and the sale of the flats. But the political complacency involved is alarming. Presumably the article about the scheme can be taken to mean that it is approved of and worthy of emulation. But this scheme seems to involve a whole new interpretation of the united front policy, and its extension to overseas Chinese is potentially disastrous politically. Just as anything goes provided it is prefixed by the word 'Socialism', it also appears that any economic tie involving overseas Chinese people or their capital can be deemed positive so long as the parties involved (on either side) adopt the label 'Patriotic'. In my view, the danger to socialism and self-reliance is likely to come much more from such contacts and from indigenous capitalist elements (both within and outside the Party) than from normal foreign trade and even potential penetration by Western

314

capital.

Special Economic Zones

In 1978, the three special municipalities (Beijing, Tianjin, Shanghai) and the two south coast provinces of Guangdong and Fujian, were granted special status in the development of foreign trade on a highly aut- onomous basis (China Trader 3, 4 Dec. 1980:40). There have been hints from Premier Zhao Ziyang that other areas may follow, for instance Dalian (Dairen) in Liaoning Province and Qingdao in Shandong (Beijing Review 51, 1981). Shanghai and the two coastal provinces of Guangdong and Fujian are not- able since they are the places from which the vast majority of overseas Chinese all over the world ori- ginate. It is interesting though perhaps not surp- rising that Fujian and Guangdong should be the first two provinces in which Special Economic Zones (SEZ) have been established. Of the three SEZ in Guangdong, one is adjacent to Macao (the Zhuhai SEZ) one is bordering Hong Kong, in the area of Shenzhen, and the third in Shantou, another 19th century Treaty Port. At present, Fujian has only one SEZ under way, at Xiamen (Amoy). Like Shantou, Xiamen is the home of many thousands of overseas Chinese.

The Special Economic Zones closely resemble the export processing or free-trade zones of other Third World countries. Though China may be in a position to resist multinational companies' manipulation, as with Joint Ventures, the policy is a political ret- reat of considerable importance. It is also one of a rather sensitive nature, since the foreign con- cessions at Treaty Ports were one of the major tar- gets of the anti-colonial campaigns. The zones do represent a yielding of sovereignty over these lim- ited areas. Taxes and customs duties will be re- duced, the foreign factory owners will have the right to manage, hire and fire, and to determine what is produced.[23] In fact, the Western part of the Shenzhen SEZ, at Sheko (west of the New Terri- tories) is entirely managed and planned by a Hong Kong company; the China Merchant Steam Navigation Co. has already spent $20 millions in levelling land for the site (Monsoon 3.2, 1980:19)

One of the key components of the political and economic control necessary for the government to restrict the impact of the Special Economic Zones outside their territory is to have clearly defined limits to this territory and the concessions perm- itted within it. Such safeguards are mentioned by

one of the officials of the Xiamen Zone in Fujian
Province, Lu Zifen (China Reconstructs, June 1981).
He cites Lenin in support of the idea of using bour-
geois capital (without mentioning the retreat which
Lenin said was inherent in the NEP), and goes on to
say:

> Thirty years of experience has made us realise
> that it is difficult for a developing socialist
> country to base itself solely on the state-
> owned economy. Various other forms of economy
> must also be used - among them, imports of
> foreign capital and joint-venture enterprises.
> In other words, allowing a little profit for
> foreign businessmen can give us a great deal
> of benefit. We do not consider these measures
> temporary or makeshift (72, my emphasis).

He described the zones as a special organisational
form under China's socialist system limited to a
given area.

It is very surprising then to see that in
neighbouring Guangdong it has been announced that
the concessions and privileges granted within that
province's Special Economic Zones are to be extended
to many towns and cities including Guangzhou
(Canton), and to many of the rural areas too (Xinhua
Weekly Issue 643, 11 June 1981). In other words, a
major political constraint on the activity of foreign capital is to be removed. There is likely to
be an even bigger influx of overseas Chinese capital
into the province, and an increased integration between the two economic systems.

At present, Guangdong's own export trade is
relatively small, and in 1980 was around $200 mill-
ions (only about 1.2 per cent of the nation's total).
But earnings from agreements to process goods for
foreign businessmen were in 1979 already double this
figure. The vast majority of the processing contracts are with overseas Chinese, and in the short
period since the policy began to operate over 2,600
such deals had been made as of July 1980 (China
Trader 4, 1 Mar. 1981:22). There is plenty of scope
for more overseas contact, and Guangdong province,
itself already delegated a great deal of power by
Beijing, has granted a lot of autonomy to its own
constituent local authorities. One county, well
known for its connections with overseas Chinese, has
established several contracts including one to produce ceramic floor tiles in a commune (an investment
of $1.6 million). As a result of a trade delegation

the county sent to Hong Kong, two contracts were
also made with Japanese companies (Ibid:223).
   Generally, though willing to accept funds and
contracts from any foreign businesses, Guangdong
province places special emphasis on overseas Chinese
An investment corporation has been formed, the
Guangdong Trust and Investment Corporation (GUTIC),
to attract funds:

> Provincial officials, fully aware of the close
> family ties that span the border and the emo-
> tional bonds of overseas Chinese to their home-
> land, have structured GUTIC to appeal to the
> particular investment interests of Hong Kong
> and Macao citizens, although anyone is welcome
> to participate. To emphasize the close assoc-
> iation, the deputy governor of Guangdong,
> Guo Dihuo, serves as Chairman of the Board,
> while board appointments include such prominent
> Hong Kong and Macao businessmen as Ho Yin,
> Tong Bin Tat and Daniel Koo (Ibid:31).

The trust is issuing shares in Hong Kong and US
dollars as well as Renminbi, (the currency of the
People's Republic of China) and these are apparently
transferable from relatives outside to those in
China. The funds raised by GUTIC will be used
either to support existing enterprises or to establish new joint ventures, either with indigenous
units or overseas businesses. In theory, this means
that foreign shareholders or conceivably their
Chinese relatives in China may hold part ownership
not only of specially set up joint enterprises but
also of indigenous enterprises.

Compensation Trade and Processing Agreements

It has been difficult to discuss the SEZ without
referring to the extension of their supposedly restricted inducements to other parts of Guangdong, and
to mention other forms of investment from foreign
sources. In fact compensation trade and processing
agreements (together with joint ventures) are policies applicable in all China. These financing
arrangements have been defined as follows by
Zhang Yennian, (Deputy Managing Director of the Bank
of China, Beijing/London):

> Compensation trade: Foreign companies or in-
> stitutions will be invited to provide technol-
> ogy, equipment and essential capital goods with

317

which our enterprises will exploit mineral resources, develop the production of agriculture,
forestry, animal husbandry, fishing, light industry, textile industry or other industries.
Outputs of the above sectors will be used to
re-pay import value of technology and equipment
by foreign suppliers. ...
Processing of material and assembling of spare
parts i.e. components, T.C. from abroad:
Foreign companies will supply samples and
essential raw materials or spare parts. Then
our factories will be engaged in production
according to quality and specification as required by foreign suppliers and will deliver
the finished products for them to sell. We
shall obtain reimbursement of expenses or commissions for processing or assembling.24

In compensation trade the arrangements range from
oil exploration and coal mining to the assembly of
calculators, cassette recorders and televisions.
China agrees to allow the foreign investor to export
all of the output for an agreed period of years,
after which time the factory and equipment reverts
to Chinese ownership and control.

The advantages are obvious; jobs are provided,
skills acquired, management experience gained, and
at the end China is left with a paid-up factory or
enterprise. However, by that time equipment may be
worn-out or outdated. Further, under this scheme
the foreign investor has much greater control over
what is actually produced: China may sacrifice this
to get the jobs or infrastructure which goes with
the investment. And fundamentally it is still a
retreat, since the Chinese labour is being exploited
by foreign capital.

The level of activity in compensatory trade is
relatively high, perhaps because foreign businessmen
have been less concerned about the legal and contractual problems than in joint ventures. The number of compensatory trade agreements made in 1979
alone was 140, but there were also more than 2000
'contracts on processing materials for overseas
customers' (Xinhua Weekly Issue, 582, 10 Apr. 1980).
By the end of June 1981, the number of compensation
trade ventures was 'over 300', excluding the SEZ.
(Xinhua Weekly Issue 663, 29 Oct. 1981). The much
larger number of processing agreements (far larger
than compensation trading, itself much greater than
the number of joint ventures) indicates the smaller
financial outlay needed by the foreign business, as

well as the less complex and more certain legal situation.

It is worth mentioning the particular role of Shanghai in processing deals and compensatory trade. It again demonstrates the strong links with Hong Kong, though of course not all deals with firms there will be with overseas Chinese. In roughly a year up to September 1979, Shanghai had signed more than 600 contracts for processing and assembly. 'Hong Kong holds the lion's share, making up 70 per cent of the joint undertakings; after Hong Kong comes Japan which accounts for 15 per cent. (Cai Behua, 1980). Of the 62 compensation trade deals made in the same period, Hong Kong and Japan appear to be the most prominent partners.

Processing agreements show the problems of 'expanded' or non-socialist trade in its most transparent form, for they involve already existing Chinese enterprises in diverting labour and means of production from the manufacture of goods for the Chinese population to the processing for foreign businesses of goods which are destined entirely for export in order to raise foreign exchange.

Export of Labour and Overseas Contracts

The final category of external financial arrangements by which China intends to earn foreign exchange is by means of so-called 'walking exports'. In fact these schemes do constitute much more than just the export of labour, although originally it does appear that groups of different numbers suitable for particular types of project were being made available for hire as a 'package'. This did not take off very well, owing apparently to the high charges asked by China and inflexibility in the sizes of work groups offered.

Now the 'package' offered seems to be much more of a kind of contract bidding mainly for civil engineering projects like roads, airports and factories. Recently, for example, a new corporation has been set up in Sichuan province, which will

> design and build, among other projects, public and industrial buildings, highways and bridges, and will provide customers with technical and labour services, industrial equipment and spare parts. (Xinhua Weekly Issue 662, 15 Jan. 1981)

The devolution of this activity, which seems designed to earn foreign exchange for this particular

319

province, may be because it is losing out in other ways as there are very few overseas Chinese from Sichuan.

People working abroad in this way receive their normal wage plus a supplement, and because the Government or corporations engage the contract with the foreign client, Chinese workers are not being treated as cheap migrant labour. But, apart from the fact that this still constitutes foreign exploitation of China's workers, the squads being offered include skilled workers, engineers and technicians. The question arises as to whether their labour, skills and equipment could be more fruitfully employed in China.

Conclusion

There is no doubt that in spite of all the criticisms of the non-socialist aspects of the external financial arrangements, they can produce certain benefits for China. By judicious use of these schemes, the economy can benefit from the introduction of new technology in areas determined by the Government to be in need of rapid development.[25] Such imports of technology can improve self-reliance through the normal route of import substitution. Even when foreign exchange funds are obtained by exporting valuable and irreplaceable oil, or by exporting needed textiles, the imported technology might include machine tools to make more looms or equipment for oil exploration and extraction, thus enabling greater self-reliance to be established.

There is, however, evidence of concern within China about some aspects of the new trade and investment projects. For instance, early in 1981 the People's Daily argued for a curb on the rapidly rising imports of a number of products, including cassette recorders and other consumer goods. The article singled out vehicle imports, which have cost, since 1949, 'three or four times the total investment in China's burgeoning auto industry'. Commenting on machinery and electrical products, it stressed that imports 'must serve to protect and foster (our) native machine-building industry. While it is wrong for China to try and make everything it needs, it is also wrong to buy everything from other countries. (Xinhua Weekly Issue 626, 12 Feb. 1981). Evidence of a very different point of view comes in an article by some economists who argue for an international division of labour in which China would concentrate on those products in

which there was supposedly a natural advantage
(Yuan Wenqi et al, 1980).

I have indicated that much of what is happening
already in foreign trade and investment policies is
non-socialist, and that the methods being used to
finance imports and cover the trade deficit are more
than just necessary retreats required in the short
or medium term. In other words, aspects of the
external financial arrangements described above involve what could be termed a 'disguised' trading
deficit, and one which is being structured into the
political economy in China's new model of foreign
trade. In disguising the deficit in this way, it
becomes clear that what could have been legitimate
retreat policies in trade are not isolated but are
linked to the existence of retreats in other areas
of policy and economy, and that overall, these have
gone beyond 'retreats' as such to become part of a
process of capitalist restoration.

The increasing integration of overseas Chinese
capital (and to a lesser extent Japanese and Western) with the Chinese economy is particularly
dangerous, especially as there are indications of a
growing integration with China's own ex-capitalists.
At least there are a few economists who are willing
to discuss recent developments of the Open Door
policy as involving capitalism in China's modernization. Referring to the SEZ, Xu Dixin (1981:14)
describes their economies as being predominantly
state capitalist:

> Processing, compensatory trade, co-operative
> enterprises and joint ventures are all state
> capitalist economic activities. Strictly
> speaking, the enterprises run by foreign or
> overseas Chinese capital constitute a kind of
> capitalist economy, but the activities of such
> enterprises are subject to control and regu-
> lation by the governments of the special
> zones. As a result they are special kinds of
> capitalist enterprises.

Although reflecting some of Xu's statements,
Xue Muqiao has gone much further, significantly in
a talk at a Hong Kong seminar on China's economy,
held in 1980.[26] He said that since China had allowed foreign interests to participate in state and
private joint ventures, there was no reason why similar joint ventures could not be established with
the participation of former industrialists, and with
that of staff and workers in their own enterprises.

Foreign Investment and Trade

Asked about whether China should guard against capitalist restoration, Xue said:

> We do not encourage the revival of capitalism.
> But nor should we be afraid of it. A little
> capitalism is all right. Now we are in no pos-
> ition totally to eradicate capitalism.
> (Eastern Horizon 20.9, Sept. 1981:8).

Unfortunately, it is more than a question of not being afraid of capitalism. In a series of policy retreats there has to be concerted awareness of and
preparation for the consequences in social relations. It is not sufficient to give 'special attention to the ideological education of people in the
special zones' to guard against the effects of capitalist ideology; in his article Xu Dixin can happ-
ily describe the zones as 'experimental units in
economic structural reform and as schools for learning the law of value and the regulation of production according to market demands' · (1981:16-17).
Since these 'laws' are now officially seen as an in-
tegral part of the socialist economy, it is curious
to find that the social relations engendered in the
SEZ are 'predominantly state capitalist' and yet are
regarded as examples for the rest of the 'socialist'
economy.

Some of these writers have begun to view the
Open Door policy and China's other economic changes
in relation to the Soviet experiences of the early
1920's. Indeed there are some similarities with the
New Economic Policy (NEP). But there is a strong
current in Lenin's analysis which admits that what
was being done was a retreat, a necessary (if temporary) reintroduction of capitalism. In 1921 Lenin
discussed this in relation to the freedom granted to
the peasantry to trade their surplus produce:

> Within the limits indicated, however, this is
> not at all dangerous for socialism as long as
> transport and large-scale industry remain in
> the hands of the proletariat. On the contrary,
> the development of capitalism, controlled and
> regulated by the proletarian state (i.e. "state"
> capitalism in this sense of the term), is ad-
> vantageous and necessary in an extremely devas-
> tated and backward small peasant country (with-
> in certain limits, of course), inasmuch as it
> is capable of hastening the immediate revival
> of peasant farming. This applies still more to
> concessions: without denationalising anything

> the workers' state leases certain mines, forest
> tracts, oilfields, and so forth, to foreign
> capitalists in order to obtain from them extra
> equipment and machinery that will enable us to
> accelerate the restoration of Soviet large-
> scale industry ...
> The payment made to the concessionaires in the
> form of a share of the highly valuable products
> obtained is undoubtedly tribute which the
> workers' state pays to the world bourgeoisie;
> without in any way glossing over this, we must
> clearly realise that we stand to gain by paying
> this tribute, so long as it accelerates the
> restoration of our large-scale industry and
> substantially improves the condition of the
> workers and peasants. (1964 edition:626).

The remarkable parallel with China is thrown
into contrast if it is recalled that the NEP came
only four years after the October Revolution and
prior to any collectivisation on the land. Further
credit goes to the Russian Communists for openly
accepting that they were having to take a step back
in order to make progress in the future. The dangers inherent in the policy were clearly spelt out,
and the retreat recognised as such.

In China there are few signs of such awareness,
or willingness to concede that the new policies are
retreats. While particular economists may admit
that some of the new trade and investment practices
are capitalist (Xue Muqiao) or 'state capitalist'
(Xu Dixin), there is a tendency in state propaganda
to describe them all as socialist measures. It can
be accepted that many leading economists, government
and party officials do genuinely believe that in the
long run the development of socialism and China's
transition to communism is best served by the new
policies. Should a significant and influential number change their minds having seen the effects, the
machinery is still there at the present for the policies to be reversed.

However such a change is not going to be easy
if, as I believe, there are sections of the party
and government who prefer capitalism to socialism.
Moreover, the consequence of the new policies is to
create significant sections of the people in various
sectors of the economy who have a strong vested interest in not ending the 'retreat'. Amongst the
peasantry, those who get rich may do so partly at
the expense of others, though it will mainly be because of changes in land tenure and marketing

relationships which favour family peasant proprietorship. They (and the many more who will want to try to get rich rather than re-collectivise) will bitterly defend such a new economic form, and the numbers involved may be a large section of the population. Providing landlordism does not re-emerge, such new social relations are less likely to produce class conflict in the countryside (and hence little renewed pressure for increased socialist collectivism) than they are to precipitate antagonism between the peasants and the government over investment subsidies and crop procurement prices.

The Open Door policies are also indicative of changes in social relations which may be far-reaching in spite of the relatively small size of foreign trade, investment and indebtedness. Exploitative ruling classes are by definition small, and we need not be surprised that changes in the relatively small party leadership can create conditions favourable to capitalist restoration. Likewise changes in economic policy concerning relatively small quantitative shifts in certain sectors may be very significant in terms of class formation. With the Open Door policies several elements are involved. The changed political status of ex-capitalists and the involvement that they have in industry and with overseas Chinese is, I feel, very significant. There is also the reduction of central government control over provincial affairs, together with the increasingly independent role of localities and individual enterprises, and the new methods by which production costs and profitability are calculated.

The effect of the new policies, whether willed (by those who wish to see capitalism emerge) or not (as by those who accept the need for temporary retreat policies), is to create a situation in which a network of new links can be established between exploiters within and from outside China. It is the coincidence of policies which promote non-socialist trade and investment with the potential for capitalist class formation that is damaging. Such a dangerous marriage may eventually be exposed and opposed by sections of the party and people, but not before the policies which bring some benefits in modernization of the means of production have done damage to socialist consciousness and once flourishing developments in socialist relations of production.

NOTES

Editorial Introduction

     1. Lin C.C. (1981). A much more extensive account will be contained in his doctoral dissertation.

     2. These and the following figures are compiled from China Trade and Economic Newsletter, May 1981 and NCNA, 11th November 1982, with information on recent corrections of the 1980 figures kindly supplied by Roland Berger, while the figure for gross industrial growth 1974-1976 is based on Field et al (1978:242).

     3. This calculation is based on the lowest figures given in Maxwell, N. (1976:818).

     4. Thanks to Richard Kirkby for providing this information from Zhang Changgen et al (1981).

Chapter 1. Chinese Economic Debates

     1. Chinese economists are beginning to realize this fact themselves, as can be seen in the present popularity of W. Brus, O. Lange, and others in China

     2. For practical purposes, inverted commas around Marxism ('Marxism') have been omitted through out the chapter.

     3. On the association between Xue Muqiao and Chen Yun in the mid '50s see Schurmann, F. (1968:196 ff). Xue at that time headed the State Statistical Bureau and Chen was vice-premier in the State Council and head of the Ministry of Commerce.

     4. In the January 1979 issue of Hongqi, Xue Muqiao wrote (p.64):

> some comrades say that ... the law of value
> neither can nor ought to be restricted. I
> have always been in disagreement with this

> opinion, I think that it is in fact possible
> to reduce the sphere of influence of the law
> of value.

As a matter of fact Xue has not pressed this point
in later publications, in spite of the defiance of
the passage just quoted.

5. Xue Muqiao, 'Jiazhi guilü zai Zhongguo
jingjizhong de zuoyung' (The function of the law of
value in China's economy) in his collection of essays, Xue Muqiao (1978:18)

6. Sun Yefang, 'Ba jinhua he tongji fang zai
jiazhi guilü de jichushang' (Local planning and
statistics on the basis of the law of value), in the
collection of his essays, Sun Yefang (1979:1-14).

7. Ibid pp. 83-137. An up-to-date version of
Sun's theory of value has been published in English,
(Sun Yefang 1980b).

8. For a short presentation of these early
departures, see Xinhua Yuebao, 2, 1980:60 ff.

9. Zhang Chunqiao, who later became the think
tank of the Shanghai school, had his debut at the
national level of theoretical debates with a small
article entitled 'Puchu zichanjieji de faquan
sixiang' (Smash the ideology of bourgeois rights) in
Renmin Ribao, 13 October, 1958. It is quite representative of what came to be called the Communist
Wind of 1958.

10. There are several versions of Mao's
'Reading Notes', a convenient translation being Mao
(1977). It is worth noting that the Notes have
never been published in China. They were circulated
among higher-level cadres in the 1960s and Red
Guards, who got hold of this classified material,
later took copies to Hong Kong. The 'Reading Notes'
are in fact one of the many points of reference for
the left-wing current in Chinese economic thinking,
laying some of the foundation for the later Shanghai
school. In recent years, surprisingly, one still
sometimes comes across references to the 'Reading
Notes', one example of this being Xue Muqiao (1979b:
3). Xue quotes approvingly from them but without
specifying the source.

11. Xue Muqiao et al (1979a:314). The reference occurs in an article by Qi Feng and Zhao
Zhenying with the title 'Shehuizhuyi jingji jihua he
shichang' (Plan and market in the socialist economy)

12. Hu Qiaomu, 'Anzhao keguan jingji guilü ban
shi, jiakuai shixian sige xiandaihua' (Do things in
accordance with objective economic laws, speed up
the realization of the four modernisations), in

Renmin Ribao, 6 October 1978, tr. in Beijing Review, 45, 46 and 47, 1978.

13. Luo Gengmo, another veteran economist, takes exception to the general view, faithful to a highly individual theoretical line that can be traced back to the late 1950s. Luo has consistently argued that the socialist economy is characterised by 'socialist products', not commodities. He finds theoretical justification for this approach in the writings of Lenin in the early 1920s. For an English-language version of his views see Luo Gengmo (1980). It is remarkable that there is no public criticism of Luo's approach; perhaps his main function is that of being a symbol of the possibility of disagreement.

14. See Liu Guoguang and Zhao Renwei, 'Lun shehuizhuyi jingjizhong jihua yu shichang de guanxi' (On the relation between plan and market in the socialist economy) in Xue Muqiao et al (1979a: 53ff). Excerpts from this article have been translated into English in Beijing Review, 31, 1979.

15. For a theoretical discussion, see Bettelheim, C. (1975:184-243).

16. For an evaluation, apparently rather representative of the ideological establishment, of Sun's economic thought, see Ma Jiaju (1980), in particular the critique on pp. 222 ff.

17. A typical example of the mainstream is the article by Lin Zili and You Lin (1978). Summaries of discussions are available in the articles by Liang Wen (1980), and, in English, Xia Liang (1980).

18. It might be added, to be noted well, that Marxism in a way was no easy choice. Marxism has been quite difficult to translate into the Chinese language and culture, giving rise to a rather partial knowledge of Marxism in China, even amongst top leaders. Mao, who was a voracious reader, apparently never read through Capital, and even the expert in the field of economic theory Xu Dixin, a leading Party theoretician for more than forty years, never had time to make a careful study of Capital until he was locked up by the Red Guards during the Cultural Revolution. See the short autobiography by Xu Dixin in Xinhua Yuebao, 2, 1980:196ff.

Chapter 2. The Shanghai School

1. According to Guangming Ribao, 17 April 1978, in July 1975 contact was established between the group in Shanghai working on the Political Economy of Socialism and a group from Nankai University of

Tianjin working on a parallel book. Presumably the
two groups continued to cooperate. The book written
by the Tianjin group was printed and distributed as
late as November 1976, but then confiscated and criticized like the book written in Shanghai.

2. For more on the connection between Mao's
theory and the theory of the Shanghai school, and on
the theoretical development of the Shanghai school,
see Christensen and Delman, 1981.

3. This was Zhengzhi Jingjixue Jiaocai
(shehuizhuyi bufen) (Teaching Materials on Political
Economy (Socialist Section)), Shanghai People's
Publishing House, 1961.

4. This information is from Renmin Ribao
24 November 1977. The titles of the manuscripts
are: Shehuizhuyi Zhengzhi Jingjixue (Zheng Qiu
Yijian Gao) (Political Economy of Socialism (Manuscript for comments)), Shanghai 1972; ... (Mo Ding
Gao) (... (Final Draft)), Shanghai 1973; ... (Mo
Ding Gao Di Er Ban) (... (Second Edition of the
Final Draft)), Shanghai 1975; ... (Mo Ding Gao Di Er
Ban Taolun Gao) (... (Discussion Draft of the Second Edition of the Final Draft)), Shanghai, 1975;
and finally Shehuizhuyi Zhengzhi Jingjixue (Political Economy of Socialism), Shanghai, 1976.

5. Peking Review, 14 February 1975. Together
with two articles written by Zhang Chunqiao and Yao
Wenyuan, published in Peking Review, 7 March and
4 April 1975, this instruction provided the start to
a campaign to study the theory of the dictatorship
of the proletariat.

6. Dong Fureng is now deputy director of the
Institute of Economics, Chinese Academy of Social
Sciences, Beijing. An article written by him was
published in English (1980).

7. In an article, 'Continue the Revolution
under the Dictatorship of the Proletariat to the
End', Peking Review, 6 May 1977

8. See also John Gittings, 1975:6.

Chapter 3. Economic Reforms in Eastern Europe

1. Beijing Review (14, 6 April 1981:3-4) and
(32, 10 August 1981:12-17). Those engaged in agriculture account for 75% of the labour force.

2. Beijing Review (4, 26 January 1981:3) and
(14, 6 April 1981:3-4).

3. A. Nove (1978:Chapter 3).
T. Bauer and L. Szamuely (1978).

4. A. Eckstein (1977:132-134).
Beijing Review (5, 4 February 1980:21-22).

5. V. Novozhilov V. Nemchinov and
L. Kantrovich in, A. Nove and D. Nuti (1972).
        C. Bliss (1972).
6. I. Friss (1973) and (1978).
        R. Nyers and M. Tardos (1978).
7. T. Bauer and L. Szamuely (1978).
8. W. Brus (1979).
        A. Fornalczyk (1980).
        M. Melzer (1981).
9. I. Berend (1974).
10. Li Yue and Chen Shengchang (1981).
        Beijing Review (14, 7 April 1980:26-27),
and (6, 9 February 1981:3).
11. Yu. Shvyrkov (1980:32).
12. J. Berliner (1976:Chapter 14).
        A. Kosygin (1965) in A. Nove and M. Nuti
(1972).
13. Berliner (1976:Chapter 14).
        M. Cave and P. Hare (1981:Chapters 3 and 9)
14. T. Bauer (1978).
        R. Nyers and M. Tardos (1978).
15. Xue Muqiao (1981:Chapter III).
        Du Runsheng (1981).
16. Beijing Review (12, 24 March 1980:14-20)
and (26, 29 June 1981:3-4).
17. G. Bennett (1978:Parts I and II).
18. L. Johansen (1978:Chapter 5.9).
19. On the Soviet Union see Berliner (1976:
Part II).
        On Hungary see P. Hare (1977)
        For a general discussion see W. Sztyber
(1970-71).
        On China see Xiao Zhuoji (1980), and
Beijing Review (20, 18 May 1981:21-22).
        20. P. Hare (1981) in P. Hare, H. Radice and
N. Swain (1981).
21. Beijing Review (43, 27 October 1980:18-21).
22. For a general discussion of a similar
thesis see, I. Berend (1978).
23. For a discussion on wage determination in
Hungary see G. Revesz (1979), F. Renversez and
M. Lavigne (1979), and M. Marrese (1981) in
P. Hare, H. Radice and N. Swain (1981).
        For a discussion of wage determination in
the Soviet Union, see A. Nove (1978:Chapter 8).

Chapter 5. China's New Agricultural Revolution

1. Preference has been given in the quotation
of sources to materials available in translation,
and especially to the monitoring reports of Chinese

broadcasts published by the BBC (British Broadcasting Corporation) and the FBIS (Foreign Broadcast Information Service). The first publishes a Summary of World Broadcasts, Part III, the Far East, abbreviated here to SWB. The second publishes China Daily Report, abbreviated here to FBIS. These have the advantage of including coverage of provincial as well as central material, particularly valuable for the subject of this chapter.

2. SWB 6560/BII/3, Henan, 17 October 1980.
3. SWB 6567/BII/4, Jilin, 17 October 1980.
4. SWB 6567/BII/1, Renmin Ribao, editorial, 1 November 1980.
5. SWB 6695/BII/5, Anhui, 3 April 1981.
6. FBIS 072/O5, Jiangxi, 13 April 1981.
7. FBIS 088/O2, Shandong, 6 May 1981.
8. FBIS 125/T2, Shaanxi Ribao, 26 May 1981.
9. SWB 6783/BII/2, Renmin Ribao, 21 July 1981.
10. FBIS 161/R1, Shaanxi Ribao, 22 July 1981.
11. FBIS 174/K7, Renmin Ribao, 1 September 1981
12. FBIS 167/R1, Heibei, 16 August 1980.
13. FBIS 038/S6, Liaoning, 25 February 1981.
14. SWB 6484/C6, Hubei, 25 July 1980.
15. SWB 6437/BII/5, Guangming Ribao, 10 May 1980.
16. FBIS 101/L11, Renmin Ribao, 15 December 1980.
17. SWB 6427/BII/1, Renmin Ribao, 14 May 1980.
18. SWB 6437/BII/5, Guangming Ribao, 10 May 1980.
19. SWB 6568/BII/5, Renmin Ribao, 3 November 1980.
20. On the faults ascribed to grass-roots cadres see especially: SWB 6568/BII/5, Renmin Ribao 3 November 1980; FBIS 253/L42, Renmin Ribao, 13 December 1980; FBIS 238/W2, Hong Kong Ming Pao, 6 December 1981, reporting Xin Guancha.
21. On peasant burdens see especially: FBIS 225, Renmin Ribao, 6 November 1979; SWB 6479/BII/1, Guizhou, 20 July 1980; FBIS 145/T1, Renmin Ribao, 11 July 1981; SWB 6814/BII/1, Xinhua, 25 August 1981; SWB 6826/C/3, Xinhua, 4 September 1981; SWB 6843/BII/2, Renmin Ribao, 17 September 1981.
22. FBIS 238/W2, Hong Kong Ming Pao, 6 December 1981, reporting Xin Guancha.
23. FBIS 174/K7, Renmin Ribao, 1 September 1981
24. FBIS 253/L42, Renmin Ribao, 12 December 1980.
25. ibid.
26. FBIS 044/Q1, Xinhua, 4 March 1981.
27. FBIS 238/W2, Hong Kong Ming Pao,

6 December 1981, reporting Xin Guancha.
    28. FBIS 093/K5, Guangming Ribao, 25 April 1981
    29. FBIS 101/L11, Guangming Ribao, 15 December
1980.
    30. SWB 6666/BII/1, Renmin Ribao, 2 March 1981
    31. FBIS 212/02, Jiefang Ribao, 10 October 1980
    32. FBIS 118/K9, Hebei Ribao, 20 May 1981.
    33. FBIS 145/T1, Renmin Ribao, 11 July 1981.
    34. FBIS 048/L2, Jingji Guanli, 1, 1981
    35. FBIS 222, Guangming Ribao, 6 November 1979.
    36. SWB 6294/C/5, Shaanxi, 3 December 1979.
    37. SWB 6919/BII/1, Kyodo, 3 January 1982.
    38. SWB 164/01, Xinhua, 19 August 1980.
    39. FBIS 145/T1, Renmin Ribao, 11 July 1981.
    40. FBIS 238/W2, Hong Kong Ming Pao,
6 December,1981, reporting Xin Guancha.
    41. SWB 6427/BII/1 Renmin Ribao, 14 May 1980.
    42. SWB 6351/BII/11, Jiangxi, 16 February 1980.
    43. FBIS 113/K19, Banyuetan No.10, 1980.
    44. FBIS 238/W2, Hong Kong Ming Pao,
6 December 1981, reporting Xin Guancha.
    45. SWB 6570/C1/1, Xinhua, 5 November 1980.
    46. SWB W1170/A/4, Jingji Yanjiu, 12,
20 December 1981.
    47. Nongye Jingji Wenti No.9, 1981.
    48. SWB 6695/BII/1, Xinhua, 1 April 1981.
    49. SWB 6705/BII/24, Xinhua, 20 April 1981.
    50. FBIS 145/T1, Renmin Ribao, 11 July 1981.
    51. SWB 6479/BII/1, Guizhou, 20 July 1980.
    52. ibid.
    53. FBIS 205/L13, Renmin Ribao, 13 October 1980
See also SWB 6774/BII/9, Shaanxi Ribao, 20 June 1981
FBIS 080/Q1, Guizhou, 24 April 1981; FBIS 202/R1,
Shaanxi Ribao, 29 September 1981; SWB 6875/BII/1,
Renmin Ribao, 30 October 1981; FBIS 209/L22,
Banyuetan, 26 October 1980.
    54. FBIS 090/P5, Hunan, 8 May 1981.
    55. SWB 6575/BII/6, Jilin, 8 November 1980.
    56. SWB 6572/C/5, Hongqi, 19 October 1980.
    57. This was of particular interest to the
author, who has always maintained that a system like
that of the Danes would have been a far better basis
for Mao's rural economic strategy than the commune.

Chapter 6. China's System of Industrial Economic Planning

    1. At the National People's Congress of
September 1980, the unrealism of the ten year plan
was recognised. It was abandoned and preparation of
a new ten year plan for 1981-1990 initiated.

2. The new policies of readjustment etc. are also forms of reform, but since reform in China often carries the connotation of decentralisation the term is not used in the discussion to follow.

3. Since I have virtually no knowledge of agriculture, agricultural production units are not discussed in this chapter.

4. Khozraschet is a Russian word meaning, roughly, economic accounting. Economic units on khozraschet are required to keep separate accounts for their financial transactions, and their revenues are normally expected to cover their operating costs.

5. There have actually been several waves of decentralisation to regional, or more often provincial, level with intervening partial recentralisations. Thus the 1958 decentralisation to provinces was reversed in 1959 but a limited decentralisation occurred in 1964, followed by further measures in 1972-1973. For further details of the earlier changes see Schurmann (1968:195-210).

6. There is some ambiguity about the timing here; central agencies and the Shanghai Municipal Planning Commission agreed that guidelines were issued in October, whereas the Shandong Province SPC claimed that it began to study the main directions of government policy as early as June or July.

7. According to the Shanghai Municipal Planning Commission, this number has now been reduced to 32, with other products allocated in a more flexible way. Even more confusingly, the BMA was reported as suggesting that 'the planned allocation of materials be reduced from 256 kinds to 68 kinds' (NCNA, 699, 7 August 1980:3).

8. This discussion concentrates on the allocation of means of production; it should also be noted that the Ministry of Commerce and its lower level counterparts deal with the allocation of consumer goods, labour bureaux allocate manpower, and the Foreign Trade Ministry handles overseas transactions.

9. The above comments about investment, including the references to the CCC, only apply to state investment. The small proportion of total investment accounted for by cooperatives and small collectives is organised differently and may well experience different problems. However, I have no information to report about that.

10. For discussion of pricing principles applied in Eastern Europe and the Soviet Union, and the practical problems involved, see Hare (1976),

Nove (1977), Berliner (1976) and Abouchar (1977).

11. It is important to emphasise here that enterprise-level investment decisions will still only
account for a very small proportion of total investment.

12. For discussion on this point see Ren et al
(1980) and Tian (1981).

13. This means that in principle the enterprises should only be in a position to replace existing capacity as it wears out, rather than undertake
significant expansions of their operations.

14. There are also some changes in the areas of
labour allocation and foreign trade regulations,
which fall outside the scope of this chapter. See
chapters 8 and 9 in this volume.

15. Some aspects of reform in the banking system are discussed in Zhang (1981).

16. As before, I am not in a position to comment here on agriculture, foreign trade or the labour
allocation system. These are all discussed elsewhere in this book.

17. Some new forms of economic unit are discussed in He (1981) but there is no space here for a
detailed analysis.

Chapter 7.   Enterprise Management - Moves Towards Democracy?

1.   For further details on the collective sector, see Lockett (1981) and (1981b).

2.   In practice this distinction is less clear
as the continual reportage of cases of economic mis-
behaviour such as bribery in the Chinese press
shows. For example, according to Beijing Review
(14 September 1981:7) 'extorting "commissions" is
rather common in the course of commodity circulation
in China today'. In particular the 'hybrid' system,
in which reform has only just begun, gives rise to a
large number of opportunities for profitable but
illegal or 'unethical' deals due to the lack of fit
between parts of the economy at different stages of
economic reform. Some of these will disappear if
reforms are carried through in the whole economy and
in areas like the price system.

3.   This occurs even in cases where the nature
of the production technology and work organisation
makes such schemes inappropriate on economic grounds.
For example, in visits to enterprises in 1981, incentive schemes for maintenance workers based on the
number of repairs had been introduced, giving incentives for less efficient repair work - a problem

which has led many UK factories to abandon such schemes. In another case, an industrial corporation was pressing an enterprise to introduce piecework-type bonuses for production workers whose work pace was fixed by automated machinery, and where the main source of variation in output was a result of repair time.

4.   For example, according to Wan (1980), the Shanghai Number One Machinery and Electricity Bureau surveyed 2000 'production management cadres in 64 enterprises' and found that only 1.6% were graduates or the equivalent. Another survey of leading cadres in over 2000 enterprises in the machinery industry showed 14.3% had university level education, 21.4% senior middle school or college level, and 64.3% primary or junior middle school education. He concluded, unfairly in my view, that 'The bureaucratic system of economic management in China is the worst and most backward in the world'.

5.   Deng's policies were very similar to those advocated by Lai Ruoyu and Li Xuefeng at the 8th CCP Congress in 1956 (see Lockett, 1982, for details also Lai, 1956, and Li, 1956).

6.   These three sections are based on Lockett (1982) but have been developed and updated both from visits to Chinese enterprises in summer 1981 and more recently published material.

7.   Within a Chinese factory, the lowest level of formal organisation is a workgroup or workteam, typically with 10 to 30 members. Above this is the workshop level, although there may be an intermediate level of a shift in some factories. The factory level is above the workshop although in large plants there may be an intermediate level of 'sub-plants' or similar. At factory level there will be various administrative sections or offices. Thus the main levels of organisation are (i) workgroup (ii) workshop (iii) factory, as well as (iv) sections. The associated management posts are (i) workgroup leader (ii) workshop director/head/manager (iii) factory director/manager and deputies, (iv) section heads.

8.   Information from a discussion with the International Section, All-China Federation of Trade Unions, (ACFTU) Beijing, September 1981. The same situation exists for the figures (below) on elections of factory directors.

9.   Information from discussions with the Beijing Municipal Trade Union Council and Sichuan Provincial Economic Commission. In Chongqing a representative of the Municipal Economic Commission

said that no factory directors had been elected.

10. The figure of 60% was said to be based on 'incomplete statistics' by the Sichuan Provincial Economic Commission; the figures for Chongqing were from its Municipal Economic Commission. Both were the latest figures available in September 1981 but their exact date is not known, and their degree of accuracy is uncertain.

11. Very similar figures were given in September by the ACFTU as well as the Beijing and Shanghai trade unions. Other reports giving the same picture include Tian (1980:24) on Tianjin and SWB (14 March 1981).

12. The sums involved were 3% of the wage fund if 4 of the 8 standard targets were met, and 5% if all 8 were met. (Beijing Review, 12 January 1979).

13. These forms of organisation resemble to some extent the workers' management teams which emerged out of the Cultural Revolution, described by Bettelheim (1974). Many factories also had a system of 'responsible people' (dayuan) within work-groups, namely workers with responsibilities for particular aspects of management within the group (for more discussion, see below). Ironically in one part of what was the General Knitwear Mill, described by Bettelheim (1974:Ch.1), visited in September 1981 such forms of organisation seemed to have disappeared, except for workers within groups who collected attendance and output figures. In fact in the No.3 Knitwear Factory (part of the old General Knitwear Mill), the Revolutionary Committee was abandoned as early as 1975 in favour of a 'leading group' (lingdao xiaozu) of managers as the main policy and management body.

14. This is a summary of the arguments of Jiang (1980b), Ma (1980) and of discussions with Jiang Yiwei and other members of the Institute of Industrial Economics under the Chinese Academy of Social Sciences, who are prominent in providing an intellectual case for the proposed reforms in the enterprise leading system. It should be stressed that they saw these reforms increasing the effectiveness of Party leadership through changing its form.

15. In practice membership is not 100% as new recruits to the labour force do not formally join trade unions immediately. In the factories visited the lowest figure given was in the Sichuan No.1 Cotton Mill where it was 83%, with most others being over 90%. Membership of trade unions in the collective sector will be much lower than these figures.

16. For example, according to the Beijing

municipal trade unions, in a machinery factory, workers' representatives refused to attend the workers' congress to put pressure on the factory directors who had been allocated more housing than they were entitled to.

17. In discussions, ACFTU cadres saw moves towards greater democracy in industry as an attempt to prevent a 'Polish situation' in China, while stating that they hoped Solidarity would 'continue to play a very important role in safeguarding the sovereignty and vital interests of Polish workers'.

18. Taiwanese 'intelligence sources' claim that leaflets calling for independent unions have been circulating in Chongqing and other parts of Sichuan Province (Free China Weekly, 17 May 1981). ACFTU cadres said they did not know of any enterprises in China where workers wanted to set up an independent trade union, although 'a few' Chinese workers might support the idea of such unions.

19. Discussion with Jiang Yiwei, September 1981. He also argued that unions should be a link between the CCP and the 'masses'.

20. The impact at shopfloor level in a less successful factory in the Hungarian economic reforms has been described by Haraszti (1977). In this book, about piecework in a tractor factory, he details increases in work norms, management appeals for harder work, and pressure for overtime to get a profit-related bonus followed by no bonus, with the factory journal explaining that, 'In spite of production reaching the planned schedules, the money allocated for bonuses has already been spent in paying for overtime' (123). While some of the conditions in Hungary do not exist at present in China, for example large profit-related bonuses for managers, Haraszti's book does illustrate graphically some of the pressures likely to be created as one aspect of economic reforms.

21. This included a comparison of all workgroups according to five factors, weighted to make up 100 points: (a) 'good politics' 20; (b) 'good tasks' 40; (c) 'good management' 26; (d) 'good culture' 6; (e) 'good unity' 8. Production and management therefore make up two-thirds of the group rating.

22. Illustrating the contrast in views, the director of the Beijing TV Set Factory thought that the more 'scientifically' work was organised, the more fragmented jobs would be. However, because they were in a socialist society, workers would accept such boring work 'because they are class

conscious'. For him democratic management was a
separate issue for it was political rather than
technical. On the other hand, advocates of scientific management at Fudan University, Shanghai, were
critical of the way in which it saw 'workers as
talking, living machines'; stressed managing workers rather than 'arousing their initiative and enthusiasm', and stated that behavioural science find-
ings to some extent contradicted it.

23. Though only impressionistic information was
obtained in this area, it has been confirmed by
other recent visitors. However, although there was
much more concern expressed with this when I visited
China in 1975, of course this did not necessarily
lead to effective action (see Lockett, 1978:33-34).

Chapter 8. Urban Employment and Labour Allocation Policies

1. For a discussion of labour questions in the
1960s and early 1970s, see Howe (1973), and for an
evaluation of the employment situation as of the
middle of the 1970s, see Karcher (1975) and Rawski
(1979).

2. The noted Chinese economist, Xue Muqiao
(1981:68), puts the matter as follows:

> What distinguishes the capitalist relations of
> production from those under slavery and feud-
> alism is, first and foremost, the complete
> freedom of the labourer from personal bondage.
> Although he doesn't possess any means of prod-
> uction he enjoys freedom of the person, free-
> dom to sell his labour power. A capitalist is
> an owner of the means of production and is in
> a position to buy labour power as a commodity
> and unite it with the means of production for
> the production of surplus value.

3. Agence France Presse report from Peking,
13 February 1981.

4. For Chongqing see Sichuan provincial radio,
Chengdu, 16 February 1979, in FBIS 22 February 1979;
for Shanghai, see Shanghai city radio, 7 February
1979, in FBIS 8 February 1979, and Yan Yin, 'Resol-
utely stop the "return to Shanghai" wind', Jiefang
Ribao 16 February 1979, in FBIS 26 February 1979.
For similar problems in Shejiang province, see FBIS
9 February 1979 and 'Shejiang labour bureau director
discusses jobs for youths', Hangzhou provincial
radio, 13 March 1979, in FBIS 21 March 1979.

5. For Heilongjiang, see the report on the provincial work conference on urban youth employment 20 June 1980, in FBIS, 124, 1980; for Jilin see Xinhua 25 July 1980, in SWB, 6486, which shows the new effort to provide urban jobs for youth who would otherwise have been sent to the countryside. Jilin also pioneered reform of the system of 'unified' labour allocation: see the report of 4 August 1980 in SWB, 6497.

6. Xinhua, 12 August 1980, in FBIS 13 August 1980; and editorial, 'The fundamental way to solve the labour employment problem', Renmin Ribao, 13 August 1980, in FBIS 20 August 1980.

7. Xinhua, 23 November 1981 carried the decisions, tr. in SWB, 6891.

8. For example, see Li Chengrui and Zhang Zhuoyuan (1980), Zhuang Qidong et al (1981), on Shandong province, Shao Lukuan (1980), and Xue Muqiao (1981:185-189).

9. For an example of such proposals see Feng Lanrui (1981). For statistical reports on readjustment of the educational system in Shandong, see Zhuang Qidong et al (1981): for example, the ratio of general to specialised/vocational middle school students in the province was changed from 98.45:1.4 in 1978 to 83.5:16.5 by the end of 1980. The proportion in 1965 had been 58.4:41.6.

10. Xue Muqiao (1981:186-189), Feng Lanrui (1981), Zhang Zehou and Chen Yuguang (1981:71-78).

11. For broad discussions of the urban collective economy, see 'Pay serious attention to the study of the theory of an urban collective economy ... ', Guangming Ribao, 19 December 1979, in FBIS, 11 January 1980; editorial, 'Persist in the assumption of responsibility for their own profits and losses - on the management principle of collectively owned enterprises', Renmin Ribao 6 June 1981, in FBIS 12 June 1981. Concerning individual economy, see Wei Xianming (1981).

12. For the official regulations on private economy, see State Council 'Regulations of a policy nature on non-agricultural urban self-employment', in Xinhua, 15 July 1981, tr. in SWB, 6783. For reports of successful business-people see 'Entrepreneurs take on help', China Daily, 30 July 1981:4.

13. For an example of the contract system in Beijing see 'Beijing's new policy on youngsters in the countryside', NCNA, 1 December 1980. There appears to be a good deal of policy variation among cities and provinces.

14. For controls on rural immigration, see

Jiangxi provincial radio, 14 October 1980, in FBIS, 203; for Shandong, see Zhuang Qidong et al (1981); and see Guangdong provincial radio, 12 September 1981, in SWB, 6837. As these reports show, the problem is very difficult to handle.

15. For example, see He Jianzhang (1979), Kuang Rian and Xiao Liang (1979), and Liu Guoguang and Zhao Renwei (May, 1979).

16. For examples see the article cited by Zhao Lukuan, Feng Lanrui, Ye Ming and Chan Guangzhen (1979).

17. For an appeal on behalf of intellectuals, see Wu Lu (1980:4).

18. For critical analyses of the 'iron rice-bowl (tiefanwan)', see Zhong He (1980) and Huang Zhengshen (1980).

19. For an approving retrospective view of the 'two-track' system see Huang Zhengshen (1980).

20. This measure was included in the 'new employment policy' promulgated after the CCP's national conference on labour and employment in August 1980, and repeated in the State Council decisions of October-November 1981, which also proposed the establishment of a national China Labour Service General Company.

21. Zhong He (1980). By contrast, Jiang Yiwei (1979:21) suggests that 'the problem of livelihood for the dismissed workers should be safeguarded by the state in the form of social insurance and the responsibility for ensuring their livelihood should not be assumed by the enterprise concerned'.

22. For example, see Kuang Rian and Xiao Liang (1979:15); compare this with Zhong He (1980), Wu Lu (1980) and He Jianzhang (1979).

23. For examples see Liu Guoguang and Zhao Renwei (1979) and Xue Muqiao (1981:67-73).

24. Beijing Ribao, 18 September 1979, tr. in CREA, 21, 16 October 1979.

25. 'A worker's worry', Gongren Ribao, 10 January 1981:2, tr. in FBIS, 23 January 1981.

26. 'Prospects of employment', Beijing Review, 2, 11 January 1982:3.

27. This rough calculation is based on an estimated urban population of 128 million in 1979 (13.8% of the total population) and a ratio (admittedly calculated for 1981) of 1:1.78 between urban population and urban workforce. The total urban population figure is cited in Zhang Zehou and Chen Yuguang (1981:73). See the next note for citation of the ratio.

28. NCNA, 18 January 1982.

29. For example, in Peking there were more un-employed in 1981 than in 1980, a fact partly attrib-uted to the pressures of readjustment (Beijing Ribao, 6 March 1981, tr. in SWB, 6692).

30. For a systematic attempt to calculate the relationship between employment growth in the spheres of material and non-material production, see Zhang Zehou and Chen Yuguang (1981:65-69).

31. For example, see Feng Lanrui (1981) for a critique of the policy of encouraging state enter-prises to set up affiliated collectives.

32. For an example of an attempt to rebut such a charge, see Xiao Wanyuan (1980).

33. These attitudes reflect not merely official ideological distinctions between state and non-state economy and the impact of elitist schooling, but also traditional Chinese attitudes toward certain 'mean' (xiajian) occupations. Xue Muqiao appears to underestimate this problem when he argues (in July, 1979) that the 'capitalist loopholes' of individual economy should be opened up in the cities. In res-ponse to the objection that only peasants are will-ing to take these jobs and urban youth refused jobs in the service trades although labour bureaux tried to 'force the crow to build its nest', he argued that such a refusal was natural since service jobs may not have squared with their skills and training – an unconvincing reply. Moreover, to the extent that urbanites do move into sectors hitherto domin-ated by mobile peasants, they may encounter resist-ance from the latter.

34. Yang Yichen, reported by Heilongjiang pro-vincial radio, 2 May 1981, tr. in FBIS 4 May 1981.

35. For an example of such conflict, see 'What does the "bowl-smashing incident" indicate?', Xinhua 16 August 1980, tr. in FBIS, 18 August 1980. In this incident an employee of a government-run rest-aurant in Changsha smashed a bowl belonging to an individually operated food stall; moreover, 'some responsible persons of the department concerned act-ed to shield the smasher and blame the stall owner'. 'Some comrades' apparently alleged that 'allowing the operation of an individually owned catering ser-vice is taking away business from state-owned rest-aurants'.

36. This general judgement should be qualified in view of regional variation. In Jilin province, for example, the process of reform seems to have been taken further than elsewhere (Jilin provincial radio, 4 August 1980, tr. in SWB, 6497).

37. For a discussion of these innovations, see

Shirk (1981:576).

38. For the activities of these companies see Xinhua, 9 July 1981, tr. in SWB, 6775, on Gansu province, and see also Jilin provincial radio, 24 November 1981, tr. in SWB, 6891.

39. Guangdong provincial radio, 22 October 1981 tr. in SWB, 1162.

40. Xue Muqiao makes this point (March 1981).

41. Agence France Presse, Hong Kong, 22 April 1981, in FBIS, 23 April 1981.

42. For example, see the report by Bonavia from Beijing in The Times, London, 8 May 1981.

43. It is dangerous to generalise even about workers in state enterprises. As Shirk (1981:591) points out, different types of workers may have different attitudes to the reforms.

44. Compare Shirk's distinction (1981:590-592) between 'organisation-oriented' and 'efficiency-oriented' enterprises, adapted from Dore (1973).

Chapter 9. Foreign Investment and Trade

1. For a Chinese 'dissident's' expression of similar views see Wang Xizhe's article (1980), translated from the unofficial magazine Philosophical Studies, 1979. Wang Xizhe was one of the authors of the Liyizhe wall poster 'Concerning socialist democracy and the legal system' which became famous in China. He was imprisoned after it was put up in Guangzhou (Canton) in 1974. For an account of the background see Brugger (1981:179-180). On the problem of the role of party power see D. Fernbach, 'Revolution, socialism and authoritarianism' China Now, 96, 1981, and my response in China Now, 97, 1981.

2. Resolution on Certain Questions in the History of our Party ... is available in, amongst other sources, Beijing Review, 29, 20 July 1981. It represents the current party leadership's attempt to summarise the political history of the CCP. In particular it forms an assessment of Mao Zedong's role and presents a balance sheet of the Cultural Revolution. For a discussion of it see China Now, 100, January/February 1982.

3. 'Some progress was made in our economy despite tremendous losses. Grain output increased relatively steadily. Significant achievements were scored in industry, communications and capital construction and in science and technology. New railways were built and ... a number of large enterprises using advanced technology went into

operation ... ' (Section 23 of the Resolution, in Beijing Review, 27, 1981:24).

    4. See Xu Dixin's elaboration of the policy for the Special Economic Zones (1981:14).

    5. See for instance the data presented by Heyman (1975:19).

    6. O'Leary (1980) has a useful analysis of this correlation.

    7. C. MacDougall, Financial Times, 3 May 1976.

    8. The policy was identified by the 'ultra-left' as one that led to 'worshipping foreign things'. That a fierce struggle was in progress is evidenced by the articles attacking open foreign trade, appearing in Beijing Ribao and Hongqi. This campaign reached a peak in 1976 after Zhou Enlai's death, and was linked to the purge and criticism of Deng Xiaoping and his 'slavish compradore philosophy'. In an article in Hongqi, (April 1976) it was argued that an unprincipled exchange of exports for imports would lead to a situation where

> we import everything that we can produce without restriction, export everything that is badly needed in the country without restriction, buy what is advanced from others, produce what is backward ourselves, and even give others the sovereign right to open up mineral resources. Then, as time passed, would we not turn our country into a market where the imperialist countries dump their goods, a raw material base, a repair and assembly workshop, and an investment centre?

(Cited in Eckstein, 1977:242). In this section I have utilised aspects of Eckstein's analysis.

    9. This policy is summed up in Mao's speech 'On the ten major relationships', 1977 edition, p.28:

> Our policy is to learn from the strong points of all nations and all countries, learn all that is genuinely good in the political, economic, scientific and technical fields and in literature and art. But we must learn with an analytical and critical eye, not blindly, and we must not copy everything indiscriminately and transplant mechanically'.

The problem is of course how to interpret this policy, what it means for self-reliance, and what degree of trade and financial arrangements to pay for it are to be allowed. Other references, ostensibly to Mao's views, are made in Li Zhiang (1977).

10. See for example Szuprowicz and Szuprowicz (1978) who estimate the Gross National Product (GNP) of 1976 at $207 billion (p.33), making foreign trade 4.3% in that year. MacDougall (ed.) (1980) gives a GNP figure for 1978 of $407 billion, making the trade ratio 5.1%. (Her GNP figure for 1976 is $342 billion).

11. In 1980 the figure was 7,300 million Yuan, or 17% of total spending on Fixed Capital Investment. The figure comes from Wang Bingqian, Xinhua Supplement, 16 December 1981.

12. Xinhua Weekly, 668, 3 December 1981. The category 'Fixed Capital Investment' has appeared sometimes as a sub-section of capital construction data, but I have not seen a definition.

13. CITIC had its capital increased in 1981 to 600 million Yuan (Xinhua Weekly, 667, 26 November 1981). The other organizations include: China Investment Bank, formed in December 1981 to raise foreign funds for domestic investment and credit and to handle loans from the World Bank. It provides investment loans for joint ventures (Beijing Review, 1, 1982:8); China International Economic Consultants Inc. is a subsidiary of CITIC, and its function is to provide economic and legal consultation services for investment activities. Operating capital is 10 million Yuan. Its Chairman is Bi Jichang, who was Vice-Governor of Fujian province, an interesting link with a province significant for its connections with overseas Chinese. There are also more than twenty organisations set up specifically to deal in the import and export of particular ranges of goods and equipment.

14. Li Qiang was still Foreign Trade Minister in 1978 when he made the remarks about accepting foreign loans (Financial Times, 19 November 1978), but he lost his post in September 1981 (Guardian, 11 September 1981) at the age of 76.

15. In the energy field, one of the things I find most disturbing is the eagerness of some of the leadership and scientists to import and construct nuclear power stations.

16. At the end of 1981 the investment in the Baoshan works was still under severe restriction, although it had been agreed between China and the principal suppliers (mainly Japan,to complete stage one of the project (Xinhua Weekly, 658, 24 September 1981).

17. The value of textile and garment (including woollens) exports in 1980 was 4,800 million Yuan, in

fact 12% more than in 1979 (<u>Xinhua Weekly, 628</u>,
26 February 1981). Textile and garment exports also
represent a substantial portion of the total of textile output value: 13% of 16,800 million Yuan in
1980 (<u>Xinhua Weekly, 648</u>, 16 July 1981). As 'expanded trade', this cotton-import-textile-export business seems to be a good example. It is seen as a
particular form of 'Foreign Economic Co-operation',
viz. processing imported raw materials (<u>Beijing
Review, 50</u>, 14 December 1981). It would seem to be
rather a precarious industry to be involved in,
given Western desires to restrict textile imports,
and the already fierce competition among Third World
textile producers.

18. <u>Xinhua Weekly, 669</u>, 10 December 1981. For
an intriguing description of growing finance and
trade connections between Hainan and its own sizeable overseas Chinese, see 'Hainan, the Treasure
Island', <u>China Reconstructs, 30</u> and <u>31</u>, 12 December
1981 and 1 January 1982. It includes the news that

> at the invitation of a group of overseas
> Chinese, Japanese experts have come several
> times to survey the island's resources and
> present proposals on exploiting the resources
> in a balanced way. Overseas Chinese business-
> men have held a number of talks with local
> officials on joint investment and compensatory
> trade, two areas which will undoubtedly be
> increasingly important in rebuilding Hainan's
> economic structure. The patriotic concern of
> these people who are far from their homeland
> has won wide public acclaim and the support
> of the government. (December, 1981:62).

19. Amongst other reports see <u>Guardian</u>,
2 December 1981, and <u>Xinhua Weekly, 666</u>, 19 November
1981, giving details of smuggling by Chinese along
the coasts of Guangdong, Fujian and Zhejiang provinces.

20. By 'overseas Chinese' I mean to include
those in Hong Kong and Macao, though technically
they are of course citizens of 'foreign occupied
Chinese territory'.

21. Similar, definitive verdicts have appeared
in the <u>Resolution on certain questions</u> ... (see note
2 above). For my comments on this subject see <u>China
Now, 100</u>, January/February 1982, and 'Foreign films
and alien developments', <u>China Now, 97</u>, July/August
1981.

22. The Honorary Chairman of CITIC is

Rong Yiren, another Shanghai ex-textile millionaire.

23. Details of the operation of SEZ and concessions available are given in Beijing Review, 50, 14 December 1981, and in Sun Ru (1980).

24. Zhang Yannian, 'Financing possibilities', in China's New Economic Strategies, Proceedings of an International Symposium at the Zentrum für Unternehmungsfuhrung, Zurich, 9-10 June 1980:128-129. Definitions are also given in Beijing Review, 50, 14 December 1981:16. Co-operative schemes or enterprises are also mentioned, which I have not discussed separately in this chapter as they appear to be contracts which combine the joint venture idea with processing deals and compensatory trade.

25. The impact of new technology on the structure of indigenous industry needs further discussion. For instance, in the new economic policies for enterprise management more emphasis is put on enterprise autonomy and profit-seeking. The re-tooling of a particular factory with modern foreign technology may reduce its unit costs of production in relation to more backward enterprises in the same line of production. Already there have been reports of many closures of high-cost or loss-making plants. If foreign technology is contributing to this it may well generate the kind of opposition seen in the Cultural Revolution, but for much more material reasons.

26. Xu Dixin is Vice-President of the Chinese Academy of Social Sciences. Xue Muqiao is Economic Advisor to the State Planning Commission.

REFERENCES

English-Language Translation Services

CREA abbreviation for: Joint Publications Research Service, China Report: Economic Affairs.

FBIS abbreviation for: Foreign Broadcast Information Service, Daily Report: China.

NCNA or Xinhua abbreviation for: Xinhua (New China) News Agency.

SWB abbreviation for: British Broadcasting Corporation, Summary of World Broadcasts: Far East.

Periodicals in Chinese

Banyuetan (Fortnightly Talks).
Beijing Ribao (Beijing Daily).
Caiwu Yu Kuaiji (Finance and Accounting).
Gongren Ribao (Workers Daily).
Guangming Ribao (Glorious Daily).
Guizhou Ribao (Guichou Daily).
Hebei Ribao (Hebei Daily).
Jiefang Ribao (Liberation Daily).
Jihua Jingji (Economics of Planning).
Jingji Guanli (Economic Management).
Jingji Yanjiu (Economic Research).
Ming Pao (Ming Bao)(Bright Daily, Hong Kong).
Nanfang Ribao (Southern Daily).
Nongye Jingji Wenti (Problems of Agricultural Economics).
Renkou Yanjiu (Population Research).
Renmin Ribao (People's Daily).
Shaanxi Ribao (Shaanxi Daily).
Shanxi Ribao (Shanxi Daily).
Xin Guancha (New Observer).
Xin Jianshe (New Construction).
Xinhua (New China News).
Xinhua Ribao (New China Daily).

References

Xinhua Yuebao (New China Monthly).
Zhongguo Funu (Chinese Women).
Zhongguo Shehui Kexue (Social Sciences in China).

ACFTU (All-China Federation of Trade Unions) (1981), The Chinese Trade Unions (mimeo), Beijing.
Abouchar, A. (ed) (1977), The Socialist Price Mechanism, Duke University Press, North Carolina.
Andors, S. (1977), China's Industrial Revolution, Martin Robertson, London.
Baark, E. (1980), Techno-economics and Politics of Modernisation in China, Research Policy Institute Paper No. 135, Lund.
Barnett, A.D. (1981), China's Economy in Global Perspective, The Brookings Institution, Washington D.C.
Bastid, M. and Domenach, (1976), 'De la Revolution Culturelle a la Critique de Confucius' in C. Aubert, L. Bianco, C. Cadart and J. Domenach (eds), Regards Froids sur la China, Editions du Sueil, Paris.
Batsavage, R.E. and Davie, J.L. (1978), 'China's International Trade and Finance' in Joint Economic Committee, The Chinese Economy Post-Mao, Vol.1, U.S. Government Printing Office, Washington D.C.
Bauer, T. (1976), The Contradictory Position of the Enterprise Under the New Hungarian Economic Mechanism, East European Economics, Fall:3-23.
Bauer, T. and Szamuely, L. (1978), The Structure of Industrial Enterprises in the European CMEA Countries, Acta Economica, Vol.20, No.4:407-415.
Bennett, G. (1978), China's Finance and Trade, Macmillan, London.
Berend, I. (1974),'Ways and Peculiarities of Enterprise Development in the Twentieth Century Hungarian Industry', Acta Historica Academiae Scientarium Hungaricae, Vol.20:363-384.
Berend, I. (1978),'Ten Years After - Instead of a Balance Sheet', Acta Economica, Vol.20, Nos.1-2: 45-60.
Berliner, J.S. (1976), The Innovation Decision in Soviet Industry, MIT Press, Massachusetts.
Bettelheim, C. (1974), Cultural Revolution and Industrial Organisation in China, Monthly Review Press, London.
Bettelheim, C. (1975), The Transition to Socialist Economy, Harvester Press, Sussex.
Bettelheim, C. (1978), China Since Mao, Monthly Review, New York.

347

References

Bliss, C. (1972),'Prices, Markets and Planning', Economic Journal, Vol.82:87-106.

Boltho, A. (1975), Japan: An Economic Survey, 1953-73, Oxford University Press.

Brugger, W. (1976), Democracy and Organisation in the Chinese Industrial Enterprise 1948-53, Cambridge University Press.

Brugger, W. (ed) (1981), China: Radicalism to Revisionism, 1962-1979, Croom Helm, London.

Brus, W. (1972), The Market in a Socialist Economy, Routledge and Kegan Paul, London.

Brus, W. (1973), The Economics and Politics of Socialism, Routledge and Kegan Paul, London.

Brus, W. (1975), Socialist Ownership and Political Systems, Routledge and Kegan Paul, London.

Brus, W. (1977), Socialisation and Political Systems, Danish translation, Copenhagen.

Brus, W. (1979),'The East European Reforms: What Happened to Them?',Soviet Studies, Vol.XXXIII, No.2 April:257-267.

Cai Behua, (1980), 'Shanghai's Foreign Trade and its Prospects', tr., from a Hong Kong seminar held in Hong Kong by the Chinese Government, in Chinese Economic Studies, 14, 1, Autumn.

Cave, M. and Hare, P. (1981), Alternative Approaches to Economic Planning, Macmillan, London.

Chang, (1975), see Zhang (1975).

Chen, N. and Galenson, W. (1969), The Chinese Economy under Communism, Edinburgh University Press.

Christensen, P. and Delman, J. (1981), 'A Theory of Transitional Society; Mao Zedong and the Shanghai School', Bulletin of Concerned Asian Scholars 13, 2.

Clark, R. (1979), The Japanese Company, Yale University Press.

Cole, R.E. (1971), Japanese Blue Collar: The Changing Tradition, University of California Press.

Cole, R.E. (1979), Work, Mobility and Participation: A Comparative Study of American and Japanese Industry, University of California Press.

Crawcour, S. (1978), 'The Japanese Employment System', Journal of Japanese Studies 4, 2.

Deng Xiaoping, (1978), 'Greeting the Great Task', Peking Review, 21, 20 Oct.

Deng Xiaoping, (1980), 'A Speech at the Enlarged Meeting of the Politburo of Central Committee (delivered on August 18; passed after discussion by the Politburo on August 31)', tr., in Issues and Studies, 17, March 1981.

Dernberger, R. (1979), 'Prospects for the Chinese Economy', Problems of Communism, Sept.-Dec.

References

special issue.

Doeringer, P. and Piore, M. (1971), <u>Internal Labour Markets and Manpower Analysis</u>, Heath Lexington Books.

Dong Fureng, (1980), 'Some problems concerning the Chinese economy', <u>China Quarterly</u>, 84, December.

Donnithorne, A. (1967), <u>China's Economic System</u>, Allen & Unwin, London

Dore, R.P. (1973), <u>British Factory - Japanese Factory, The Origins of National Diversity in Industrial Relations</u>, University of California Press, Berkeley.

Dore, R.P. (1979), 'Industrial Relations in Japan and Elsewhere', in A.M. Craig (ed), <u>Japan: A Comparative View</u>, Princeton University Press.

Du Runsheng, (1981),'Good Beginning for Reform of Rural Economic System',<u>Beijing Review 48</u>, 30th November:15-20.

Eckstein, A. (1977), <u>China's Economic Revolution</u>, Cambridge University Press.

'Economic Readjustment off to a Good Start' (1980), by a leading member of the SSB, <u>Beijing Review</u>, 20, May 19th.

Edwards, R. (1979), <u>Contested Terrain: The Transformation of the Workplace in the Twentieth Century</u>, Heinemann.

Fan Jigang, (1980), 'The cause of the emergence and existence of commodities', <u>Social Sciences in China</u>, Vol.1, No.2.

Feng Lanrui, (1981), 'On Factors Affecting China's Employment', <u>Renmin Ribao</u>, 16 Nov. tr. in <u>SWB</u>, 6888.

Feng Wenbin, (1981), 'On Questions of Socialist Democracy', <u>Beijing Review, 24</u>, Jan. 26.

Field, R.M. McGlynn, K.M. and Abrett, W.B. (1978), 'Political Conflict and Industrial Growth in China', in US Congress Joint Economic Committee, <u>Chinese Economy Post-Mao</u>, US Government Printing Office, Washington D.C.

Fornalczyk, A. (1980),'Integration of Enterprises in a Socialist Economy', <u>East European Economics</u>, Spring:3-33.

Friedman, A.L. (1977), <u>Industry and Labour</u>, Macmillan, London.

Friss, I. (1973),'Objective Conditions of the Economy and the Extent of Centralisation and Decentralisation', <u>Acta Economica</u>, Vol.10, No.3-4:303-314.

Friss, I. (1978),'Ten Years of Economic Reform in Hungary', <u>Acta Economica</u>, Vol 20, Nos 1-2:1-19.

Gittings, J. (1975), <u>How to study China's Socialist development</u>, Institute of Development

Studies, Communication 117, Sussex.

Gongren Ribao (6 Oct. 1980), 'Workers and Staff Must Have the Right to Manage Enterprises', tr., in Beijing Review, 24, 20 Oct.

Gongren Ribao (10 Oct. 1980), 'Trade Union Life', tr., in CREA 26:34.

Gordon, D.M. (1972), Theories of Poverty and Unemployment, Lexington Books.

Granick, D. (1975), Enterprise Guidance in Eastern Europe, Princeton University Press.

Gray, J. and White, G. (eds) (1982), China's New Development Strategy, Academic Press, London.

Guardian (30 Jan. 1980), 'Solidarity in China', London.

Guo Maoyan, (1977), 'Expose the Conspiracy of the "Gang of Four" in Attacking Foreign Trade Policy', Hongqi, 4, tr., in Chinese Economic Studies 11, 1.

Halliday, J. (1975), A Political History of Japanese Capitalism, Monthly Review Press, London.

Halliday, J. (1980), 'The Struggle for East Asia', New Left Review, 124.

Haraszti, M. (1977), A Worker in a Workers' State, Penguin, Harmondsworth, London.

Hare, P. (1977), 'Industrial Prices in Hungary', Soviet Studies, Vol.28, Nos.2-3:189-206 and 362-390.

Hare, P.G. (1981), 'The Investment System in Hungary', in P.G. Hare, H.K. Radice and N. Swain (eds), Hungary: A Decade of Economic Reform, Allen and Unwin, London.

Harper, P. (1971), 'Workers' Participation in Management in Communist China', Studies in Comparative Communism, 4, July/Oct.

Harrison, B. (1972), 'Education and Underemployment in the Urban Ghetto', American Economic Review, 62.

Hazama, H. (1981), 'Japanese Industrialisation and Labour-Management Relations, 1860-1930', mimeo. Paper presented at the SSRC Conference on Business and Labour History, March.

He Jianzhang, (1979), 'Problems in the Planned Management of the State Economy and Orientations of Reform', Jingji Yanjiu, 5, tr., in CREA, 5, 3 Aug.

He Jianzhang, (1981), 'Newly Emerging Economic Forms', Beijing Review, 21, 25 May.

He Jianzhang, (1982), 'Basic Forms in the Socialist Economy', China Reconstructs, 31, January.

Heyman, H. (1975), '"Self-Reliance" Revisited: China's Technology Dilemma', in B.B. Garth (ed), China's Changing Role in the World Economy, Praeger,

References

New York.
    Hidasi, G. (1979), 'China's Economy in the late 1970's, and its Development Prospects up to the mid-1980's', Acta Oeconomica, 23.
    Hilton, I. (3 May 1981), 'China - The Great Leap Backwards', Sunday Times, London.
    Hirschman, A.O., (1958), The Strategy of Economic Development, Yale University Press.
    Horie, Y. (1965), 'Modern Entrepreneurship in Meiji Japan', in W.W. Lockwood (ed), The State and Economic Enterprise in Japan, Princeton University Press.
    Hough, J. (1980), Soviet Leadership in Transition, Brookings, Washington D.C.
    Howe, C. (1973), 'Labour Organisation and Incentives, Before and After the Cultural Revolution', in S.R. Schram (ed), Authority, Participation and Cultural Change in China, Cambridge University Press.
    Howe, C. (1978), China's Economy, Elek Books, London.
    Howe, C. (ed), (1981), Shanghai: Revolution and Development in an Asian Metropolis, Cambridge University Press.
    Hu Qiaomu, (1978), 'Do Things in Accordance with Objective Laws, Speed up the Realisation of the Four Modernisations', Peking Review, Nos. 45-47.
    Huang Zhengshen, (1980), 'Some Thoughts on the Origins of the "Iron Rice Bowl"', Beijing Ribao, 16 Jan. tr. in CREA, 49, 21 Mar.
    Jiang Yiwei, (1979), 'A Discussion of "The View that the Enterprise is the Fundamental Unit" - Tentative Remarks on the Nature of Enterprises under Socialism and their Relations with the State', Jingji Guanli, 6, 25 June, tr. in CREA, 18, 30 Oct.
    Jiang Yiwei, (1980), 'The theory of an enterprise-based economy', Social Sciences in China, Vol.1, No.1.
    Jiang Yiwei, (1980b), 'On the Basic Characteristics of Socialist Enterprise Management', Jingji Guanli, 11, tr. in CREA, 170.
    Johansen, L. (1977), Lectures on Macroeconomic Planning, Vol.1 and 2, North Holland.
    Karcher, M. (1975), Unemployment and Underemployment in the People's Republic of China, IBRD Reprint Series No.25.
    Kerr, C. Dunlop, J.T. Harbison, E. and Myers, C.A. (eds) (1973), Industrialism and Industrial Man, Penguin, Harmondsworth.
    Klatt, W. (1979), 'China's New Economic Policy: A Statistical Approach', China Quarterly, 80, Dec.

References

Kornai, J. (1975), <u>Mathematical Planning of Structural Decisions</u>, second ed., North Holland, Amsterdam.

Kornai, J. (1980), <u>Economics of Shortage</u>, Vols. A and B, North Holland.

Kosygin, A. (1965),'On Improving Industrial Management', in A. Nove and M. Nuti (eds), Penguin, Harmondsworth, London.

Kuang Rian and Xiao Liang, (1979), 'On the Law of Value and the Right of Enterprises to Independent Action', <u>Jingji Yanjiu</u>, 5, tr. in <u>CREA</u>, <u>6</u>, 6 Aug.

Kumar, K. (1978), <u>Prophecy and Progress: The Sociology of Industrial and Post-Industrial Society</u>, Penguin,Harmondsworth.

Kunio, Y. (1979), <u>Japanese Economic Development</u>, Oxford University Press.

Lai Ruoyu, (1956), 'Speech' in <u>Eighth National Congress of the Communist Party of China</u>, Vol.2, Foreign Languages Press, Beijing.

Lardy, N.R. (1975), 'Economic Planning in the People's Republic of China: Central-Provincial Fiscal Relations', in Joint Economic Committee, <u>China: A Reassessment of the Economy</u>, U.S. Government Printing Office, Washington D.C.

Lardy, N.R. (ed), (1978), <u>Chinese Economic Planning</u>, M.E. Sharpe, White Plains, N.Y.

Lenin, V.I. (1921), 'The Third Congress of the Communist International', in his <u>Collected Works</u>, Vol.3, 1964, Moscow.

Levine, S.B. and Kawada, H. <u>Human Resources in Japanese Industrial Development</u>, Princeton University Press.

Li Chengrui and Zhang Zhuoyuan, (1980), 'Comprehensive Planning for People Awaiting Employment and Making Full Use of Manpower Resources', <u>Jingji Yanjiu</u>, 8, 20 Aug. tr. in <u>CREA</u>, 88, 2 Oct.

Li Xuefeng, (1956), 'Speech' in <u>Eighth National Congress of the CCP</u>, Vol.2, Foreign Languages Press, Beijing.

Li Yue and Chen Shenchang,(1981),The Scale and Structure of Industrial Enterprises', <u>Social Sciences in China</u>, No.2:49-65.

Li Zhiang, (1977), 'Distinguish the Correct Line from the Incorrect Ones: Actively Develop Socialist Foreign Trade', <u>Hongqi, 10</u>, tr. in <u>Chinese Economic Studies, 12</u>, 1-2.

Liang Wen, (1980), 'San nien lai zhengzhi he jingji zhijian guanxi wenti taolun' (The debates in the last three years on the relation between politics and economics), <u>Zhongguo Shehui Kexue</u>, 6.

Lin, C.C. (1981), 'The Reinstatement of

References

Economics in China Today', China Quarterly, 85.

Lin Guoguang, (1979), 'Views on Several Major Issues of Economic Restructuring', Jingji Guanli, 11 tr. in CREA, 46.

Lin Pei, (1980), 'Establish and Perfect the System of Workers' Congresses', Renmin Ribao, 6 March, tr. in SWB 6403/B11, 24 April.

Lin Zili and You Lin, (1978), 'Lun zhengzhi he jingji de guanxi' (On the relation between politics and economics), Jingji Yanjui, 1.

Lin Zili, (1980), 'Initial reforms in China's economic structure', Social Sciences in China, Vol. 1, No.3.

Liu Guoguang and Zhao Renwei, (May 1979), 'The Relationship Between Plan and Market in a Socialist Economy', Jingji Yanjiu, 5, tr. in CREA, 6.

Liu Guoguang and Zhao Renwei, (1979), 'Socialist Economic Planning and the Market', Beijing Review, 31.

Liu Guoguang, Wu Jinglian, Zhao Renwei, (1980), 'Relationship Between Planning and Market as seen by China in her Socialist Economy', Atlantic Economic Journal.

Loasby, B.J. (1976), Choice, Complexity and Ignorance, Cambridge University Press.

Lockett, M. (1978), Chinese Industry: Management and Division of Labour, Dept. of Employment, Work Research Unit, Occasional Paper No.1, London.

Lockett, M. (1981), 'Producer Cooperatives in China, 1919-1981', mimeo. Paper presented at the International Conference on Producer Cooperatives, Denmark, May/June.

Lockett, M. (1981b), 'Self-management in China' Economic Analysis and Workers' Management, Vol.15, No.1.

Lockett, M. (1982), 'Organisational Democracy and Politics in China', International Yearbook of Organisational Democracy 1982, Wiley, London.

Lu Luping, (1980), 'Several Questions in the Accelerated Development of Light Industry', Jingji Yanjiu, 2, tr. in CREA, 58, April.

Luo Gengmo, (1980), 'Lenin's Analysis of Four Kinds of Relations of Exchange in Russia after the October Revolution', Social Sciences in China, Vol. 1, No.1.

Ma Hong, (1980), 'Tentative Study on Reform of Leadership System in Industrial Enterprises', Jingji Guanli, 12, tr. in CREA, 116.

Ma Hong, (1981), 'On Several Questions of Reforming the System of Economic Management', Jingji Yanjiu, 7, tr. in CREA, 175.

353

References

Ma Jiaju, (1980), 'A Pioneer Work on Economic Reform', Social Sciences in China, Vol.1, No.1

MacDougall, C. (1980), 'China Takes Lesson from Poland', Financial Times, 30 Oct. London.

MacDougall, C. (ed) (1980), Trading with China: A Practical Guide, McGraw-Hill, Maidenhead.

MacDougall, C. (1982), 'Policy Changes in China's Foreign Trade Since the Death of Mao, 1976-1980', in J. Gray and G. White, eds. (1982).

Main Documents of the Second Session of the Fifth National People's Congress of the People's Republic of China, (1979), Foreign Language Press, Beijing.

Manpower Bureau (Laodongli Ju) of the Ministry of Labour, (1980), article in Zhongguo Funu, 9, precis tr. in FBIS, 17.

Mao Tse-Tung, (1956), 'On the Ten Great (or Major) Relationships', originally 1956, to be found in S. Schram (ed), Mao Tse-Tung Unrehearsed, Penguin London, (1974), or in Mao Zedong, Collected Works, Vol.5, or separately in 1977 by Foreign Languages Press, Beijing.

Mao Tse-Tung: Critique of Soviet Economics, (1977), tr. Moss Roberts, Monthly Review Press.

Marrese, M. (1981), 'The Evolution of Wage Regulation in Hungary', in P. Hare, H. Radice and N. Swain (eds), (1981), Hungary - A Decade of Economic Reform, Macmillan, London.

Maxwell, N. 'Recent Chinese Grain Figures', China Quarterly, 1976.

Melzer, M. (1981), 'Combine Formation in the GDR', Soviet Studies, Vol.XXXIII, No.1, January:107-124.

Miyazawa, K. (1964), 'The Dual Structure of the Japanese Economy and its Growth Pattern', reprinted in K. Sato (ed) (1980), Industry and Business in Japan, Croom Helm, London.

Nakamura, T. (1981), The Postwar Japanese Economy, University of Tokyo Press.

Ni Zhifu, (1981), 'Implement the Guidelines of the Sixth Plenum, Give Full Play to the Initiative of the Workers as Masters of the Land, and Strive to Rush the National Economy Forward', Gongren Ribao, 13 Oct. tr. in SWB 6870/B11, 3 Nov.

Nolan, P. and White, G. (1981), 'Distribution and Development in China', Bulletin of Concerned Asian Scholars, Vol.13, No.3.

Norman, E.H. (1940), Japan's Emergence as a Modern State, Institute of Pacific Relations.

Nove, A. (1969), An Economic History of the USSR, Penguin, Harmondsworth.

References

Nove, A. (1977), The Soviet Economic System, Allen and Unwin, London.

Nove, A. (1978), The Soviet Economic System, Allen and Unwin, London.

Nove, A. and Nuti, D. (1972), Socialist Economics, Penguin Harmondsworth, London.

NUM (National Union of Mineworkers) (1980), 'Delegation to China, Report', mimeo.

Nyers, R. and Tardos, M. (1978),'Enterprises in Hungary Before and After the Reform', Acta Economica Vol.20, Nos.1-2:21-44.

Okita, S. (1980), The Developing Economies and Japan, University of Tokyo Press.

O'Leary, G. (1980), 'China's Foreign Relations: The Reintegration of China into the World Economy' in W. Brugger (ed), China Since the "Gang of Four", Croom Helm, London.

Orchard, J. (1930), Japan's Economic Position: The Progress of Industrialisation, McGraw Hill, New York.

Piore, M.J. (1972), 'Notes for a Theory of Labour Market Stratification', Working Paper No.95, Department of Economics, M.I.T.

Qian Junrui, (1980), 'Eliminate Feudal Vestiges in Economic Work', Beijing Review, 23, 29 Dec.

Rawski, T.G. (1979), 'Economic Growth and Employment in China', World Development, 7.

Ren Tao, Sun Huaiyang and Liu Jinglin, (1980), 'Investigation Report - Enterprises in Sichuan Province Acquire Greater Independence', Social Sciences in China, Vol.1, No.1

Renversez, F. and Lavigne, M. (1979), Regulation et Division Internationale du Travail, L'Experience Hongroise, Economica, Paris.

Revesz, G. (1979),'Regulation des Salaires et Stimulants des Entreprises dans L'Economie Hongroise' in F. Renversez and M. Lavigne (eds).

Research Trip (1981), Interviews conducted by C. Littler, M. Lockett and P. Abell in Beijing, Chengdu, Chongqing and Shanghai with members of industrial enterprises, trade unions, and Economic Commissions.

Richardson, G.B. (1960), Information and Investment, Oxford University Press.

Rosovsky, H. (1961), Capital Formation in Japan Free Press, New York.

SSB (1979), Statistical Work in New China, State Statistical Bureau, Beijing.

State Statistical Bureau (SSB) (1981), 'Communique on the fulfilment of the 1980 National Economic Plan', Beijing Review, 24, 18 May.

References

Schram, S.R. (1981), 'To Utopia and Back: A Cycle in the History of the Chinese Communist Party' China Quarterly, September.

Schurmann, F. (1968), Ideology and Organisation in Communist China, California University Press.

Shao Lukuan, (1980), 'Several Problems of Labour and Employment in Our Country', Renmin Ribao, 19 Aug. tr. in FBIS, 4 Sept.

Shirk, S.L. (1981), 'Recent Chinese Labour Policies and the Transformation of Industrial Organisation in China', China Quarterly, 88, December.

Shu Hongliang, (1980), 'To Regain Workers' Confidence in their Unions', Gongren Ribao, 18 Nov. tr. in CREA, 120.

Shvyrkov, Yu. (1980), Centralised Planning of the Economy, Progress Publishers, Moscow.

Smith, T.C. (1955), Political Change and Industrial Development in Japan: Government Enterprise, 1868-1880, Stanford University Press.

Stalin, J. (1972), Economic Problems of Socialism in the USSR, Foreign Languages Press, Beijing.

Statistical Handbook of Japan (1980), Bureau of Statistics, Office of the Prime Minister.

Sztyber, W. (1970-71), 'Theoretical Basis for the Reform of Sale Prices', East European Economics: 91-131.

Sun Ru, (1980), 'The Conception and Prospects of the Special Economic Zones in Guangdong', tr. from a Hong Kong seminar held by the Chinese government, in Chinese Economic Studies, 14, 1, Autumn.

Sun Yefang, (1979a), Shehuizhuyi jingji de nuogan lilun wenti (On some theoretical problems of a socialist economy), Beijing.

Sun Yefang, (1979b), 'Lun zuowei zhengzhi jingjixue duixiang de shengchuan guangxi' (On the relations of production as the object of political economy), Jingji Yanjiu, 8.

Sun Yefang, (1980a), 'Tantan gaohao zonghe pingheng de jige qianti tiaojian' (On some preconditions for creating overall balance), Jingji Yanjiu 2.

Sun Yefang, (1980b), 'What is the origin of the Law of Value?', Social Sciences in China, Vol.1, No.3.

Szuprowicz, B.O. and Szuprowicz, M.R. (1978), Doing Business with the People's Republic of China: Industries and Markets, Wiley, New York.

Taira, K. (1970), Economic Development and the Labor Market in Japan, Columbia University Press.

Tian Sansong, (1980), 'Democracy in Factories', Beijing Review, 23, 1 Sept.

References

Tian Yun, (1980), 'One Step Back, Two Steps Forward - Readjusting Capital Construction', <u>Beijing Review</u>, 29, July 21.

Tian Yun, (1981), 'More Authority for Enterprises Revives the Economy', <u>Beijing Review, 14</u>, April 6.

Tissier, P. (1979), 'The Economic Policy of the New Chinese Leadership in 1977 and 1978', <u>Capital and Class, 9</u>, London.

Turner, B.A. (1975), <u>Industrialism</u>, Longman, London.

Valkenburg, F.C. and Vissers, A.M.C. (1980), 'Segmentation of the Labour Market' : The Theory of the Dual Market', <u>The Netherlands Journal of Sociology, 16</u>.

Vogel, E.F. (1979), 'Nation-building in Modern East Asia: Early Meiji (1868-1890) and Mao's China (1949-1971)' in A.M. Craig (ed), <u>Japan: A Comparative View</u>, Princeton University Press.

Volkoff, A. (1981), <u>The Role of Foreign Trade in China's Current Development Strategy</u>, Unpublished M. Phil. thesis, Institute of Development Studies, University of Sussex.

Wan Xiang, (1980), 'From Bureaucrat to Manager' <u>Jingji Guanli, 11</u>, tr. in CREA, 110.

Wang Xizhe, (1980), 'For a Return to Genuine Marxism in China', <u>New Left Review, 121</u>, London.

Wei Xianming, (1981), 'Permitting Individual Operation Does Not Mean Negating the Transformation of Private Ownership', <u>Gongren Ribao</u>, 27 July, tr. in <u>FBIS, 151</u>.

Westney, D.E. (1980), 'Patterns of Organisational Development in Japan: The Spread of the Incorporated Enterprise, 1888-1918', in D. Dunkerley and G. Salaman (eds), The <u>International Yearbook of Organisation Studies 1979</u>.

White, L.T. (1978), <u>Careers in Shanghai</u>, University of California Press.

Whitehill, A.M. and Takezawa, S. (1968), <u>The Other Worker</u>, East-West Center Press, Honolulu.

Wu Lu, (1980), 'Thoughts on Soliciting Job Applications', <u>Renmin Ribao</u>, 5 July, tr. in <u>FBIS</u>, 16 July.

Xiang Rong, (1980), 'A Glimpse of Factory Life' <u>Beijing Review, 23</u>, 17 March.

Xiang Xuanpei and Du Lingfeng, (1980), 'The Question of Retention of Profits by Enterprises', <u>Jingji Guanli, 14</u> (in Chinese).

Xiao Liang, (1980), 'Politics and economics - how are they related?', <u>Social Sciences in China</u>, Vol.1, No.4.

References

Xiao Wanyuan, (1980), 'Individual Economy is not Capitalist Economy', Nanfang Ribao, 23 Aug. tr. in CREA, 97.

Xiao Zhuoji, (1980),'The Law of Price Movement in China', Social Sciences in China, No.4:44-59.

Xu Dixin, (1981), 'China's Special Economic Zones', Beijing Review, 50, 14 Dec.

Xue Muqiao, (1978), Shehuizhuyi jingji lilun wenti (Theoretical problems of a socialist economy), Beijing.

Xue Muqiao et al, (1979a), Shehuizhuyi jingjizhong jihua yu shichang de guanxi (The relation between plan and market in the socialist economy), Vol.1, Beijing.

Xue Muqiao, (1979b), Zhongguo shehuizhuyi jingji wenti yanjiu (Research on some problems of China's socialist economy), 1979.

Xue Muqiao, (1979c), 'Liyong jiazhi guilu wei jingji jianshe shiye fuwu' (Make use of the law of value in the service of economic construction), Hongqi, January.

Xue Muqiao, (July 1979), 'My Views on the Problem of Urban Employment', Beijing Ribao, tr. in CREA, 22, 22 Oct.

Xue Muqiao, (1980), Dangqian Woguo Jingji Ruogan Wenti (Certain Questions Concerning our Present Economy), People's Publishing House, Beijing.

Xue Muqiao, (June 1980), 'A Probe into the Question of Changing of the Economic System', Jingji Yanjiu, 6, 20 June, tr. in CREA, 81.

Xue Muqiao, (1981), China's Socialist Economy, Foreign Languages Press, Beijing.

Xue Muqiao, (March 1981), 'How Should We Handle Correctly the Relationship Between Readjustment and Reform?', Gongren Ribao, 13 Mar. tr. in SWB, 6681.

Xue Muqiao, (December 1981), 'Addendum to "China's Socialist Economy"', Beijing Review, 49.

Yamamura, K. (1964), 'Zaibatsu Prewar and Zaibatsu Postwar', Journal of Asian Studies, 23.

Yamamura, K. (1975), 'A Compromise with Culture: The Historical Evolution of the Managerial Structure of Large Japanese Firms', in H.F. Williamson, (ed), Evolution of International Management Structures, University of Delaware Press.

Yoshino, M.Y. (1968), 1971 edition, Japan's Managerial System, M.I.T. Press, Massachusetts.

Yoshino, M.Y. (1974), 'The Multinational Spread of Japanese Manufacturing Investment Since World War II', Business History Review, 28.

Yuan Wenqi, Dai Lunzhang and Wang Linsheng, (1980), 'International Division of Labor and China's

References

Economic Relations with Foreign Countries', <u>Social Sciences in China</u>, Vol.1, No.1.

Yue Guangzhao, (1981), 'Several Questions on Increasing Employment and Raising Labour Productivity', <u>Renmin Ribao</u>, 23 Nov. tr. in <u>SWB, 6898</u>.

Zhang Changgen, Liu Minghao, Hu Yanzhao, (1981) 'Shanghai shi dou renkou zhuangkuang he wenti yiji women du jianshe' (Urban construction and the condition and problems of Shanghai city's population), <u>Renkou Yanjiu, 2</u>.

Zhang Enhua, (1981), 'On Banking Reform', <u>Beijing Review, 29</u>, July 20.

Zhang Chunqiao, (Chang Ch'un-ch'iao), (1975), 'On Exercising All-round Dictatorship Over the Bourgeoisie', <u>Beijing Review, 18</u>, April

Zhang Zehou and Chen Yuguang, (1981), 'On the Relationship Between the Population Structure and the National Economic Development in China', <u>Social Sciences in China</u>, Vol.2, No.4.

Zhao Lukuan, Feng Lanrui, Ye Ming and Chen Guangzhen, (1979), 'Enterprise Management Must Adapt to the Demands of Great Changes', <u>Caiwu Yu Kuaiji, 3</u>, 20 Mar. tr. in <u>CREA, 7</u>, 14 Aug.

Zhao Lukuan, (1980), 'Several Problems of Labour and Employment in our Country', <u>Renmin Ribao</u>, 19 Aug. tr. in <u>FBIS</u>, 4 Sept.

<u>Zhengzhi jingji xue jiaocai (shehuizhuyi bufen)</u> (Teaching materials on political economy (Socialist section), (1961), People's Publishing House, Shanghai.

Zhi Exiang, (1979), 'The Election for Shop Heads', <u>China Reconstructs, 28</u>, May.

Zhong He, (1980), 'Some Views on Reform of the Labour System and the "Iron Rice Bowl"', <u>Beijing Ribao</u>, 16 Jan. tr. in <u>CREA, 49</u>, 21 Mar.

<u>Zhongguo Baike Nianjian 1981</u> (China Encyclopaedia Yearbook, 1981), Beijing.

<u>Zhongguo Jingji Nianjian 1981</u> (Chinese Economy Yearbook, 1981), tr. in <u>CREA, 185</u>.

Zhou Xiuqiang, (1980), article in <u>Renmin Ribao</u>, 23 July, tr. in <u>FBIS</u>, 25 July.

Zhuang Qidong and Sun Keliang, (1981), 'The Problem of Urban Unemployment During the Period of Readjustment', <u>Hongqi, 11</u>, 1 June, tr. in <u>SWB, 6775</u>.

Zhuang Qidong (et al) (1981, 'A Long-term Employment Policy is Needed ...', <u>Guangming Ribao</u>, 16 Aug. 1981, tr. in <u>FBIS, 169</u>.

INDEX

Index